L

(Love's Joy)

FRITZ KREISLER

VIOLIN

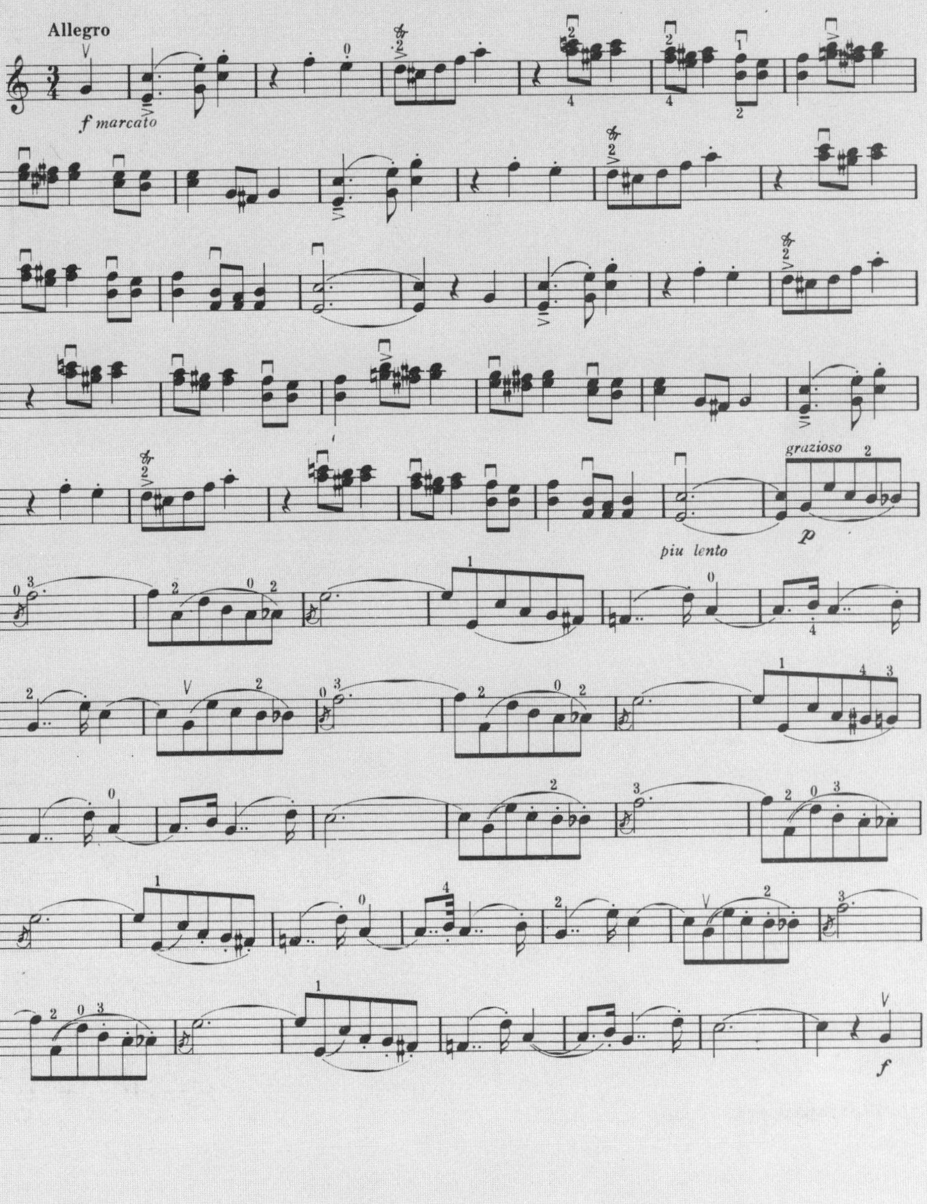

Allegro

f marcato

grazioso

piu lento

p

f

Fritz Kreisler

Kreisler, circa 1915. (Courtesy Sylvia Rupp)

Fritz Kreisler

Love's Sorrow, Love's Joy

by Amy Biancolli

Amadeus Press
Reinhard G. Pauly, General Editor
Portland, Oregon

Endpapers: Printed scores of *Liebesleid* and *Liebesfreud* by Fritz Kreisler reproduced with permission of Carl Fischer, Inc. All rights reserved

Copyright © 1998 by Amadeus Press
(an imprint of Timber Press, Inc.).
All rights reserved.

Amadeus Press
The Haseltine Building
133 S.W. Second Avenue, Suite 450
Portland, Oregon 97204 U.S.A.

Printed in Hong Kong

ISBN 1-57467-037-9

Library of Congress Cataloging-in-Publication Data

Biancolli, Amy.
Fritz Kreisler : love's sorrow, love's joy / by Amy Biancolli.
p. cm.
"List of works" : p.
Discography : p.
Includes bibliographical references (p.), and index.
ISBN 1-57467-037-9
1. Kreisler, Fritz, 1875–1962. 2. Violinists–Biography.
I. Title.
ML418.K9B53 1998
787.2'092–dc21
[B] 98-12200
CIP
MN

To the memory of my parents:

Louis Biancolli,
who loved and celebrated music, and
Jeanne Mitchell Biancolli,
who once dreamed of playing quartets in heaven
with Fritz Kreisler.

Contents

Art ought to be a priesthood,
and every artist should be a priest.

—Fritz Kreisler

Preface, Acknowledgments, and a Few Words About Louis Lochner

Liebesleid and *Liebesfreud:* Fritz Kreisler's meditations on love's sorrow and love's joy have found a cozy and frequent home in my stereo for the last few years, and I have struggled to play the former piece (not the latter—not yet) on my own violin in my own earnest but amateurish style. I know as well as any how subtle and surprisingly difficult his pieces are, and how impossible it is for anyone, amateur or professional, to conjure in the late twentieth century the spirit of the nineteenth that bore them. Whatever success I have had with my fiddling and with this book I owe in no small part to Kreisler himself—a man with no regular pupils, but a teacher in the most essential sense. Although my generation and relative youth mean that I never had the opportunity to interview Kreisler or hear him perform live, I nevertheless feel that in the time I have spent researching and writing this I have become fully and intimately familiar with him. I had been working on this biography for about a year and a half when I ran across tapes of an old radio interview with him; for the first time, I heard the great man's heavy accent, high voice, and persistent lisp. It was odd, hearing him speak through the decades, wondering how—whether—he might have responded to the questions I would have liked to ask. Yet I felt somehow that his was the voice of a friend, someone who had opened up his life for me to see and (I hope responsibly) interpret. He was a delightful and inspiring personality to study, and I never tired of his acquaintance.

I must also thank another man I unfortunately never met, Louis P. Lochner. Lochner wrote an exhaustively detailed biography of Kreisler that was first published in 1950 and remains on the shelf of many a listener and music library; I am grateful to him for this massive effort, as I am grateful for the generosity evident in the donation of his Kreisler-related papers to the Library of Congress. Lochner was not quite Boswell to Kreisler's Johnson, but he came close: the violinist kept no journals of his own, so his biographer served as diarist of a life that otherwise might never have been fully chronicled.

Which leads me to an inevitable question, and one that several who helped me with this volume wanted to know: Why would I bother writing a new biography of Fritz Kreisler when Lochner did the job so thoroughly back in 1950? What, they wanted to know, could I possibly hope to add?

For those and for others who may ask the same question, I have two answers. My first is the simplest and, I believe, the most persuasive: I wrote a new biography of Fritz Kreisler because I fear he is in danger of being forgotten. Three and a half decades have now passed since his death, almost five since his retirement, and in that time the world of music—and the prevailing definitions of violin artistry—have changed drastically. New, young violinists with techniques demonstrably better than Kreisler's have little awareness of his deeply human playing and his mystical relationship with the instrument, which can seem to contemporary observers either ridiculously cockeyed or embarrassingly quaint. Similarly, audiences whose ears are accustomed to literal contemporary performances may find Kreisler's more liberal interpretations shocking in their deviations, intended and unintended, from the printed page.

With this in mind, I worked with the hope that a new biography of Kreisler will reintroduce an artistic figure of towering importance to a generation of listeners who have, perhaps, forgotten how to hear the very intimate message of his playing. Lochner was faced with no such task; he wrote his biography for a readership still infatuated with his subject. He needed only to inform, not persuade.

This brings me to my second reason: Lochner's biography, as exhaustive as it is, contains some glaring (and fascinating) gaps. Because Kreisler's wife, Harriet, served as censor for the final manuscript, the published volume fails to describe with any candor either Harriet's control over her husband's life or the intense dislike she aroused in nearly everyone she met. It also overlooks the matter of Kreisler's ethnic and religious heritage and the complex forces behind his flight from Germany in the late 1930s. On the flip side, Lochner's biography at times contains too much—Kreisler was an infamous fibber, and several of the yarns spun in those pages are prevarications of the most thoroughly spurious sort. Many of them are by their very natures impossible to confirm or debunk, but I have done my best (in a chapter dedicated to the subject and throughout the rest of the book) to examine them with a critical eye and a good-natured appreciation for their literary worth.

I should also add that I have nothing but the sincerest admiration for Lochner, a considerable scholar and good friend of Kreisler's whose affection for and understanding of his subject comes through on every page. Lochner enjoyed an access to Kreisler that for obvious reasons I did not have; having been born a year and a half after the violinist's death, I was forced to rely on interviews and several of Kreisler's own writings in my search for lively quotations. Lochner was also able to interview many prominent musicians, now long dead, whose analyses and anecdotes I could only gather from secondary sources. Although I have done my best to locate and interview as many people as possible, few who knew Kreisler personally are still alive. Throughout my book I have turned by necessity to Lochner's for facts and comments that I have been unable to find anywhere else, and for that—and to him—I am hugely grateful.

This book is as much about Kreisler's legacy as it is about his life and accomplishments. I have tried to place his career in context, discussing his influence on subsequent generations of musicians and the evolution of violin playing into a contemporary standard far removed from the example he provided. The structure of the book reflects this emphasis on context; unlike Lochner's biography, which provided a straight chronology of Kreisler's career, mine is more analytical and less linear. Although the chapters are organized in a loosely chronological manner, many sections are topical in nature and function as essays rather than direct accounts of Kreisler's life.

The resulting biography is, I hope, an interesting, discerning, and readable portrait of a man whose impact on music, and indeed on twentieth-century popular culture, is profound, unprecedented, and often overlooked. My wish is that it will be regarded not as an attempt to replace or refute Louis Lochner's important work but as an updated assessment of a career remarkable for its intensity and span. Fritz Kreisler was born at the end of the nineteenth century, found fame at the start of the twentieth, and retired smack in its middle. Now, as the world tilts wildly toward the twenty-first, the sad-faced man from Vienna may be more relevant than ever.

I owe many other debts of gratitude. Thanks go first to my splendid husband and eleventh-hour proofreader, Christopher D. Ringwald, whose unending, uncomplaining, and unqualified love and support gave me the time and wherewithal to accomplish this. My daughters I must thank for their happy distractions; my relatives, real and surrogate, for their love. I would also like to express my gratitude to the many friends and co-workers who in the last few years have asked innocent small-talk questions about Fritz Kreisler only to be swept away by my in-depth replies.

To Frederic Kreisler I owe my appreciation for his candid and affectionate reminiscences of his beloved Uncle Fritz, for his input and perusal of the manuscript, and for his permission to quote from Kreisler's documents. I would also like to thank Robert Lochner, Louis Lochner's son, who welcomed my efforts with this new book, gave me his blessing for its completion, and permitted me to quote from his father's papers. And I would like to acknowledge my late father-in-law, Eugene C. Ringwald, who gave me many suggestions, guided me to Kreisler's mausoleum in Woodlawn Cemetery, and recalled for me his fondest memories of hearing Kreisler play in Carnegie Hall.

The heartiest thanks must also go to my assistant in Washington, DC, Regina Verow, who helped me with research at the Library of Congress. David De Angelo provided similar help in Pittsburgh. David Sackson in New York City generously supplied me with clippings, photos, recollections, inspiration, time, insights, and—last but most certainly not least—cassette tapes of his two extraordinary interviews with Franz Rupp, the German pianist who often served as Kreisler's accompanist in the 1930s. Eric Wen, a Kreisler scholar, assisted me in numerous ways, furnishing heaps of enthusiasm, many sage comments, and the discography found at the back of this book. Susanne Dopierala Richardson was gracious about helping me with several idiomatic German translations.

I am grateful to my editors at Amadeus Press, Reinhard G. Pauly and Eve Goodman, for their support, insight, and endless well of patience. A "thank you" as well for Joshua Leventhal, also at Amadeus, who edited my manuscript with generosity and a razor eye.

Many more deserve my thanks. Among them: Sylvia Rupp, Oscar Shumsky, Harold Coletta, Sir Yehudi Menuhin, Philip Dreifus, George Gingold, the late Josef Gingold, Michael Tree, Harold Schonberg, Ross Parmenter, Sylvia Rabinof Rothenberg, George Neikrug, the late Joseph Fuchs, Sam Kissel, Paul Nubauer, Edward S. Naumburg, Andy Stein, Alix Williamson, WQXR and George Jellinek, Robert Mann, the Blessed Sacrament Church in New Rochelle, and Melvin Spitalnick. I am grateful to Carl Michaelson and Bill Rhoads at Carl Fischer, who provided information for the list of works. I would additionally like to thank the many people who responded to author's queries that were printed in various publications, and to the individuals and publishers who granted permission to use their materials.

The libraries, archives, and other institutions to which I owe acknowledgments include: the New York State Library in Albany, the New York (City) Public Library (the main branch and the Library for the Performing Arts), the Butler Library at Columbia University, the Library of Congress (which houses Kreisler's and Lochner's papers and is home to the stunning oil painting by Howard Chandler Christy reproduced on the cover, with added thanks to Maxine Christy Peters and Elbert Yerian), the Albany

Public Library, the Atlanta Public Library, the State Historical Society of Wisconsin, the library of the State University of New York at Albany, the New York Philharmonic Archives, the Philadelphia Orchestra Archives, the Curtis Institute of Music, the Boston Symphony Orchestra Archives, and the Carnegie Hall Archives.

Finally, I am sincerely indebted to two great mentors, Toni Bosco and Fred Wagner, who taught me, inspired me, and encouraged me to write.

In addition to the individuals mentioned above, kind appreciation is offered to the following for permission to reprint copyrighted material:

Excerpts from *The Way They Play* by Samuel and Sada Applebaum, 1972, reprinted by permission of TFH Publications and of Michael Tree.

"Kreisler's Berlin Home Destroyed" (7 July 1945) reprinted by permission of the Associated Press.

Excerpts from *Joys and Sorrows* by Pablo Casals and Albert E. Kahn, reprinted with the permission of Simon & Schuster. Copyright © 1970 by Albert E. Kahn.

Excerpts from "Heifetz Unrivaled on Violin" by Richard Dyer, 12 December 1987, reprinted by permission of *The Boston Globe.*

Excerpts from "L'Amico Fritz" by David Ewen, August 1935, reprinted courtesy of *Esquire* Magazine and the Hearst Company.

Excerpts from *The Art of Violin Playing* by Carl Flesch, 1930, reprinted by permission of Carl Fischer Inc.

Excerpts from *The Spell of the Vienna Woods: Inspiration and Influence from Beethoven to Kafka* by Paul Hofmann, © 1994 by Paul Hofmann. Reprinted by permission of Henry Holt & Co., Inc.

Excerpts from *Fritz Kreisler* by Louis Lochner, reprinted with the permission of Simon & Schuster. Copyright © 1950 by Louis P. Lochner; copyright renewed © 1978 by Louis P. Lochner.

Excerpts from *From Russia to the West: The Musical Memoirs and Reminiscences of Nathan Milstein* by Nathan Milstein and Salomon Volkov. Translated by Antonina W. Bouis. Copyright © 1990 by Nathan Milstein and Salomon Volkov, translation © 1990 by Antonina W. Bouis. Reprinted by permission of Henry Holt & Co., Inc.

Excerpts from "The Kreisler Revelations: Debit and Credit" (24 February 1935) and "An Open Letter to Fritz Kreisler: The 'Classical Manuscripts'" (17 March 1935) by Ernest Newman, reprinted by permission of the Times Newspapers.

Excerpts from "Music: The Great Kreisler" (25 March 1940), "Grand Old Man" (13 February 1950), and "The Paragon" (12 February 1962), reprinted by permission © 1940, 1950, 1962, Newsweek, Inc. All rights reserved.

Excerpts from *The New York Times* copyright © 1888, 1905, 1909, 1912, 1914, 1916–1919, 1921, 1924–1926, 1928, 1933–1935, 1939, 1941, 1942, 1944, 1946, 1947, 1955, 1960, 1962 by the New York Times Company. Reprinted by permission.

Excerpts from "And So to Mr. Kreisler" by Winthrop Sargeant, reprinted by permission, © 15 April 1961, The New Yorker Magazine, Inc. All rights reserved.

Excerpts from *Forbidden Childhood* by Ruth Slenczynska and Louis Biancolli, 1958, reprinted by permission of Ruth Slenczynska.

Excerpts from "Audience Pays Stirring Tribute to Kreisler" by Helen Knox Spain, 12 November 1949, reprinted by permission of *The Atlanta Journal Constitution.*

Excerpts from *Rise to Follow* by Albert Spalding, © 1943 by Albert Spalding. Reprinted by permission of Henry Holt & Co., Inc.

Excerpts from *The Human Side of Greatness* by William L. Stidger, © 1936 by Harper & Brothers. Reprinted by permission of HarperCollins Publishers, Inc.

Excerpts from "Instinctive Partnership" by Dennis Rooney and "L'Amico Fritz," January 1987, reprinted by permission of *The Strad.*

Excerpts from "Kreisler's Art Thrills Large Audience Here" by Edgar S. Van Olinda, 29 January 1942, reprinted by permission of the Albany *Times Union.*

Additional thanks are offered to those who granted permission for use of materials but who are not named individually in these acknowledgments. While every reasonable effort has been made to contact copyright holders and secure permission for all materials reproduced in this work, we offer apologies for any instances in which this was not possible and for any inadvertent omissions.

One

Vienna

The Vienna of Fritz Kreisler was a city of brilliant facades. In the late nineteenth century it was the seat of the Habsburg Empire, a municipality struggling under the harshest burdens of economic and moral decay, of class struggles, racism, poverty, prostitution, and ingrown political corruption. But that was not its public face. The Vienna that bewitched the world was a city of pleasures, sophisticated and plebeian, self-conscious and pure, a capital ruled not by the Emperor Franz Josef but by music and dance, twin arts whose charms crossed social strata and converged in that singularly Viennese creation, the waltz. The city crackled with intellectual and social activity, from cafes to public gardens to the carefully planned living rooms of the middle class. Cultures met and merged in Vienna, a crossroads for artists and literati from around the world. It was a global city, and the musicians it nurtured—Johann Strauss the Elder, Johann Strauss the Younger ("the Waltz King"), Anton Bruckner, Franz Lehár, Johannes Brahms—conquered Europe and beyond.

This Vienna was as much an idea as it was a city, and as such it relied on a particularly fickle confluence of philosophical and political winds. In the second half of the nineteenth century all was in flux. The Habsburgs, who had ruled Vienna for the better part of six centuries, began to fray quite visibly around the edges; the artistic community, always bubbling disagreeably over one issue or another, split with unusual vitriol between traditionalists and self-designated "Secessionists" who developed their own credo, funding, and architecture; and the medieval walls that had surrounded the *Innere Stadt*, the ancient heart of the city, were razed and replaced with the grandly designed Ringstrasse. Old Vienna was starting to age; but it aged like a wrinkling diva—still graceful, still seductive, still so confident of her own appeal that the young sopranos in the wings were all but overlooked. The old dame was stubborn, and stubbornly attractive. In the end, it took the full destructive force of World War I, and the collapse of the Habsburgs, to shoo her off the stage.

In some regards, Vienna was no different from many other *fin-de-siècle* European cities, most of which were torn between the push toward modernism and the pull of history. At best, the struggle sent Europe lurching wildly toward the twentieth century; at worst, it ripped it apart. Vienna of that era offers, in many ways, a snow-dome view of the problem: small, crystalline, and contained. Because the city was at the same time global and insular, progressive and mired in tradition, the forces at work on the rest of the continent swelled to exaggerated dimensions once they found their way to the seat of the Habsburg Empire. As Carl E. Schorske illustrates in his fascinating book of essays, *Fin-de-Siècle Vienna: Politics and Culture*, the disintegration of the old order and the formation of the new led an entire generation of artists to ponder the most fundamental questions of creativity and existence. "Not only Vienna's finest writers, but its painters and psychologists, even its art historians, were preoccupied with the nature of the individual in a disintegrating society," Schorske wrote. "Out of this preoccupation arose Austria's contribution to a new view of man."[1]

In 1875, the year of Fritz Kreisler's birth, Vienna had not yet entered the new urban era but was approaching it, slowly, hesitantly, not at all sure of its hospitableness. The dismantling of the inner walls in 1857 was one of the bolder lurches toward modernization, displaying an admirable if ultimately confused effort on the part of Franz Josef and Mayor Karl Lueger to give the city a new profile in an artistic as well as a literal sense. The broad, circular Ringstrasse edged toward modernity while nervously looking back: its architectural plan was self-consciously nostalgic, comprising an oddly eclectic amalgam of historical styles that conveyed nothing so much as an abundant lack of direction. The new university, for example, was assuredly renaissance; the parliament building was classical; the Hofburgtheater was early baroque; and the Rathaus (city hall) was gothic. "In Austria as elsewhere," wrote Schorske, "the triumphant middle class was assertive in its independence of the past in law and science. But whenever it strove to express its values in architecture, it retreated into history."[2]

Schorske attributes such architectural anachronisms—and the philosophy behind the Ringstrasse in general—to political and ideological shifts that pulled Vienna away from imperialism and the Catholic Church and toward the liberal, secular, and constitutional principles best evoked by past architectural styles. But another cause may be a pervasive Viennese stodginess that manifested itself in typically conservative aesthetic judgments; those who planned the street could not allow themselves to take real risks, perhaps because doing so would have plunged the city undeniably—and irretrievably—into the future. When it is too terrifying to move forward, move back.

Such intransigence was obvious throughout the arts community, particularly in the tensions that built toward the end of the century between the city's traditionalists and those who strove for a new style, an art nouveau. So firm was the traditionalists' lock on city funding and attention that a group of rebellious artists, frustrated with the establishment's narrow view of acceptable art and architecture, formed a frankly named Secession movement with its own champions and funding. Among those active in the Secession were architect Otto Wagner and artist Gustav Klimt, whose erotic, gold-toned female forms tweaked traditional conceptions of femininity; among the movement's best-known and most striking projects was the boxlike, windowless House of the Secession, an 1898 Josef Holbrich creation topped by an enormous sphere. Such innovation was intended to push Vienna forward, yes, but also to portray establishment artists as bloated, spoiled, and dull. It was not difficult to achieve.

In music, too, Vienna was torn between old and new, established and trailblazing. Regardless of how later generations regarded them, in the late nineteenth century Johannes Brahms and Anton Bruckner (and, by extension, Gustav Mahler and Richard Wagner) were at the center of a bitter music rivalry. Brahms was the adored, the successful, the unofficial composer laureate of Vienna; Bruckner was underappreciated and often ignored by a populace enchanted by traditionalism and turned off by his massive Mahlerian symphonies, which tilted stubbornly toward the future. The two men inspired a ferocious partisanship that was typical of Vienna's dual, and dueling, personalities: one charged forward while the other shuffled back.

Physically and geographically, the city was a mix of old and new, traditional and radical, urban and sylvan. Surrounding Vienna but lying at least in part within city boundaries were the Vienna Woods—the large, rolling, sweetly melancholic expanse of land that had sparked Beethoven to compose his Pastoral Symphony and Kafka to write passionate letters to his lover, Milena. The woods have for centuries been a refuge for the Viennese, a place where the rigorous financial and social demands of the city could be escaped and forgotten. Manhattan's Central Park has been called "the lungs of New York"; if so, the Wienerwald is Vienna's heart.

In his brief but lyrical book, *The Spell of the Vienna Woods*, Paul Hofmann described the allure of the forest that cradles Vienna.

> The many shades of green, the affecting autumn foliage, the dark firs, the soft contours of hill after hill with their vineyards and ruined castles, a few spectacular gorges and cliffs, the ancient towns and village taverns: all have inspired painters, poets, and especially composers.[3]

To that list of artists he might also have added violinists. Fritz Kreisler's rolling rhythms and melodies spoke as eloquently of the Vienna Woods as they did of the easy joviality of the waltz. Both were fetching and accessible escape routes from the city's collapsing structures, and both contributed to what writer Hermann Broch once referred to as the "joyous apocalypse"[4] of late-nineteenth-century Vienna: the pervasive, pan-cultural denial that allowed the Viennese to ignore the omens of massive societal change.

There were many such omens. In Vienna, as in the rest of turn-of-the-century Europe, the social and even some of the physical foundations that symbolized and supported the city's oldest structures were crumbling, slowly but inevitably. In this regard Vienna was no different from any other city. Yet Austrians, idiosyncratic and rebellious yet paradoxically staid, made sure that their own peculiar growing pains were sharper, and more sustained, than anyone else's. Liberalism—an experiment hatched by the intelligentsia, championed by the middle class, and feared by the elite—died a slower death than in other European countries, suffocated by the mass movements it helped create. Artists attacked the status quo with more acid and greater energy. The monarchy took longer to fade. New ideas are a threat to any order, but particularly to one as conscious of its past, and as reliant on it, as that of Vienna. In an era marked by social and political upheaval throughout the continent, the land of the Habsburgs was the most reluctant to change.

Friedrich "Fritz" Kreisler, born on 2 February 1875, was the last, best ambassador of nineteenth-century Vienna to a twentieth-century world. He was also the perfect embodiment of the city's struggle between old and new. His father, Salomon (possibly Samuel) Severin Kreisler, was a doctor, a native of Krakow, Poland, and an amateur violinist who adored music but never displayed the inclination or the talent to become a professional. A gentle and genuinely caring man, he rarely charged his many impoverished patients and made barely enough money from his medical practice to pay his own bills. Somehow, however, he was able to support his family—squeezed into a modest six-room house in Wieden, a borough of Vienna—along with a penchant for exotic animals (fish, birds, even crocodiles) that required attentive care and specially heated sand. Kindly and quiet, Salomon disliked discipline and never struck his eldest son. "My father had a full beard, a deep voice, which, however, was always soft spoken. Nothing stentorian emerged from him," Kreisler recalled many years later. "He had a fine sense of humor. I don't remember ever being punished by him, except that he could reproach one verbally."[5]

Discipline was the mother's territory. Anna Kreisler was a devoted but apparently quick-tempered mother and wife whose disposition may have had something to do with a chronic case of myelitis—an inflammation of the spinal cord or bone marrow—which partially paralyzed her and kept her in constant pain; Kreisler once remarked that he never saw her walk.[6] She made up for her husband's meekness by ruling the household with a firm hand and a punishing one, keeping the children in line with regular physical discipline. She was also, according to her son, wholly unmusical, although she accommodated and indeed encouraged Salomon's hobby by cooking a Saturday meal for his weekly chamber-music gatherings.

Fritz was the second of five children. The first, a girl, died when Fritz was still extremely young and had not yet formed an impression of her; the third, Ludwig, died young in an accident; the fourth and fifth, born ten years after Fritz, were the twins Ella and Hugo. Hugo died in 1929 in Vienna, after a distinguished career as a cellist in the United States and Austria. Ella died in the United States in 1939 and is buried in Hackensack, New Jersey. Anna Kreisler died in 1909; Salomon Kreisler, in 1921.[7]

In many ways, the Kreisler family was typical of the Viennese middle class of the time. Despite periodic financial problems, they were educated, musical, and professional—just the sort of burghers whose liberal politics pushed for reform in the courts and removed education from the control of the Catholic Church. At the same time, they were the old guard—not royalty, to be sure, but bourgeoisie who benefited most from the preservation of old ways and laws. In other words, they were establishment. (They were also, as will be discussed at length in Chapter 8, at least partly Jewish.)

In this setting Kreisler acquired an Old World aesthetic untouched by New World angst. He was a child of the ländler, the Wienerwald, the Emperor, and he remained as such for the rest of his life. It was a durable imprint. To the world at large he represented Old Vienna decades after Old Vienna itself had vanished. After 1938 he never returned to his birthplace, preferring to visit the less capricious, and vastly more romantic, city in his mind. He knew that Vienna; he embodied it. With his courtly mannerisms and the waltzing lilt that lifted everything he played, he preserved the city as no one else could—conveying its charms, its fondnesses and frivolities, while handily ignoring most of the troubles that characterized the end of the century. This was not a Vienna of world-class scandals, dying Habsburgs, creaking finances, oppressed classes, virulent anti-semitism, widely patronized prostitutes, and attendant disease; this was a Vienna of beauty and grace, of carefree pleasures that smacked of the divine despite their temporal nature. It was intoxicated without seeming drunk, sensual without being seedy. It was, in short, a city that had never really existed.

Except in music. In the operettas of Strauss, Lehár, von Suppé, in the dense orchestral works of Brahms, Bruckner, Mahler, and in the less grand but no less significant tradition of *haute* middle-class amateur musicianship, late-nineteenth-century Vienna was a vital and vivid city whose pulse beat always in three-four time. That Vienna—the Vienna of *The Blue Danube*, of *Die Fledermaus*, of *The Merry Widow*, and of *Tales from the Vienna Woods*—was a city of storybook proportions, unassailable in its cheer and unrivaled in Europe as home to the arts. From there had launched or languished many a musical career: Gluck, Haydn, Mozart, Beethoven, Schubert, Liszt. The list stretches over several centuries and includes performers and composers, commercial successes and those who died destitute and ignored. Even those who hated Vienna (Mozart among them[8]) could not resist its lure; much like New York City today, it was a place where careers were made and broken.

That it did neither for Fritz Kreisler is a quirk of his adult professional life that resonates with irony but in no way lessens the significance of the city's impact on his earliest development. Regardless of how Vienna advanced (or failed to advance) his later career, Kreisler's childhood exposed him to the cultural and historical traditions that were to remain abiding influences long after his final departure from Austria. Charismatic and fickle and seductively alive, the seat of the Habsburgs gave the nascent musician a liberal perspective, a relaxed familiarity with art, and a connection with past masters that would serve him—and serve as cause for nostalgia—for the rest of his life. His artistry and his outlook were profoundly and permanently shaped by his place of birth.

(One fascinating aspect of Vienna's influence is its role in forming Kreisler's attitude toward his own Jewish roots. So significant is this, and so complex were its ramifications throughout the violinist's life, that it will be examined closely in Chapter 8.)

By all accounts, young Fritz was a normal boy who enjoyed a normal childhood, neither more nor dramatically less privileged than any other son of Vienna's middle class. The capital of the Austrian Empire was an insular town with a clubby intellectual stratum, a prominent and energetic cafe society that moved comfortably and obviously through the academic and artistic community. Everyone knew everyone else, generations of geniuses overlapping one another and connecting eras of musical history with a seamless thread of acquaintances; anyone who knew which coffeehouse to frequent had a perfectly reasonable chance of meeting any of the music circle's most celebrated members. Thus it was far from unusual that Salomon Kreisler, whose path crossed with many of Vienna's intellectuals, counted among his friends an amateur fiddler named Sigmund Freud, whose bearded presence entered the Kreisler house for many an evening of chamber music. Such amateur nights occupied every bourgeois home; music was as much a part of the living room as it was part of the Opera House.

So Kreisler grew up, as many Viennese did, surrounded by music-making. Yet he was distinguished from the beginning by his natural affinity for the violin, not the easiest of instruments, and an innate musicality that gave him prodigious insights into anything he played. "I was born with musical feeling," he once said. "I knew music before I knew my ABCs, so I deserve no credit, no thanks for my art. Do people praise fishes for their swimming, or birds for their singing?"[9]

Kreisler first started playing on a toy violin at age four, a fairly advanced age compared with the starting points of some other well-known prodigies. His first teacher was his father. Legend has it that the younger Kreisler mastered the instrument so quickly that Salomon, discouraged by his own relative inability, stopped playing the violin and turned to the cello. When Fritz's brother Hugo studied and mastered that instrument, he, too, surpassed his father—and eventually moved on to a respected concert career. At that point the older man, perhaps too exhausted to switch to the double bass, promptly set about learning the viola. With that instrument he remained for the rest of his life.[10]

Young Fritz showed promise almost immediately. Another story from Kreisler's childhood, which may or may not be apocryphal, describes the boy's swiftly learned and altogether stunning ability to read music. According to this tale, Kreisler had been noodling around with a cigar-box fiddle when a member of his father's quartet, thinking the boy might indeed have talent, gave him a musically functional toy instrument. Thus equipped, he soon began to pester the grown-ups to let him sit with them as a fifth player in their quartet. One day the group was playing an arrangement of the national anthem when they paused suddenly; Fritz, absorbed and oblivious, kept on. To the adults' mutual amazement, the little four-year-old finished the piece in perfect time and intonation.[11]

At age seven he was admitted to the Vienna Conservatory—thanks to his mother, who gamely lied about his age—making him the youngest pupil hitherto accepted. The conservatory offered a six-year program: three years of secondary-school training, three undergraduate. Amazingly, Kreisler was admitted as an undergraduate.

His first teacher was Joseph Hellmesberger, Jr., a member of Salomon Kreisler's string quartet and a prominent Viennese violinist who composed several operettas. (According to *Baker's Biographical Dictionary of Musicians*, Kreisler studied at age six with Jacob Dont and later with Jacques Auber.) Fritz took lessons on a half-size Thir violin, which carried him through his three years at the conservatory and upon which, at the age of ten, he won the institution's gold medal for violinists. Along with the accolades he then received a three-quarter-size Amati, a beautiful little instrument that he subsequently brought to his studies at the Paris Conservatoire.[12]

But back to Vienna. There the young aspirant studied composition with Bruckner himself, a man Kreisler later described as "a combination of genius and simpleton" whose entire being revolved around music and his deep faith. "Religion was very real with him," Kreisler said. "If the near-by bells tolled, he would either fall on his knees in the midst of a class lesson and pray or, more often, would leave and rush over to the church for his devotions."[13]

While at the conservatory Fritz taught himself the piano, an instrument that his family had never owned. He later claimed to have spent more time at the piano than he did on the violin—a doubtful assertion, considering its source's tendency to exaggerate—and in fact became the accompanist for many of Hellmesberger's other pupils.[14]

In his memoirs, Carl Flesch recalled his introduction to Kreisler's playing, when Kreisler was just ten years old. Flesch was visiting the conservatory in 1885 to have his talents assessed by the institution's director, Joseph Hellmesberger, Sr., when it was suggested that he and his mother listen in on a student rehearsal. There he heard a small boy perform Sarasate's *Faust* Fantasy with orchestral accompaniment. "I sat gaping, for such fiddling I had never heard before." When young Flesch told Hellmesberger how impressed he was with the ten-year-old violinist, Hellmesberger replied, "Yes, little Kreisler will cause a great stir in the world; if only he had better posture!"[15]

Despite his love of music, his evident gifts, and a healthy appetite for learning, the promising young student was not a particularly hard worker. A lifelong aversion to practice was formed (not surprisingly) in childhood, when little Fritz resorted to every manner of subterfuge in an unending effort to escape rehearsal. Only through repeated parental pestering was he induced to spend any productive time at all with his instrument—an image that refutes the stereotype of the workaholic *Wunderkind* and illustrates, as do many other aspects of his boyhood, under what unorthodox circumstances Kreisler's gifts evolved.

The prize he won upon graduation, unprecedented for a child his age, indicates that he indeed must have attended to his studies with some seriousness of purpose. Nevertheless, in later discussions of his years at the Vienna Conservatory Kreisler spoke not of hours toiling under Hellmesberger's tutelage, not of furiously practicing out of ambition or of fear, but of more usual school-boy preoccupations. On the day he won the gold medal he was also elected chief of his gang of friends, an honor that left a much deeper impression than any scholastic honor.[16]

> I was only seven when I attended the conservatory and was much more interested in playing in the park, where my boy

> friends would be waiting for me, than taking lessons on the violin. And yet some of the most lasting musical impressions of my life were gathered there. Not so much as regards study itself, as with respect to the good music I heard. Some very great men played at the conservatory when I was a pupil. There were Joachim, Sarasate in his prime, Hellmesberger, and Rubinstein, whom I heard play the first time he came to Vienna. I really believe that hearing Joachim and Rubinstein play was a greater event in my life and did more for me than five years of study![17]

There were others: Vienna was awash in music, from Wagner operas to chamber recitals (many featuring the violinist Arnold Rosé) to Brahms premieres to appearances by Adelina Patti. A musical child such as Kreisler no doubt attended many of the city's offerings, giving him an ear for live performance—and exposure to a broad span of musical styles—that continued to serve him long after he left the city. There was no better place than Vienna at the turn of the century to rear a young musician. His childhood there shaped his understanding not only of the arts and urban life but of the world beyond, the international community of aesthetes and intellectuals who passed through Vienna and gave its residents a sense, part real, part illusory, of having a truly global perspective. Kreisler grew up believing he knew the world. That air of cosmopolitanism, combined with a faith in humanity and what Yehudi Menuhin later described as a "feminine" sophistication, contributed greatly to his public persona, both onstage and off. Few musicians are so defined by their youth as Kreisler was by his; his views, his behaviors, were eternally, curiously childlike. Few, too, have so evoked musicians heard and admired during boyhood. They were as much a fixture of Kreisler's childhood as were excursions to the city's great park, the Prater.

Even as a boy, Kreisler moved in a circle of performers and composers that included the likes of Johannes Brahms. In a 1955 radio interview with WQXR, a classical music station in New York City, Kreisler recalled his early familiarity with the composer and his first memories of the magnificent Violin Concerto in D Major, Op. 77, which, he said, was "associated with my childhood and with my life until I was twenty-one years old. . . . I first heard it played—which is funny—by Bronislaw Huberman, in Vienna. He was fourteen years old and I was about twelve or eleven years old."[18] (In fact, Kreisler was seven years older than Huberman. Huberman, a successful prodigy, played the Brahms concerto in Vienna in 1896, with the composer in the audience. He was indeed fourteen years old, or nearly so, but Kreisler was twenty-one.)[19]

As for the composer himself, Kreisler remarked in the 1955 interview:

> Oh, I knew Brahms from the minute I was a pupil at the [Vienna] Conservatory—that was when I started, at seven years. In Vienna there was in the conservatory itself a little restaurant, which was a musicians' club, and Brahms was the president. There was music every week, mostly chamber music. And the works of Brahms were very often played there—particularly when he had just composed them and wanted to hear them. And I remember I once played the G minor trio. He gave it to me and asked me to play it, and he wanted to know . . . whether it could be played. And I said to him, "Master, I couldn't play it, because my fingers aren't long enough for that, but it is playable."
>
> So you see, he gave me that to play before it was published.[20]

In an interview with Olin Downes of *The New York Times* in 1942, Kreisler recounted chamber sessions with Brahms in even greater detail.

> I had the inexpressible good fortune to sit in quartets to whom he more than once brought the manuscript of a new chamber composition, for us to run it through for him. He would stop us, and change a note or two, or discuss the scoring of a passage. To talk to an Olympian like that, to actually be present at the creation of superb music, was priceless—and a lasting possession which does not fade or suffer from comparisons made with the perspective of time.

> We knew then a wine of the spirit. We were preoccupied with beauty. And thank God, the spell did not wear off. How distinctly I remember the circumstances of my early years.[21]

Vienna was not Kreisler's only childhood home; Paris was a city of lasting if less formative impressions. During his two-year stay at the Paris Conservatoire Kreisler developed the basis of a lifelong affection for France that was reciprocated, during his adult career, with one of the most consistently loyal audiences he enjoyed anywhere. He found in Paris not kindred spirits so much as complementary ones, people whose cosmopolitanism and love of music were rooted in separate but similar traditions. As a child he lapped up the language and the culture.

Chaperoned by his ever-ailing mother, Fritz quickly distinguished himself as one of the most talented pupils enrolled at the prestigious Paris Conservatoire. There he studied violin with Joseph Lambert Massart and composition with Léo Delibes, admiring the former for his emphasis on feeling over technique and humoring the latter in his pursuit of the opposite sex. According to one yarn, probably more fictive than factual, so dizzy was Delibes when it came to women that young ladies of his acquaintance would materialize in the middle of a lesson and whisk him away to go dancing. Off he would run, leaving his young pupil to continue with some composition or other that Delibes had left unfinished. Thus Kreisler took credit, in later years, for no less a work than the "Coppelia" waltz in Delibes's ballet of the same name; the motif, he claimed, was all his.[22] (This is a charming tale, but it is not even remotely possible: *Coppelia* was produced in 1870, five years before Kreisler was born! Whether Kreisler confused the waltz with one of Delibes's later works or concocted the entire story from his own extremely fertile imagination is open to speculation. Giving him the benefit of the doubt, we will assume that Kreisler was in fact charged with working on one of his teacher's compositions as a pedagogical exercise. The question of the composer's flightiness with women remains for Delibes scholars to consider.)

So successful was young Fritz in his studies—no matter how little he practiced—that, two years after his entry into the conservatory, he won the Premier Premier Prix, the highest juried prize awarded by the institution. In so doing, he surpassed four adult violin finalists. In addition to the award, he was presented with a bright red Gand-Bernardel violin, the first full-size instrument he ever owned and by far one of the ugliest.[23] He was then twelve years old. On the lip of a prodigious career, he went home to Vienna.

Kreisler would return to Vienna, in music if not in fact, for the rest of his life. His hallmark was always the light-footed yet muscular grace that characterized his playing and compositions alike, a buoyant dynamism harnessed through tightly controlled tempo and rhythm. This insistent pulse, rooted in and reminiscent of the waltz, impelled everything from Kreisler's miniatures to his fiercely driven interpretations of Beethoven and Bach. Many of his compositions were in fact indirect descendants of ancient Austrian folk dances, which in the hundred years before Kreisler's birth wound their way from the peasant villages of Upper Austria into the ballrooms of Vienna. One such Alpine dance was the ländler (from *das Landl*, or "little country"), a likely grandchild of a medieval round dance that incorporated a slow pair dance with elaborate turns, steps, and, in the case of the Tyrolian *Schuhplattler*, rhythmic clapping *(Platteln)* on the hands, legs, lederhosen, and shoe soles. There were 3/4 and 4/4 versions of the ländler, but it was the seductive pulse of the 3/4 dance that mutated, over the decades, into the Viennese waltz. Stripped of its intricate turns and twists, this new dance focused on the ländler's elegant and intimate ending—the closing steps, when man reunites with woman and circles her waist with his arm. "It is hardly believable," wrote Katharina Breuer, "what storms of indignation were raised by this new and supposedly indecent dance."[24]

Kreisler's understanding of the waltz and its ancestors was intuitive, complete, and very clearly expressed in the irrepressible dancelike qualities of so many of his works. *Liebesleid*, for example, was conceived as a concert version of the ländler (indeed, the ländler tempo is designated at the top of the sheet music) and retains its pointed emphasis on the dotted quarter note. Even more striking are the highly similar rhythmic figures shared by his *Caprice Viennois* and an ancient ländler. Consider the latter section of the *Schuhplattler*, as practiced in Kastelruth in the Austrian province of Tyrol (Example 1):

Example 1. *Schuhplattler* of an ancient ländler from Kastelruth, Austria.

Compare the above with the più lento passage in *Caprice Viennois* (Example 2); despite clear melodic differences, the two passages boast rhythmically identical opening bars (dotted quarter, eighth, quarter) that lend both works, in turn, their gentle, swinging gait:

Example 2. From *Caprice Viennois*, 1910.

Almost as striking are the rhythmic figures shared, with some variation, by *Liebesfreud* and another Austrian folk dance. Example 3 shows measures 4–8 of *Liebesfreud:*

Example 3. From *Liebesfreud*, 1910.

The opening bars of the *Steyrischer* (Example 4), from Grundslee in the Austrian province of Styria, repeat a similar rhythmic figure—

the difference being the substitution of two eighth notes for a quarter note in the third beat of every other measure.

Example 4. *Steyrischer* from Grundslee, Austria.

Indeed, several others of Kreisler's short pieces are based directly or indirectly on Austrian dances, including *The Old Refrain*, *Im Paradies*, *Schön Rosmarin*, and the *Marche Miniature Viennoise* (one of the few in 2/4 time). These, in turn, informed such larger works as his String Quartet in A Minor (written in early 1919) and his *Viennese Rhapsodic Fantasietta*, both ringing reminders of Austrian dance.

The rhythms of Austria also propelled Kreisler's performances. More than any other single technical aspect of his playing, Kreisler's rhythmic gift seized the listener's attention and accounted for the violinist's intangible appeal. As the late violinist and pedagogue Josef Gingold recalled:

> Once I had an aisle seat in Carnegie Hall in the orchestra [section], and he was playing *Schön Rosmarin* as an encore. I was saying to myself, "What is it about this man that he goes to everybody's heart?" And I happened to look down on the floor, and everybody's foot was beating time to the waltz.[25]

Or, as Carl Flesch observed in *The Art of Violin Playing:*

> The adept waltz player, as he was formerly frequently found among the Viennese artists, made a point of again and again attempting to restore the original tempo by unnoticeable retardations. The peculiar charm which is a feature of Kreisler's playing is mainly due to his clinging so firmly to the original rhythm.[26]

He clung to it, it clung to him; decade after decade, the rhythm appeared in his operettas, his arrangements, and his late *Rhapsodic Fantasietta*, lusciously dated to our ears. Even at the close of his career, when other powers had abandoned him—when deafness led to a loss of intonation, when age led to a loss of vigor—Kreisler's rhythmic acuity remained. It was his most enduring and salient quality: Vienna.

How fitting, then, that graceful old Vienna brought forth the most bewitching of all nineteenth-century and ultimately twentieth-century performers. Just as Vienna resided in that tense position between history and progress, so did Kreisler appear always to be a figure existing in two eras at once. He was then and he was now, established and unorthodox, connected to the tradition of violin virtuosos but radically apart from it. As he grew older and entered further into the twentieth century, he planted himself even more deeply into the place and time of his youth. Vienna consumed him; or he embraced it. "He was always animated by the spirit of Vienna," said Ross Parmenter, a former music critic for *The New York Times*. "I think he spoke with a voice of an earlier age."[27]

Fritz Kreisler could not have been born anywhere else. He realized this and referred to it, implicitly if not explicitly, throughout his career—whenever he played *Caprice Viennois* for an encore, whenever he spoke lovingly of the Emperor, in every brief, gracious bow before performing. He was the city's great apologist. In some ways he was also its worst Pollyanna; where in Kreisler's Vienna was the classism that killed the monarchy, or the racism that brought it infamy? Where was the stubbornness, the disease, the sagging economy? Nowhere—none of that had relevance when Kreisler played or spoke. Such was one of the violinist's greatest and most enigmatic gifts that everything he expressed was naively, guilelessly ignorant of ugliness; he seemed capable of perceiving and communicating beauty alone. Even during World War I, when Kreisler fought with the Austrian army and later paid for his patriotism by being ostracized from the American stage, his protestations in support of the dying monarch (and monarchy) always rang with sincerity. He seemed driven by the purest, and most innocent, of motives: the desire to seek and convey only what is noble. The poise of an aging emperor is noble. The camaraderie of the front is noble. Patriotism is noble. Music is noble.

Few public figures have managed to convey both childish idealism and cosmopolitanism in the same graceful gestures. One who did was nurtured by the city most celebrated for escapism. Vienna always represented, and on some level continues to represent, that which is artistic and artificial: the opera, the waltz, the appealing sheen of formality that accompanied the bourgeoisie's well-groomed walk through life.

Kreisler was Vienna, right down to his mustache. Fittingly, as the decades passed he lost neither his facial hair nor his resolutely Viennese mien; despite his many years spent married to an American woman, living on American soil, bearing American citizenship, he never seemed anything but a figure from a Franz Lehár operetta: robust, polite, appealingly soldierlike, and alive with music. "He was born in a city that was once romantic, joyous and free," a critic for *The New York Times* wrote on 29 May 1941. "Those qualities are in him, despite the sadness that came over all who knew and loved that city." Unlike the city that peaked and struggled, Kreisler carried his old, waltzing Vienna well into the new century. Perhaps it is just as well he never returned to visit the genuine article. Had he, he could not have maintained the portrait of the city that he preserved so carefully, for so long, in the canvas of his music. As it was, Vienna's pastel colors remained unsullied, and Kreisler cradled his beloved city for as long as he lived and played.

Two

Prodigy

Fritz Kreisler was not the first, last, or greatest prodigy ever to lift a violin to his chin, startling the public with pristine techniques and precocious musical sensibilities. There has been and probably always will be a morbid fascination with youthful players—morbid because the prodigy seems an unnatural or even anti-natural phenomenon, a creature that has diverged so dramatically from what is perceived as normal human development and maturation that it seems, somehow, an affront to God or Nature. "Your musical prodigy has his use," wrote a critic for *The Independent* just after the turn of the century, "which is to purvey good music, along with astonishment, to a certain class of people who would not think of going to hear the same music played by a mature master—and, sometimes, to develop, with the added years, into a great musician."[1] The most gifted prodigy is a challenge to the adult soloist, for a child who performs with the skills of a ripened player may seem to cast unspoken aspersions on the mere grown-ups who matured at a more usual pace. If an eight-year-old can play a Paganini Caprice with the panache of a thirty-year-old, what is the thirty-year-old left to do?

Jascha Heifetz was one of the most staggering prodigies of modern history for many reasons, not the least of which is the terror he instilled in the adult virtuosos who heard him perform as a child. Pre-pubescent or not, he was already a colleague and a rival, and a substantial one.

The young Kreisler was no such bombshell. Gifted in many ways and a clear master of his instrument, he managed a middling career as a prodigy without ever breaking into the kind of success enjoyed by Heifetz, or Menuhin, or many others. He gave concerts, he toured, he won awards, he impressed his elders, he inspired all sorts of predictions about his future promise, but he never quite seized the public's attention. When his term as a prodigy ended—in 1889, well before his fifteenth birthday—it ended abruptly, with little fanfare and with no apparent regrets on either the violinist's part or that of his parents. He had attempted an early career and it had not worked. Life presented other opportunities, and he took them: heading back to Gymnasium, then medical studies, then army service. As a boy he had never focused on the violin to the exclusion of all else, so it was not difficult for him to pursue other avenues; then as in later years, he was a person of varied interests. Distracting him from the violin was always a fairly simple task.

This may, in fact, have been the saving grace of Kreisler's career. Because his time as a *Wunderkind* was both uneventful and brief, he was spared some of the more arduous and potentially damaging trials faced by other prodigies, who have succeeded brilliantly in premature approaches to the stage only to watch their careers—and sometimes their lives—crumble under the dual pressures of concertizing and adolescence. For some prodigies, early triumph is a burden that crushes the development of a later career. "My life was moving toward a crisis," recalled the pianist Ruth Slenczynska in *Forbidden Childhood*, an agonizing account of her years as an abused prodigy.

> Some such turning-point arrives in the life of every child prodigy: the day when allowances cease to be made on grounds of youth; the time for reappraisal; the need for re-adjusting to new values. Father must have thought the career could go on indefinitely at the pace and pitch he had set for his wonder-child. If people paid to hear me at eight and nine

> and ten, why not at thirteen and fourteen and fifteen? Surely there were many more good years to his golden goose. But the warnings were multiplying.[2]

Kreisler himself was highly critical of parents and teachers who push their children too soon into a career. In a conversation with Carleton A. Scheinert in *Etude*, Kreisler contended that

> children should grow simply in music and not be forced into it for business reasons. . . . For myself, I have been protected by the broad intelligence of a wonderful wife, with ideals of life and great good sense in treating me as a man, subject to the same laws of health, or right and progress as any other man.[3]

He might have been speaking simultaneously of his parents, who never forced him into concertizing but simply followed what they believed were his wishes and inclinations.

Scheinert's short article made no mention of the violinist's own prodigious beginnings but harshly described the pressures that drive young students into early professional careers.

> If we look back to music student days we remember children younger than ourselves, more advanced, possibly more talented. Already some were making public appearances, being hurt not only musically but egotistically and physically by unreasonable adoration and expectations. We wonder where they have disappeared! Reaching at last their early twenties, physique gone, vitality drained, they are unable to continue the pace. . . . Too much, too fast progress! The talented child should be treated as any normal child.[4]

As a boy Kreisler faced no such trials, for he scored no such triumphs. His gifts did not bring him world fame at a young age. In cutting short his tenure as a prodigy, Kreisler benefited from an unremarkable public reception that guaranteed he would never burn out from overwork or overattention. He simply was not successful enough as a child to become a ruin later.

That Kreisler's later career flourished not in spite of but because of his lack of success as a prodigy is a compelling irony, and one that will be considered at length later in this chapter. But what of Kreisler as a young professional, the boy in short pants who earned prizes wherever he studied and who performed the most rigorous works in the repertoire with what must have been surprising grace? Naturally, no recordings exist from this period—still too early for the gramophone—so students of the instrument who are curious to understand Kreisler's early career are left with a disappointing gap. What does remain is a sampling, albeit small, of music reviews from his 1888–1889 tour of America with Moriz Rosenthal, a pianist whose international stature was significantly greater than his young colleague's and who drew, unfortunately for these purposes, most of the pair's critical attention.

Kreisler was, at that point, thirteen years old—he celebrated his fourteenth birthday on tour in the New World. Having won the Premier Premier Prix at the Paris Conservatoire, he was by the dawn of adolescence an instrumentalist of considerable talent and poise, a natural for an early solo career and just the type of boy wonder that observers would have expected to conquer the critics without much trouble. Indeed, he seemed ready to strike out on his own; his departure from the conservatory was also a departure from formal teaching, for he was never again to take instruction in the violin. Massart was his last teacher; whatever Kreisler learned after that he learned on his own or from listening to others—a key contributor, no doubt, to what became a highly distinctive style. Kreisler sounded like no one else in part because, after his exit from the Paris Conservatoire, he studied with no one else. The self-creation that defined him musically began at an early age.

The American tour with Moriz Rosenthal was a logical next step. Rosenthal, a pupil of Liszt's, was invited by Edmund C. Stanton, manager of the Metropolitan Opera, to make a tour of the United States. At the time, few soloists were expected to carry a program alone, and Kreisler seemed a fair choice—he had grabbed some attention by winning his conservatory prizes, and Rosenthal had heard him perform. The pianist therefore arranged for the young violinist to appear with him in fifty concerts in the United States. Although he also arranged for Kreisler's mother to accompany them on the journey, she was too ill to travel and remained behind.[5]

In October of 1888, Rosenthal, Fritz's accompanist, Dr. Bernhard Pollak, and Fritz—carrying a beautiful Grancino violin, a gift for which his father had saved the equivalent of a thousand dollars—set off from Vienna to northern Germany (Hamburg or possibly Bremen). There they boarded a small steamer equipped with sails as well as an engine. After three weeks punctuated by miserable episodes of *mal de mer* on young Kreisler's part, the group arrived in New York City. Seeing Manhattan, he later said, "was one of the greatest thrills of my life."[6]

Another thrill was his United States debut on 9 November in Boston. By most accounts a geeky-looking fellow—his longish hair was parted in the middle, he wore knee-high trousers and a huge bow tie, and he clunked onstage in massive tassled boots—the young Master Fritz Kreisler made a solid if ultimately unspectacular impression on fresh American audiences. Critics at the time appear to have spent nearly as much newsprint musing about the lad's appearance as they did commenting on his artistic merits: he was awkward, ungraceful, even, as one reviewer commented, "heavy-footed."[7]

As for his potential, there was no overall consensus; reviews were divided between those who regarded him as a youthful if unripe genius and those who dismissed him as just another talented juvenile. "He plays like a nice, studious boy who has a rather musical nature," wrote Howard Malcolm Ticknor in the *Boston Daily Globe*, ". . . but cannot be ranked among prodigies or geniuses."[8] The *New-York Daily Tribune* gave the Boston concert the briefest possible mention in its 10 November edition, devoting two sentences to Rosenthal, one to the orchestra, and one to "Master Fritz Kreisler, the Austrian violin boy." *The New York Times* was more generous: "He is at present not a phenomenon but a promising youth, who plays in an honest, straightforward style and from whom good things may be expected."[9] (Kreisler's Boston appearance was significant for at least one other reason: the occasion marked his introduction to Franz Kneisel, then concertmaster of the Boston Symphony and first violinist of the renowned Kneisel Quartet. The two would become close friends.)[10]

Despite the lack of consensus among reviewers in Boston and elsewhere regarding the promise of this "violin boy," critics seemed to agree that, whatever his relative merits, he needed to work on his right arm. His intonation was good—his left hand was quick, accurate, and agile—but his bowing was weak, and several critics commented unfavorably on the smallness of his tone.

Typical in this regard is a review that appeared on 11 November in *The New York Times*, which gave Kreisler no small mention following his New York debut in Steinway Hall. Appearing on the same program were German pianist Conrad Ansorge and Anton Seidl's orchestra in the conductor's "Grand Orchestral Concerts" series.

> Master Kreisler has come to this country under the management of E. C. Stanton of the Metropolitan Opera House. He is a lad of 14 [sic] who has already carried off a first prize from the Paris Conservatoire and has played with success abroad. His tone is as yet quite small and not at all times absolutely pure; yet it has a pleasant cantabile quality which will probably develop in time into true instrumental song. His stopping is generally good, though by no means perfect, but that would be expecting much from so young a player. His bow arm is, unfortunately, stiff, and he appears to be sadly deficient in flexibility of wrist. To counter-balance these technical faults, which study will doubtless remove, he has an honest, unaffected style and an evident appreciation of effects. He pleased the audience greatly, and not without reason, and he was recalled several times.[11]

The Independent, a New York weekly, gave the young soloist considerable attention, analyzing Kreisler's strengths and weaknesses with observant and often prescient insights. Although the critic overstated the prodigy's age as "15 or 16," he quite accurately pinpointed the nature of Kreisler's disarming—albeit underdeveloped—gifts.

> The attitude of the critics and the public toward young artists so heralded may well be more conservative than ever at present; and in the case of young Kreisler, so far as he illustrated the other night what is in him, there appeared to be no extraordinary warrant for enthusiasm, tho there is

> ample material for warm interest and bright prophecies as to the future. He is a handsome, manly looking lad, of fine physique, and a bold, mature face. In the favorite Mendelssohn concerto he showed a refined and superior musical intelligence and sympathy and a degree of executive skill at times strikingly developed, but on the whole far from being adequate to the work itself, or to what, we dare say, are his musical intuitions. He has less fullness of tone than [Brazilian prodigy Maurice] Dengremont, and his inaccuracy is occasionally disagreeably marked. In stopping he is hardly what one anticipates of a violin prodigy; and he does not give me the impression that he has reached, as a pupil, the stage of technical training and freedom which a relatively little time would bring to pass, greatly to his good. The boy, however, has two things—expression and, already, that distinctly French quality of style. His playing is again and again charming, if not astonishing, and especially in the slow movement of the concerto he showed some very happy and musicianly traits.[12]

"Charming, if not astonishing": writing decades before Kreisler achieved any measure of fame, an anonymous critic for a New York periodical used the single word that has been most often identified with Kreisler's playing. Even then—even when his playing was immature, unpracticed, and, according to some observers, deeply flawed—he already had the innate and inimitable ability to beguile his listeners. If only his bowing had matched his charm.

The *New-York Daily Tribune*, which otherwise gushed over Master Kreisler's two Manhattan appearances, joined a chorus of critics when it identified a pithless right arm as the main hurdle that stood between him and a significant international career. Its coverage of the prodigy's 10 November performance reported that "the lad Fritz Kreisler" had given a "most favorable impression." Furthermore,

> Throughout the evening admiration was held by the faultless purity of his intonation; unfortunately, however, his tone is extremely small, and he hurried the tempo unduly, and denied

> his listeners the pleasure which comes from a reposeful performance. That he has much talent is indisputable, and we would prefer to postpone judgment till after his appearance at the Rosenthal concert on Tuesday.[13]

Tuesday's concert only confirmed the reviewer's opinion: good left hand, bad right. Although Kreisler made a "much more favorable impression" than he had with Seidl's orchestra three nights earlier, Kreisler's bowing and tone production were somewhat flawed. Otherwise, he might "measure himself with some of those who stand highest in the world's admiration."[14]

That the young man was criticized for having a small tone, fast tempo, and unimpressive bow control is interesting and in retrospect ironic, since a warm tone, moderate tempos, and masterful bow work were later regarded as among the mature Kreisler's greatest and most appealing assets. It is possible that the thousand-dollar Grancino was ill-matched for large concert halls; it is also possible that Kreisler simply had not developed his distinctive bowings. (Either way, the weakness was not corrected, as had been urged by American critics, through concentrated study and rehearsal. Thanks to some unidentifiable sleight of hand, it appeared to correct itself—through a seven-year period of almost total disuse.)

In New York as in Boston, the kid in short pants persevered. At the second of his two concerts in Manhattan he played Henri Vieuxtemps's *Fantaisie-caprice*, with piano accompaniment (and with "admirable tone and accurate intonation," wrote *The New York Times*).[15] In Chicago, on 1 March 1889, he rendered Henri Wieniawski's *Fantaisie brillante* on themes from *Faust*, inspiring lukewarm to good reactions among the local critics (although one found his playing "crude and frequently out of tune").[16] Accounts of his appearances at other venues are hard to come by, due to the performer's relative inconsequence and the nonexistence or generally poor quality of newspaper indices of the time. What is known is that Kreisler performed across the continent for the duration of the 1888–1889 season, stopping off in Cleveland, St. Louis, Kansas City, New Orleans, and many other unidentified locations. In all probability it was a grueling affair that involved daily train travel and nights spent in small hotels, no easy routine for a gangly adolescent traveling without his parents. According to Lochner, Kreisler killed time by reading omnivorously and throwing himself into the study of English, a language that he would later master—with no small assistance from his future wife—with surprising fluency.[17]

Lochner cast the American tour in a wholly positive light, balancing its scant financial success (most of Kreisler's $37-a-week fee[18] went toward expenses) against the intellectual and spiritual benefits of exposing a young mind to a new culture. This is certainly true, and it may well be that Kreisler's early introduction to the United States, like his time spent in Paris, contributed to his cosmopolitan outlook and unbending faith in humanity.

Yet his concertizing with Moriz Rosenthal must have been a frustrating experience on some level, for it drove him to quit. He no sooner returned to Vienna than he decided, with his parents' blessings and advice, to set aside musical pursuits while he finished his education. Although his motivation for giving up music at this point was complex and will never be completely understood, it is at least clear from the abruptness of the decision that he desired to break free from what promised to be a narrow life. According to Charles D. Isaacson, Rosenthal himself repeatedly chided his young colleague for having a limited view of the world. He teased: "You are only a fiddler, Fritz. You know nothing but how to play those strings. You can't even talk about anything else." As a result, Isaacson wrote, "When Fritz returned to Europe he had an overwhelming ambition to confute the taunt of narrowness. As a result, he went headlong to the opposite pole."[19]

So Kreisler returned to his studies at the Piaristen Gymnasium, run by Catholic lay brethren. With added tutoring from his father, he was able to fulfill the requirements for his Abitur (roughly the same as high school plus two years in college) before his eighteenth birthday.[20]

Thus in 1892, unsure of what direction to take next and aware of the mandatory military duty that awaited him two years hence, Kreisler enrolled in the medical school of the University of Vienna. The years he spent studying medicine were to remain with him, in one form or another, for the rest of his life: in his mastery of Greek and Latin, in his understanding of his own physical ailments, and in his obsession with collecting antiquarian books, many of which were medical texts. In medical school he toiled over corpses, sandwich in hand, and appeared in no significant way different from his fellow students; a former classmate recalled for Lochner that no one knew or spoke of Kreisler as a musician, and that the only characteristic that distinguished him from the others was his ability to perform dissections without looking at his hands. Lochner attributed this quirk to Kreisler's repulsion at the stench of the corpse and his habit of turning his head (that is, his nose) as far from it as possible.[21] This may be, and it presents a comical picture, but how anyone of any manual dexterity could accurately take apart a human body while staring in the opposite direction is beyond imagining. If true, the old and infirm of Vienna were deeply fortunate that Fritz Kreisler never became a doctor.

Even in medical school Kreisler did not pursue a degree single-mindedly. "In those youthful days," he said, "I had some very weird thoughts about my future career. I envisaged myself operating on a patient in the morning, playing chess in the afternoon, giving a concert in the evening, and (in anticipation of a glorious military career) winning a battle at midnight."[22]

After two years of school, Kreisler abandoned his medical studies and entered the imperial Austrian army as a soldier in the Kaiserjaeger Regiment. At some point during the next twenty-four months, between hours spent in military training and further hours spent socializing, he returned to the violin that had lain dormant during his years in Gymnasium and medical school. He made no great effort at practice or study—he had no time—but picked up the instrument now and then to entertain his comrades. At the same time, he earned a reputation as an accompanist to his commanding officer, the Archduke Eugene of Habsburg, who was a grand-nephew of the Emperor and an amateur singer of some skill and greater enthusiasm. The Archduke and the fresh-faced volunteer performed together at sporadic music recitals that were arranged for the regiment's officers and their dates.[23]

Although little information exists concerning Kreisler's youthful service in the Austrian army, what does emerge from the turn of the century is a portrait of a young man, intelligent and musically gifted, who had no firm ambitions and no clear idea of which direction his life should take. Attractive, articulate, well-liked, and mature in many ways, he nevertheless lacked the self-awareness to recognize what must have been obvious to anyone who knew him: that his future was bound, undeniably and inextricably, to the violin. He could learn to be a doctor or prepare to become a soldier, but Fritz Kreisler was already a violinist. No seven-year sabbatical could change that.

Finally, in 1896, after finishing his mandatory service in the army, he faced once again the matter of his as-yet unsettled career. Still unsure of his ambitions, he returned to serious study of the instrument that he had treated so casually for so long. It may be that, as Lochner contended, Kreisler simply decided to "return to his first love and make the violin the chosen instrument for expressing what his soul felt and strove and yearned for."[24] It may also be that the twenty-one-year-old, like many young adults of any era, was in dire need of something to do. A medical career would have required three more years of study. A military career also would have meant a commitment to serve for a set block of time. A musical career, however, required nothing more and nothing less than holing himself up with his instrument and practicing—hard—until his technique was up to par. The violin was familiar; the violin was safe. That the violin also presented his best, last chance at realizing an extraordinary musical and communicative gift was probably, at that stage in his life, not even considered.

Nevertheless, Kreisler returned to the violin, and he returned with gusto. With his father's help, he obtained room and board at a tavern outside Vienna, where he reacquainted himself with the instrument and fiddled now and then for patrons in the adjoining saloon. In those quarters he remained for eight weeks, working on manual dexterity and a repertoire that he had not approached in several years. Kreisler later said that he used some of the time to complete one of his arrangements of a Paganini piece, although he did not identify which one.[25]

Those eight weeks and the stretch that followed proved to be a period of surprising productivity. Besides the Paganini, Kreisler probably composed during this period the first of his three celebrated cadenzas for the Beethoven Violin Concerto in D Major, which, though now less frequently played, are significant additions to a standard member of the repertoire. Writing them at such a young age was a vote of confidence in his own future, as Kreisler had not yet made enough of a name for himself to secure jobs as an orchestral soloist and could not have foreseen a time when he might. To have composed a cadenza for a concerto he had not yet performed publicly with an orchestra was an act of blind faith.

The few years following Kreisler's release from the army also marked the start of the period during which he wrote his infamous "fakes," the faux eighteenth-century manuscripts that will be discussed at length in Chapter 7. Embarking on what would prove to be an agonizingly slow ascent to prominence, Kreisler capitalized on his relative anonymity by creating for himself a repertoire of works—the fakes as well as others penned under his own name—that would showcase his own unusual strengths as another composer's music could not. These works were in fact key elements in the development of a singular musical personality that evolved less from his loosely romantic interpretations of established works than from his graceful and eccentric reflections on his own musical conceits. More than any other violinist (including, arguably, Pablo de Sarasate and Nicolò Paganini), Kreisler shaped his career from his own compositions; they were malleable clay.

This was, then, a time of emergence and simultaneous disappointment for Fritz Kreisler, an interval of creative advancement that had little direct connection to the state of his professional career—which encountered one hurdle after another. An attempt to join the Vienna Hofoper orchestra failed when the concertmaster who auditioned him, the renowned Arnold Rosé, complained that Kreisler "kann nicht vom Blatt lesen" (can't sight read, or read music cold).[26] There is another possibility: dissatisfaction with Kreisler's sense of rhythm, an even stranger complaint.[27] The unexpected setback of his unsuccessful audition with the Vienna Hofoper, probably the result of professional jealousies as well as real errors on Kreisler's part (it is not hard to imagine him showing up for an audition without having practiced), directed the young musician toward a solo career as a successful audition would not have. As often occurs with great artists, Kreisler's early career was propelled not by triumphs but by failures that sent him trundling down unplanned but ultimately fruitful paths. Had he caught fire as a prodigy, he might have quickly burned out; had he earned a position at the second desk of the Hofoper orchestra, he might have remained a workaday ensemble player for years to come.

There is some indication that Kreisler's expectations of himself were, at this point, actually quite low. Carl Flesch recounted his second introduction to Kreisler, when the Austrian was still a youth (Flesch said twenty; in all likelihood, he was twenty-one). Kreisler, he wrote years later, "had the misfortune to grow up too swiftly, and to enter puberty all too early—an age which is usually so momentous for artistic development." As a very young man, Kreisler seemed "a big, strong, broad-shouldered fellow whose facial expression showed a lively temperament with a touch of brutality, and who was amiably superficial and dashing in character."[28]

According to Flesch, Kreisler's early efforts in Vienna amounted to little more than appearances in other musicians' recitals: he "passed as a local celebrity who had all but gone to the bad; he had in fact resigned himself to ending up as an orchestral player." Kreisler's main problem, beyond his fondness for cafe society and his incurable loafer's heart, was the "unrestrained orgy of sinfully seductive sounds" that flowed from his violin—too unfettered, too emotional, too instinctive, too much. Only by maturing musically and personally and by taming undisciplined affect in his playing was Kreisler able, Flesch believed, to finally present in public an artistry that audiences could accept and eventually embrace.[29]

Flesch took a harsh view of the limbo between Kreisler's years as a prodigy and his eventual return to the violin as young man; in Flesch's opinion, the interval nearly destroyed his career. But there is an alternate way of looking at Kreisler's temporary divorce from the instrument, a less severe perspective that sees in Kreisler-the-mature-musician a virtuoso who was indeed formed and informed by Kreisler-the-prodigy—but in a wholly unorthodox manner. It is possible that he "found himself" (to borrow Isaacson's words) not by embracing the violin as a youth but by running directly away from it. At a point when most soloists would have flung themselves headlong into an early and in most cases lucrative career, the "Austrian violin boy" with the high boots and mournful eyes chose to deny what to any outsider must have seemed a predestined vocation; he chose to avoid, or at least postpone, the rigidity required of those who spend their lives in music. He freed himself to explore other interests and facets of his personality, a personality later realized in his own distinctive music-making. He freed himself, in other words, to mature as a human being before he matured as an artist.

Had Kreisler resumed his musical education upon returning to Vienna in 1889, he might have emerged scant years later as a young performer of the highest order and might as well have enjoyed international fame at a much earlier stage in his life. He might also, arguably, have taken instruction from one or two more pedagogues whose influence might have had slight but significant impact on their pupil's approach to the instrument. What that impact might have been is impossible to say, but further education may well have affiliated Kreisler with one particular school of playing, be it French or Belgian or Leopold Auer's, and in so doing effectively muzzled an original voice. Kreisler was who he was in no small part because he took no formal instruction on the violin past the age of twelve. In consequence he was able to develop a nakedly personal, manifestly idiosyncratic style that refuted all attempts to categorize him and made his ultimate successes both more extraordinary and harder to attain. Beyond an obvious association with the musical traditions of Vienna and a suggested kinship with Eugène Ysaÿe, his playing offered no clear reference points, no pigeon holes, no hooks upon which to hang a handy appellation. He belonged to no school of playing but his own.

As a result, Kreisler's adolescent retreat from the instrument ensured that his eventual return would succeed or fail on the violinist's own peculiarly individual merits. It also guaranteed that the adult Kreisler would in large measure avoid comparison with the younger one, a common frustration for prodigies who mature musically in the public eye. As Ruth Slenczynska wrote:

> The fact that I made my concert debut twenty-eight years ago puts me in a rather odd position. People recall me as an old-timer. I am someone they heard far back in their youth. Yet I am only thirty-two. Time and again they have come up to me and said, "I remember you when . . ." as if I were twice my age. Wherever I go there is always somebody who heard me play as a child.[30]

By the time Fritz Kreisler returned to the concert stage, the ripples from any splash he had made as a boy were long since scattered. He was, if not an unknown, a lesser-known instrumentalist than those who had concertized during the time of Kreisler's sabbatical, so listeners were less inclined to compare him (favorably or unfavorably) with the ghosts of Kreisler's past. Too much time had passed; too little attention had been paid him as a child. Despite the American tour, despite all the conservatory prizes, despite the occasional prescient insights from reviewers about his skills and potential and underlying charm, Kreisler's prodigious beginnings did not secure or even directly aid his adult career. His accomplishments as a pupil and moderate if unremarkable achievements as a child soloist provided a technical and practical base on which he relied for the rest of his professional life; they also gave him an ease, a naturalness, in performance that amplified his onstage charisma and fared him well through every manner of musical mishap. If Kreisler seemed to belong onstage, his juvenile concertizing was one reason why.

Beyond such indirect influences, however, Kreisler's later career had no direct relationship with his earlier one. When he left the army in 1896 and holed up in a tavern for eight weeks, he was, essentially, starting from scratch. For all intents and purposes, Fritz Kreisler began his solo career at the age of twenty-one.

Three

From Ysaÿe's Shadow to the Birth of a Pop Star

At first consideration, Kreisler's youthful debut on the American concert stage may appear to teach us nothing useful about the artist as a very young man. Or it is useful only by default: it perhaps gives us a glimpse of what Kreisler might have become but did not. He did not soar as a child performer. He did not practice hours upon hours each day. He did not, and his parents did not, single-mindedly pursue his career in music. He seduced neither audiences nor critics. So little critical attention was paid to Fritz's share of the program during his maiden tour of the United States that what we know of his playing at the time—beyond the standardized praise that seems to have been accorded all prodigies, then as now—is limited to those same cursory if occasionally revealing descriptions of weak bowing and good intonation. Yet as we have seen, Kreisler's boyhood concertizing had the profoundest impact on the remainder of his career, simply because it seems to have had no impact at all. That few took notice of his entry into and exit from the American stage did not bode well for his potential as a soloist on either side of the Atlantic, but it did promise that whatever advances Kreisler ultimately made would be made cleanly, honestly, and from a dead start: he could not rest on any laurels, for he had no laurels on which to rest.

When Kreisler re-entered the concert arena as a young adult, he did so as an underdog. He had no prominent pedagogue to mentor and champion him, no poseur's love of the limelight to draw attention to his playing, no spectacular technique or diabolical virtuosity to ignite the interest of an audience filled with savvy listeners. There were already enough violinists in circulation to keep Vienna occupied; the city did not need or seek another. Kreisler's failure to obtain a position as a section player in the Hofoper orchestra showed just what a struggle he faced in trying to establish a career as a professional musician, much less a soloist, for he had given up as a child the one descriptive label—prodigy—that distinguished him immediately and positively from other violinists. He was no longer a prodigy; he was not yet recognized, or even recognizable, for stylistic and technical innovations that would later establish him as one of the great figures in twentieth-century performance. He was merely one of many violinists in a broad field of virtuosos.

Chief among European virtuosos was Eugène Ysaÿe, a lion of a man who loomed so large on concert stages everywhere that anyone who aspired to the same position was doomed to unflattering comparisons. Ysaÿe was simply unapproachable.

> Who is there among contemporary masters of the violin whose name stands for more at the present time than that of the great Belgian artist, his "extraordinary temperamental power as an interpreter" enhanced by a hundred and one special gifts of tone and technic, gifts often alluded to by his admiring colleagues?[1]

So effused Frederick H. Martens in his 1919 collection of interviews, *Violin Mastery: Talks with Master Violinists and Teachers*, a remarkable document of the history of violin performance. A 1918 photograph of Ysaÿe, his wavy hair below the collar, his profile granitic in its bluntness, dominates the cover of the book and its frontispiece. Martens's interview with Ysaÿe takes up the first chapter, and the above quotation in fact opens the book. The author could have chosen no better way to begin his volume, for it summed up perfectly both the sentiments of concertgoers around the world and the dilemma facing Kreisler at the start of his career: Ysaÿe was all. The Belgian's huge stature overshadowed all others, making his predecessors seem dusty and his contemporaries sound wan by comparison. Kreisler was neither dusty nor wan, of course, but he was different—and different in a way that did not immediately impress the crowds that had been subdued so thoroughly by Ysaÿe.

Born in Brussels in 1858 and a student of Vieuxtemps's and Wieniawski's, Ysaÿe was the pre-eminent violinist of his generation, a soloist of such enormous popularity and equivalent critical acclaim that he was tapped, inevitably, as successor to the great Hungarian violinist Joseph Joachim. But unlike Joachim, who built his reputation on lambent classicism, purity of expression, and an elegant, temperate style, Ysaÿe burst onto the European stage like a tiger let loose from his cage. He was a tall man, big-boned, large-headed with thick features, and his heft was expressed in his music: he played the violin with fire and fierce attack, astonishing his audience with the virtuosity, the masculinity, the sheer size of his performance. He was not a soloist of soft-spoken or simple pleasures.

"When he appeared on the platform, one felt the presence of a king," Pablo Casals once said. "He had a fine presence and was of great stature, looking like a young lion with piercing eyes. His gestures also; the way he moved about; he was a show in himself. . . . One could not fail to be carried away by the strength of his personality."[2]

He had his detractors. George Bernard Shaw had little patience for Ysaÿe, praising his technical skill and conceding the man's broad public appeal, but nevertheless deriding him as "an unsympathetic player." Ysaÿe "is declared by experts the most dexterous of living fiddlers," Shaw wrote. "I can answer for it that he is the most bumptious; but I do not rank bumptiousness high as an artistic quality: perhaps because I am myself singularly free from it."[3]

Kreisler was Ysaÿe's heir in some ways, his opposite in others—particularly in personality and presentation, which were altogether less theatrical ("bumptious") and thus less instantly attention-grabbing. Philip Dreifus, a Cincinnati violinist of many years, was fortunate to meet both Fritz Kreisler and Eugène Ysaÿe in the early part of the century. He played for Kreisler in 1914, taking a handful of lessons from him before Kreisler's brief service in the Austrian army during the early months of World War I; he studied under Ysaÿe during the last years of the maestro's life, while he was living in Cincinnati. The differences between Kreisler and Ysaÿe as musicians and as men were stunningly, instantly obvious. "It was about the difference between white and black," Dreifus said. Kreisler's inimitable grace contrasted with Ysaÿe's more solid style of playing.

> Ysaÿe was a big man with a large stomach, and he didn't have the grace that Kreisler had. Kreisler had a particular Viennese lilt and style in his playing and a style that wrapped you up. Ysaÿe, he was big, he was very heavy . . . [and] he played that way. You just can't compare them.[4]

Ysaÿe was, in fact, obese. By the second decade of the twentieth century he had filled out every inch of his big-boned frame, becoming a man of such fulsome proportions (if drawings, photographs, and descriptions of him are to be believed) that it is a wonder he lived as long as he did. "He really wound up eating himself to death," said Dreifus. "[But] I had only the greatest admiration for him. It was probably one of the greatest experiences of my life, studying with him and studying with Fritz Kreisler."[5]

Even earlier, Ysaÿe's corpulence gave him the appearance of one whose playing, like his physique, bespoke indulgent excess. Consider this description from a turn-of-the-century musical commentator named Arthur Symons:

> I looked at Ysaÿe as he stood, an almost shapeless mass of flesh, holding the violin between his fat fingers and looking vaguely into the air. He put the violin to his shoulder. The face had been like a mass of clay waiting the sculptor's thumb. As the music came, an invisible touch seemed to pass over it; the heavy mouth and chin remained firm, pressed down on the violin, but the eyelids and the eyebrows began to move as if the eyes saw the sound and were drawing it luxuriously, with a kind of sleepy ecstasy, as one draws in perfume out of a flower.[6]

In his memoirs, *Rise to Follow*, Albert Spalding recalled hearing Ysaÿe perform the Beethoven sonatas in London.

> Ysaÿe was at his leonine best. His tone was not large, but it had an expressive quality impossible to describe. His famous Guarnerius tucked under his chin looked like a half-sized fiddle, too small for the great gamut of emotions it was to run. How well I remember the tremendous drama of the C Minor Sonata. . . . The eight-bar exposition of the theme by the solo piano paves the way for its still more telling repetition by the violin. Ysaÿe used to hold that G—sustained through three-quarters of a bar—a fraction of a second over time so that the figure of four sixteenth-notes precipitated themselves with extra speed, resolving the phrase with an explosive quality. It gave you goose flesh![7]

Spalding regarded Ysaÿe as the connection between two divergent approaches to violin playing: Joachim's and Kreisler's. As he commented in an interview with Louis Lochner:

> Fritz Kreisler is as different from Joseph Joachim as the romanticism in architecture of the pre-Renaissance period is different from the Gothic of the thirteenth and fourteenth centuries. In a sense Ysaÿe was the bridge between the two styles of playing. Interestingly enough Joachim's playing was quite different from what he did pedagogically. He played with a fire which he would never have tolerated in his pupils.[8]

A closer look at the three styles of playing supports Spalding's observations. Joachim, born in 1831, was separated from Ysaÿe (born in 1858) by one generation and from Kreisler (born in 1875) by two. Although the violinists overlapped by many years—Kreisler was thirty-two and approaching world fame when Joachim died in 1907—the generation gaps yawned between them, yielding differences in technique and philosophy so marked that the forty-four years between the births of Joachim and Kreisler can only be regarded as a period of the utmost change, even revolution, for violin artistry.

Consider an old, faint, but remarkably telling recording of the bourrée from Bach's Partita in B Minor, rendered in 1903 by Joseph Joachim.[9] It is a peculiar little performance for many reasons, not the least of which is the jarring confluence of recording technology—which signals modernity, or at least its approach—with an obsolete playing style. It is cool, hygienic, almost entirely devoid of vibrato (Kreisler's heavy use of vibrato, as we shall see, was to be a central part of that virtuoso's legacy), and sometimes glaringly out of tune; nowhere in the piece are there any obeisances to sentiment in particular or audience preference in general, and every passage is rendered with the interpreter's restraint for which Joachim was famous.

Ysaÿe, by comparison, startled the world with his sheer animal energy—tempered by an obvious desire, usually indulged, to play directly to the audience. His performances in many ways were studies in contradiction: hugeness of personality versus lightness of tone, flashiness of interpretation versus precision in technique. In Ysaÿe's playing—his version of Wieniawski's "Obertass" from Two Mazurkas (on the same compact disc as Joachim's bourrée from the Bach partita) is a fair example—can be heard quicksilver phrasing, firecracker energy in the fast passages, and a few clear precursors to Kreisler's trademark glissandos. A light, warbling vibrato colors his legato but virtually disappears in fast sections and double stops.

This style of playing is distinct from but clearly related to Kreisler's, which took Ysaÿe's relationship with the audience and made it at once the most intimate and obvious characteristic of his playing. The tone of Kreisler's playing was darker, fuller; the romantic ornaments more evident; the link with his listeners more intensely personal. Ysaÿe's playing differed from Kreisler's in dimensions rather than in ideology: it was built on a larger scale. Everything about it (and, ultimately, him) was bigger, broader, more confrontational, and took up more space on the stage, giving listeners no room to doubt anything they heard. Kreisler suggested; Ysaÿe informed.

A further study of the two styles can be made by comparing their respective recordings of Brahms's *Hungarian Dance* No. 5 in G Minor. Ysaÿe's version, an arrangement by Joachim, was recorded in 1912[10] and displays in full the brash charm that startled audiences who had been accustomed to the much starker beauties that had characterized Joachim's approach. Marked by exaggeratedly gutsy attacks on the downbows, a shining tone in the dancing middle section, and wild variations in tempo, Ysaÿe's interpretation surprises the listener—even a listener separated by three-quarters of a century—with the utter self-confidence of its player. There are no "maybes" in this piece, no ambiguities, no unanswered questions or intrusions of pathos and pain. It is simply a big, flashy, outrageously entertaining piece of work.

Kreisler's reading of the Brahms was recorded at roughly the same time as Ysaÿe's (actually a year earlier)[11] but shows a notably different approach to the music and the instrument itself. The violinist's tone is darker—if it were a color, it would be brown to Ysaÿe's gold—and more resonant, supported by a vibrato that cuts faster and deeper into the path of the music. In Kreisler's hands it is a heavier-sounding piece, layered and reverberative, with less voracious downbow attacks, more sonorous double stops, a more consistent tempo (although some license is taken), and an overall lack of certitude. This is one man speaking, not a chorus of Ysaÿes. Most interesting of all is the airiness, the roominess, of Kreisler's reading, an easy fluency that gives the impression of a leisurely tempo despite the fact that Kreisler's recording is much faster than Ysaÿe's. Perhaps as a result of his rhythmic precision or his ever-busy vibrato, Kreisler's version seems to have more space between the notes. There is so much detail in Kreisler's playing—his pulse is so incisive, his tremolo so fast—that the feel of his performance is under tempo.

In contrast with the elder violinist's massive sound and virtuosic style, Kreisler's was subtler, more human, less of a shout than a dialogue with his listeners. It is no wonder that he was not an immediate hit. To audiences still mesmerized by Ysaÿe, Kreisler must have presented a perplexing amalgam of old and new, virtuosic and subdued. Here was a tall man, nearly as broad as Ysaÿe, reared in the same city that had embraced the demonic charisma of Paganini, heir to the same traditions; here he was, producing a sound of such casual intimacy that he might have been speaking with his voice instead of his violin. He was the first to use his violin as an instrument of conversation, the first whose style was a relaxed and natural expression of his own musical personality. John McCormack was one among many who compared Kreisler's playing to the human voice, and it is an apt analogy; the vocal qualities of his style, a mix of rhythmic vigor, precise articulation, and lingual emphases, were both the cause of early audience indifference and the reason for his ultimate success.

Even more specifically, Fritz Kreisler introduced to violin playing one practice that had never been exploited to quite the same extent: the continuous vibrato. Forerunners on the instrument used vibrato judiciously and with some frequency but did not employ it everywhere—it was reserved as an ornament, primarily for use in long or held notes. Although Ysaÿe used the technique more often, more beguilingly, and to greater effect than any of his predecessors (Kreisler himself credited Wieniawski's "French vibrato" as a significant influence[12]), he did not vibrate in virtuoso sections of a work and often played entire passages without it. Kreisler's nonstop vibrating was remarkable for its rapidity, its evenness, and its employment even in the fastest runs of eighth or sixteenth notes; the resultant quiver added depth to his bow work and yet another conversational quality to his tone. If his playing sounded vocal, the unfading vibrato was one reason why.

As Carl Flesch wrote in *The Art of Violin Playing:*

> What has become of the day of Joachim and Sarasate, when one was permitted to vibrate only on those tones whose importance with regard to the melodic line seemed to justify this special expressional garnish? Kreisler defends the principle of lending soulfulness even to the passage-work that seems apparently dryest, by means of a slight vibrato which fuses with the actual tone to make an indivisible unit. On this basis he has formed for himself a style of performance which represents the contemporaneous ideal of beauty in violin playing in its perfection.[13]

More than any other characteristic of Kreisler's approach to the violin, this one has endured; few instrumentalists performing today may appreciate its origins, but all continue to exploit what was, at the turn of the century, a subtle but startling innovation. Its widespread contemporary use carries some irony, for despite how commonly it is utilized now, it perplexed concertgoers at the time and was not quickly embraced by Kreisler's colleagues. Listeners accustomed to a more linear tone—a tone generated by the right arm as much as or more than the left—were forced to adjust their expectations of the instrument and what sounds it can produce. The violin became in Kreisler's relaxed cradle an instrument whose tonal character was not merely influenced but shaped by the labors of the left hand.

"Violinistically, [Kreisler] was certainly a new kind of fiddler," said Eric Wen, a Kreisler scholar and record producer.

> It is true that Kreisler had this quality, this ability, to bring in the fast passages, and he had this wonderful kind of warmth that he could manage in sheer violin playing. It is true that the vibrato was concrete—and people often take to things, or qualities, that are [imitable], like the constant vibrato. He had this deep musicianship, an expression, a soulfulness, that was so part of his nature. But there is that quality of playing or at least attribute of playing that did influence a lot of people.[14]

Kreisler stood out from his contemporaries in other regards, exhibiting as a young man all or most of the qualities that would later become his hallmark: a relaxed yet active left hand (hence the vibrato); intensely focused articulation, which used martelé, détaché, and portato strokes in extremely economical bow work; a striking use of portamento; and a keen sense of rhythm, expressed in an elastic but precisely metered rubato. These attributes, combined with the active vibrato, gave Kreisler's playing an energetic, natural style that at once calmed and excited its listeners.

Wen continued:

> His playing was very focused, but on the other hand, Kreisler also sounds very relaxed. If you see the oscillations of the tone itself, it's incredibly alive, intense, and buzzing—yet when you hear him play anything, it's so charming, it puts you at ease. He had this incredible mixture, this intensity in his playing style, and yet he could exude the most

> calm, relaxed style. . . . He certainly was a unique, personal kind of artist.[15]

Not all scholars of the violin regard Kreisler's nonstop vibrating as a desirable or even benign development, however. Hans Keller, in an economical and biting essay on the evolution of violin technique, excoriates the "chronic vibrato" popularized by Kreisler's multitudinous recordings. While praising the violinist's individual charms, Keller criticizes the example he set for generations of performers to follow, who distilled his technique to its tangible qualities and tried desperately to imitate the inimitable.

> I am not implying that [Kreisler's playing] harbored hidden unmusicality—or rather, it did, not for Kreisler himself, but for all his plentiful conscious and unconscious imitators. . . .
>
> Legion were the students of the violin who listened to his gramophone records over and over again, utterly unalive to the fact that as an artistic act, any performance is unrepeatable. Why? There were plenty of reasons, and from the so miscalled musical point of view, it was his characteristic "sweet tone" that was chief amongst them. But from the technical standpoint which, by then, had become disturbingly isolated, there was one single puzzled, baffled, mystified preoccupation—Kreisler's intriguing vibrato in quick passages, his ability to employ vibrato in the fastest scale and yet keep it crystal-clear.
>
> When he came in, the all-pervasive vibrato had progressed well beyond the danger point anyhow; as soon as one heard and saw that he was capable of employing vibrato in the very places which one had learnt to keep free of vibrato in order to retain their clarity, "Let there be vibrato!" became more unconditional than "Let there be light!," for God divided the light from the darkness, whereas Kreisler didn't divide his vibrato from anything.

As a result, Keller concludes, "Vibrato tone as the norm has so firmly established itself that a player will, as it were, start vibrating as he ascends the platform. The devastating influence the chronic vibrato has had on the envelopment of the right arm's expressive power cannot be overestimated."[16]

Although some of Keller's hyperbole might be overlooked (comparing Kreisler to God, for example), his assessment of Kreisler's technical impact is indisputable: forever after, tone production in modern violin playing has been dependent upon the left hand's constant wiggle. Whether this is preferable to the *senza vibrato* tonal variations once produced by the bow arm alone is a matter of personal (and, by now, cultural and historical) prejudice. Certainly Kreisler saw no harm in it. Conceding that Joachim disliked Kreisler's use of the vibrato, Kreisler said, "No, if a human voice uses the tremolo unnaturally, that is bad. With the violin, however, the tremolo comes natural."[17]

Natural or unnatural, viscerally appealing or musically disastrous, Kreisler's fleet vibrato helped carry violin technique into the twentieth century. Technique would later be carried further—by Jascha Heifetz—but at the time, this rising Viennese instrumentalist offered a strange and finally seductive new sound. The challenge to audiences was to accept him without comparing him to Ysaÿe. The challenge to fellow violinists was whether, and how, to imitate him.

Despite the dissimilarities between Kreisler and Ysaÿe—and despite the fact that, clearly, they competed for the same audience—the two men were never true rivals. They respected, supported, and befriended each other in a manner that in retrospect may seem naive in its sincerity and in fact proves that Kreisler belonged as fully to the previous century as he did to this one. That the two men enjoyed each other's company and dedicated works to each other (Kreisler his *Recitativo and Scherzo Caprice*, Ysaÿe one of his celebrated Six Sonatas for Solo Violin) indicates just how little ill will passed between them. "We were all friends," Kreisler told an Associated Press reporter in 1958. "We helped each other. We were solidly and fondly together in the field of music. The fact is, there wasn't the competition that I see today."[18]

Furthermore:

> We all acted in the same way. We had our simple pleasures together. In Germany in summer, we strapped on our

> rucksacks, we carried perhaps a toothbrush and an extra pair of shorts. Sending on heavier things in somebody's wagon . . . we'd set off on a twenty- or thirty-mile walk through the Black Forest.
>
> We walked alone at first. Then we walked with girls. Then we walked with our wives. It cost us perhaps $1 a day, we had beer or wine, or maybe only milk or water. The man who carted our stuff might charge seven cents. My wife and I would hike as far as from here [New York City] to Albany.[19]

Kreisler's friendship with Ysaÿe began when the older man was at the apogee of his popularity and continued, against all common sense and most human nature, well past Kreisler's own rise to the top. The Austrian had long since displaced Ysaÿe as the world's top violinist when, in 1928, he visited his friend at his studio in Brussels. Josef Gingold was then a student of Ysaÿe's and had just wrapped up a lesson when Kreisler materialized. Gingold recalled:

> It was his first appearance in Belgium after the First World War. . . . During the concert, Kreisler played three concerti: the Mozart D major, the Beethoven, and Vivaldi, the likes of which I've never heard since. He came to Brussels and immediately went to see the master, and they embraced, and Ysaÿe said, "Where is the gendarme?" And Kreisler said, "She's downstairs. She'll be up in a moment."[20]

Ysaÿe's reference to Harriet Kreisler, Fritz's wife, as "the gendarme" (or "constable") reveals no small familiarity with Kreisler's personal life and illustrates as well the relaxed nature of their friendship. (Chapter 4 provides a detailed discussion of Harriet and her role in Kreisler's life.) Two such Old World gentlemen could enjoy and admire each other without allowing anything so crass as ambition (or a cranky wife) to stand in the way.

Fritz Kreisler had grabbed Ysaÿe's attention very early on in his career—years before gaining a substantial international following, a decade or more before anyone realized he had displaced the Belgian as the uncrowned king of string players. The turn of the century had not yet arrived when Ysaÿe first remarked upon Kreisler's potential. The occasion was Kreisler's 1899 Berlin debut, a musical coming-out so startling for its intensity and suddenness that it is hard to fathom, in retrospect, why his career did not skyrocket immediately thereafter. "His name was on all lips," recalled Flesch. "It was felt that with him a new era was beginning in the history of violin playing."[21]

Among those who sensed the significance of Kreisler's debut was, not surprisingly, Eugène Ysaÿe. Many years after the fact, Arthur Abell—a writer and chronicler of musical greatness—wrote for Kreisler's seventy-fifth birthday dinner a long letter of appreciation that recalled Abell's early introduction to Kreisler's artistry, and recalled conversations Abell subsequently held with six musical figures of towering importance: Ysaÿe, Joachim, Max Bruch, Arthur Nikisch, Richard Strauss, and Lilli Lehmann. Abell's account is an extraordinary piece of history and a lucent illustration of Kreisler's connection with the late nineteenth century.

Abell's first anecdote, an account of remarks made by Ysaÿe, concerns Kreisler's "sensational" Berlin debut of March 1899. Stunned by the performance he had just heard, Abell asked Ysaÿe—who, according to Abell, "was one of the many celebrated violinists who sat in Beethoven Hall that evening"—what he thought of Kreisler's rendition of the Vieuxtemps Violin Concerto in F-sharp Minor and Paganini's *Non Più Mesta*. Ysaÿe replied: "Fritz Kreisler is the Wieniawski of our day. I know whereof I speak, for I studied with the great Pole and I heard him play many times. Kreisler has a brilliant future before him."[22]

Eight months later, Abell heard Kreisler again, this time as soloist with the Berlin Philharmonic, conducted by Nikisch.

> In the box next to me sat the great Joseph Joachim, a fascinated listener, while you [Kreisler] played the Mendelssohn concerto, which he had studied and played with the composer more than forty years before. After the concert I asked Joachim for his opinion of your playing, and he said, "I am very much impressed. Kreisler is not only a great and very individual violinist, but also a pronounced musical personality."[23]

Abell said that he had heard Kreisler as a soloist with the Berlin Philharmonic Orchestra under Nikisch on at least five occasions between 1899 and 1913, and that during that time Kreisler appeared with the conductor more than had any other violinist "except the renowned Ysaÿe."

> After your rendition of the Brahms concerto in 1909 I asked Nikisch how he reacted to your playing. He replied, "It is always a great pleasure to conduct for Kreisler because of his interesting and highly individual conceptions and his rare musicianship. He has a very appealing tone and impeccable taste in everything he interprets."[24]

Also in 1909, Kreisler performed Max Bruch's *Scottish Fantasy*, with the composer himself at the piano, at a gathering held in Abell's Berlin home. Bruch later said of the violinist's abilities: "Kreisler's playing sends out a rare magic. He has a wonderful tone, and his beautiful style of phrasing especially impressed me."[25] Later that same day in 1909, Kreisler startled Bruch by plunking himself at the piano and playing a selection of Strauss waltzes. Amazed, Bruch remarked, "Why, Kreisler plays the piano almost as well as he does the violin! Only a born Viennese can play Strauss waltzes with such charm."[26]

Even Richard Strauss was among those with early (and, thanks to Abell, documented) opinions of the young Viennese performer. Following the world premiere of Strauss's opera *Ariadne auf Naxos* at Stuttgart in 1912, under Strauss's personal direction, Abell asked the composer to name his favorite violinist of that time.

> His reply was characteristic of Strauss. He said, "In my youth I was much interested in the violin as a solo instrument, and I composed a concerto and also a sonata for it. Of late years, however, I, to quote Richard Wagner, 'think of the violin only in the plural,' but when I hear such ravishing tones as Eugène Ysaÿe and Fritz Kreisler draw from their instruments I love to think of it again in the singular. Formerly Joachim was my ideal violinist, but today I have two, Ysaÿe and Kreisler."[27]

Finally, a bit of a detour: Abell's generous reflections include his account of a May 1926 meeting with the great soprano Lilli Lehmann, then seventy years old, at her home in Berlin. After visiting with Lehmann and her sister Marie, Abell and the two aging ladies took a stroll down to Kreisler's house, only to find that the violinist was not at home. Abell was disappointed, but the aborted visit presented an occasion for him to ask, once again, his favorite question: What did she think of Kreisler's playing? The reply began with a quote from the poet Johann Ludwig Uhland: "Singen wem Gesang gegeben" (Those should sing to whom song is given).[28] Lehmann continued:

> All my life I have followed Uhland's advice. I love the violin, and I have always thought of it as an instrument of song. In my youth Wieniawski was my favorite violinist. How he could make the Mendelssohn concerto soar and sing, shine and sparkle! In the eighties Joachim, Sarasate and Wilhelmj were my ideals. Today I prefer Fritz Kreisler because he sings on his instrument as does no other living violinist. I greatly admire his virtuosity too, because in my youth I used to sing such coloratura roles as Philine, Violetta, and Leonora.[29]

Lehmann finished her reply in German so idiomatic that Abell declined to translate it: "Kreislers bebende Töne gehen zum Herzen. Sein Spiel ist wirklich genial. Ich sehe in ihm mein geigerisches Ideal verkörpert." Or, in English: "Kreisler's vibrating tones go to the heart. His playing is really brilliant. I see my violinistic ideal embodied in him."[30]

Despite all the (belated) accolades, it took the young Fritz Kreisler much time and concertizing before he was able to draw the crowds that those who heard him believed he deserved. He nevertheless persisted, touring Britain and the United States throughout the century's first decade and drawing consistently good notices wherever he performed.

It was a feverish period, marked by frequent travel. At the turn of the century Kreisler brought his new wife to London, where the couple lunched and dined with Enrico Caruso at a side-street restaurant while the great tenor happily drew cartoons for them. In 1900

Kreisler appeared at a children's Christmas concert in New York City arranged by Walter Damrosch and was rewarded by the young ones with a huge ovation. In the same year he performed in, among other venues, New York and Chicago (where reviewers praised his artistry but groused about a poor-quality violin); the following season he was back in Vienna, on hand to greet Rachmaninoff when the pianist arrived.[31]

It was during this period, or sometime in the few years following, that Kreisler made an unexpected, unpublicized, and justly famous impression as a pianist. According to this possibly apocryphal tale, the soloist arrived at a London concert hall after traveling all night to rehearse the Mendelssohn violin concerto with an amateur orchestra. Frazzled and exhausted from the trip, the absent-minded Kreisler showed up without his instrument; his solution, to the surprise of everyone in the hall, was to deposit himself at a nearby piano and play the entire work from memory, transcribing it extemporaneously for the keyboard. So exact was his transcription and so precise his instructions to the orchestra that the performance went perfectly later that evening.[32]

He returned to New York City several times in the next few seasons, appearing onstage with Jean Gérardy in 1902, with a noticeable limp in 1904 (why was unclear), and with Josef Hofmann in 1905. On each occasion he was greeted warmly, but never with the capacity crowds or the fervid anticipation that were to be his popular rewards less than a decade later.

Critics remained skeptical of his gifts. In a fascinating essay published in the 19 January 1905 issue of *The Independent*, the author (uncited) compared the artistry of three violinists: Ysaÿe, Kreisler, and a Hungarian prodigy named Franz von Vecsey. Vecsey was dismissed as a "likeable little boy" with a "big, luscious tone" who displayed some promise but did not "play like a man, with a man's feeling and comprehension." So much for Franz. Ysaÿe, in the same pages, was lionized as "more than a virtuoso" and given a glowing account of his sundry gifts.

> He is a great musician; a masterly interpreter of music's content and meaning. He plays the loftiest music. . . . His tone is that of a dozen virtuosos in unison, clear, limpid, sonorous and singing. He handles that big, magical tone

> with marvelous delicacy and reposefulness. In the brilliant passages Mr. Ysaÿe is strong and satisfactory, but hardly develops the leonine power and magnificence one might expect, from a glance at the man, to be the chief characteristic of his playing. It is in the remarkably delicate phrasing and shading, continued throughout every measure of all that he plays, and the depth of feeling and sentiment with which his playing is imbued that the real excellence of his work is found.[33]

Having thus established Ysaÿe as the be-all and end-all of all things violinistic (how could any soloist hope to surpass "a dozen virtuosos in unison"?), the critic then turned to Kreisler, who arrived on the New York concert scene "after a few years absence, having in the interim added several cubits to his musical stature." The Austrian "fairly challenged comparison with Ysaÿe by placing on his first program the great Beethoven concerto, which the Belgian had already played—with the same New York Symphony under Walter Damrosch." Thus challenged, the author complied:

> It must be said at once that Kreisler is a great virtuoso, an artist of rare abilities. His technical skill is amazing. His temperament is fiery. His style is vigorous and aggressive, yet polished. His tone is penetrating, but it is thinner, less sweeping in depth and volume than Ysaÿe's. He lacks the intelligence, the musical comprehension, the musicianship of the older man. He is deficient in well-rounded emotionality. Ysaÿe's laurels are secure. He remains the great wizard of the bow.[34]

The idea of anyone damning Kreisler for deficiencies in tone, intelligence, or "emotionality" may seem peculiar now, but at the time and in context it made perfect sense: here was an upstart violinist, so distinct in tone and personality, who was forced to walk in the shadow of one of the most magnetic characters in the history of solo performance. Ysaÿe had inspired a passionate following. Why should any of his admirers, be they reviewers or average listeners, have heard in Kreisler's playing any indication of his future eminence? Or why, if they heard it, would they have switched their allegiance from the older man to the younger, from the Belgian to the Austrian?

Most astonishing of all, in retrospect, is the fact that Kreisler made any career advances whatsoever during Ysaÿe's lifetime. Yet it was not long after *The Independent*'s dismissive article that Kreisler began to acquire both the critical reputation and the widespread popularity befitting a soloist on the ascent. This was many years before Ysaÿe's name would fall from the list of the world's foremost performers; but Kreisler's, in the meantime, was on the rise.

By 1907 Kreisler began to make his mark. He toured the British provinces, sold out Queen's Hall, claimed the hard-won affection of Boston (previously known as a pianist's town), and earned a reputation as a specialist in seventeenth- and eighteenth-century music, in great part—and with delightful irony—because of his cache of hoaxes (to be discussed in detail in Chapter 7). He also received some praise for his taking up of the Brahms concerto, which critics said had never been truly mastered by the elderly Joachim. That Joachim died the same year was a fitting and bittersweet coincidence.[35]

In the years that followed, Kreisler's career continued to climb toward a summit that he finally reached, after much effort, during the century's second decade. He performed frequently in Europe (including an appearance with Willem Mengelberg in Carlsbad) and the United States (where a 1908 tour was interrupted by an acute case of typhoid, and a 1909 run of the West Coast peaked with triumphs in San Francisco and Seattle), yielding more raves and bigger crowds at every turn.[36] At the same time, he found himself the subject of more frequent and increasingly in-depth magazine and newspaper mentions, which discussed once again his fondness for the Brahms concerto, his combing of French monasteries for those celebrated manuscripts (that is, the fakes), his love of chamber music, and his high opinion of American musical sophistication. Kreisler had many strong opinions and much to say. Finally, people were beginning to listen.

As "W.E.B." wrote for *The Musician* in 1909:

> [Kreisler's] art contains so much that appeals to one's sympathies that one is apt to overlook his enormous technical equipment. Idealism, repose, dignity and charm are perhaps

> its most salient features, combined with a broad eclecticism that makes him at home in whatever he undertakes, be it Bach, Beethoven, or a mazurka by Zarzycki. I suppose the highest form of musical interpretation is that which does away with all idea of work, schools, and quibblings as to details, and leaves the hearer free to enjoy the music pure and simple; and if this be so, Mr. Kreisler has won his place among the few elect—the very few, I might say.[37]

According to the article, Kreisler's position in the music world was, at this point, "unassailable"—and indeed, he seemed to have reached an apex of critical acclaim. In 1910 conductor and contrabass player Serge Koussevitzky helped Kreisler arrange a tour of Russia that included stops in St. Petersburg, Moscow, and several other Russian cities.[38] So established had Kreisler become in the brief years since *The Independent* dismissed him as subpar Ysaÿe that, in the January before his Russian tour, no less mainstream a publication than *Harper's Bazar* was inspired to remark upon Kreisler's United States appearances with the baldest hyperbole.

> The return of Fritz Kreisler—to many minds the greatest of modern violinists—is one of the delights of the musical season. . . . No more beautiful music has been heard than that this great master of the violin has given us. This, considering his art, goes without saying. A deserved tribute should be offered, however, to the courage which makes Mr. Kreisler ignore an appeal to "popular" taste in the preparation of his rare and exquisite programme, and leads him to hold firmly to those high ideals for which he is noted on both sides of the ocean.[39]

This excerpt is interesting for a few reasons, not the least of which is its characterization of Kreisler as a musician who overlooked mainstream tastes while planning his programs. So he was—but he was also one to showcase his own works, some of which had not yet been identified as such and many of which went on to become some of the most widely beloved pieces in the violin repertoire. Decades later, a typical Kreisler recital included more "popular" music than any other prominent violinist was willing—or able—to present.

The route to such popularity began, not surprisingly, when Kreisler started committing his music to 78 rpm records. The newly vigorous gramophone industry gave birth to one of its biggest, and first, recording stars in 1910, when the Victor Phonograph Company signed the violinist to an exclusive contract. The move was prescient on Victor's part, for it displayed a keen understanding of Kreisler's appeal long before it was universally recognized and it made possible a type of popular stardom that had never before been achieved. As performer and composer, no one—not even Ysaÿe—was better suited for mass consumption, simply because no one boasted that same insouciant knack for delivering a catchy tune.

Even today, generations after his earliest work with Victor, Kreisler's unmistakable mix of sincerity and charm cuts through all the scratches and static, his vibrato singing, his charisma simple but eloquent. Sound recording brought Kreisler's playing into the world's living rooms, where it had really always belonged; the warmth of his style translated perfectly to the phonograph, which gave the listener the same intimacy, the same sense of a personal connection with the violinist, that added such a seductive quality to his live performances. He was just the sort of performer that the audience wanted to bring home—and thanks to the gramophone, they could. Kreisler was made for the 78.

In this regard Kreisler was similar to his friend Caruso, another performer with a genius for connecting with his audience, and another who became a hugely popular recording star with the advent of new technology. They were, in fact, the world's first true pop stars—long before Elvis Presley or Frank Sinatra, Kreisler and Caruso were turning out "singles" that were successes (even "hits," to borrow a term from popular music) around the world. As musicians they were revered. As public figures they were idolized. The main difference between them, besides their instruments of expression, was the fact that Kreisler composed much of the music on his own recordings, while Caruso did not; during this period Kreisler continued to turn out one short piece after another, crafting their length and character to the limitations—and the appeal—of the 78 rpm format. There is reason to wonder whether his output as a composer would have included many longer and more "serious" works had he not been so successful on disc (and had Harriet not pestered him to produce only commercially viable work). This may be so, but it is also true that Kreisler's particular gifts as a composer were well-suited to short forms and in fact may have been better realized in his "lollipops" and light arrangements than in his two longest and weightiest works, the string quartet and the *Rhapsodic Fantasietta*. No one asks why Johann Strauss did not write oratorios; to wish he had would mean underappreciating or overlooking the nature and extent of his gifts.

Whatever the long-term ramifications, the 1910 agreement with Victor marked a turning point in Kreisler's career, for it completed his transformation from an artist overshadowed by the accomplishments of his predecessors into a figure poised to become a celebrity of theretofore unheard-of proportions. Certainly his career was already established—certainly his public profile had grown tremendously—certainly he would have continued to succeed in concert halls had he never recorded a 78. But sound recording gave him a form and breadth of exposure that had not been possible in earlier decades and helped create, in Fritz Kreisler, a mass-media celebrity the likes of which the world had rarely seen. Decades before the Beatles, he was a pop star.

Clearly, by the start of this century's second decade Kreisler had made undeniable advances in concert halls and recording studios. Not to be overlooked was his popularity as a composer of sheet music: in 1908, B. Schott's Söhne, a music publisher based in Mainz, Germany, started publishing about twenty of Kreisler's short pieces and "arrangements"; by 1911, the publishers announced, they had sold seventy-thousand copies of Kreisler's music.[40]

The year 1909 proved fruitful in several regards. Besides meeting and "performing" with Max Bruch in Berlin, Kreisler maintained a breakneck schedule that hurried him through thirty-two concerts in a thirty-one-day tour of Germany. He also appeared as a soloist at the second Brahms Festival at Wiesbaden.[41]

Fritz Kreisler was heavily in demand and hugely admired. His ascent to the top of his profession, which had endured so many early setbacks, finally seemed secure: there was no longer any question of his place among the world's top string players, and many had already started referring to him as the foremost violinist. Just how far he had come was symbolized by a series of informal gatherings that began in 1910 and continued regularly for several years. At the start of every summer, a small army of eminent musicians—Kreisler, Ysaÿe, Georges Enesco, Jacques Thibaud, Pablo Casals, Alfred Cortot, Harold Bauer, and Raoul Pugno—gathered at Thibaud's house in Paris for marathon sessions of recreational ensemble playing that allowed each man the simple pleasures of chamber music.

As Pablo Casals detailed in his memoirs, *Joys and Sorrows*, written with Albert E. Kahn:

> Those sessions in Thibaud's place would begin in the late spring or early summer, at the end of the concert season, when our tours were finished. Our group would come together, like homing pigeons, from all parts of the globe. Ysaÿe would have just returned from a tour of Russia, Kreisler from the United States, Bauer from the Orient, I perhaps from South America.[42]

Casals described the loosely organized sessions as evenings of the purest entertainment: world-class performers making music for the joy of it.

> How we all longed for that moment! Then we would play together for the sheer love of playing, without thought of concert programs or time schedules, of impresarios, box-office sales, audiences, music critics. Just ourselves and the music! We played duets, quartets, chamber music—everything and anything we felt like playing. We would constantly change around: Now one would play the first or second violin or viola, now another. Sometimes Enesco would be at the piano, sometimes Cortot. Usually we met after supper, and we would play and play. No one paid the slightest attention to time. The hours flew past—we stopped occasionally for something to eat or drink. Often when we finished, it was early morning as we left Thibaud's.[43]

Ysaÿe and Kreisler, the once and future paragons of violin artistry, took turns on viola. Finally, after years of concertizing, they were equals.

Violinists and scholars may take exception to such generalizations, but even a cursory glance at the history of violin technique and performance suggests a hierarchical, even monarchical, progression from one reigning soloist to another. There are indeed potentates of the violin, and though their time in power may be relatively brief (as short as a decade), their influence on entire strata of aspiring instrumentalists can be profound and nearly irreversible. Allegiances formed in youth to a ruling sovereign can last a violinist's lifetime; Ysaÿe had his loyalists, as did Kreisler, as does Heifetz still today.

Carl Flesch reflected on this situation in his 1930 work, *The Art of Violin Playing:*

> The violin playing youths of the years between 1860 and 1880 regarded the seriousness and grandeur of Joachim's manner of playing as a goal worthy of their efforts. Between 1880 and 1890 Sarasate's lightness was considered the most precious quality. And when Ysaÿe's star rose radiant in the violinistic heavens, all were convinced that intensity and freedom of expression constituted the artist's noble attribute. Today, again, the vital blood-current with which Kreisler infuses his tone, his racy, rhythmic power, is the aspiring violinist's ideal.[44]

Why, then, was the listening public so lax in responding to this "vital blood-current?" Why did Kreisler take so long to establish himself in recital halls? Why were his gifts unrecognized—or, at least, underappreciated—until he was well into his thirties?

Obviously, his stunted career as a prodigy was partly responsible; had he persevered as a child and not abandoned the instrument during his teenage years, there is every likelihood that he would have achieved the heights of fame at a much earlier age. (What that would have meant for him artistically is another matter altogether.)

Just as obviously, Kreisler's entry into the upper ranks of solo performance was stymied by the continued prominence of Eugène Ysaÿe. So influential, and so long, was Ysaÿe's reign as king of the violin that no brooding Viennese with an unidentifiable and unprecedented style was about to dethrone him—not easily. Ysaÿe's grip on the instrument was firm, his grip on the audience firmer.

But perhaps the best explanation for Kreisler's slow rise to prominence was articulated, once again, by Carl Flesch. In Kreisler Flesch saw the nineteenth-century soloist whose artistry crossed into and in fact helped define violin performance in the twentieth century. Kreisler, Flesch wrote, "was the first who most nearly *divined in advance* and satisfied the specific type of emotional expression demanded by our age. This is the reason why, in spite of his astonishing violinistic precociousness, his actual participation was recognized and appreciated at a period comparatively so late" (italics are Flesch's). Further:

> Thirty years ago his manner of performance, borne on the wings of tempestuous sensuality, supported by an exacerbant, intensive vibrato, and communicating an excitement which whipped up its auditors, was not yet in conformity with the then ruling taste of the time. Gradually the interval between the two was bridged. Kreisler grew more clarified the more turbulently our epoch behaved itself. In his style, in his tone, with its seductive yet ennobled sensuality, in the compelling rhythmic nature of his specific bowing technique, in that impulsive "itinerant musician" quality which, for all its directness, never oversteps the limits of good taste, our time appears mirrored in a transcended, ennobled conception of art.[45]

In other words, Kreisler failed to succeed as a turn-of-the-century violinist because his musical conceptions and techniques belonged to a wholly different—and future—era. When the world caught up with him, he succeeded. He was ahead of his time.

Four

Fritzi and Harriet

Everything I am as a violinist I owe to Harriet.[1]

It is entirely possible, although some more ardent Kreisler devotees may deny it, that without Harriet Kreisler there to nudge him—to needle him into practicing, to raise his fees, to protect him from the masses—Fritz Kreisler would not have had his career. He would have had *a* career, perhaps, achieving a modicum of respect and some fame on the basis of his own extraordinary gifts, but it is reasonable to suppose that he would not have attained quite the same status as a global celebrity. To begin with, he was not nearly as ambitious as Harriet and seemed to prefer the company of friends, the dusty comfort of antique books, and the thrills of the poker table to anything approaching hard work. As he and everyone who knew him confirmed, he hated to practice. He did not simply avoid it himself; he was evangelical on the subject, advising colleagues not to spend too much time rehearsing. Excessive practice numbs the creative spirit, he admonished.

Harriet forced him. Some accounts, possibly fictitious, tell of Mrs. Kreisler locking Mr. Kreisler and his fiddle into a room and not letting them out until he practiced. Others, of more verifiable origin, describe her efforts to limit his gambling, drinking, book-collecting, and other apparently aimless activity, in an effort to focus his attention on musical matters. By all accounts, she was the practical half of the marriage, the one who kept her eye on the coffers and made sure "Fritzi" was given his due. She was, too, a ferociously protective woman who guarded her husband jealously, forbade him to socialize with other women while on tour, and raged mightily whenever he appeared to disobey her. She married him, managed him, made him. She controlled him.

Fritz Kreisler met Harriet Lies in 1901. Kreisler was returning to Europe on the *Prince Bismarck* following an American tour with Josef Hofmann and Jean Gérardy; Harriet, having maneuvered her way into the graces of a young, well-connected, and Continent-bound acquaintance, was a passenger on the same ship. Kreisler entered a barber-cum-gift shop on board the *Bismarck* when he spotted the flame-haired Harriet trying on a hat. "I saw the reflection of a beautiful red-headed American girl in that mirror," he recalled in William Stidger's *The Human Side of Greatness*. "I fell in love with her instantly, for she smiled at me then and there; and I smiled back. That was the beginning and the end for me."[2]

That last comment ("the end"? of what?) might have an ominous ring to it, but Kreisler meant it as a broad romantic gesture. Harriet was his world; she defined his boundaries, boosted his stature, and accompanied him on every step of his life and career, even when she was not with him physically. Her presence loomed, always, everywhere. She made no effort to retreat into the background.

Nor did it take long, after that first meeting, for her to solidify her role or to establish herself as a no-nonsense presence in his life. While aboard the *Prince Bismarck*, the couple recalled eight years later, the ever-charming Kreisler had taken to entertaining passengers with his considerable pianistic skills. He was so engaged in a salon full of ladies when Harriet broke in, annoyed at their attempts to impress the violinist with their erudition and fine taste. "One after another they asked him to play Chopin nocturnes and Beethoven sonatas, opus this and opus that," Mrs. Kreisler remembered. "I was getting very much bored. Finally I said, 'Oh, Mr. Kreisler, won't you please play the Florodora Sextette,' and he did the rest of the way over!" As Fritz himself put it: "It struck me as delicious frankness."[3]

Harriet Lies was the divorced wife of a man named Fred Woerz and the only child of German-American tobacco merchant George P. Lies. Born at Second Avenue and Tenth Street in Lower Manhattan, Harriet was later fond of recalling her childhood propinquity to fashionable New York families (among them the Astors and the Stuyvesant Fishes) and bragged, to friends and acquaintances, that her parents hailed from among the oldest Catholic lines in the city.[4]

This sort of boastfulness aggravated Franz Rupp, Kreisler's accompanist in Europe during the 1930s, who did not believe Mrs. Kreisler's claims and regarded her as an exceptionally coarse and offensive woman. Yet there is no question that her father was a wealthy man and that he did, ultimately, pass that wealth to his only child. After his death in May of 1924, George Lies left to Harriet the bulk of his estate, willing her $791,042 in real estate and other holdings—a whopping fortune for that era. (His entire estate was appraised at $882,042 and included, among other assets, realty at 7 and 9 Waverly Place, 43 and 51 West Fourth Street, 106 East Seventy-Eighth Street, and 1510 Avenue A. It also included a $454,205 trust deed of property that he gave to his daughter two weeks before he died.)[5]

Whatever his lineage, George Lies was not pleased that his daughter would marry a fiddler. According to Stidger, Lies "felt that it was lowering the standards of the family a little to have a daughter marry a mere musician."[6] He might have been justifiably nervous; he was probably dimly (if at all) aware of the groom's career and knew only that his daughter's first marriage was a failure. But thanks to Kreisler's considerable charm, and Harriet's even more considerable willfulness, it was not long before Fritz and his future in-laws were on familiar terms.

Physically, the tall, big-boned Harriet was a fair match for Kreisler, whose stature and build made him one of the more commanding presences on the musical stage. A description published six years after their marriage portrays Mrs. Kreisler as tall, "of fine proportion and grace, and with a face whose beauty and evidence of depth of forceful and high-aspiring character grows on one."[7] Photos of them taken at the time of Kreisler's World War I stint show a handsome couple, dour and stiffly uniformed. Fritz is wearing an Austrian army reserve uniform, his left hand handling a sword with the same light touch that he used to grasp the violin scroll just before playing. In a few photos Harriet is dressed in the long white garb of a Red Cross nurse.

Harriet and Fritz got engaged immediately after their first meeting—while still on the *Prince Bismarck*, in fact. Just as quickly, Harriet began to alienate Fritz's friends. According to one story of untraceable origin—repeated by the late Franz Rupp—her attachment to Kreisler so irked Josef Hofmann that he exclaimed, after meeting her, "Who's that horrible woman?"[8]

After landing in Bremerhaven, the smitten couple went to Berlin, where Harriet surprised several of Fritz's friends with her brash display of youthful ardor. One of those friends, Edith Stargardt, recalled that "Harriet in an exuberance of affection plumped herself on the lap of her loving swain. We considered it at the time less shocking than amazing."[9] Rupp commented that at parties Harriet "would get vulgar. She got drunk, put her legs up on a coffee table."[10] Evidently, Harriet's prohibition of alcohol for Fritz did not apply to her own habits; she drank, and in no small quantities.

A year later, in 1902, the two were married in New York City. A second ceremony, conducted by an Austrian ambassador in London, followed shortly thereafter. According to Kreisler, the latter nuptials were arranged "to satisfy the national and church requirements—and our double marriage took!"[11]

In truth, there is evidence that their second marriage was followed not long after by a third. Apparently, some technicality overlooked in one of the first two ceremonies drove the couple once again to seal their marriage, in Hoboken, New Jersey, in 1905. This minor but interesting fact was included in Louis Lochner's original notes for the *Fritz Kreisler* manuscript but did not survive Harriet's scrutiny for final publication. (Harriet's role as censor for the Lochner book will be discussed further later in the chapter.) Why will remain a mystery, but the biography does mention Fritz and Harriet's *final* nuptials—in 1947, following their instruction in Catholicism by Fulton J. Sheen. Thus they were married a grand total of four times.

As a result of her efforts to control Kreisler and his career, Harriet was feared and despised by many. She was "bossy," "domineering," "a virago"—all of them appellations assigned by Kreisler's colleagues, many of whom used an even less flattering and considerably more vulgar word to describe his wife. Few other terms surfaced so often in interviews with people who were acquainted with Harriet, and few were uttered with such lingering anger. Judging from the accounts of Kreisler's acquaintances, Harriet was (and is) almost as universally disliked as her husband was adored: she was regarded as the source of his melancholy, as an obstacle in the way of any and all recreation, and as a cause for much speculation among friends who could not fathom why, beyond the obvious practical benefits, Kreisler remained with a woman who repeatedly and obviously mocked and embarrassed him. It was, for many, an enduring mystery of his life.

"I didn't like her. As a matter of fact, I hated her," said Franz Rupp. Rupp, who called Harriet "the worst" of the difficult women he knew from his career as a pianist for Emmanuel Feuermann, Marian Anderson, and others, recalled the stringent rules of conduct Harriet imposed on Fritz in almost every facet of his life.[12] While touring in particular, Kreisler followed—or was told to follow—a strict code, being forbidden by Harriet from entering gambling houses or appearing at any social function that might be attended by women. He was not to stray. Any failure to obey the law was swiftly and soundly punished.

In 1935 Kreisler and Rupp embarked on a much-publicized zeppelin tour of South America, stopping in Brazil, Argentina, and Uruguay. "He promised his wife he wouldn't go to parties [and] that he would never give an interview to a woman," Rupp said. In Rio de Janeiro, however, Kreisler in fact appeared at a function with a member of the opposite sex—"very beautiful, too"—and a bystander, not realizing the consequences, snapped their photo. Somehow that photo made it out of Brazil, back to the United States, and into the hands of Mrs. Kreisler, who greeted her husband upon his return to Germany with the picture jammed in her fist. Kreisler and Rupp had no sooner alighted from the zeppelin when Harriet attacked. "Rachmaninoff was there, his daughter was there," Rupp recounted. Harriet came to the zeppelin "with her fist in the air. And you know what she said? 'You son of a bitch!'—before other people!"[13]

In an interview published in *The Strad* magazine in 1987, Franz Rupp told of a concert in Amsterdam:

> The manager had engaged a pretty girl to turn pages for me, since he knew that was my preference. Just as the encores were getting underway, who showed up from Berlin but Harriet? She was furious on account of the page turner and made quite a scene backstage. Kreisler blamed me, of course! She was very rude to me and I thought that she would slap him, as I actually had seen her do once but had pretended not to.[14]

Harriet often ridiculed her husband in public. Various people have told of her dismissive attitude toward his genius, reviling his abilities and announcing, for any who would hear, that Fritzi might have amounted to something if only he had practiced. "You god-damned good-for-nothing," Ernest Schelling's wife, Lucie, once overheard Harriet say to Fritz, "you aren't even a fiddler!"[15] Violist Harold Coletta recalled dropping by the NBC studios one day in 1949 or 1950 when Kreisler, then in his seventies, was performing on the "Bell Telephone Hour."

> I got there just near the control booth to see Fritz walk out and play his first piece—and an elderly woman was standing outside, next to where I was. . . . So after the first number, during the applause, while the announcer was [introducing]

> the next piece, I turned to her and I said, "Isn't it wonderful to still hear Mr. Kreisler play so beautifully?" She said, "I am sick and tired of that damn fiddle." That was the end of our exchange.[16]

Even at concerts, it is said, Harriet did her best to control and humiliate him. So intimidating was her presence that, according to Rupp, it negatively affected his playing: Kreisler played beautifully when he was alone, less so when his wife hovered nearby.[17] The violinist "was sort of an easy-going, good-for-nothing type who'd rather sit in the bar than practice," said George Neikrug, the cellist and string teacher based in Boston. "She'd be yelling at him, and he'd be stooped over backstage. As soon as he was onstage, he was this heroic figure—and as soon as he got through [the concert] and came off stage she'd yell at him, and he'd be stooped again."[18]

What was she yelling about? Sir Yehudi Menuhin, who admired, emulated, and befriended Kreisler and to this day speaks of him with reverence, said that Harriet actually told Fritz which encores to play. In 1929, when young Yehudi was a prodigious thirteen-year-old, he attended a Kreisler concert in Berlin. "There she was backstage," he said, "ordering him about."

He described her behavior at a concert Menuhin performed in Paris. "I was playing with an orchestra—the Beethoven concerto," Menuhin recalled. "She was quite a virago. She was. And she nudged Fritz and said, in a very, very loud, audible whisper, 'Now, Fritz. You never played your cadenzas as well as that, did you?' "[19]

Harriet stories abound. "I met [Kreisler] once at a dinner and had the misfortune of sitting next to his wife. Well, she was horrible," said Edward S. Naumburg, an amateur violinist and a lifelong compiler of Kreisler lore and recordings. "She was very bossy. He was henpecked. She was brash."[20]

Alix Williamson, a press agent for numerous performers, saw Fritz and Harriet in a restaurant in New York City, not long before Kreisler died. The two were in the middle of an impressive row. "She was bawling him out at the top of her lungs. He looked so embarrassed, because everybody knew who he was. He put his head down in his hand," Williamson remembered. "I felt sorry for him. . . . She was bawling the hell out of him in a loud voice. 'Now, Fritz!' And he just sat there and hid his face."[21]

According to another anecdote, this one told by violinist Philip Dreifus, Harriet was so ferociously controlling that she did not permit Kreisler to be paid by check; instead, she demanded that payment be handed directly to her, from which she allowed her husband an extremely frugal stipend. As a result, Dreifus said, Kreisler "had nothing to live on when on the road." A Cincinnati impresario, aware of the situation, arranged for Kreisler to play at a private concert in the city and gave a portion of Kreisler's payment to the violinist in cash. Not accustomed to this arrangement, Kreisler was unsure what to do with the money and—according to Dreifus—hid it under the rug in his apartment. The solution worked fine until Harriet "decided the floor needed waxing" and lifted the rug, revealing thousands of dollars.[22] (If true, the story underscores Kreisler's casual ways with cash. Fond of the stock market and fascinated with gambling, he was far from skilled at handling money and allowed Harriet to supervise all financial aspects of his career.)

Even the more private family moments revealed Harriet's domineering side. Kreisler's great-nephew Frederic remembers visits with the aging couple when he was a boy.

> She was a formidable person. She was a very opinionated and domineering sort of individual, and I really didn't enjoy being with her much. She gave orders about what he could eat and what he couldn't eat, because he was on a strict diet during those last few years. He had heart trouble himself. He was quite heavy at the end, and she wanted to make him lose some weight.[23]

The late violinist Jacques Thibaud, a good friend of Kreisler's, called Harriet "Harri-OT" behind her back and often told tales of the Kreislers' marital antics. Pianist Sylvia Rabinof Rothenberg recalled Thibaud's descriptions of Kreisler as a man pursued by harpies: "He'd run away to hide from her because she was like a madam principal with him, an army general." Kreisler, who never did stop collecting rare books despite his wife's efforts to the contrary, used to hide old medical texts and Greek and Latin works under the rug (apparently a popular spot for concealing contraband). There Harriet would find them, then confiscate them for Fritzi's own good. "He was forever hiding books from her," Rothenberg said.[24]

To be fair, Thibaud himself sang a slightly different tune in Louis Lochner's biography of Kreisler, which paints Harriet as a strong-willed but essentially benevolent creature whose very bossiness stemmed from an unselfish desire to help her husband. Because Lochner was a friend of Kreisler's, and because Harriet had veto power over the contents of the book, it is safe to assume that more acidic portraits of her character either never reached her eyes or, once scanned, were swiftly discarded. That the biography appeared in any form was a testament to Harriet's regal lenience: so complete was her control over the book that there was some question whether she was going to allow it to be published at all.

The main hurdle was her failing eyesight—it was so far gone that Lochner had to read aloud the finished manuscript word by word for her approval. He dreaded doing it and complained about the chore in correspondence to Charles Cunningham during August of 1949. "Fritz is pressing me for getting the agony over with in the course of next week," Lochner wrote, "lest Harriet change her mind at the last minute and say she doesn't want the book to appear."[25] Charles Foley believed that Harriet did not "care a damn" what the book said about Fritz—her main concern was what Lochner wrote about her.[26]

In this light, Thibaud's comments in the Lochner biography should be regarded as truthful but probably incomplete—not bowdlerized so much as edited, carefully and willfully, by a woman with a clear picture of how she wanted to appear. They address Harriet's contribution to Kreisler's career.

> If we later had the great Fritz, we owe it to Harriet. Harriet saved Fritz. He began to practice, to write, to stop playing poker all night. Wherever he was, in Paris, Berlin, London, or elsewhere, she made him practice, made him do his very best. She can be credited with a great percentage of his success.
>
> In the Kreisler career there were two capitals: the artistic capital, the genius, was supplied by Fritz; the moral and physical capital came from Harriet. Harriet was absolutely necessary to Fritz.[27]

Harriet may have been necessary for Fritz, but so were his escapes from her. He took flight regularly from her company. One of his favorite oases in his later years was Charles Foley's, the sheet-music publisher that handled the violinist's work. Located in mid-town Manhattan, it provided a convenient yet secluded hideaway from Harriet's control. "When he had enough of Harri-OT he would go up to Foley's, and the minute they saw him walk in they would pull down the dark window shade with the 'closed' sign on the door," recalled Rothenberg, corroborating Foley's own description of Kreisler's visits. There, snug in a worn, black-leather arm chair, the violinist who had supped with dignitaries around the globe would eat his favorite lunch: a hot dog, canned beans, a roll, and a beer. "They always did that for him."[28]

Menuhin drew a similar picture: "I went to see him once [at Foley's]," he said. "Usually I went to see him at the River House—he used to live at the River House overlooking the East River—but this time I went to see him alone, and he asked me to come see him at Foley's." Menuhin did.

> And there was dear Fritz, in only his shirt sleeves, seated on an arm chair which had seen better days. The image was stuffing coming out on a hot day in June, and there was Foley and Kreisler, just reminiscing about old times. He used to go there almost every day.[29]

There are those who have told similar stories of Kreisler's escapes to Foley's; others described his taste for alcohol, a potentially destructive inclination squelched by Harriet at every opportunity. Harriet strictly policed his drinking, forbidding him to imbibe on tour and giving him periodic and sometimes public breath checks. On one occasion, as Nathan Milstein described, Mrs. Kreisler "sniffed the air suspiciously" after her husband had surreptitiously downed no fewer than four double martinis. She confronted him:

> "Fritz, were you drinking?"
> "No!"

"Fritz, open your mouth and breathe at me!"
"Don't be silly."

"He got away with it that time," Milstein concluded. "The usual storm didn't break."[30]

Harriet had good reason to keep an eye on Fritz's drinking; his fondness for alcohol was well-known and, under different circumstances (and with a different wife), might have become problematic. In his breezy and entertaining book of memoirs, Milstein described in great detail a visit to a German restaurant, where the two violinists were presented with monstrous pitchers of beer spilling over with foam. "Kreisler was happy!" Milstein wrote. "He went pink in splotches, the way young ladies did in the days of my youth when they were propositioned. I was rather dismayed that my idol could get so excited over beer and rathskeller food." Kreisler was over-enthusiastic with the beer, lingering in the restaurant until shortly before he was scheduled to perform. He was, Milstein said, "not at his best when he went out onstage."[31]

Kreisler was equally fond of gambling, be it card games or casino tables or stock market speculation; he took such a tumble in the stock market crash of 1929, NBC producer Wallace Magill once said, that he had to borrow ten thousand dollars each from three friends to cover his losses.[32] Many who knew Kreisler described his frequent if clandestine attendance at poker games, another form of recreation prohibited by Harriet. Violinist Sam Kissel recalled trying out one of Kreisler's bows at the shop of Rembert Wurlitzer, the well-known Manhattan luthier. He promptly fell in love with the bow, and, at Kissel's request, Wurlitzer asked Kreisler whether he was willing to sell it. The reply was Yes, but, "On one condition: Don't tell his wife about it, because he wants to use the money for gambling." Kissel agreed, and bought the bow for a paltry two hundred dollars.[33]

Kreisler's thirst for gambling was not easy to slake. Milstein recalled touring in Monte Carlo with Vladimir Horowitz in the late 1920s. There the two instrumentalists met up with Kreisler, who asked them, "Tell me, boys, do you gamble in the casino?"

> We simply didn't have the money to gamble, so we honestly replied, "No, we don't." Kreisler nodded approvingly.

"Good, good, you're doing the right thing. I don't go there, either."

Some time later, Mr. Putnam, our manager in Monte Carlo, proposed, "Would you like to watch them play at the casino? You shouldn't bet, but just taking a look is all right. It's an amusing spectacle." And he gave us passes. And what did we see the moment we got in? Kreisler gambling away at roulette, putting stakes on different numbers, completely caught up in the game and utterly delighted! We left in a hurry before he noticed us. We didn't want to make him uncomfortable.[34]

Another tale from Franz Rupp, recounted in *The Strad*, described the only occasion in Rupp's memory that Kreisler lost his temper. "Harriet once asked me to tell him not to bet for such high stakes," Rupp said, "so I did, and he told me in no uncertain terms to mind my own business! I never mentioned it again." In the same article, Rupp told of Fritz and Harriet riding in a car in France. Harriet goaded her husband so thoroughly, making him so desperate with her barbed attacks, that when the vehicle slowed for a curve he flung open the door and jumped out. Off balance, he fell to the ground and smacked his head.[35]

There was, however, another side to Harriet Kreisler. The white Red Cross nurse's uniform (as shown in the early photograph of the couple) fit Harriet well in more ways than one; for it was during Kreisler's service in World War I that the flip side, the positive side, of Harriet's controlling nature became fully apparent. While Fritz was off in the trenches, his wife was working for the Red Cross, busily tending to wounded soldiers. To many on their death beds, she eased their worry by promising that she and her husband would provide for their orphaned children. Harriet thus instituted what was to become the couple's celebrated commitment to war orphans, destitute children, and other needy people, pumping a considerable percentage of Fritz's postwar income into charitable causes.

Kreisler never complained publicly about his wife's philanthropic urge, even when she indulged it unilaterally. More often than not he expressed admiration and gratitude for the influence she had on his life, her habit of giving and the conviction, frequently articulated, that the less fortunate should benefit from the Kreislers' largesse. "Mrs. Kreisler," he said, "is chiefly responsible for this social viewpoint."[36] That her generosity was coupled with a clearly self-centered taste for luxury—Elsa Maxwell once said Harriet wore an emerald "larger than the Hope Diamond"[37]—was an irony blunted by her own ferocious independence. Clearly, Harriet's philanthropy and her unabashed egoism were simply facets of the same driving personality trait. She did what she wanted, when she wanted, and she did it with focus, conviction, and confidence.

Harriet and Fritz spoke often and blithely of the insignificance of money in their lives. In so doing they fashioned for themselves public personas that seemed otherworldly in their disdain for material possessions and their fondness for simple things; such ferocious zeal marked their commitment to giving that it is easy to mistake the devotion in their remarks for conventional religious piety. "I am constantly endeavoring," Kreisler once said, "to reduce my needs to a minimum. . . . In all these years of my so-called public success, we have not built a home for ourselves. Between it and us would stand all the homeless of the world."[38] (The remark discounts the mansion in Germany where they lived for almost fifteen years.)

Or again:

> Mrs. Kreisler and I live simply. We do not ask for more money for ourselves than it takes to live, and we live simply. We do not go in for society and show. . . .
>
> In talking to a wealthy New Yorker recently, she was asked this question: "You do not seem to get much kick out of social life, out of meeting the elite of New York?"
>
> And my wife replied in my hearing, "No! I get more kick out of feeding poor children. I would rather dine with them than with the rich. I get my kick out of bringing a stray dog home and feeding it. I just get my kick in a different way!" That is the spirit of my wife and I have absorbed it from her.[39]

There were some who questioned her motives. Albert Spalding and his wife, Mary, believed Harriet was furiously jealous of her husband and his fame.[40] Rupp went even further, telling *The Strad:* "Harriet had a gift for publicity but no interest whatever in music.

To her, music was just so much noise. She was strictly business. Even a donation to charity would be done for business reasons." She had what in German is known as *Herrschsucht*, an urge to be "bossy, domineering." "She was nobody but wanted to be somebody," Rupp added. "I always thought that she would make a good circus manager."[41]

In the same 1987 interview with Dennis Rooney of *The Strad*, Rupp said he once asked Kreisler why he had never composed a sonata or a symphony. Kreisler's reply: "My wife always said there was no money in it."

In later, unpublished conversations, Rupp repeated his characterization of Harriet as a stubbornly unmusical woman, someone who was more interested in boxing matches than anything anyone—including her own husband—might do on a concert stage. She was so fanatic about the "Sweet Science," in fact, that "she was very mad that I didn't remember the names of boxers. . . . For her, I think, when [Kreisler] played it was just a noise. She was unmusical. Completely unmusical."[42]

Frederic Kreisler made similar observations, describing Harriet as utterly ignorant of history, literature, and music—an ignorance she often masked "through liberal use of bombast." Her vituperative ignorance, Frederic observed, contrasted sharply with Fritz's knowledge and love of philosophy and his lifelong reflections—through words and music—on the meaning of truth and beauty.[43]

Of all the ironies in Fritz and Harriet Kreisler's marriage, one stands out: the strongest half of the equation was also, physically, the weakest; Mrs. Kreisler was subject to frequent bouts of extremely poor health. Among the saddest mysteries of the Kreislers' union was their childlessness, which they never discussed publicly (such topics having been *verboten* until fairly recently) but which might indeed have been related to Harriet's shaky constitution. Frederic Kreisler has said "there were pregnancies" of which the family was aware, but there were, unfortunately, "no surviving children."[44] How many failed pregnancies over how many years is unknown, as is the effect these may have had on their marriage.

Correspondence between Kreisler and friends during the 1940s and '50s refers to frequent, and usually vague, illnesses afflicting his wife, from severe bouts of influenza to a condition that sounds possibly psychosomatic. In January of 1937 Harriet was felled by a bad flu ("What worries me," Kreisler wrote, "is the weakness of the heart action"). In July of the same year, she suffered from a malady, undisclosed, that was serious enough to slow down the couple's travels and keep them in Carlsbad until the end of the month. So shaky was her health that Kreisler was not certain they would be able to attend the Paris Exposition, scheduled for the end of August.[45]

As the years passed, her health only deteriorated. In a letter to Louis Lochner, written from Heaton Hall in Stockbridge, Massachusetts, and dated 1 July 1948, Kreisler reported that Harriet was resting quietly and would "certainly recuperate better if she did not excite herself constantly." He continued:

> Unfortunately I am quite powerless in this respect for even if I can segregate her from people and reporters I cannot from the mail, the telephone, the papers and the radio. At any rate she feels much better in this quiet spot than in the turmoil of Babylon on the Hudson.

A few months later, the situation was similar: Harriet had suffered from "much excitement here lately and is much in need again of an absolute rest."[46]

Even in good health, Harriet was likely to spin into a rage with the smallest provocation. If there was a medical connection between her health and her moods, it may well have been high blood pressure; although there is no mention anywhere of such a diagnosis, accounts of her more outrageous tantrums nevertheless seem tacitly hypertensive. She did have a tendency, as her husband so delicately put it, to "excite herself." Even she admitted as much. In a letter to George F. Denney, Jr., Harriet expressed her admiration for his radio talk show, "The Forum," and told him that she and her husband were frequent listeners. Then she added: "Frankly, I get awfully angry when the audience irritates me by being so one sided, but that is not your fault! My limbs are tired from kicking and the radio and table suffer in consequence."[47]

The radio and table are, unfortunately, unavailable for close examination. Were that possible, the inevitable nicks and dents would probably reveal that the demonstrative Mrs. Kreisler had not exaggerated at all.

Certain questions cry out to be answered. How did Kreisler withstand Harriet's behavior—her rages, her edicts, her unyielding rule? Why, through constant verbal cudgeling, did he stay with her? He never hinted at divorce and, despite his travails, seemed resigned to her rule. He usually obeyed her prohibition against socializing on tour. Perhaps not surprisingly for one so uncombative by nature, he complied with many of her demands. Those that he skirted—her rules against gambling and book-collecting, for example—he did so with an almost innocent cheer, his punitive snap at Rupp a shocking and obvious exception. Perhaps his moral code did not permit him to break the union; perhaps he shied from change or confrontation; perhaps he feared that without her, his career, and indeed his life, might have dwindled to nothing. So thoroughly and in so many ways did she control his daily existence that the thought of breaking free—as liberating as that might have seemed to an outsider—must have been too terrifying to entertain.

From one perspective, Kreisler's attachment to his domineering spouse made perfect sense, for it echoed Salomon Kreisler's decades-long marriage to the short-tempered Anna. Like his father, Fritz Kreisler was a sweet-natured and impractical man who shunned confrontation and indulged a fondness for collecting (manuscripts and violins rather than exotic animals); and, like his father, he married a woman who structured his world and held him in an unbending iron grip. Anna and Harriet were both practical women, both prone to rages, both ill (Anna chronically; Harriet often), both unmusical, both capable of violence, and both wholly, undeniably devoted to their husbands. It sounds hackneyed and almost quaintly Freudian to say so, but Fritz Kreisler married his mother. He fell in love with Harriet and remained with her for sixty years because, given his upbringing, he could not have imagined himself with anyone else. He married a difficult, tone-deaf woman because difficult, tone-deaf women were all he knew.

Rupp proposed a different theory. He was convinced that Harriet "had something" on Fritz—something dangerous enough to persuade him never to cross her, never to leave, never to speak of divorce. What that something might have been is open to the purest speculation. "I think she knew some secret, because he always didn't say anything," Rupp said. "There must be something. I never found out."[48]

So reads Rupp's hypothesis. Another is appealingly simple: Kreisler stayed with his wife because he wanted to, he loved her, he could not live without her. Period.

Yehudi Menuhin drew this portrait of the marriage.

> He loved her because she actually saved him from drink and drugs and gambling and women. Not that he was longing for that, but nonetheless he realized that she was his barrier against his vulnerability to temptation. . . . Whenever he traveled without her he lamented, "Oh, Harriet isn't with me, Harriet isn't here." But I suspect he had a better time.[49]

Possibly. But the Kreislers did seem to share a certain rapport, at least in print. In October of 1934 the two granted an unusual double interview to *The New York Times*, which noted both Kreisler's chipper demeanor and the spirited verbal jousting that marked his exchanges with his wife. The occasion was the couple's arrival in the United States on the liner *Europa*; Kreisler "appeared happy again, because his wife, who, he explained, had managed, bossed, teased and cajoled him for thirty-two years, was also back again after more than a year's absence enforced by illness."[50]

The *Times* piece described Fritz arguing amiably with Harriet, declaring that his wife was "really the boss" and complaining that she "divides her love between two dogs and me. First comes our Airedale." According to the article, Kreisler maintained that Harriet "held a whip hand over every moment of his life and that he liked it, but Mrs. Kreisler, calling him 'Poppa' and 'Fritzy' alternately, pictured him as a willful, temperamental martinet, who kept her constantly jumping to please his whims."[51]

When Kreisler started waxing romantic about the difficulties of translating an ancient book—it was like "striving for love in a dream," he said—Harriet interrupted:

> Now how will that sound in the papers, Poppa? What with fiddle plays, and now this "striving for love in a dream," and the way girls already make eyes at him. Listen, boys, he has been coming here too much without me; he's gotten out of hand. You see, when he travels alone he does not practice, but remains upstairs in the lounges. When I am here he works. He would be a good fiddler if he would only practice. . . . Don't let him fool you, standing there, amiable like that. Often other women come to me and say sweetly, "Oh, the dear Mr. Kreisler." And to myself I think, "Oh, boy, if you only had to handle him for six months."

She concluded: "You know, I like him. He is no good, he buys books, and he won't work, and he refuses to play the piano enough (he plays that better than the fiddle), but I like him anyhow."[52]

Many years later, in a 1958 profile of Kreisler that appeared in the *Los Angeles Times*, the ever-prickly Harriet spoke joshingly—with obvious impatience and even more obvious affection—of her husband's penchant for book-collecting. She said she was "a little jealous of his books and ancient manuscripts" and complained that most of the time he spent on books should go toward composition.

> But I can't do anything with him. When we were first married, and had hardly a dollar to spare, he would spend that dollar on some old book. And now, after all these years, when he goes to bed at night, you can't see the man for books. They are piled all about him, around him, under his head, and down the neck of his pajamas.
>
> He is as honest as the day, about everything but books. Whenever he finds himself with a bit of extra money in hand, he will hide it away for the purchase of old parchments. He will hide it in books, or on top of the wardrobe,

> or under the rug, then he will forget where he has hidden it. Months later the maid will come to me and say, "Look, Mrs. Kreisler, here is some money I found hidden under Mr. Kreisler's dress shirts." I always know what it is. It's his book-money.[53]

It is a charming picture: the bookish, disorganized Kreisler, burying himself in manuscripts and surreptitiously stashing the cash, while his commanding wife worked hard to bring order to her husband's unruly ways. She set the rules, he broke the rules, she set him straight. That was the procedure, and it served them well through the six decades of their marriage.

The arrangement seemed to satisfy them both, Fritz no less than Harriet. By his own admission, he enjoyed her "whip hand" hold on his life and appeared to love her deeply. In early 1933, after arriving, Harriet-less, to honor a full schedule of state-side concert engagements, Kreisler told a reporter how being separated from his wife for so long made him "feel really lost." His woebegone condition, he continued, supported his belief that "love is above all else, even the career of an artist or a musician. Cynicism to the contrary, love is first and success is next. Love, health and a job. The job may be laying bricks or composing sonatas—it is all work. But without love it is not life."[54]

In Stidger's *The Human Side of Greatness*, Kreisler devoted a fair portion of his autobiographical chapter to Harriet's role in his life. He is a quiet, fearful man, he explained; his wife is outgoing. On the subways, he is the "last to get in and the last to get off," one who is constantly jostled by other people's elbows. "My wife is different," he said. "She jostles them, stands on her own feet. That is the American in her. I am timid. She is confident. She knows how to take care of herself and of me also. . . . She looks after the baggage, my violins—and me also. I'm impractical."[55]

In the same essay, Kreisler wrote:

> She is a very remarkable woman with a fine brain and an uncanny intuition. She is a self-sufficient person and, in that respect, has what I most lack. I needed her and she has made the way easier for me all these years for she has

> looked after me in a natural everyday way. When I say such things about her she says: "That's right, Pop!" She calls me "Pop" and "Fritzy"—and I like it.[56]

At the close of the essay he gave a definition of happiness that is remarkable for its crystalline idealism and its aching declaration of marital love. "What makes for happiness is a chance to do something for others, to serve others," he said, "and to love one woman for life, living in the buttressing strength of her faith and confidence; in her love, more certain of her understanding than of all else in life."[57]

If Kreisler's own scribblings are to be believed, his wife was a source of tremendous strength and an object of lifelong affection. She also, clearly, loved him in return, her combativeness on occasion as playful as it was pugnacious. Hilde Lochner described Harriet's smitten behavior at one of the countless dinners honoring Kreisler at the close of his career: with no clear sight through the crowd, Harriet squirmed girlishly for a glimpse of her swain on the dais. When she finally spotted him, Lochner said, "she beamed with joy."[58]

That Harriet Kreisler drove her beloved to distraction is, in this regard, almost beside the point; the pair's devotion was mutual and lifelong and seemed, if anything, to increase with age. For Kreisler's part, he remained a gracious and generous man, and never appeared to turn bitter despite his battling bride. "He was a wonderful person," said Josef Gingold, "when Harriet let him be one."[59]

Who, then, was Harriet Kreisler? Was she an unfeeling, brutal shrew with a desire to torture her husband? Or was she merely a strong woman who ran her husband's career, protected him fiercely, did the dirty work he shunned, conducted herself with supreme self-confidence, and angered a lot of people—men in particular—in the process?

Kreisler liked to drink; Harriet tried to control him. Kreisler liked to gamble; Harriet tried to control him. He ate too much, too heavily, and the wrong things; as far as she could, she controlled him. Milstein once recalled eating dinner with the Kreislers at the home of Yolanda Mero-Irion, the wife of Hermann Irion, general manager of the Steinway and Sons in Queens, New York. "My wife, Therese, was sitting next to Kreisler and diligently filling his plate," the violinist described. "Suddenly Mme Kreisler, seated at the opposite end of the table, cried out, 'Therese, stop killing my Fritz!' She watched everything like a hawk!"[60]

Had Harriet been a man, observers might have forgiven her for seizing control and might even have admired her spousal devotion and ceaseless industry. As a woman she was given no such latitude. History tells us that Harriet was impossible, a sorehead, a harridan. Surely she was abrasive; just as surely she was difficult to like. Yet without her—without her there to badger her husband, discipline him, manage him, police his vices, and make him practice—the world might never have known its greatest violinist. "One thing is certain," Kreisler's occasional accompanist, Michael Raucheisen, once remarked. "Without Harriet Kreisler, there would be no Fritz Kreisler."[61] In his place would have appeared a gentle man, well-educated and charming, whose fondness for games of chance and pitchers of beer might have overridden all desire to make of his talents a significant career. He might have been, in other words, what Harriet had always said he was: a good-for-nothing loafer who drank too much, dreamed too much, and quietly wasted his talent.

Five

Shunned: An Enemy in America

It is my fond hope that after the war has ended we artists will be in a position to carry first the message of peace through all the countries. Surely art and religion will be the first forces that will set about the great reconstruction of world sympathy.

If, for instance, the dignified figure of Ysaÿe were seen on the concert stage of any country which had been hostile to his in the war, would there be any one equal to expressing animosity? I don't know what I myself will be able to do, because I have fought, and they may not be able to forgive me at first. I fear art and artists will suffer.

When peace comes, although art will try to speak its message, will not all the energies of the nations be devoted to re-establishing the material things that are of first urgence? I fear all other things will have to wait for them.

Then there are so many artists who have fallen. They may not be world-famous, but, after all, the art of a country

> is the sum of what all its artists are, and the individual does not loom large.[1]

By the summer of 1914 Fritz Kreisler was at the top of his profession and, it seemed, the civilized world. Wherever he toured, he packed houses; however he played, he earned raves. Nowhere was he more popular than in the United States, where his musical panache, combined with a movie-idol charisma, made him one of the most universally recognized celebrities on the concert circuit. His poised, mustachioed presence drew thousands into music halls around the country.

Fritz and Harriet were far from American shores—they were taking in a cure at Swiss medicinal baths—when the Austro-Hungarian empire went to war. In his memoirs of his experiences during World War I, *Four Weeks in the Trenches: The War Story of a Violinist*, Kreisler recalled the outbreak of hostilities:

> On the 31st of July, on opening the paper, I read that the Third Army Corps, to which my regiment (which is stationed in Graz) belonged, had received an order for mobilization. Although I had resigned my commission as an officer two years before, I immediately left Switzerland, accompanied by my wife, in order to report for duty. As it happened, a wire reached me a day later calling me to the colors.[2]

The couple returned to Austria by way of Munich, where authorities had stopped all traffic and Kreisler and his wife were allowed through "only due to the fact that I revealed my intention of rejoining my regiment in Austria." By 1 August they had reached Vienna, which, Kreisler wrote, had been transformed by "feverish activity everywhere."

> Reservists streamed in by the thousands from all parts of the country to report to head-quarters. Autos filled with officers whizzed past. Dense crowds surged up and down the streets. Bulletins and extra editions of newspapers passed from hand to hand. Immediately it was evident what a great leveler war is. Differences in rank and social distinctions had practically

> ceased. All barriers seemed to have fallen; everybody addressed everybody else.[3]

After preparing in Vienna and at Graz, Kreisler's regiment was sent to Lemberg; on 10 August, they reached the fighting line, where their task was to "fight day and night without rest" in an attempt to hold off seven Russian outfits. Kreisler was quickly introduced to the realities of war. As he later explained upon his return to the States:

> It is all a vague, blurred impression in my mind. I cannot call it even a nightmare, for it lacks the definite impression that a nightmare sometimes creates. . . . For instance, when you hear the first shell burst, it is a terrible thing; the whining in the air, the deafening crash, and the death it spreads around it. That is what you think of your first shell. But you think less of the second and third, and after that they pass out of your mind.
>
> The first man you see die affects you terribly. I shall not forget mine. He sat in a trench and suddenly he began to cough—two or three times—like an old man. A little blood showed at his mouth and then he toppled over and lay quiet. That was all.
>
> Very shortly none of these things affect you. It has made me mournful when I have thought how quickly we all threw over everything the centuries have taught us. One day we were all ordinary civilized men. Two or three days later our "culture" had dropped aside like a cloak and we were brutal and primeval.[4]

Conditions were hard in the trenches. Kreisler and his fellow soldiers ate little, subsisting on soup, bread crusts, and the occasional cow that was found, shot, butchered, and consumed immediately. A toothbrush "was not imaginable," nor was a change of clothes. Kreisler left all thought of his violin behind him, he said, just as he had left behind every semblance of civilized existence. In the trenches with him were "a Prince, a sculptor, a mathematician, and a professor, and nobody asked them who they were, or cared. We forgot everything except the work we had to do. Why should I claim immunity as an artist?"[5] (Many years later, Pablo Casals described his reaction, at the time, to his friend's conscription. "It was hard to imagine," he recalled, "that gay and gentle genius in a soldier's uniform.")[6]

Kreisler's musician's background distinguished him on the field in one discernible way. According to his account in *Four Weeks*, his trained ear allowed him to track the distance and arc of enemy missiles and, in so doing, estimate their place of origin.

> Every shell describes in its course a parabolic line, with the first half of the curve ascending and the second one descending. Apparently in the first half of its curve, that is, its course while ascending, the shell produced a dull whine accompanied by a falling cadence, which changes to a rising shrill as soon as the acme has been reached and the curve points downward again.

After informing an artillery officer that he could pinpoint the exact position of a missile reaching its acme, he was sent on a reconnoitering tour to do just that—the results of which, he was told, enabled officers to determine the nearly exact range of the Russian guns. "It is the only instance," he said, "where my musical ear was of value during my service."[7]

That service was cut abruptly when, on 6 September, his regiment's trenches were attacked by Russian Cossack forces.

> It was about 11:30 when they attacked us. I can remember being hit by one horse and knocked down. While I lay I saw a second Cossack reach down to finish me. He got me in the hip, but as he struck me I fired my revolver. I remember seeing him fall and the riderless horse gallop on. Then I became unconscious.[8]

His orderly found him several hours later, using the Russian he had killed as a pillow. The orderly revived Kreisler with brandy and helped him back to the lines and, eventually, to a field hospital.

Harriet, who was volunteering for the Red Cross in Vienna, had heard no word from her husband for the three and a half weeks he was in the trenches. "None of my field postcards had arrived," he recalled, "and she was suffering extreme nervous strain from the long anxiety and suspense, which she had tried in vain to numb by feverish work in her hospital."[9] When she did hear word, it was that her husband had died—a rumor that spread, unsubstantiated but undeterred, to the United States. Kreisler later blamed the mix-up on a mistake made by a field hospital surgeon, who confused the violinist with the dying man in the bed beside him. When the neighbor succumbed, the surgeon reported the death as Kreisler's.[10]

After spending several days being moved from one field hospital to another, Lieutenant Kreisler at last sent a telegram to his wife announcing that he would return the following afternoon—10 September—to Vienna. This information, following weeks of no news, then bad news, from the front, sent Harriet into a whirl of excited preparation. A few days later, she mailed a letter to her "Dearest Mama and Papa" that fairly bursts with relief:

> When I finally saw him limp off the train, my knees went out from under me from shock. He had a three weeks' growth of beard, which was more gray than black, and was hollow-eyed and cheeked. He had lost about twenty pounds in weight, and limped from a bruised nerve center in his leg. Well, I was so glad to see him alive that I soon recovered my courage, for he was my first thought. Thank God, it is nothing serious; it is really more soul and nerve shock than anything else.[11]

From the field hospital Kreisler was transferred to Vienna, where a party of Red Cross nurses and doctors included ("to my great joy") Harriet. After further time recuperating in the Vienna hospital —either a few days or a few weeks, depending on the account— Kreisler left with his wife for Baden, where he spent three weeks taking a cure at the sulphur baths. He then was examined by a commission of surgeons and pronounced unfit for military duty. Finally, after being promoted from lieutenant to captain, the violinist received his formal discharge due to permanent disability in mid- to late October of 1914. From start to finish, Fritz Kreisler's World War I service in the Austrian army lasted less than three months.

Back in the States, Kreisler's war experience was reported, at first, in the scantiest bits and pieces. On 16 September—long after Kreisler had been wounded—*The New York Times* passed on word that the violinist was guarding bridges in Vienna. Only a few days later word of his injury reached the American press.

Once Kreisler was discharged, however, the floodgates were flung wide open: suddenly, passionately, and with what would later emerge as extreme irony, the wounded veteran was greeted by the American public with nothing short of adulation. Because the United States had not yet entered the war, there was no conflict between being a loyal American and being infatuated with a retired Austrian lieutenant. He was simply a war hero. That he was a war hero for the "Huns" was a subtlety that had not yet gripped the national psyche.

From the moment he touched American soil—stepping down from the liner *Rotterdam*, accompanied by his wife and a cane—Kreisler was greeted with something close to awe. Upon arriving, he told of the Cossack horse charge that left him with a gash in his leg, gamely describing the heroism of his regiment and his own contribution; his heroic story appeared in the 25 November edition of *The New York Times*.

Such was the start of his honeymoon with America, a period of American fascination with the violinist that was to continue for the next several months. His limp alone proved curiously alluring. Consider Kreisler's post-service debut at Carnegie Hall, where his rapturous reception had as much or more to do with the romance of war as with the art of music. An article in *The New York Times* stated:

> The hall has probably never held a greater throng; all the seats were filled, and as many were put upon the platform as it would hold, and people stood as well. The greeting that was given him when he appeared was long continued, warmly demonstrative and enthusiastic. He has not returned

> wholly unharmed from the war, for he came upon the stage with a limp. But his admirers were fain to notice that the limp was minimized as far as it could be. It was not exploited as a subject for commiseration, as it conceivably might have been by some. Mr. Kreisler is too much an artist and a gentleman to do that; he possesses too many assets of an artistic kind. It immediately appeared when he began to play that he was in full possession of them all.[12]

On the program that evening were a number of Kreisler favorites, pieces familiar to anyone who had heard him before the war: Handel's A Major Sonata, Tartini's *The Devil's Trill*, the Chaconne from Bach's D Minor Partita, and a variety of smaller pieces. In performing the works, the *Times* article continued, Kreisler "was at his best; his tone was beautifully warm, rounded, and poignant in its quality; his technical proficiency seemed to have suffered no lapse, and these things were made the means of interpretations of commanding nobility."

A week later, two hundred friends and admirers gathered at the Hotel St. Regis to pay homage to the veteran. Every variety of VIP attended the event, from Harold Bauer and Walter Damrosch to Alexander von Nuber, the Austro-Hungarian consul general (who hailed him as "Kreisler, the Austrian patriot"). Kreisler, seized by his usual modesty, thanked his friends and downplayed his country's decision to send such a treasured artist to the front. "The fighting men are measured not by rank," he said, "but by capacity for suffering."[13]

A second Manhattan recital, given on 30 December 1914, was even more of a success than the first. The audience was so huge that it filled not only the usual seating—floor, boxes, galleries—but a stage area set aside to accommodate the entire chorus of the Oratorio Society, which had performed earlier in the week.[14]

Nor was New York alone in its enthusiasm. By the beginning of the new year Kreisler's renewed popularity—expressed most often as a sort of euphoria—was evident around the country, as newspapers and magazines filled with fawning portrayals of the brave and strapping Austrian. On 3 January 1915 the *Montgomery Journal* ran a huge spread on Kreisler's war service, complete with photographs, speculative drawings of Kreisler in battle, and a thick black headline that declared, "HOW IT FEELS TO KILL ANOTHER MAN." Publications normally devoted to staid musical essays and reviews gave over pages of space to Kreisler's derring-do in the trenches; no one, it seemed, was immune. Even the ever-acerbic George Bernard Shaw had his say. It was probably around this time that someone remarked to Shaw that the Muses had placed a violin in Kreisler's arm at birth. Shaw quipped: "And a bow in [his] leg." Then, turning to Kreisler: "You're an Austrian cavalry officer, aren't you?"[15]

At times, the violinist's celebrity seemed to overshadow his musicianship; anyone who has witnessed the giddy reception given contemporary rock idols is familiar with the sort of pop fanaticism that greeted Kreisler in early 1915. Always something of a heart-throb—for good reason did Harriet train a wary eye on any woman who approached him—Kreisler found himself, on his tour of the States, the music world's equivalent of a matinee idol. Judging from accounts of audience response, it was sometimes difficult to distinguish between ovations recognizing the violinist's musical prowess and those approving his stardom. He was a leading man in a one-reel war movie; his mere presence onstage, his military bearing, and his generous black mustache were enough to cause the female half of his audience to go politely berserk.

A good example of this can be found in the 16 January 1915 edition of the *St. Louis Globe Democrat*, in which Richard Spamer described an appearance at the Odeon with the St. Louis Symphony Orchestra. According to Spamer's account, "The women shouted shrill cries of joy at seeing again this idol among violinists. The men stamped their feet with such vigor that [Conductor Max] Zach looked about him a bit uneasily."

By March, Kreisler's tour had become such a monstrous success that Henry T. Finck was driven to write in *The Nation:*

> Fritz Kreisler is the lion of the musical season.
>
> In Greater New York he has already played fifteen times to overflowing audiences, and that figure might easily be doubled before the end of the season were it not for the

> urgent calls from other cities, where his success is equally pronounced; so the greatest of living violinists has at last come into his own.[16]
>
> America, it seemed, could not get enough of Fritz Kreisler.

Kreisler-mania abated only slightly in the months that followed. Adding to the hoopla was the publication of *Four Weeks in the Trenches*, which was referred to or excerpted in a number of publications. On 29 May 1915, *The Literary Digest* quoted whole the long passage from the book devoted to the violinist's keen ear in tracking enemy shells, and earlier—in late 1914—*The New York Times* had published an account of Kreisler's wartime experiences, patched together from interviews and other information. But nothing so advanced the notion of musician-as-war-hero as the performer's own slim volume. Read today, *Four Weeks* remains an energetic and astonishingly literate war story, filled with advancing Russians and the agonizing cries of wounded men. Whether all of it is true (and there is reason to doubt that it is, considering Kreisler's predilection for creative storytelling) is, in this regard, a moot point, since the book was widely accepted as fact and its effect on the public was obvious and real. It solidified his image as a loyal Austrian. What no one could have guessed was how that image would come to be used against him.

Some time after Kreisler arrived in the United States from the front, he attended a concert given by Jacques Thibaud, a close friend and fellow violinist. Thibaud had served in the French army and had also returned with a limp. Profoundly affected by the war, Thibaud, in his first recital after returning, performed an impassioned rendition of Chausson's *Poème*, which his own emotion forced him to abort midway through, tears streaming down his face. Konrad Bercovici recalled walking the stricken Thibaud back to his New York City hotel, where Kreisler also was staying. As they entered the hotel, Kreisler was in the lobby. "When he saw us come in, with Thibaud leaning heavily on me, pale as a ghost, he took a few steps forward, as if he wanted to speak to his old friend," Bercovici later wrote, "but he remembered that he was still an officer in the Austrian army and turned away before the Frenchman had seen him."[17] A few days later, Thibaud and Kreisler met on the street; the two soldiers saluted each other and passed on without speaking a word.

Shortly after that, Bercovici—a Romanian by birth—attended a Kreisler recital at Carnegie Hall.

> The war had not been kind to my kin. I had lost several close blood relatives. I felt a little like a traitor to their memory to listen to the playing of one of their enemies; one who perhaps had directed the attack in which they were killed. Yet—there I was. I sat in the center of the hall and had the illusion that Kreisler played for me personally. He worked the blue of the Danube river and snowcapped, pine-covered mountains into his tones. Vienna sang and danced in every stroke of the bow. . . . Gay Austria! Polite Austria! Enchanting and peaceful.
>
> When Kreisler ceased playing, the applause was deafening. I looked up. Jacques Thibaud was in a box. I hadn't known he would be there. He didn't know I was there. When everybody had stopped applauding, his hands were still clapping. He rose, when Kreisler took the tenth bow, and cried at the top of his voice: "Bravo! Bravo!"

Thibaud, Bercovici, and Kreisler met in the hotel lobby following the concert. The two violinists "hesitated for a moment, then rushed to each other with outstretched hands. The war was ended as far as they were concerned."[18]

The remainder of 1915 and 1916 passed without incident, as Kreisler and his wife settled down in the States. In mid-1916 he started work on his first operetta, *Apple Blossoms*, for theatrical producer Charles B. Dillingham. At the same time, he continued to perform, always to positive reviews, inevitably before large and almost obsessively appreciative crowds. (It was not uncommon for audiences to demand four, five, or six encores from the violinist, and on at least one occasion, reported in the 11 December *New York Times*, management had to cut the hall lights to get the throng to leave.) A good number of his concerts were benefits—for children's causes, hospitals, and destitute musicians of all nationalities trapped in Vienna by the war—all of which reinforced his reputation as a philanthropist and, if anything, furthered his popularity with the general public. But even the recitals that were not benefits raised money that passed only briefly through Kreisler's wallet; so demanding were his philanthropic commitments that his busy schedule was more a matter of necessity than frank ambition. Besides the destitute musicians, his concertizing supported forty-three Russian, Serbian, and Austrian orphans whose fathers Harriet had tended while working for the Red Cross. He also sent money to his own father, who had lost everything in the war. Kreisler may have been living on these shores, but his attention was focused on Europe.

At no time was this more apparent than in late 1916, shortly after the death (on 21 November) of Austro-Hungarian Emperor Franz Josef. Ever the patriot, Kreisler vigorously defended his home country and former monarch, attacking any implication that either was responsible for the war. In an interview with *The New York Times*, the violinist waxed eloquently on Franz Josef's paternal nature and unassuming way of life. The emperor

> had the same qualities that make children love the right sort of grandfather, only he was that sort of grandfather to all of his people. . . . A farmer would write that his cow had died and that nobody would lend him money to buy another—wouldn't the Emperor please buy one for him? And the Emperor always would, and get ample compensation in chuckling over the queer letter.

On the subject of the American press—specifically, its editorial pages, which had by and large condemned Franz Josef—Kreisler was adamant and angry:

> The American papers have been very bitter. All the editorial writers have seemed to say to themselves before going at their task: "Now we must not show this dead Emperor any pity or any sympathy because he was an old man, because he

> is now a dead man. We must say nothing good of him. He was bad. He was cruel. He was reactionary. He caused the war. . . ."
>
> It was Russia that had the motive—possession of an ice-free port. It was a Russian officer who trained the assassin in pistol practice before the killing of the Archduke Francis Ferdinand at Sarajevo. It is a cruel mistake to hold the old man who has just died responsible for all the suffering that has come to the world in the last two years. It must be left for history alone to render definitive judgment concerning the personality and the work of the late Emperor, a personality by which the entire history of the Austro-Hungarian monarchy has been decisively influenced.[19]

Significantly, even at this relatively late date of December 1916, *The Outlook*, which reprinted a portion of the interview, chose to cap such fiercely nationalistic ramblings with a bit of gushing admiration for their speaker. "Even those who do not agree with Mr. Kreisler as to the cause of the war," it concluded, "can appreciate this great artist's chivalry and his tribute to his Emperor."[20]

Franz Josef was not all that preoccupied Kreisler during this period; if his own comments (and those of his wife) are to be believed, the violinist had already begun to feel the squeeze of anti-Austrian and anti-German sentiment that had been building, slowly but perceptibly, over the months. He said:

> As an Austrian and a soldier, I owe every drop of my blood, every dollar that I can earn, to my country; but as an artist I am above all politics and owe my best to the world. If the time ever comes that I am unwilling to play the beautiful music of France, or Russia, or any other country, I hope to forget our own Austrian Hymn.[21]

Similarly,

> I would be ashamed of Austria if she resented my playing the music of the world. But Austria never will. In Austria and Germany today they are giving the plays of Shakespeare,

> they are playing the music of Russia and France. In Vienna it is still no crime to use the French language. The band of the Prussian Guard has kept the march from *Carmen* throughout the war.

Mrs. Kreisler carried the point even further, complaining that her husband could not perform the Austrian hymn on American programs without being criticized for spreading what might be perceived as propaganda. "I am afraid that too much of the bitterness of the war is here in nonbelligerent America," she said.

> On the field does the nurse or the surgeon stop to ask "What is the nationality of this wounded man?" Not at all, but doesn't America stop to ask that? . . . Doesn't human red blood flow from a wounded Austrian as from a wounded Italian or Russian? Can't a mother or wife of Austria suffer too? Can't an Austrian child starve?

The violinist concluded:

> People tell me that I am all right, personally, but that Austrians as a nation cannot be accepted. I will have none of that. I am an Austrian. We are all alike. Why hate us? Why hate any people because of disagreement and disapproval of the political government of that people?
>
> I am not only an Austrian but, more than that, I am a human being and have no right to hate anybody, because we are all brothers and should be able to think of individual men as such, no matter what we may be doing to each other as members of political groups. I have not cut off a single friendship because of the war and I have friends who are of every belligerent country.[22]

Kreisler remained an in-demand artist and a revered public figure through the beginning months of 1917. In May *The Musician* ran a twelve-stanza poem, "When Kreisler Played," by a Reading, Pennsylvania, businessman named Nathaniel Ferguson. In a brief preface to the poem the editors referred to Kreisler as "one of the great favorites of the concert field today" and opined, "It is especially significant that a man of this type should respond so splendidly to the power of music to take hold of and to direct the thought. It is a striking proof of the interest which men of influence in financial and industrial affairs are beginning to show in music." Whatever its didactic value, Mr. Ferguson's poem shows an unabashed reverence for Kreisler's art, using florid imagery to describe the reverie inspired by his playing:

I saw the ships go out to sea,
To far mid-ocean's gales;
I saw them gray in havens fair
Let down their tattered sails.

I saw the snow of frigid zone,
The frost upon the pane;
The fury of the tropic storm,
Black clouds, and then the rain. . . .

But then, in joyous sensuous strain,
The measures of the waltz
Rang in the gladness of the world
And mercy to the false.[23]

It is not known whether the violinist ever read Mr. Ferguson's verse, but one hopes that he did. In the long months that followed, love poems dedicated to Fritz Kreisler were an increasingly scarce commodity.

As 1917 wore on, it became ever more apparent that the United States was bound to enter the war on the side of France and Britain. With an eye on impending U.S. involvement—and an understanding of the ramifications for resident aliens—President Woodrow Wilson released a statement that, had it been heard and heeded, might have pre-empted any later controversy. Dated 6 April, it said: "So long as they [enemy aliens] shall conduct themselves in accordance with the law, they shall be undisturbed in the peaceful pursuit of their lives and occupations and be accorded the consideration due to all peaceful and law-abiding persons."[24]

It was a curiously prescient announcement. Unfortunately, like so many other presidential proclamations, it was recorded, reported, and forgotten.

On 28 April 1917, Congress passed a draft bill, and on 18 May President Wilson signed it, issuing a proclamation that fixed 5 June as the day American men would register for the national army. By 27 June the first American troops had landed in France.

The entry of the United States into the war had two obvious, and almost immediate, effects. The first was the demonization of all things German and Austro-Hungarian—an unavoidable social byproduct, and one that has reappeared subsequently in American attitudes toward the Japanese, the Vietnamese, and more recently, the Iraqis. During United States involvement in World War I, the Germans and their allies were "Fritzes," "Huns," and "Krauts," incomprehensibly evil creatures whose humanity was somehow different from our own. Sauerkraut was renamed "Liberty Cabbage," and German nationals were banned from the eastern shores of the United States. German music disappeared from music halls around the country.

This being the case, the second clear effect of America's entry into the war—namely, the social ostracism of all "enemy aliens" on home turf—was both predictable and, to a certain extent, inevitable. That Kreisler became one of the more prominent examples obeyed a certain logic, since he not only claimed citizenship with a country allied with enemy forces but had actually proven his allegiance to it by serving in its army. It hardly mattered that he served at a time in the war when the United States was not yet involved; nor were his popularity here and his obvious fondness for this country likely to persuade skeptical "patriots" that his presence in American concert halls was entirely benign. His four weeks in the trenches were too publicized, his profile as a soldier too pronounced. He had served on the wrong side in the war. To a public obsessed with its enemy, Kreisler presented an unsettling and manifest threat.

Pittsburgh provided a case in point. Always popular in the city, Kreisler was scheduled for two performances in Pittsburgh in early November 1917: an 8 November recital in Carnegie Music Hall and a 10 November appearance in the Union Arcade Auditorium as, of all things, accompanist for Russian baritone Reinhold Warlich. Kreisler was an accomplished pianist, and, as *The Pittsburgh Post* commented, a chance to hear him perform as accompanist "is as if the audience were given a glimpse of the master-musician at his favorite recreation."[25] Both appearances were heralded by Pittsburgh music writers with an unbridled excitement that belied the trouble already brewing.

On 4 November the Pittsburgh *Gazette Times* ran a damning front-page article that quoted representatives of the city's self-ascribed patriotic organizations who were opposed to Kreisler's impending recitals. Kreisler's photo ran alongside that of Karl Muck, the Boston Symphony Orchestra conductor who created a stir when, several months earlier, he refused to include *The Star-Spangled Banner* on his regular program. The association with Muck was entirely negative and, for Kreisler, did damage to a public image that was already severely battered. Just how battered was clear from the angry, fearful, xenophobic voices featured in the story.

The consensus among them was based on reasoning so simple (and, to a warring nation, so compelling) that the danger of Kreisler's presence in this country could barely be contested. Simply stated, all enemy aliens were regarded as spies. Because Kreisler was clearly, and by anyone's definition, an enemy alien, he was also just as clearly a spy. One particularly robust example of this logic was offered by Colonel Thomas W. Griffith, the ranking United States Army officer in Pittsburgh at the time, who questioned Kreisler's motives for touring and declared: "The Austrian Army is not letting its officers off on prolonged furlough without a definite object. . . . It is time we Americans woke up to some of these things." Another angry citizen, a musician who had traveled through Germany before the war and returned with an eye for German devilry, flatly referred to Kreisler and Muck as "artist spies." She urged: "Let them trek back home, where they can live on war bread and horse meat."[26]

Thanks primarily to Dr. Muck, much of the discussion regarding Kreisler, at this point, was preoccupied with the matter of *The Star-Spangled Banner*. Two county commissioners resolved not to rent out Memorial Hall to any musician who would not perform the national anthem. Although driven to concede that Federal authorities had no jurisdiction over performers who refused, the district attorney at the time, Lowry Humes, nevertheless proclaimed: "If a man refused to play the national anthem at the proper time and in the proper place without giving a good and sufficient reason, his conduct might lead to an investigation."[27]

On 11 November 1917 the *Post* contributed to the debate with an editorial outlining its opposition not to "Fritz Kreisler, the violinist," but to "Fritz Kreisler, an officer in one of the armies that is supporting our enemy, Germany, in its barbaric warfare." The editorial, headlined "Lionizing Hun Musicians," began by attacking the principle rather than the person—it would be a "lasting disgrace to the community," were an Austrian artist allowed to perform while American soldiers were giving their lives to fight the enemy—but concluded with an overheated diatribe against all things German and the highfalutin thinkers who regarded art in a realm beyond politics. Consider:

> We have music enough of our own to serve our purposes during this war without laying out American dollars to fatten musicians of the enemy. Common sense tells us that it would not look right to let Prussian landmasters go through our country playing only their music and showing contempt for *The Star-Spangled Banner* and the people it represents, or to give any artist of the enemy an opportunity to be lionized in public by the disloyal or those who do not think. It is not in harmony with Pittsburgh's contributing thousands of its sons to fight the enemy and subscribing many millions of dollars to back them up. If such things represent the "artistic temperament" then the hour has arrived for showing the "artistic temperament" who's who in America.[28]

Clearly, the *Post* was reflecting a mood—and a peculiar wartime dialectic—common to Americans of the time. It was a simple argument, powerful, and not likely to be ignored by a populace obsessed with the enemy.

Nor was it. The *Post* was hardly acting in a vacuum; protests had been piling up from the Women's Club of Pittsburgh, the Pittsburgh Teachers Association, Red Cross auxiliaries, and numerous other women's and civic organizations, including the Daughters of 1812, the Daughters of the American Revolution, and the Daughters of Betsy Ross. One such group, the Pittsburgh chapter of the United Daughters of the Confederacy, drafted a resolution that promoted the city's own musicians and condemned as disloyal anyone who attended a recital performed by "an enemy." "Let us rejoice," the statement read, "that Pittsburgh has given the world also those eminent musicians, Ethelbert Nevin and Charles Wakefield Cadman."[29]

Such protestations had their intended effect: on 5 November Charles Hubbard, the city's director of public safety, suggested that Kreisler might not receive a permit to perform, adding that "the patriotic angle will be taken into consideration." (On the same day Karl Muck and the BSO were banned from performing in Baltimore.)[30] Only two days later, Hubbard ordered the Pittsburgh police to deny Kreisler permission, effectively banning him from the stage. Kreisler's second scheduled performance in the city was taken care of the same day, when May Beegle, the concert manager for the Union Arcade, cited objections that had been "brought prominently forward" and canceled the recital.[31]

The *Post* could hardly contain its satisfaction with the ban—an editorial in the 8 November edition of the paper commended the decision for its good taste and used the occasion, once again, to attack Dr. Muck for a program that offended "red-blooded Americans"—nor could its rival, *The Pittsburgh Sun*, which advocated in more measured language an equally strong censure of "enemy performers":

> What is personal and what is impersonal must be considered. Our fight is personal with the individual who represents autocracy, and who is responsible for the war, its horrors and its prolongation. With German and Austrian art, which is impersonal, we are and always will be at peace, for art is universal. It is not German or Austrian music of which we complain, but the "loyal subjects" of Germany and its allies who travel about this country in luxury and security, drawing thousands of dollars from American purses which might well be used elsewhere, and which will be ere

> this conflict ends. . . . Our protest is not against what Muck or Kreisler plays, but against Muck and Kreisler.[32]

Long months later, after Kreisler had announced in the spring of 1918 the cancellation of his American tour, this question of the personal versus the political remained a central component of the reaction against enemy aliens. On 10 March 1918 *The Washington Post* published a startlingly harsh editorial condemning "Lieutenant Kreisler."

> Kreisler argues that art is international and that discrimination should not be made against an artist on account of his nationality; but artists are not. And Austrian lieutenants certainly are not. When the war is over, and peace reigns throughout civilization, America will again welcome Kreisler, the violinist. Meanwhile, Lieut. Kreisler might remember that he is in the enemy's land by sufferance.

The editorial further warned: "Lieutenant Kreisler should remember that there are a number of internment camps in this country where enemy aliens are detained, and that among them are a great many men who could present a better argument for their freedom than he has."[33]

Interestingly, this debate—about the personal or impersonal, the political or apolitical nature of music and musicians—went through several rounds during United States involvement in World War I, as music by German composers disappeared from the programs of various American music halls. The debate shifted considerably over the decades, mainly due to the rise of Nazism and its promotion of Richard Wagner's music. As a result of this association, bolstered by his advocacy of Nietzsche and his own avid nationalism, Wagner was thus linked with the horrors of the Holocaust, so much so that the Israel Philharmonic went for more than half a century without playing any of his music. When, in 1991, Zubin Mehta attempted to break the ban and conduct Wagner's works unannounced, the audience rose and left.[34] Music is a powerful form of communication, and its language can speak eloquently of liberty or oppression; of that, the works of Dmitri Shostakovich are clear and unsettling proof. Whether individual performers can wield similar power is a matter of opinion.

Kreisler's response to the Pittsburgh ban was passionate and swift. His statement was published in *The Pittsburgh Sun* on 8 November 1917:

> There have been continuous statements in Pittsburgh papers designed to prejudice and arouse public opinion against me. It has been said that I am an Austrian officer on furlough and that my funds were sent abroad to give comfort to enemy arms. In this morning's papers these statements are intensified by positive and violent accusations to that effect.
>
> Those statements are utterly baseless and untrue. I am not on furlough here. At the outbreak of the war in July, 1914, I served for six weeks as a reserve officer of the Austrian army on the Russian front, and after receiving a wound was pronounced an invalid and honorably discharged from any further service. There has been no attempt whatever by my government to recall me into service.
>
> It is true that I sent money to Austria. I have sent a small monthly allowance to my father, a medical doctor and professor of zoology, who has lost everything during the Russian invasion of Austrian territory in October, 1914, and has been prevented by a subsequent paralytic stroke from exercising his profession. He is aged 74. I have sent monthly allowances to the orphan children of some artists, personal friends of mine who fell in the war. In fulfillment of a pledge undertaken by my wife, at the deathbed of some Russian and Serbian wounded prisoners whom she nursed during my stay at the front, I have sent 11 individual allowances to their destitute orphans in Russia and Serbia through the medium of the Red Cross in Berne, Switzerland.
>
> The bulk of my earnings, however, has gone to the Brotherhood of Artists, founded by me for the purpose of extending help to stranded artists and their dependents regardless of their nationality. For a full three years my contributions were the sole and unique support of 17 British,

Russian, French and Italian artists and their entire families who found themselves stranded and utterly destitute in Austria at the outbreak of the war. I have been bitterly and violently attacked by Chauvinists in Vienna for diverting my earnings to that channel. On the other hand, I am in honor bound to state that I have never been rebuked for my actions by any official of my government. I have not sent a penny to Austria since the entrance of the United States in the war and I have not had a word from abroad for fully eight months. The ironical aspect of the situation is that some three score of British, French, Russian and Italian children may now be actually dying of want because I, technically their enemy, am prevented by the laws of this country, their friend and ally, from saving them.

During every minute of my three years' stay in this country I have been conscious of my duty to it in return for its hospitality. I have obeyed its laws in letter and in spirit, and I have not done anything that might be construed in the least as being detrimental to it. Not a penny of my earnings has ever, nor will it ever, contribute to the purchase of rifles and ammunition, no matter where and in whatsoever cause. The violent political issues over the world have not for an instant beclouded my fervent belief in true art as the dead center of all passion and strife, as the sublime God-inspired leveler of things, as the ultimate repacifier, rehumanizer and rebuilder of destroyed bridges or understanding between nations.

It is to the cause of crystallizing and purifying this true vocation of art and to the preservation and marshaling of its forces, the priesthood of artists all over the world, against the coming day of their mission, that every penny of my earnings has been and shall be devoted as long as I shall be permitted to exercise my profession. No sordid consideration of my material welfare enters for a moment into my mind. After four years' successful tour of this country, I have less money to my name than many a prosperous bank clerk. I have no personal interests at stake. I shall serve the cause I am devoted to undismayed by personal attacks as long as the deep sentiment and feeling I bear this country will not be

> thrown into conflict with the fundamental and unalterable principles of my honor as a man and artist. I make no appeal for sympathy, but for justice and respect.
>
> But come what may, my deep gratitude for past kindness, hospitality and love shown me by the American public will be forever engraved in my heart.[35]

On the same page in the *Sun*, one column over, was an article about the decision to prohibit the Philadelphia Orchestra from playing music by composers of German or German-allied descent when performing in the city of Pittsburgh. According to the article, the group responsible for the ban, the Pittsburgh Orchestra Association, believed that "it is the duty of loyal American citizens to show in every public act emphatic disapproval and rejection of all that savors in the slightest degree of German influence, recognition or sympathy." To do otherwise would "give moral support to the living enemies of all art and progress."[36]

The city of Pittsburgh was not alone in its rejection of Kreisler. Officials in the town of Sewickley, Pennsylvania, prefigured the trouble in Pittsburgh when the Women's Club of Sewickley Valley and the Edgeworth Club engineered a ban against the violinist;[37] among other things, that incident served to equip Pittsburgh protesters with an effective example of so-called patriotic spirit and action. The hoopla in Pittsburgh, in turn, appeared to act as a catalyst for similar protests around the nation. Only days after Kreisler was banned from Carnegie Music Hall, he met a similar fate in Youngstown, Ohio, which also canceled performances by Metropolitan Opera soprano Frieda Hempel "for her alleged pro-German sentiments." Hempel responded to the ban much as Kreisler had in Pittsburgh, dismissing as "malicious and unqualified falsehood" the idea that she had ever uttered an anti-American sentiment.[38] In her case, however, the ban was lifted; it seems Hempel had proved herself by volunteering to sing for soldiers, doing needlework for the Red Cross, urging Dallas residents to buy War Bonds, and planning to marry an American.[39] That Kreisler was already married to one apparently did not matter.

There was other trouble. The mayor of Newcastle, Pennsylvania, responded to complaints from Civil War veterans and canceled Kreisler's appearance, and in Wilkes-Barre, Pennsylvania, the Rotary Club led an effort to remove the violinist's name from a promoter's schedule. Their reason was Kreisler's donations to destitute Austrians. Clarksburg, West Virginia, took a pre-emptive strike in the controversy when a prominent women's organization called the Marcato Music Club banned anyone or anything of German influence—artist or composer—from performing or being performed. Farther north, a concert promoter in Providence, Rhode Island, squelched any potential controversy by publishing the nationality and patriotic accomplishments of every performer on his roster.[40] And in Louisville, Kentucky, singer Ernestine Schumann-Heink side-stepped what would have been a shower of arrows when she removed from her program all German music and replaced it with songs in English.[41]

Violinist Philip Dreifus remembers avoiding lines of protesters to hear Kreisler play in Cincinnati. "That was horrible," he recalled. "People walked in front of the concert hall with banners, horrible banners. It wasn't very pleasant. It upset me very much, I assure you, but it didn't affect Kreisler's playing—and it didn't keep many people away."[42]

A particularly fervid attack on the Austrian violinist came from a Brooklyn minister named Newell Dwight Hillis, who denounced Kreisler from his pulpit in Plymouth Church only a few hours before Kreisler released a statement to the press announcing that he was canceling his American concert tour. Hillis accused Kreisler of funneling American money to the German-Austrian war effort. Kreisler was an Austrian captain, he argued, who had obtained release from the military by promising to send the government a portion of his income; as a result, "every night that Kreisler is paid a thousand dollars Austria can buy fifty rifles with which Germany can kill our American boys." Hillis contrasted Kreisler's treachery with the bravery and sacrifice of Albert Spalding, the young American violinist, who gave up lucrative contracts to fight Germans on thirty dollars a month. Would "real patriots" give their money to "an enemy state"—that is, Fritz Kreisler—knowing it would be used to purchase rifles "with which to kill Albert Spalding"? Surely, he urged, "there must be some law" that could enjoin music hall directors from hiring the likes of Kreisler.

Kreisler responded quickly and angrily to Hillis's charges, calling them "cowardly, irresponsible and unethical" and demanding that the minister retract them. In particular, the assertion that Kreisler had secured his release from the army with a vow to forfeit a percentage of his income was "a baseless and malicious lie"; that Hillis was a man of God led Kreisler to doubt that he "uttered this lie in full cognizance of its falsity and import." *The New York Times* further noted that Kreisler demanded of Hillis the chance to confront him "as man to man," so obvious—and curiously romantic—a challenge that the *Times* could not resist an added comment: "Kreisler's earnestness in making the demand recalled to his interviewers an old story to the effect that the Austrian had in his time fought three duels in Europe and that he bore on his face the scar of one such encounter."[43] Beware the avenging Hun!

Amid all the angry outcry rose a few, barely audible voices of dissent. The New York periodical *The World* bucked the common wisdom when it ran an editorial in November 1917 supporting Kreisler and attacking the "enemy-music-phobia" that was then in vogue. "We are not at war with Austria," it protested, "and the violinist's bow is technically no more an enemy weapon now than it has been these many years." Criticizing and mocking the "supersensitive militarist imagination" that saw in Kreisler's music-making a Germanic bogeyman of the direst sort, the editorial pondered:

> Is there any further length to which enemy-music-phobia can go? Will the little German bands be allowed to play "Stille Nacht" when Christmas comes? Are we indeed getting ready to sing our own "Hymn of Hate" against all things German, music and musicians most of all? . . .
>
> Cabinet officers did not hesitate to attend and applaud the Boston Symphony Concert in Washington. Why must local officials imagine a vain peril to the nation in a musical performance?[44]

In truth, not every American municipality protested Kreisler's appearances. In New York City, known for its warm receptions of the artist, an audience packed with sailors in uniform unleashed "a tumult of roaring acclamation rarely heard in a concert hall."[45] Nor did Kreisler have trouble filling houses in Baltimore and Washington, DC, where his audience included members of the Diplomatic Corps. In Hartford, Connecticut, a concert went on by strict order of the mayor, and in Fall River, Massachusetts, his performance was paid for, in part, with a thousand dollars in Liberty bonds.[46] A potential controversy was defused in New Haven when the treasurer of Yale University refused to cancel a Kreisler appearance despite warnings from the chief of police. "It does not appear to me that for us to seek to repudiate our written agreement would help our country," he wrote, adding, "For any community to tolerate the placing of a ban upon the playing of such a musician as Kreisler would be in effect for it to declare a war against Art."[47]

For its part, *The New York Times* ran Kreisler's Pittsburgh statement (more than two weeks after it was released) along with a spray of letters on the subject of German music and artists. Unlike other newspapers, which ran the statement straight, the *Times* prefaced it by noting that "Mr. Kreisler's letter is in English, which he speaks as one who has spent most of his career in America since childhood."[48] Immediately following the statement was a letter from Spanish pianist Alberto Jonas, who extolled Kreisler's virtues—his "sympathies and love for America," his marriage to an American citizen, his many years spent performing in the country—and reminded readers that when Kreisler returned from his stint in the Austrian army "and limped onto the concert stage, the whole American people cheered him for his manly, simple, unostentatious behavior. . . . How could he be made to suffer now, for what Americans deemed right then?" To push Kreisler off the American stage "would be the greatest injustice to this incomparable master of the violin," Jonas wrote. "It would be an irretrievable loss to America. It would mean to drive him away, not only now, but perhaps forever."[49]

Not forever, of course, but no sooner had Jonas's letter appeared in the paper than Kreisler issued a second statement, this one announcing the cancellation of his American tour—contracts that would have earned him roughly eighty-five thousand dollars. In his statement he referred to the "bitter" attacks that had been made upon him as an Austrian and a former officer, and said that he had also been criticized for fulfilling contracts that had been made "long ago." He asked for the release from all such contracts and promised to play only—and without compensation—for charities to which he had pledged his assistance. It concluded: "I shall always remain deeply sensible of my debt of gratitude to this country for past kindness and appreciation of my art."[50]

The World again stepped forward to berate and ridicule the "popular hysteria" that led to Kreisler's retirement, sarcastically characterizing the outcome as "a great victory" for a certain brand of patriot and asking, with obvious distaste: "Does a violin disguise sedition?"[51]

Apparently, *The World*'s editorial writers were not wholly alone; Kreisler's manager, Charles A. Ellis, said that twenty-four hours after the violinist's announcement a flood of requests arrived from around the country, asking him to fulfill the engagements he had canceled. As *The Boston Transcript* wryly noted: "Some even who have been mistrusting the violinist as an 'alien enemy' have swiftly and passionately discovered that the 'alien enemy' makes money for them."[52]

The *Times*, on the other hand, applauded Kreisler's decision on its editorial pages, admitting that the violinist had every legal right to carry on unmolested but noting nonetheless:

> Had he obstinately stood on his legal rights, he would have continued to offend no inconsiderable part of the American public, and though in almost any of our larger cities he could have attracted large and enthusiastic audiences, they would have been made up mainly, as they have been here, of people who applauded him as a Teuton rather than as a violinist, and who took the opportunity he provided to demonstrate that they, too, were in mind antagonistic to our national policies. Sooner or later this would have resulted in disturbances that might easily have developed into violence.

Although its characterization of Kreisler's audiences as a sea of Teutonic sympathizers is, in retrospect, of doubtful veracity—was the Diplomatic Corps opposed to American policies?—the *Times* was correct in its conclusion. If Kreisler had pursued his American career, his recitals might, in fact, have ended in bloodshed. "As it is," the editorial concluded,

> Mr. Kreisler can withdraw temporarily from view, and he will take with him an amount of approval as a good musician who was a good soldier and who has a sense of

> propriety and expediency that not all artists possess. This appreciation will be of value to him and to his country when come the better days for which we are all hoping.[53]

In other, less scripted, comments, Kreisler spoke of his retirement with resignation and control. "I propose to live quietly," he said, "and devote myself to composing some serious works that I have long had in mind."[54]

Unfortunately, Kreisler's retreat from the American stage was hardly the end of the controversy. Barbs continued to fly—and land—in Kreisler's direction. For a time it seemed that certain segments of the population were disappointed with his announcement, not because they longed to hear him play but because they longed to use his concert tour as a chance to make broad, and broadly public, patriotic gestures. *The Christian Science Monitor* used the occasion to take an added slap at the violinist, scrutinizing his payments to his impoverished father in Austria. "In all seriousness," the article pondered, "would it not be better policy, on the part of the United States, to bring the father over to the son and place both in a comfortable internment camp, where they would be under no living expense whatsoever?"[55]

It took several months for the brouhaha to settle down entirely—in part because Kreisler, out of stubbornness or hope or charity commitments he chose to keep, kept popping up here and there to give recitals. Illness prevented him from performing at a 3 December 1917 benefit for poor children (specifically, for the Christmas Fund of *The New York American*) at the Hippodrome,[56] but a few weeks later he appeared in the first of a series of three scheduled chamber recitals with three former members of the Kneisel Quartet. His performance with them created no obvious stir, possibly because Kreisler's share of the proceeds went to a fund for needy musicians sponsored by the Bohemians Club, an artistic association in New York.[57] Accounts of the recital—which earned favorable reviews—alluded only in passing to the troubles that preceded it.

The new year started quietly enough. Fritz and Harriet settled into a fairly simple life; Fritz occupied himself professionally with work on his operetta for Charles Dillingham, *Apple Blossoms*, and, still, the occasional benefit recital. A second concert with the Kneisel Quartet drew little attention, barring one critic's observation that at times the violinist "soared so noticeably to heights inaccessible to his three fellow musicians that it somewhat impaired the team work of the quartet." Nevertheless, the review maintained, "his playing was an unfailing source of delight to his hearers. Their enthusiasm increased progressively through the concert."[58] It seemed, at least initially, that Kreisler would be allowed to retain the vaguest shadow of his former public profile.

Yet the tenor of the times had hardly changed. In March of 1918 the New York State Senate barred "disloyal and seditious" books from the schools, aiming to "prevent any more of Germany's insidious propaganda from creeping in." On the same day, a resident of Orange, New Jersey, protested Kreisler's scheduled appearance at a local high school, expressing amazement that any self-respecting resident would agree to hear the Austrian.[59] It was the old story. Kreisler might have ignored the incident and continued on with his charity concerts, but he was, no doubt, tired of such protests and longing for some measure of anonymity, if not acceptance.

A few days following the protest in Orange, Kreisler made another announcement: he would not appear at an upcoming engagement in Passaic, New Jersey (where he was scheduled to perform, once again, as accompanist for Reinhold Warlich), and he would not appear anywhere else thereafter for the duration of the war.[60] The following month he asked Charles Dillingham for release from his contract to write *Apple Blossoms*,[61] thereby excusing himself from the last of his wartime commitments. For as long as the United States was at war, Fritz Kreisler would lead an exclusively private existence, unseen, unheard.

It was a difficult ostracism. So bitter were feelings toward Kreisler and his wife that the couple found themselves shunned by former acquaintances. Friends who remained loyal to the Austrian were also snubbed. Geraldine Farrar, in a book of memoirs titled *Such Sweet Compulsion*, described the "ban" imposed on Kreisler throughout the war years:

> Friends turned aside when he passed on the street, and because he and his wife were honored guests at a Christmas

> party in my home, their presence brought me a sheaf of scurrilous—and, of course, anonymous—letters about the occasion. I was taken to task as well, by a recently naturalized citizen, for my loyalty to old friends.[62]

Press and public alike were unforgiving; Kreisler was a pariah.

It was not long before the war in Europe drew to a close. By late 1918 Bulgaria had surrendered, and so had the Turkish and Austro-Hungarian empires. Germany followed when its empire crumbled under the strain of revolution and its emperor, the Kaiser Wilhelm, gave in to the Allies. On 11 November 1918, the war to end all wars was finally over.

Kreisler, however, did not venture back into the limelight for another year after the end of the war, and for good reason. The United States, while no longer losing soldiers to enemy bullets, was nevertheless in limbo over the Treaty of Versailles, a document it refused to sign because of American opposition to the League of Nations. An atmosphere of edginess persisted despite the end to open hostilities. And, not surprisingly, the American populace was in no mood to open its arms to the foreigners it had so recently shunned; wartime prejudice is virulent and powerful, far more stubborn than the politicians who make peace where once they made war. "I predict," the violinist said before his wartime retirement (indeed, before the protests began), "that one week after the war ends the artists of France, of Russia, of all the now hostile countries, will be welcomed in Vienna." Quickly corrected by his wife—"Not in a week, make it a year"—he extended the length of time, adding, "They will not only be welcomed, they will be received with enthusiasm." He made no such predictions about the United States and its readiness to receive formerly "enemy" artists.[63] But his decision to stay in the shadows for a full twelve months was well informed and, under the circumstances, necessary.

In the meantime, he occupied himself with *Apple Blossoms*. Composed by Kreisler and Victor Jacobi with a libretto by William

Le Baron, the operetta offered Kreisler a chance to indulge in one of his lifelong passions: light music. As he announced at the time:

> I'm crazy about light music. I adore waltzes, and have always wanted to write them. Into an operetta one can put all the fire and verve, all the charm and color, which have made this form of entertainment so popular abroad. We are not pioneers. Gilbert and Sullivan, Victor Herbert, Reginald De Koven, showed what might be done. And the public greeted them with delight. In the meantime, too often musical comedy has been so vulgarized that many have lost sight of its artistic possibilities.[64]

Further:

> I have always thought that in America there was a great demand for good operetta. An operetta is a homogeneous work in which everything is based on a central idea. No work of art can be without that. And there should be dramatic impulse, good scenic effects and a romantic touch. It should be a combination of musical charm and dramatic idea. . . .
>
> Art is not great because it is austere, and you cannot measure it by its seriousness. A good operetta deserves its place in art. Art in itself is in large part accidental. At least it is involuntary.[65]

A tale of young love gone awry, *Apple Blossoms* concerns the plight of Dickie, who is in love with Nancy, who is, unfortunately, engaged to marry Philip. Philip, in turn, is in love with a young widow. Nevertheless, Philip and Nancy trade wedding vows and head off on their honeymoon, where Dickie and the widow inevitably appear. Nancy's father, realizing Nancy and Philip should not have been forced to marry, goes about getting them a divorce. But in due time the young couple realize that they enjoy being married and, by operetta's end, resolve to stay together.

Accompanying this rather fluffy plot were nineteen songs: nine of them Kreisler's, eight of them Jacobi's, two of them written jointly. Kreisler wrote all but one of the waltzes; Jacobi, all but one of the one-steps and two-steps. Among the numbers, which charmed audiences at the time but have long since disappeared, were "The Marriage Knot," "Star of Love," "I Am in Love," "A Girl, A Man, A Night, A Dance," and, appropriately, "The Second Violin."[66]

For Kreisler, writing the operetta offered him one of his only real escapes from the war and his own musical exile. "It was the only thing which saved me," he remarked later. "In seeking to write songs which should amuse people and make them happy, if only for a moment, I found I could forget myself."

Indeed, he was so enchanted by the experience that when the operetta finally went into production, in the fall of 1919, he threw himself into rehearsals with tremendous zeal. As Jacobi observed:

> It was no uncommon sight to see the famous violinist with a dozen of the beauties of the chorus clustered around him as he hummed a bit of the refrain, marking time with the nervous right hand which has thrilled thousands as it wields a violin bow. Or, again, to see him sweep aside the man on the piano stool with an impatient gesture and seat himself, to swing into a dashing accompaniment for a pair of little dancers who remained quite unmoved at the extraordinary spectacle of a world genius willingly accepting suggestions as to tempo, while they went through their steps without a quiver.[67]

Apple Blossoms opened 7 October 1919 in New York City's Globe Theater, with Charles Dillingham producing (despite Kreisler's previous retreat from the contract), and ran for more than a year. In its cast, in relatively minor parts, were Adele and Fred Astaire.

Greeted warmly by the audience as well as the critics—Heywood Broun of the *New York Tribune* called it "good music, pleasant to hear, melodious and interpretive of the lyrics . . . pleasant, high-class entertainment"—the premiere of *Apple Blossoms* appeared at first to herald the end of Kreisler's ostracism. As Broun remarked, "We were glad to observe that the war on violinists has ended."[68]

It had not. No sooner had Kreisler made a few small steps toward resuming his concert career, in the waning months of 1919, than the old ghosts of xenophobia came back to haunt him. Although he was allowed to play unimpeded in Lawrence,

Massachusetts (once the American Legion, which had asked Kreisler not to play any German music, announced that it would not interfere), other municipalities were not as liberal: in nearby Worcester, concerned citizens protested a planned Kreisler recital, while an appearance in Lynn was yanked off the schedule when the mayor of the city allowed a permit for a program of sacred music only. According to his decision, a jury of twelve musicians would determine whether Kreisler complied with the permit; if he did not, police appointed to patrol the recital would arrest him on the spot. Not surprisingly, his performance there was canceled.[69]

Just as he had a year and a half earlier, Kreisler faced some of his most determined opposition in cities of the American heartland. Despite the occasional voice raised in defense of the violinist—the Duluth *Tribune*, for one, published an earnest explication of Kreisler's behavior during and after the war—public sentiment across the nation's heartland appeared to be set against foreigners, firmly and irrevocably. In Battle Creek, Michigan, a group called the Ministerial Association spearheaded a protest against the violinist, causing him to cancel, while in Grand Rapids the American Legion played a similar role, with similar results. The performance there was struck from the schedule after an attempt at a compromise—moving the concert from an armory to a more symbolically neutral venue—failed to appease the city's more zealous citizens. The Grand Rapids *Herald* objected to the notion "that there can be one 'American' rule for the armory and another for the rest of the city."

Louisville, Kentucky, played host to an impassioned uproar over Kreisler's impending appearance—led, again, by the American Legion. The most eloquent plea came from a Commander McKeekin:

> I can understand how those who were not taken from the ordinary paths of life and thrown into the maelstrom of war, those whose very souls were not wrung in the ordeal, may be able to forget within a year. But we can not forget so soon. The bursting shells of Château-Thierry, the Argonne, and Champagne are too vivid in our memory. Companions who failed to come back, victims of the Prussianism for which Kreisler unsheathed sword, are held in recollection too sacred for us to remain indifferent.

Or, in the words of *The Courier Journal*: "Must perfectly normal, national feeling give way to an ill-timed art venture?" Apparently not. In response to the protest, Kreisler's concert was postponed "indefinitely."[70]

In the Northeast, cooler heads were at least trying to prevail. New York City's American Legion post made a peace offering of sorts when it invited Kreisler to perform at a "testimonial" concert at the Hippodrome on 28 December (the tenor John McCormack was also scheduled to perform[71]), which Kreisler promptly accepted, only to learn a few days later that the invitation had been revoked. It appeared that the American Legion's national headquarters did not share the New York local's more lenient attitude toward foreigners, and ordered the branch to cancel its offer. (Besides, they added, the Hippodrome had already been secured for that date by the Big Brothers.)[72]

None of this was, or should have been, surprising, given the continued prejudice against anything or anyone of Germanic or Austro-Hungarian origin. The war may have been over, but the demonization was not.

Nevertheless, the fiddler persevered, and ultimately—with nowhere to go but back to the stage—his perseverance paid off. He ignored protests in Ithaca, New York, where the mayor had ordered a proclamation urging citizens to boycott the violinist, and played through a recital that very nearly turned into a riot. Midway through Kreisler's performance a contingent from the American Legion, which had tried unsuccessfully to force their way into the concert, cut electricity to the building and bathed performer and audience alike in total darkness. For another forty minutes Kreisler played in the dark hall, doing his best to ignore the cries of "Hun! Hun!" that wafted in from the crowd outside. Inside, the audience countered with noisy cheers.[73]

Similar success was met in Worcester, where the initial protest collapsed under the weight of support for the violinist—so popular was his concert there that four hundred people were left standing outside the hall, unable to cram inside. Boston, too, greeted Kreisler with warmth. Even the *Herald* reasoned aloud, "It is not likely that in his native country, Austria, there is to-day any affection for Germany."[74]

Kreisler found perhaps his greatest welcome in New York City. Appearing at the Metropolitan Opera House on a program with company singers, he attracted one of the largest audiences of the season and drew an ovation the likes of which, according to *The New York Times*, "old frequenters of the house had not seen for any star in years."

> It was the violinist's entrance midway in the proceedings that stirred the crowd to its extraordinary demonstration. Wave on wave of applause swept from floor to galleries as Kreisler bowed; the orchestra players clapped, and presently stood up to greet him at a nod from Conductor Hageman, and when finally hissing for silence was heard, the applauding 4,000 gave one round more to show this was no divided welcome.[75]

Although there remained a few bumps on the road back to acceptance, Kreisler found less and less resistance from "patriotic" organizations. Protests subsided, music halls filled; the attacks on him were nothing more than "little pin pricks."[76] By the summer of 1920, when he and his wife sailed to Austria to help distribute food and clothing, Kreisler had been welcomed back, fully if belatedly, by the fickle American public.

The years that followed Kreisler's ostracism were spent regrouping—reestablishing his career, reconciling with lapsed friends, rehabilitating his public figure as one beloved by so many listeners. It was also a time when Kreisler concerned himself even more pointedly with the plight of his ravaged homeland and its greatly impoverished population. At the close of 1921 he spoke with anguish of Austria's starving masses:

> There are about fifty thousand living in luxury, and another five and a half million who are half alive. . . . Men and women of the best families and of the highest intelligence

> and integrity are selling their last pairs of shoes to get food. I have seen famous professors selling the coats off their backs after they had parted with their most cherished books and family heirlooms to keep them and their families from starving to death.[77]

He capped his remarks with a plea to the United States to join the other Allied nations in granting Austria a twenty-year moratorium to pay its debts.

Such eloquent pleas established Kreisler as the most prominent Austrian spokesperson on American soil and fueled speculation that he might be—or indeed, already had been—appointed Austrian Ambassador to the United States. Rumors flew so fast, and so furiously, that the U.S. State Department felt obliged to announce its support of the supposed appointment. The nonplused Kreisler publicly declined. So firmly, however, had the idea of Ambassador Kreisler been fixed in the collective imagination that the Austrian Foreign Office finally, officially denied that he had ever been named.

There is one final irony in the story of Kreisler's reemergence following World War I: the struggles he continued to have in Paris long after the last shout of disapprobation had subsided in the United States. On 11 November 1924, only two days after Kreisler played at the Paris Opera before a hugely enthusiastic audience, a second performance was canceled due to protests by French citizens piqued by vestigial rumblings of wartime patriotism. It was all in the timing: 9 November was just another raw Parisian evening, but 11 November was Armistice Night.[78] Even in 1924, ten years past Kreisler's service under an alien flag, he had not, it seemed, been entirely forgiven.

Kreisler, ever the poet, described his ideals and his role as an artist in an eloquent statement that appeared in the *Literary Digest* in early 1920.

> My message is a purely artistic one and always will be in every country under every circumstance.
>
> I will never stand for any inclusion of the national element in art. I would as quickly oppose any attempt in

Vienna to agitate against French music. The higher art goes the less it has to do with terrestrial things. It is like religion and philosophy.

Music has no vehicle in which it is held down and confined to nationalities any more than religion is for one favored people alone. . . .

Art ought to be a priesthood and every artist should be a priest. Artists should be like the great missionaries of the middle ages—those great figures in the development of religion and civilization who had a burning desire to go into all the world and preach the Gospel to every creature.

No one knows the exquisite moments an artist has in the realization of his art and the carrying of its message to the world. . . .

I feel I have a mission to bridge over the abysses between the peoples working with the universal language of art and its deep-rooted feelings of good will.

Now, to-day, my vocation is a higher, greater, finer one to live for than it has ever been before. I shall exercise that principle as long as I may be permitted—as long as my honor as a man and my ideals as an artist are left untouched.

There is a great element of reunion at work in the minds of men today. There is a getting together for humanity and progress in all lines of endeavor. Already there are thousands of Americans in Austria engaged in all sorts of activities, from making money in commerce to expending money in mercy. No one could express the human suffering that is being prevented and alleviated by America's work in Austria.

I think I shall go on here exercising my profession. My whole life is based on the great hope—that I may be able to help in the rebuilding of art and the upbuilding of artists.

I shall always use my excess earnings for that—to help and encourage unfortunate artists and to preserve their work for humanity.

I have only a deep devotion to my art, no ambitions, no aspiring desires for myself alone.

There in a broad way is my credo.[79]

Six

Tall Tale Teller: The Kreisler Apocrypha

Fritz Kreisler's ability to tell tales and spin interesting yarns has already been alluded to; he had a certain penchant for hyperbole that resulted in fictions ranging from little white lies to grand hoaxes that fooled friends, critics, and fans alike. The most extraordinary aspect of this ability was the fact that anyone anywhere ever believed him. Granted, those who knew him best—his poker buddies, his fellow musicians, those who joined him for lunch over schnitzel and a glass of beer—learned to take his stories with several grains of salt, to enjoy them, to retell them again and again, but to remember always that the truth-to-falsehood ratio in any given yarn was likely to weigh heavily on the side of falsehood. Decent and moral man that he was in so many other ways, Kreisler had few if any scruples when it came to lying. Or perhaps they should not be regarded as lies; perhaps, as the cellist and pedagogue George Neikrug said in a 1992 interview, they were simply exercises in "true fiction."

This puts us in the difficult position of having to discern when or even whether this practiced fibber was ever telling the truth. Here was a man for whom prevarication came as naturally as eating, for whom the habit of distorting reality was no more morally reprehensible than the stacks of books he collected behind Harriet's back. He liked old manuscripts; he liked gambling; he liked good food; and he liked to weave stories out of the thinnest air. Determining which of his windy little tales are based entirely in fact, which in some, and which in none is an often fruitless but always amusing undertaking that tells us more of Kreisler's personality—and his perception of himself—than any straight chronology of his life.

Admittedly, he was not always responsible for his own apocrypha; several stories that circulated during and after his lifetime have no clear relationship to anything he said, any offhand boast or flailed exaggeration, and must be attributed instead to the Kreisler mythology that emerged at the height of his career and persists to this day among new and lingering admirers. Benno Rabinof once told of being greeted upon his arrival in a small-town Ohio hotel to the sound of some distant, dreadful violin playing; informed that Mr. Kreisler was also staying in the hotel, Rabinof requested a neighboring room. He then burst into Kreisler's room, where he found accompanist Carl Lamson snoring mightily and Kreisler himself half asleep, lazily drawing bow across strings while lying flat in bed.[1] That Kreisler made his debut in London as a pianist, that he studied to be an engineer, that he was a fully certified and practicing physician—such concoctions are pure fantasy, born in a petri dish of speculation some eighty or a hundred years ago. However they started, they spread with viral diligence for several decades and will probably never be completely eradicated.

Viral anecdotes are one problem. Another is the pure theatricality of Kreisler's life, a source of stories so flatly outrageous that the most skeptical observer might be led to question whether all have been falsified for mass consumption. The difference between truth and fiction is hard to detect when even the true stories sound hyperbolic; the yarns concerning Harriet alone (she locked him in a room to make him practice? She married him *how* many times?) are bizarre enough to prove that old stranger-than-fiction maxim all by themselves. The flamboyant absurdity of so many real events in Kreisler's life makes the fabricated ones easier to swallow.

Just how easy is evident in the most famous—and surely one of the tallest—of all his tall tales, the celebrated "hoax" that presented seventeen of Kreisler's own violin pieces as the work of obscure eighteenth-century composers. So elaborate was this particular tale, so unquestioningly was it received by the music press and the public at large, and so thoroughly did it flummox people once it was revealed, that it deserves particularly close attention; thus it will be addressed at length in Chapter 7.

There remain, however, several equally colorful if smaller-scale fictions that Kreisler used to snow his listeners with repeated and surprising success. The most gullible recipients of such stories were, fittingly, those who are normally most proud of their powers of skeptical discernment—that is, journalists. Whereas Kreisler's closest friends and colleagues were familiar with his knack for storytelling and were practiced at finding the fiction in his stories, acquaintances in the newspaper business knew him only as a sort of demigod, a morally unassailable figure whose erudition and philanthropy were nearly as celebrated as his art. He was Kreisler, after all. He was articulate, knowledgeable, quotable, and charming. He spoke (albeit with a lisp) in complete sentences, with vivid imagery and a musician's ear for the natural rhythms of language. The stories that he told were so brightly and imaginatively rendered that it is no mystery why they made it into print; in the jargon of the industry, they were great copy.

Consequently, his remarks were rarely scrutinized for any reason, accuracy least of all. Embraced with equal enthusiasm were accounts of Kreisler's early life that the violinist had given, in bits of varying size and believability, throughout his career; outrageous little fibs that he had hatched during interviews in the early part of this century reappeared like mischievous specters in subsequent retellings, often in the most respected publications. Occasionally Kreisler, perhaps in a fit of belated remorse, tried to correct the misinformation that he had so freely disseminated, but after decades of public exposure, his falsehoods had accumulated the hard shell of fact. Even Kreisler's earnest (but ultimately wan) efforts at correction in Louis Lochner's *Fritz Kreisler* had little effect, mainly because he balanced those corrections with a stunning collection of fresh new yarns. (Josef Gingold claimed that many of the stories in Lochner's book are pure fancy.)

"Kreisler had a terrific imagination," said Gingold, who had an opportunity to hear many such imaginative tales in the course of a long evening spent with Kreisler during a tour of the Midwest. "And he would make up stories. Sometimes he'd tell them more or less correct and you'd wonder, when you heard this, if the ending was not the same."[2]

With this in mind, what follows is a wholly cheerful analysis of Kreisler's fictitious stories. It is by no means an exhaustive compendium; it is instead a survey of some of the more colorful, revealing, or generally entertaining examples of this oft-practiced predilection. In some cases the detours from truth are brazen and easily spotted; in others, the information available (often extremely scant) is contradictory and inconclusive. By its very nature such an analysis is unscientific and open to debate—even if Kreisler were alive to confirm or deny some of these examples, who would trust him to be honest?—and it may, as such, be a frivolous exercise in speculation. Yet Kreisler, champion storyteller that he was, would have delighted in such an undertaking and enjoyed the attempt to rewrite his life once more. It had been through so many revisions already.

The "I went to art school in Paris" Tale

Very early in Kreisler's career word got out, probably from his own mouth, that as a young man he had spent a few bohemian years studying painting in Paris. Versions of this story varied in complexity and chronology—a few had him attending art school after his medical studies, some before—but the essentials were always the same. In every version, Kreisler was a young man, talented and idealistic, obeying the aesthetic urge; he was also tortured with indecision over whether to choose a career in art over a career in music (or a career in medicine, or a career in the military). For a year or two he chose to study art, then abandoned this path and returned to his beloved fiddle (or attended medical school, or joined the army); but the time in Paris shaped his sensibilities forever.

As tall tales go this one is easy enough to believe, made easier by the fact that Kreisler had always styled himself in fiction and in fact as an incorrigible romantic, the sort of Old World fellow who regarded Art and Beauty as absolutes and pursued them as ends in themselves, not as a means to fame or adoration or money or anything quite so twentieth century. He oozed idealism. He also oozed artistic sensibility, combined with the assured worldliness of a man born and reared in turn-of-the-century Vienna. It is not difficult to picture him as an aspiring young painter.

That Kreisler was a lifelong admirer and collector of art adds to the story's plausibility, although his erudition in matters aesthetic is more likely rooted in his liberal Viennese education. Where and how the rumor began is easy to guess—it probably morphed from one of Kreisler's own exaggerations, uttered as a young man and disseminated by friends and colleagues—and the reason for its durability is not hard to fathom, considering a widespread and quite accurate conception of him as a multitalented renaissance man. The world had already embraced a violinist who composed, played piano, studied medicine, boasted arcane knowledge of book collecting, spoke numerous languages, served as a soldier, wrote beautifully, and exhibited a huge appetite for learning—so it was no great stretch to imagine him dabbing paint to canvas in *fin-de-siècle* Paris. Why not?

In fact, nothing surprises about this rumor other than the manner in which it was finally quashed. In a fit of—what was it? regret? conscience? candor?—Kreisler himself laid the story to rest in Lochner's biography, wherein he described his youthful ineptitude with maps and his near-failure of a Gymnasium geography class. "My inability even to draw a map should dispose once and for all of the rumor that I studied painting under Julien of Paris," he protested. "I have never been able to live that story down. I have not painted a picture in my life."[3]

The "My leg was seriously wounded in an attack by the Russians during World War I" Tale

To be fair, this war story is as likely to be true as it is false; the difficulty in tracing its accuracy is that apparently no one alive today ever saw Kreisler in shorts and bare feet. This may sound glib, but the truth is that nowhere exists an authoritative, believable description of the wounds that official accounts tell us released him from further service in the Austro-Hungarian army during World War I. Even Kreisler's own version, told in *Four Weeks in the Trenches* and addressed in full historical context in Chapter 5, is aggravatingly vague about the wound itself—it says only that a horse stepped on his shoulder, that a Cossack "got me in the hip," and that a "sharp knife pain" shot through his right thigh. The knife pain may have been due to a well-aimed bayonet rather than a horse, but Kreisler makes no further mention of it or the shoulder injury; the only indirect reference concerns a mixed commission of doctors and officers who, he tells the reader, gave him a medical examination by committee and determined that he was "invalid and physically unfit for army duty at the front or at home."[4]

According to this account, Kreisler's wounds were undeniably severe; and, as previously quoted, early reports of his return noted a limp and sometimes a cane. Cincinnati violinist Philip Dreifus remembered the limp in Kreisler's first American concerts following his wartime service. Harriet attributed it to a "bruised nerve center." Yet hardly anyone who knew Kreisler in his later years can recall any such impediment—Nathan Milstein, who spotted him "limping along" Madison Avenue, was one exception[5]—and no mention of it is made in later articles. Even in the closing years of his career, he was not seen limping on stage; one must assume that either he made a complete recovery from terrible wounds, or his wounds were not so terrible to begin with.

After some examination of conflicting accounts, there appear to be two possible theories that explain the riddle of Kreisler's leg injury. The first theory proposes that Kreisler's leg—it might have been right or left, although Kreisler himself said it was his right leg—was in fact gravely wounded. How gravely wounded? A shattering fracture? A near-amputation? A joint injury? Many years after the fact, an editorial writer for *The New York Times* declared that "a bullet freed" Kreisler from the army, "leaving him with a limp but not impairing his marvelous fingers."[6] Helena Huntington Smith, in a retrospective of Kreisler's career published in *The New Yorker* on 24 November 1929, claimed that the "net result" of Kreisler's World War I experience was "a wound in the foot."

The second, more radical theory suggests that Kreisler suffered no serious wounds at all, his discharge from the army resulting from serendipitously minor injuries. Kreisler's accompanist in Scandinavia,

Ernö Balogh, was one who believed that Kreisler received no wounds.[7] Franz Rupp was equally skeptical of these wounds, questioning the veracity of Kreisler's war recollections in *Four Weeks in the Trenches*. He claimed that Kreisler culled from his own imagination many if not most of the stories there told.[8]

Joseph Fuchs was the theory's most adamant proponent, convinced not only that Kreisler suffered no major injuries but that "he never was in combat" at all—in which case, *Four Weeks in the Trenches* would be a startling collection of lies. According to Fuchs, the leg injury in question was in fact a foot injury that, Kreisler boastfully claimed, resulted from a sword duel. "He lost one big toe," Fuchs said. "He said it was a duel. It never was a duel. It was an infection."[9]

Despite Fuchs's adamancy, Frederic Kreisler is equally certain that his great-uncle suffered no such debilitating injury: he did not walk with a limp, and he was not missing all or part of a foot. In Frederic's memory, Uncle Fritz never discussed the Cossack attack or any resulting wounds; indeed, the violinist never mentioned his World War I service at all.[10]

Taking the violinist at his word, the reader may decide that Kreisler was indeed stabbed in the leg and crushed in the shoulder during World War I. The leg wound, as illustrated, underwent several dramatic permutations, changing in severity and geographic location (the thigh? the hip? the foot? the toe?) through the course of Kreisler's lifetime. The shoulder wound was not mentioned again and at no point appeared to affect his playing. Kreisler never revealed whether his right or left shoulder was wounded by the Cossack's horse; it must have been the left, since a serious injury to his right shoulder would have been a debilitating blow to his bow arm.

The "I once played with a bow covered with soap" Tale ("The Soap-Bow Incident")

According to this outlandish story, Kreisler was once shaving before a concert when he accidentally dripped soap onto the middle of his bow. Why he failed to notice this little mishap is one mystery; what soap suds were doing within dripping distance of his bow is another. (Was the great man practicing in the bathroom? Was he tuning up between razor strokes? Or perhaps he was using his bow as a back-scratcher and dropped it into the sink?) No matter. The fact—and the fiction—remains that Kreisler walked out of his hotel and into the concert hall with dangerously soapy horsehair. Not one to warm up, or tune up, or even tighten up his bow before a recital (he never loosened it after playing, so there was never a need to tighten it), he simply opened his case, took out his instrument, and walked onstage. He put the fiddle under his chin and started to play.

Much to his surprise, the middle of the bow produced no sound at all. Immediately aware of the implications and gifted enough to accommodate them, he shifted his playing to the extreme ends of the bow and proceeded to perform the entire Paganini Violin Concerto No. 1 at the frog (the base, held lightly in the right hand) and the tip. This was no mean feat; the meat of a violin's sound is produced in the middle of the bow, which is easier to control than the tip and more honeyed in tone than the frog. Anyone who can perform Paganini at the ends of the bow is a musical gymnast of considerable talent and dexterity. Anyone who can even conceive of doing it has an imagination almost as dexterous as his hands. Kreisler, naturally, qualified on both counts.

This story was a favorite of the violinist's, and it circulated for years among his friends and, inevitably, the press and public. A capsule account appears in Louis Lochner's biography, the story attributed not to Kreisler directly but to workers in the violin shop of Rembert Wurlitzer—laying its believability on particularly shaky foundations.[11] According to George Neikrug, Kreisler himself told a version of the story to violinist Benno Rabinof that traveled several rotations of the music world and mutated wildly along the way. Neikrug heard it twice: secondhand from Rabinof, then firsthand from the original source. In both versions the piece in question was the Paganini; the venue was New Orleans. (Lochner sets the tale in an unnamed town in Florida.) Neikrug heard the yarn while being introduced to Kreisler following a "Bell Telephone Hour" radio broadcast in 1949 or 1950 at the NBC studios in Manhattan. When Rabinof took Neikrug backstage to meet the great violinist, Kreisler proceeded to embellish the story again. "You know," Neikrug later remarked, "Kreisler's stories were sort of true fiction. He made a good story like it was creative."[12]

Technically, this story has a single huge flaw: Kreisler rarely if ever used the extreme ends of his bow, exploiting the middle for most forms of articulation. Why he resisted playing at the frog is open to speculation, but Flesch attributed his avoidance of the tip to a physical shortcoming: Kreisler, he wrote, "ha[d] too short a right arm" in proportion to the rest of his body, and thus "never use[d] the extreme point of the bow."[13] If Flesch was right, if Kreisler had trouble reaching the tip, then we are left with an absurd impossibility: that Kreisler performed the entire Paganini concerto at the frog alone.

Whatever its credibility, the story has an amusing footnote. According to Lochner, a critic covering Kreisler's famous soap-bow recital commented favorably on the virtuoso's technique in performing the opening piece entirely at the tip and the frog. Interestingly, no source citation is given for this tidbit, nor is the mystery critic named. Because the boys at Wurlitzer's did not reveal to Lochner the year or date of the recital, confirming the origins of this little tale is close to impossible. Maybe Kreisler did, one day, drip soap onto his bow; maybe he was only practicing (one of those rare occasions) when he discovered it; maybe the mishap was discovered while performing; or maybe, were the truth known, the soap did not cover the entire bow but a small section of it, a mere spot, and the adjustments made to cover for it were more minor than he later claimed. Or maybe the mishap happened exactly as he said. Then again, maybe not.

The "I once locked myself in a flat and grew a scraggly beard over a woman" Tale

Among the wildest and most colorful of Kreisler's tales of his youth was alleged to have occurred in Paris in the late spring of 1901, weeks or perhaps days before he met and became besotted with Harriet Lies on a crossing of the *Prince Bismarck*. Unaware (one assumes) that true love lurked just around the corner, Kreisler became hopelessly infatuated with a young Parisian woman, of course named Mimi, whose affection for Kreisler was matched only by her fondness for expensive froufrou. Said Mimi was in fact so demanding of her swain that she drained him of his last franc, driving him to pawn his violin and leaving him unable to pay the rent. His landlady was none too pleased with this development and, to quote Lochner, promptly "held him virtually a prisoner on the premises" until the irresponsible young artist could pay up. This he did only after appealing to his father, who arrived in Paris with the necessary payment and rescued poor Fritz, heavily bearded and suitably hermit-like, from immurement and hauled him back to Vienna. The violin itself remained in captivity, as Dr. Kreisler's funds were depleted from paying off his son's massive bills. As a result, when Eugène Ysaÿe was forced by illness to bow out of a November engagement in Berlin, and Ysaÿe's friend Kreisler was asked at the last minute to replace him, the younger man was compelled to perform without rehearsal or any meaningful practice on an unfamiliar, borrowed instrument. Or so the story goes.[14]

Certain aspects of this tale are entirely believable. It is not hard, for example, to imagine Kreisler blowing his money on recreational pursuits of any kind (his gambling springs to mind), or treating his violin in an off-hand manner (he was cavalier with his instruments and often left them unguarded), or performing cold on a strange instrument with no chance to practice. Nor is it much of a stretch to imagine him losing his heart and dignity to a manipulative and strong-willed woman. In Lochner's *Fritz Kreisler*, Kreisler's courtship of Harriet Lies is presented as his first genuine love affair. "His relation to the fair sex hitherto had been one of 'crushes,' of infatuations, of flippant flirtations," Lochner wrote. "Nothing really serious."[15] Kreisler's French bombshell surely qualifies.

Yet this Mimi creature, according to Kreisler's story, appeared on the scene in late spring 1901—roughly the same time he was falling in love with Harriet—and proceeded to wrap him so tightly around her sassy little finger that he made himself a pauper rather than lose her love. What a tight schedule he must have followed! And what extraordinary powers of bilocation, to walk the decks of the *Prince Bismarck* while he was simultaneously being held captive by a vicious Parisian landlady. He was indeed a man of many talents.

The "I once played for a sultan" Tale

In another vivid example of Kreisler's web-spinning abilities as evidenced in Lochner's book, Kreisler describes, in ornate detail, the recital he performed for His Majesty Sultan Abdul-Hamid II of Turkey. This occasion took place some time after Kreisler had failed to qualify for the Hofoper, when the young artist was busily trying to put together a solo career. Among his acquaintances at that time was an industrialist named Guttmann, who, equipped with *joie de vivre* and the financial wherewithal to indulge it, invited a collection of friends on a cruise through the Mediterranean. In Constantinople they crossed paths with an Austrian ambassador named Calice who developed a fondness for Kreisler and suggested he return to Turkey to play for the sultan. All the arrangements were made, but once the violinist arrived it became clear that His Majesty was far too busy to hear him. According to Kreisler, he lolled about for weeks waiting for the command to play. "But I didn't mind," he later said. "I would sit with his courtiers, drinking coffee and smoking cigarettes. We could look into the imperial gardens, where the ladies of the sultan's harem were taking sun and water baths in their birthday suits!"[16]

As if that were not splashy enough, Kreisler's story continued:

> Then, finally, one day I was commanded to play. There was no time to send for an accompanist. The sultan sat there cross-legged and by a gesture indicated that I should begin. I played a slow movement from one of Bach's unaccompanied suites for the violin.
>
> After about two minutes of playing, His Majesty clapped his hands. I felt flattered. The ambassador quickly disillusioned me. "That means you should stop," he whispered. "He doesn't like your selection. Play something fast."
>
> So I played something quite inane, but with a lot of fireworks. It sounded particularly senseless without piano accompaniment.
>
> The sultan's eyes danced. He swayed to the rhythm and seemed thoroughly to enjoy the performance. I played several other fast numbers, and then he asked me whether I preferred a decoration or a bag of gold coins—one hundred Turkish pounds! I said I'd gladly take the cash. So one of the

> sultan's attendants handed me an embroidered bag from which most enticing metallic sounds issued forth.[17]

After hefting his bag of coins for the sultan to inspect (to make sure that none of his underpaid servants had pocketed the money and replaced it with rocks), Kreisler was ferried across the Bosporus and returned to the Austrian embassy. On departing the country he was handed a farewell present from a Turkish bey: "a huge box filled with nougat and with one thousand Turkish cigarettes." This he showed off with pride upon his return to Vienna, where his family "regarded it with something akin to awe." Nevertheless, he recalled, "father cast a searching glance at me. He examined my eyes, took my pulse, and said gravely: 'Unless you stop smoking immediately, you may soon be dead. There was hashish in all the cigarettes you smoked.'"[18] The young Kreisler had learned his lesson: right then and there he quit smoking. The hashish turned him off tobacco forever.

Josef Gingold remembered a slightly different version of the tale, a long, elaborate story related to him by Kreisler late one night over dinner. In this version, Kreisler was instructed not just to "play something fast" but to play it with the proper head-shaking theatrics. So Kreisler shook his head, to great effect—in one glance he spotted the sultan grinning broadly—and the violinist was rewarded with the same choice of cash or decoration. He chose the cash, but his ambassador friend immediately corrected him: royal protocol required that he accept the decoration, he admonished, and Kreisler must quickly change his mind. This Kreisler refused to do, and he accepted the sack of coins. When he opened the sack he discovered, as promised, one hundred gold pieces—and a decoration.

A few days later, Gingold recounted, "Kreisler met one of his friends, a very marvelous Russian violinist [named] Charles Gregorovitch." (Gregorovitch studied with Henri Wieniawski and Joseph Joachim, among others, and enjoyed a significant career.) Gregorovitch looked extremely sad; Kreisler asked him what was wrong. The man replied that he was returning to his conservatory in Russia following a leave of absence that had freed him up for a concert tour of Europe. Upon arrival at the conservatory he would be required to visit the committee that had given him his leave and demonstrate to them, with newspaper reviews and decorations, the fruitfulness of his tour. Unfortunately, he did not have a single decoration to show for it. At that Kreisler told his friend to accompany him to his house, where he dug out the sultan's gift and gave it to Gregorovitch. Gregorovitch objected—"I cannot do that; that's not honest"—but Kreisler persuaded him to accept it. "Look," he said. "The sultan doesn't know my name from your name, and it will do you good."[19]

That is the story. How much of it is true? Some of it, certainly—Kreisler's cruise through the Mediterranean is verifiable, as is his subsequent visit to Turkey. Gingold believed that some, if not all, of the tale was concocted, and he was similarly skeptical of other fabled Kreislerisms. At the very least, Gingold's version of the story is a good illustration of Kreisler's laxness with the facts: Gregorovitch may have had some scruples about fudging them before an academic committee, but Kreisler obviously did not. He had no trouble encouraging his friend to falsify evidence for the sake of appearances.

The "A cowboy held me at gunpoint" Tale

A delightful example of Kreisler apocrypha, this story can be traced to his tour of the United States with Moriz Rosenthal in 1888–1889. The pair appeared, often without heavy attention from the press, in towns from East to West, a route that in all likelihood introduced them to a few oddball Americans. Nevertheless, the tale Kreisler told about his stay in Butte, Montana, stretched the bounds of credibility—or it should have.

The story goes as follows:

Young Fritz (he was then only fourteen years old) had been touring with the fabulously difficult Bach Chaconne but decided, upon arrival in Butte, that the gritty mining town might prefer something a bit less strenuous. So he performed a lighter piece instead. The recital went well enough, and afterward the young instrumentalist retired to his hotel room. Some hours later he was aroused by a loud knock; upon answering the door he was greeted by a large, angry, armed Montana cowboy who, accompanied by his little daughter, demanded that Kreisler perform the work that was missing from the program. Kreisler complied—motivated no doubt by a desire to go back to sleep and by the .45 revolver that the cowboy fingered idly throughout the Bach. At the work's conclusion the angry cattleman gave his terse review—"it's lousy"—and stormed out the door, child in tow.[20]

Ignoring the characterization of Bach's Chaconne as "lousy" (perhaps he was referring to Kreisler's slumberous playing), there are several unbelievable aspects to this story. It is hard, for example, to believe that Master Fritz would have been allowed to stay unaccompanied in a lonely hotel room. Granted, Kreisler's mother did not accompany the child on his American tour, but were there no other chaperones? Where was Mr. Rosenthal? Would not the vigorous sounds of Bach have stirred and angered people in neighboring rooms? Why, were this cowboy truly peeved enough to use armed force, did he wait several hours to storm Kreisler's accommodations and make his demands there? Would it not have been simpler and more efficient to hold the violinist at gunpoint immediately following the concert?

Whether there is any truth to this story (Lochner himself debunks it[21]), it does reveal something about Kreisler's nature—specifically, his love of mythic hyperbole. The gentleman who was once a boy from Vienna must have been fascinated by tales of the Western cowboy, the slumping loner armed with a six-shooter and the iconoclastic self-reliance that figures well in tall tales. How natural for Kreisler to spin a story to fit such a character. So many other romantic archetypes figure in Kreislerian tales (the enigmatic sultan, the Carmen-esque lover, the killer Cossacks) that a gun-slinging cattleman, pictured in this context, does not seem particularly out of place. The only real surprise is that Kreisler made no mention of a horse and a ten-gallon hat.

The "Schumann would have thanked me for altering his music" Variations

The story of Kreisler's revision of Schumann's *Fantasie* in C Major for violin, Op. 131, is a revealing illustration of Kreisler's knack for fabrication, because it illuminates better than any other the inconstancy of his own stories—they were likely to change in fickle turns according to memory or circumstance.

The Schumann tale is included in Nathan Milstein's memoirs and begins with the younger violinist's characterization of the elder. "Kreisler was a mystifier," Milstein wrote. "It wasn't enough for him to change Schumann's Fantasy for violin and piano, he also wanted to prove that he had acted on the composer's personal authority!" Hence Kreisler's childhood memory, recalled to a fascinated Milstein, of being in a Vienna cafe when Brahms ("a pompous man with a beard"), Joachim, and Robert Schumann were animatedly discussing music.

> Sitting down at the piano, Schumann showed Brahms his composition, the violin fantasy! Brahms didn't like something about it. They began arguing, with Schumann trying other possibilities: Maybe this? Or this? According to Kreisler, it was his memory of those variations that prompted his subsequent revisions of the Fantasy.
>
> Kreisler told me about this remarkable encounter with such vividness and fervor that I was fully prepared to believe him. Why shouldn't Kreisler have met Joachim and Brahms? But Schumann? Alas, simple arithmetic showed that the composer had died almost twenty years before Kreisler's birth.[22]

(In fact, Schumann died in 1856—nineteen years before Kreisler was born.)

Another version of the tale, set forth in Kreisler's own hand, is less brazen in its historical inaccuracies and in fact may begin to approach the truth. It is at least a likelier story.

The document in question is a draft of program notes on the *Fantasie*, undated but probably prepared for Kreisler's premiere of the work with the Chicago Symphony Orchestra. Penned in Kreisler's unmistakable script, it says the arrangement of the piece was inspired by "a memorable evening in Vienna . . . one of the weekly gatherings of the Wiener Tonkünstlerverein."

> Brahms (a frequent visitor of these informal gatherings) and Joachim (then on a visit in Vienna) were present. The evening had started with a chamber music offering in which

> Kreisler (then 19) had taken part and at the following supper the young artist was privileged to sit in the vicinity of the two great men. During the meal the conversation between Brahms and Joachim turned to their friend and benefactor, Schumann, and in particular to his Fantasy, Op. 131. Joachim, to whom the work is dedicated, deplored its neglect by other violinists and ventured to prophecy after his death it would sink into complete oblivion. Brahms thought that the beautiful portions of the work might be saved for posterity by a judicious revision, and suggested a more concise form, the eliminating of a few meaningless passages and, above all, an elaboration of the wondrous, but far-too-short middle episode.
>
> The burning desire to undertake that revision germinated in Kreisler from that day on, but he waited respectfully, until the death of Joachim thirteen years later destroyed any further possibility of the work being undertaken by the latter. . . . After discarding two previous attempts, Mr. Kreisler now places before the public the third and final version of the revised work.[23]

This time, the dates and facts make sense: either Kreisler was careful to make the story as believable as possible (knowing that anyone who read the program notes could easily go home and check), or it occurred exactly as described. In either case, Milstein's version is both more preposterous and more entertaining, precisely because of its very absurdity. Kreisler's gift for rearranging and revising others' works is legendary. What charms in this and similar stories—including a far-fetched rationalization for revising the Tchaikovsky violin concerto that involved a supposed conversation with Tchaikovsky's friend Sergei Taneyev in one version of the tale and composer César Cui in another[24]—is the breezy manner in which Kreisler manufactured historical source references for what were probably his own conceits. A psychotherapist might find in this tendency some personal or professional insecurity (Why was he always giving credit to others for his own creations?), but in all likelihood such falsehoods were inspired by nothing more exotic than a desire to make things up. Or, again, it is possible that Kreisler's mix-ups, such as switching Taneyev for Cui or vice versa, were the result of simple memory lapses. Milstein does not date the Schumann and Tchaikovsky stories, but chances are he heard them in the late 1930s or early '40s, when Kreisler was perhaps sixty-five years old. Whether the fact-switching was intentional or accidental is, as a result, unclear.

The "I deeply influenced the development of one of the world's most celebrated chamber works" Assertion

This claim of Kreisler's might be true. It might also be false, the probability of which increases when one understands that the story is not only impossible to confirm but is just the sort of yarn that Kreisler loved to tell.

One of the more obscure Kreisler facts (or fictions), it appeared in print only once—in a March 1955 cover story in the *International Musician*, the official journal of the American Federation of Musicians. A more elaborate version traveled from Kreisler himself to Wallace Magill, producer of the "Bell Telephone Hour," who in turn passed it on to David Sackson. The tale concerns a young Austrian composer named Arnold Schoenberg, who approached Kreisler around the turn of the century with the manuscript for an extremely difficult string trio. Kreisler read it, liked it, and returned it to his friend with one suggestion: since each of the three parts was saddled with constant, extended double stops, why not divide them all into two parts and turn the work from a trio into a sextet? Schoenberg complied—and the result, completed in late 1899, was *Verklärte Nacht*.[25]

The truth or falsity of this anecdote is, unfortunately, impossible to determine. Kreisler's account in the *International Musician* does not help: it is off-handed, only vaguely illuminating (the piece "had such richness it wouldn't do for three instruments," he said), and seems, in fact, to serve primarily as a chance for the violinist to criticize Schoenberg's later experimentation with twelve-tone composing. Consider:

> [Schoenberg's] *Gurre-Lieder* is a great work. Then something seemed to happen to him. He seemed to go against all

> he had done before. During a western tour, a young reporter in a small town came to me—nice fellow he was—and told me that Arnold Schoenberg had passed that way a few weeks before and that he (the reporter) asked him what he thought of me. Schoenberg said, "Fritz—I loved him dearly, but now that stinker does not want to follow me."
>
> I refuse to follow dual-tonal noises. I once told a composer, "Goodness, violinists will play out of tune anyway, without having the score made out of tune for them!" Then, do you know, you can't read the scores of atonalists up and down—just horizontally or, rather, slantingly, as one instrument takes over from another. It's my opinion that science is having an evil influence on art.[26]

Did Schoenberg actually call Kreisler a "stinker"? Maybe. The only verifiable elements in this and related utterances are Kreisler's deep distrust of atonal music and his fondness, then as always, for vigorous hyperbole. If it was worth saying, it was worth exaggerating.

Of all the yarns that Kreisler spun throughout the years, of all the outrageous exaggerations, the most entertaining are those that illumine the florid romanticism of his youth. These stories are so far-fetched, so colorfully detailed, and so cinematic in their melodrama that it is a wonder no one purchased the movie rights and turned his young adulthood into a pulpy two-reel film. He might have starred in it himself; he had many of the qualities of an early film star (black hair, big stature, mournful eyes), and his one real flaw, that high-pitched, lisping voice, would have been perfectly cloaked in a silent movie. Jascha Heifetz occasionally played himself in films (most notably in *They Shall Have Music*, 1939), so there is no reason why Kreisler could not have portrayed a yearning young artist from Vienna. He was perfect for the part. (Unfortunately, by the time it occurred to someone—Lochner—that Kreisler's life was indeed worth filming, the violinist was too frail, and Harriet too controlling, to agree.)

Kreisler had rehearsed the role for decades. There is no question that he had a flair for the theatrical, nor is there any doubt that his musical judgment was colored by it. He was truly, even unduly, fond of emotion and admiring of its ability to shape not only the artistic sensibility but the art itself; passion informed his every choice, musical and personal. It was the essence of Kreisler's gift that he was able to convey such emotion without abandoning the erudition, taste, or historical precision required of a responsible musical interpreter. He expressed passion without over-indulging. On the violin as in life, he was ever the well-mannered gentleman. He gambled and drank and in his younger years smoked, but he did not appear to abuse such vices, did not brag about them, and did not seem corrupt as a result; he traveled the globe and met world leaders of the purplest cloth, but retained the air of the humblest democrat; he fell precipitously, suddenly, passionately in love, but then married the woman and remained dutifully henpecked for sixty years. He had a colorful life, but it was never so colorful as his stories implied. All of which gives his wildest tales added charm.

Where did this fondness for tale-telling come from? Why had Kreisler so few compunctions about tweaking the facts? Why was he always believed? Time and again he swayed listeners with implausible stories, and time and again these stories were circulated and reported as fact. Had Kreisler announced to the world that he had inspired Puccini to write *La Bohème* or had once played a concerto with a hairless bow, one can assume that such fantasies would have been printed verbatim or nearly so in publication upon publication, year after year, until some random skeptic bothered to check whether any of it were true. Kreisler certainly would not have volunteered the information. He would not have seen a need.

The real mystery, throughout Kreisler's life, is why such an intrinsically moral, resolutely principled man had such an appetite for fib-telling. It may be that his fondness for fancy overpowered his regard for the facts; it may be that he saw the truth not as a collection of literal details but as something more liter*ary*, lacking in accuracy but abundantly rich in meter and metaphor. He was a storyteller. "Kreisler had a marvelous imagination," remarked Gingold, "and thank God, did he use it through his playing."[27]

Normally Kreisler told stories with his violin, standing straight as a pin in the center of the stage, his face twitching slightly while his right and left arms wove the tales. His performances were not stories in the strictest sense—no purely instrumental music is, no matter how directly inspired by text—but they carried ideas and emotions as real, as specific, as those evoked in narrative form. Kreisler was, by nature and profession, a communicator. Helping him to communicate were his violin, his understanding of beauty, his command of languages, his talent for writing, his ability to speak extemporaneously, his love of conversation, and his deeply imagistic, unapologetically melodramatic knack for storytelling. He simply liked to talk.

Frederic Kreisler's memories of his Uncle Fritz include affectionate recollections of this fondness for storytelling but, interestingly, almost none of the violinist's famed and fictive web-spinning. According to Frederic, the aging violinist limited himself to stories of musicians he had known and places he had played. The more elaborate fictions were never recounted for family ears—at least, not that Frederic was then aware or now remembers. Upon hearing a few of the more outrageous stories retold, he responded with laughter and disbelief that any skeptical listener could have taken them seriously.

In looking back on the more elaborate stories that came from Kreisler's own lips, Frederic emphasized his uncle's pride, his deep morality, and the memory loss that marked his retirement years. Indeed, Frederic Kreisler believes that some of the violinist's later examples of truth-stretching might have been something else entirely: the lapses of an aging man, filled with dignity, who could not recall a date or detail and simply substituted another. Unlike the more whimsical and obvious apocrypha that originated during Kreisler's prime, these later falsehoods might thus be seen as poignant indicators of the great man's decline.[28]

Kreisler as web-spinner: it is a characterization that fits as well as his clothes—better, for his jacket never hung quite properly on his figure, stretching buttons against holes and fabric against flesh. In photographs he looked as stiff as a sausage, his bearing military, his mouth and eyes unsmiling, his mustache almost comically bushy. From such portraits it is hard to fathom the sagas he spun in storytelling and the liberty he took in details; it is hard to reconcile his button-down demeanor with his unbuttoned yen for embellishment;

it is hard, in short, to imagine him as a prankster. Yet he was. Despite the seriousness with which he approached his music, Kreisler was never one to take himself or the publicity that surrounded him too seriously. The opposite was true: he was at the core an unambitious, easygoing man who, were it not for a practical and highly ambitious wife, would have spent his days with friends and his money on long shots. He enjoyed drinking, eating, gambling, socializing, and a good tale, engagingly told. Few told one better than he did.

Thus we are left with a legacy of storytelling, only some of which is true. Kreisler made himself into the character he wanted to be: lover, war hero, trick fiddler, innocent held at gunpoint by a spur-clacking cowboy. In reality he was a sweet man with a shrewish wife who made such small trouble as his home life and concert career allowed.

So Kreisler concocted. Given a chance to reminisce, he often padded the truth with fabrication—and he did so freely, easily, and without self-consciousness. He lied not out of malice or failed superego but out of sheer playfulness, a recreative urge that found few other equally impish outlets for expression and overcame or simply ignored accepted social prohibitions against prevarication. Somewhere in the wash of fiction bobs one detail or another that resembles the truth; retrieving it from the flotsam is an engaging but ultimately frustrating task. For in the end, the dry facts mattered little to Fritz Kreisler. Like anyone else with a strong autobiographical streak and an urge for self-creation, he made up many of the facts as he went along. A life well-narrated is, in the end, vastly more interesting than one well-lived.

Seven

Hoaxes All: Pugnani, Vivaldi, Martini, and Kreisler

In early 1935, *New York Times* critic Olin Downes was conducting research for a lecture-cum-recital that he was scheduled to present with Yehudi Menuhin as part of the concert series Downes ran at the Brooklyn Academy of Music. Menuhin would perform several pieces and Downes would analyze them, musically and historically, for the audience's edification.

Downes had been writing reviews of Menuhin's concerts from the time the violinist was eleven years old, and they had become good friends by the 1930s. In an interview nearly sixty years later, Menuhin discussed the 1935 recital: "[Downes would] talk about the music and then he'd have the program played. And this time I had the Pugnani piece as the first piece on my program, and [Downes] wanted to know something more about it to be able to speak about it."[1]

So Downes began to research Kreisler's well-known arrangement of the *Praeludium and Allegro*. Naturally, the critic wanted to compare the arrangement with Pugnani's original.

The original, however, was nowhere to be found. Everywhere he looked, every library, every archive, turned up empty. Downes was flummoxed. He cabled Kreisler in Vienna, asking him whether and where he might locate the ancient manuscript. Kreisler's response—that no Pugnani original was available, there was no Pugnani original, Pugnani had nothing to do with the piece, and the work was, in fact, one of several such masterworks penned entirely by Kreisler himself—provoked one of the century's liveliest debates on the ethics of music and proved to be among the violinist's longest-running and most entertaining scandals. Discussion of the great Kreisler "hoax" was to preoccupy musicians, audiences, and critics for years to come; to this day, it remains one of the richest and most perplexing moral quandaries in all of modern music.

Fritz Kreisler's fondness for storytelling was addressed in the previous chapter. The stories there described were related with a certain measure of whimsy, the violinist's blithe yarn-spinning being impossible to regard in any other way. Never did his fibbing seem driven by guile. Rarely was it met with any response more severe than befuddlement; so automatic were his fibs, and so skilled was he in telling them, that even the most skeptical listeners were lulled into a Kreisler-induced suspension of critical discernment. His tales had always been part of his charm.

Yet few revelations have rattled music circles as soundly as that anticlimactic little confession of 1935. This more than any other event in Kreisler's life raised doubts about his artistic integrity, inciting apoplectic reactions from publishing's most excitable critics and causing even the unflappable ones to scratch their heads in search of an explanation. Even decades later, when Kreisler was long retired and fast approaching the end of his life, interviewers were still confronting him with the question: Why? For what reason would the world's most respected string player seemingly deceive his listeners, year after year, in a matter of such musical significance? Then as earlier, his answers came freely—as freely and cheerfully and articulately as the tales that had hatched the hoax to begin with.

The story behind the scandal is short and sweet: way, way back, when Kreisler was still a relative unknown on the European concert circuit, he wrote a number of violin works in a variety of styles that he attributed to other people. Most were eighteenth-century composers; most of those, barring a few obvious exceptions, were little known to nineteenth- and twentieth-century audiences. No one noticed any discrepancy in style between Kreisler's pieces and the other works of those eighteenth-century composers—or, if anyone noticed, no one remarked upon it and so Kreisler found no pressing reason to confess. For thirty years he toured with his collection of faux masterworks, giving them credibility and laying the foundation for a truly global hoax.

Exactly which pieces are included among the "fakes" varies according to who is counting and which catalog is used. Lochner referred several times to "a dozen" works but listed eight in the appendix and fourteen in the text. Kreisler himself fingered fourteen for *The New York Times*, but not the same fourteen that Lochner later listed. The violinist further muddied the waters by telling the *Times* that "every piece named, in fact, the entire series labeled 'classical manuscripts,' are, in every detail, my original compositions, with the sole exception of the first eight bars of the Couperin *Chanson Louis XIII*, taken from a traditional melody."[2] The problem with this confession is that the two main publishers of Kreisler's works—B. Schott's Söhne in Europe and Charles Foley in the United States—listed different works under the "classical manuscripts" heading.

After cross-checking catalogs from both B. Schott's Söhne and Charles Foley against Lochner's account and Kreisler's own comments at the time, one can compile a complete, final list of the Austrian's brilliant dummies. It contains a total of seventeen works (see also Appendix B, List of Works): *Allegretto*, in the style of Boccherini; *Allegretto* in G Minor and *Menuet*, in the style of Porpora; *Andantino* and *Preghiera* (Prayer), in the style of Martini; *Aubade Provençale, Chanson Louis XIII and Pavane*, and *La Précieuse*, in the style of Louis Couperin; Concerto in C Major, in the style of Vivaldi; *Grave*, in the style of W. F. Bach; *La Chasse* (caprice), in the style of Cartier; *Praeludium and Allegro* and *Tempo di Minuetto*, in the style of Pugnani; *Scherzo*, in the style of Dittersdorf; *Sicilienne and Rigaudon*, in the style of Francoeur; *Study on a Choral*, in the style of Stamitz; and *Variations on a*

Theme by Corelli, in the style of Tartini. Missing from this list is *La Folia*, Kreisler's transcription of a piece by Corelli. Foley/Fischer listed it as a "classical manuscript," but it is clearly an arrangement.

Olin Downes broke the story in the Friday, 8 February, edition of the paper—front page and above the fold, placement befitting a surprise revelation from the world's most prominent violinist. "Kreisler Reveals 'Classics' As Own; Fooled Music Critics for 30 Years," declared the headline, summing up with pithy economy the embarrassment faced by music journalists on both sides of the Atlantic: putting it bluntly, they had been made to look like fools. The very professionals whose experience, education, and discerning ears had qualified them for careers in music criticism had been unable to perceive the difference between eloquent classical masterpieces and melodies devised by an unabashedly romantic violinist-composer. They had been duped—and reactions to the deception ranged from shock to bemusement to philosophic resignation.

To understand the highly emotional response that Kreisler's disclosure provoked, one must remember that Fritz Kreisler was, in 1935, an artist of indubitable integrity and unparalleled fame. If anyone appeared immune from accusations of fraud, it was he. For the previous decade and a half, his career had advanced steadily—critically, popularly, and geographically. The period following his successful postwar return to the American stage included a tour of Japan and China, the composition and production of his second operetta, *Sissy*, ever-expanding record sales, preparations for a zeppelin tour of South America, and seemingly nonstop appearances in the United States and beyond. Having survived the years of demonization by American audiences during and after World War I, Kreisler emerged in the decade that followed with a stature that seemed only to swell with each passing year. His struggles in Paris notwithstanding, Kreisler's reputation in Europe never received the pummeling that it had in the States during the war; nevertheless, his reemergent presence in the United States contributed significantly to his enhanced public profile worldwide. Always an international figure, in the period before 1935 Kreisler assumed the role that he would fill until his death: the object of intense (and sometimes undiscriminating) global devotion.

A particularly interesting aspect of Kreisler's public image as it emerged during this period was his utter dominance of the press. He sneezed, and reporters covered the event. He made the news, or so it appeared, every time he arrived somewhere, or departed somewhere, or uttered some opinion on anything from atonalism ("a thing of disturbance, a product of nerves that are upset . . . a pogrom in the arts") to jazz ("transitory . . . a clever caricature . . . the majority of the jazz composers pilfered their themes and motifs from the masters") to the plight of artists in post-World War I Germany ("they are absolute beggars") to divorce ("most people who get divorces are looking for happiness and expect to find it in another mate. But they do not find it, for the reason that they have no happiness in themselves").[3] When Kreisler held the floor, people listened; his sagacious, often mystical, usually long-winded comments popped up in one interview after another.

Kreisler's 1923 tour of Asia demonstrated the truly global dimension of his fame. From 20 April through 9 June, Fritz and Harriet Kreisler and accompanist Michael Raucheisen traveled throughout Japan and China, stopping for concerts in Shanghai (where a normally taciturn audience erupted into cheers), Tokyo (where the group survived an earthquake), Yokohama, Kyoto, Osaka, Shenyang (where Kreisler gave an impromptu recital after being ejected from his train for military purposes), Beijing (where he performed separate concerts for Europeans and Chinese), back to Shanghai, and Tianjin. At each stop he was greeted rapturously, a phenomenon he attributed in part to the success of his recordings.[4]

Eighteen months later, Kreisler's remarkable popularity revealed an uglier side: he was a target. In December 1924 Kreisler's sister Ella (or possibly her twin, Hugo) received a letter in the green room during a Kreisler performance in Vienna. Inside was a demand, from "Three Unemployed Bank Clerks," that Kreisler pay seven hundred dollars or his arm would be shot off. The missive was reported, and nothing came of it.[5]

Whatever he did, wherever he did it, Kreisler's actions were noted by the international press and duly praised, boosting his celebrity beyond what it had been before the ostracism of World War I. In 1928 he attended the American debut of Leon Theremin's newfangled electronic instrument—and in one newspaper account (the 25 January 1928 *The New York Times*) Kreisler's name appeared earlier in the story than Theremin's. His concerts sold out; his recordings sold thousands; even a piece of candy called *Sissy, the Rose of Bavaria* served as proof of his genius. Had Kreisler *tried* to hurt his own career at this point, had he *tried* to ruin his reputation or earn a scathing review, the press and public would simply not have cooperated.

The success of *Sissy*, Kreisler's second flirtation with light opera, is a good example of the violinist's Midas touch during these years. The operetta opened in Vienna on 23 December 1932 to great critical and popular enthusiasm, which buoyed it through a long run; from Vienna it went on to successful stays in Amsterdam, Munich, and other European cities. Like *Apple Blossoms* before it, *Sissy* was long on charm and short on substance: its plot concerned nothing meatier nor more earth-shaking than the bumpy court romance between a fetching tomboy (Sissy, of the title) and a young Austrian Emperor. With lyrics by Ernst and Hubert Marischka and music composed entirely by Kreisler, the operetta proved a winning trifle whose best-known song is the ditty "Stars in My Eyes"—featured in the 1936 Josef von Sternberg film *The King Steps Out*.[6] *Sissy* was a popular crowd-pleaser and was well reviewed at the time. (And its popular appeal still survives, more than six decades later: a month-long run of *Sissy* at the Schönbrunn Theater in Vienna during the summer of 1997 was sold out three weeks before opening night.)

Despite one Viennese critic (quoted in *The New York Times* of 15 January 1933) who griped that he would rather hear Kreisler play the violin, such complaints were few and far between. Kreisler in the 1930s was an artist of incontestable talent and unimpeachable integrity, arguably the most respected performer on the world stage. When his admirers learned that he had faked the work of eighteenth-century composers, they were stupefied.

Colleagues and critics alike weighed in on the Kreisler hoax. Some reacted out of anger or embarrassment, while others laughed it off as typical Kreislerian myth-making. Violinist Mischa Elman, whose very playing bespoke purity of intent, was, among all of Kreisler's colleagues, the one most clearly bewildered by it all. Elman's reaction was printed in *The New York Times* on Saturday, 9 February 1935, the very day after Downes's announcement of the scandal first appeared.

> It is indeed a surprise that one who stands for all that is beautiful, noble and true in art as Kreisler should have resorted to such means in these so-called arrangements, which would take a high place of themselves, without his having to attribute his compositions to older sources, when these composers are not able to enjoy the plaudits or endure the criticisms which these compositions may or may not evoke.

In fact, most of Kreisler's colleagues responded in one of three ways. Some were nonplussed and amused. Others, like Elman, were nonplussed and offended. But the savviest violinists were not surprised at all: they claimed to have been aware of the deception all along, thanks either to their own musical perspicacity or to Kreisler's hushed admissions. Among those who belonged to this third category was Albert Spalding, who said he had believed for years that the works in question were Kreisler's own but had respected the elder man's desire to avoid claiming authorship.[7] Also in the know was Jascha Heifetz, who declared: "His style was too typical for any of us not to recognize, but since they have been proven of such vital importance to the violin repertoire, they stand merit—master works of the twentieth century in the eighteenth-century style."[8]

Supposedly, Georges Enesco, Franz Rupp, and Louis Persinger were all in the know, as was Efrem Zimbalist. So supportive was Zimbalist of Kreisler's deception that he claimed the violinist "did a great service" to music and musicians by composing the pieces—no matter who received the credit.

> The violin repertory has been wonderfully enriched by these compositions, and as Kreisler did not think it advisable to

> say they were his when he wrote them, he had a perfect right to attribute them to anyone he pleased. Any composer, living or dead, should be proud to claim them as his own. However, anyone who is really familiar with Kreisler's style of writing would recognize the infallible signs of the actual composer of these works.[9]

Menuhin's position on the matter was articulated at the time by his father, Moshe. He said:

> There is no question that this is one of the most creditable things that Kreisler has done. He had to struggle in his early days and he did not want his name to appear perpetually on a program. Georges Enesco, Yehudi's friend and recently his teacher, always praised these compositions and recommended that Yehudi study them, irrespective of their origin, because he considered them such excellent works.[10]

More recently, Yehudi Menuhin reaffirmed and reinforced his opinion of Kreisler's subterfuge. "I think it was a delightful and justified hoax," he said. "Some people overreacted at the time. They're excellent pieces."[11]

From Kreisler's point of view, the brouhaha over his ersatz masterworks was overblown, outrageous, even amusing. He had not counterfeited the pieces in the sense that a criminal counterfeits money or fakes the distinctive hand of a renaissance painter; he had not, in other words, deceived an unsuspecting public for the basest purposes of making money. Kreisler never confessed to outright deceitfulness, nor did he tolerate any attempts to portray his little hoax as willful fraudulence. No matter that he wrote the works in the styles of other composers, using the names of other composers, publishing them as though they had been written centuries before; no matter, either, that he devised long, elaborate, and indulgently colorful stories to hide their true origins. His motives, he objected, were pure.

Kreisler's explanation was simple. Around the turn of the century, a musician seeking a solo career was faced with a practical dilemma:

how to devise programs that were artistically interesting, historically orthodox, and yet, not surprising for an era preoccupied with appearances, free of anything that might be construed as arrogance.

Indeed, the solo recital itself was a relatively modern invention. Well into the nineteenth century, even the most successful instrumentalist or vocalist was expected to share an evening's program with any number of fellow performers. Those who did not—those who, such as Franz Liszt or Nicolò Paganini, presumed to fill an evening with their own solo playing—were nearly as famous for their egos as they were for their musical genius. "To be a success in those days you had to know how to make programs," Kreisler later told Louis Biancolli for an article published in the June 1951 *Etude*. "The violinist's repertory was then very small."

Bach's sonatas for unaccompanied violin were not popular and were rarely played in the early part of the century. A handful of sonatas by Schubert were available, Kreisler said, "but Beethoven's sonatas were out of the question. You had to be big to do them and you needed a big pianist to elaborate them with you, a combination, let us say, equal to Horowitz and Elman or Rubinstein and Heifetz today." The standard violin concertos were similarly taboo because "anybody playing a violin concerto with piano accompaniment at that time would have been laughed off the stage." Playing with an orchestra was impossible unless the violinist was famous enough to merit one or wealthy enough to hire one. As a result, Kreisler maintained, "If you were a concert beginner you never played a concerto. And if you were poor and unknown, no great pianist would appear with you. Therefore, no Beethoven sonatas." Furthermore, Brahms's *Hungarian Dances* were regarded as the property of Joachim and of Brahms himself, "and no one dared compete with those two giants." To make matters worse, arrangements of pieces composed for other instruments—piano or flute or voice, for example—were simply not done.[12]

What, then, was a young performer to do? How could he fill his programs?

> You fiddled around with Bach's Chaconne or *The Devil's Trill* of Tartini or sonatas by Corelli, Veracini and Geminiani. The rest of the program was made up of smaller pieces, like Ernst's *Elegie*, Raff's *Cavatina*, Wieniawski's

> Mazurkas and Polonaise, and Vieuxtemps's *Ballade*. . . . They were all good pieces as far as they went, but I wanted to play other things. And there just weren't any.[13]

Thus, Kreisler continued,

> That was why I resolved to create a repertory of my own. I then began to write music under the composers' names. I took the names of little known composers like Pugnani and Louis Couperin, the grandfather of François Couperin.
>
> Not a single composition of Couperin's was known. Maybe in faraway libraries there were pieces by him, on yellow illegible manuscripts. You had to rummage around to find them. So with Padre Martini. Naturally, Vivaldi was a bit different. Bach had made arrangements and transcriptions and even borrowed ideas from him. So had others. And his music was scattered around everywhere.
>
> Not for one moment did it enter my head to imitate them. I could have done a better job of copying their style if I had intended it. That wasn't my plan at all.
>
> I just wanted some pieces for myself . . . and I wrote them. I gave them these names. I was eighteen [sic] then and I wanted to be a violinist, not a composer. I wanted to give recitals and I couldn't put several pieces on the program and sign them all "Kreisler." It would have looked arrogant.[14]

(As usual, Kreisler exaggerated slightly: he was not eighteen, at which age he started his army service, but in his early twenties when he embarked on his career and began to write the celebrated fakes.)

Not long after Kreisler composed the works, he concocted a characteristically cute story designed to conceal their true origins. Specifically, he said he had stumbled across the entire collection of manuscripts in an ancient European monastery, or monasteries, somewhere in the vast expanse of Europe—which ones, he never said. This marvelous little tale was dispensed freely to curious journalists and colleagues who were miffed, and even scandalized, that one lone violinist should hold the copyright to a motherlode of lost classical works. "I am glad to be able to speak with authority from no less a source than the artist himself, having persuaded him to satisfy my curiosity as to the origin of the works," boasted a writer identified as "W.E.B." in an October 1909 article in *The Musician*.

> The violinist discovered a collection of manuscript music in the possession of the monks who inhabit one of the oldest monasteries in Europe, and so anxious was he to have them for his own that he copied one of the pieces on his shirt cuff. To this the monks objected, and eventually Mr. Kreisler, after much persuasion, succeeded in purchasing the whole collection for a considerable sum of money. It was a labor of love to arrange them for the concert room, and having been at so much pains and expense to procure his treasures, he naturally considers that, so long as he can play them, they are his sole property. It is only fair, too, to state that others had access to the manuscripts, but it was left to Mr. Kreisler to discover their value and utilize them.[15]

Although this story may strike the skeptical reader as absurd (an entire piece on his shirt cuff?), it was nevertheless swallowed whole by generations of music journalists. Why no one bothered to check the details mystifies the modern observer but reaffirms the esteem with which the violinist was regarded; if Kreisler said it, it had to be true—even if he devised a markedly different version of the tale each time he chose to tell it. Barely a month after he had snowed *The Musician* and its presumably erudite readership, he spun an even more ornately detailed variation for *The New York Times*. In that publication he spoke of his fondness for collecting "old furniture, or porcelain, or books," and claimed that the first of his "found" manuscripts were in fact part of a carefully amassed collection that was shown to Kreisler by a fellow enthusiast. He was in Italy, he explained, when said collector invited him to inspect a collection of objets d'art in "a certain palace." Kreisler was brought to a room in this hypothetical palace, and he began to examine its contents. Sitting in a corner was a glass case containing several ancient manuscripts; one among them had musical notation, and, "glancing at it carelessly," Kreisler realized that it boasted a gorgeous melody. He resolved to memorize it—with some help, once again, from that ever-handy shirt cuff. Upon returning to his hotel room and attempting to read through the piece on his violin, he discovered that parts of the music were "lacking" and returned to the palace the following day to fill in the blanks. To his disappointment, the owners had placed a cover over the manuscripts. It so happened that the family that owned the collection was poor—not too poor to live in a palace, however—and agreed to sell the manuscripts.[16]

It was a charming story. Almost as charming was the embellishment that followed, as Kreisler impressed that unsuspecting *Times* reporter with a description of further works discovered "in an old convent in the South of France." Between those and the palace items, he possessed fifty-three such ancient manuscripts. Five of them were valueless; the remaining forty-eight were "gems."

"I have arranged some of it for my instrument," he said. "I have made a few minor changes in the melodies, and I have modernized the accompaniments to some extent, but I have tried to retain the spirit of the original compositions." Some he had agreed to publish in the coming months, he said, "but many of the most beautiful ones I have not played in public as yet, and those I am reserving. They will not be published for many years to come."[17]

(What became of those remaining phantom manuscripts is a matter for speculation, but in all likelihood Kreisler was alluding to works he had not yet written; despite his later claims to the contrary, it is possible that he intended to produce further counterfeits for years to come.)

One critic for *The New York Times* discussed Kreisler's "arrangement" of the Vivaldi concerto, an unmistakably false work by modern standards that was heralded just after the turn of the century as the long-ignored masterpiece of an unsung composer. Thoroughly convinced that the piece was authentic, the critic spoke in glowing appreciation of Kreisler's discovery:

> [Kreisler] has resuscitated a concerto of Antonio Vivaldi, an Italian composer of the early eighteenth century, who has tasted of immortality through Bach's arrangements of many of his works. Bach admired him, apparently, more than posterity has, for his name now seldom appears on concert performances. Yet this [Kreisler's] concerto goes to confirm Bach's high opinion; [it is] a strikingly strong and vigorous piece of music, which a century and a half of neglect has

> scarcely staled, full of ideas, rather than of formalism, ideas of a really individual character, and in the slow movement of breadth and dignity.[18]

Not all were so easily fooled, however; there were skeptics among the sheep. The *Musical Courier* was one early doubting Thomas that saw through the ancient-convent canard and heard contemporary elements in the works, though it stopped short of calling the violinist a liar.

> The *Musical Courier* never has believed the story, particularly as some of the staff of this paper are acquainted at first hand with Kreisler's propensity for perpetrating harmless hoaxes. All the Kreisler arrangements of the old numbers are provided with modern harmony in the solo setting and the accompaniment, and as the original music does not seem to be easily available, it is difficult to say how much of the versions played by Kreisler belongs to the composers and with what share the clever adapter should be credited.[19]

Presumably the press included other skeptics, but those who questioned Kreisler's story did so hesitantly, tip-toeing around outright accusations of falsehood.

In many of the interviews given at the time, Kreisler discussed his "discoveries" with what seems, in retrospect, to have been a deadly poker face—that few saw through it is proof of both his remarkable gift for misleading the press and the press's equally remarkable naiveté. Which explains, in part, why the world was so surprised to learn that he had lied. That Kreisler claimed the most innocent motives for the ruse lessened the shock only slightly, as did his dubious reassurances that he had not tried all *that* hard to deceive people. As he told Olin Downes, had he actually intended to fool the world with counterfeits, he would have gone about the task more carefully—and the result would have been much more difficult to detect. "And he could have," Downes wrote.

> There is not a better musician, one with more knowledge and taste, today, whether Kreisler plays his concerto, or

> makes an arrangement; writes an original piece, or plays an exquisite piano accompaniment for a friend; or, for the fun of it, improvises a jazz piece on the ivories. He remains a supreme musician, living in his art, working and thinking in its terms—those of the eternal youth of a most poetical age.[20]

Downes could afford to be understanding; as the journalist who broke the story seven years earlier, he had no cause to harbor ill will against Kreisler. But the hoax had tricked a world of critics, and not all of them were happy about it. One, Ernest Newman of London's *Sunday Times*, published an essay on the subject so negative that it provoked Kreisler into engaging in one of the era's nastiest and most vigorous public feuds.

Newman's initial essay was flippantly written and pitched from a curious angle. Rather than attack the man directly, he instead denigrated the musical style that Kreisler had chosen to imitate—hence belittling two centuries' worth of composition. The hoax "is welcome as showing how easy it is, and always was, to write this kind of music," Newman wrote.

> The simple truth is that a vast amount of seventeenth and eighteenth century music was merely the exploitation of formulae, the effective handling of which is within the scope of any ordinarily intelligent musician to-day. From one point of view Kreisler has not gone nearly far enough in the excellent work of clearing up the world's muddled thinking on these points: for my part I could wish he had "discovered" some Bach and Handel manuscripts as well. In so far as Bach and Handel merely sat down in perfectly cold blood and ground out their morning's ration of music-according-to-the-recipe they merely produced well-sounding stuff that anyone of any intelligence to-day could turn out by the handful.[21]

Newman's argument went on in this overheated vein for several paragraphs, eventually concluding that, "as far as the merely musical point is concerned . . . there is nothing whatever in Kreisler's achievement." He then considered the hoax from an ethical standpoint, pondering whether Kreisler's revelation had cast suspicion on all such arrangements; the violinist might even be sued, Newman suggested, by some misled music lover who had bought a piece by "Vivaldi," only to learn it was written by Kreisler. All in all it was an odd and rather foolish piece of writing.

Kreisler's reply, which appeared in the 10 March *Sunday Times*, was swift and sharp, referring to Newman as a "venerable grumbler" and dismissing the critic's complaints as the grousing of one who had been (or at least felt) humiliated.

> He is hard put to explain why he, a musical augur par excellence, failed to nail down my transcriptions for the pastiches they were. There was really no necessity for Mr. Newman to worry, for the prestige of a critic with a sense of musical values is not in the least endangered because a piece, which he pronounced good, is found to have been written by another person than he thought. The name changes, the value remains.

After marveling at Newman's reduction of Bach and Handel to the overpopulated ranks of the ordinary, Kreisler then claimed that he had given the critic every opportunity to see the "arrangements" for what they were.

> Did I not do my best to save him from his present discomfiture? Did not every copy of my incriminated transcriptions since their publication thirty years ago bear a notice in three languages, covering a full page, warning Mr. Newman that "They (the transcriptions) are, moreover, so freely treated that they constitute, in fact, original works"? Is it my fault that, in spite of all these hints, the great critic failed to see the light, whereas the true authorship of the so-called "classical manuscripts" had been for years an open secret among hundreds of musicians throughout the world? . . .
>
> I beg to assure Mr. Newman that no hoax was ever intended. I did not write the pieces in question as a young man of twenty-five in the hope of tripping up the eminent critic thirty-five years later. I simply wrote them in order to enlarge my programmes, where they figured modestly "in the style of" Pugnani, Cartier, etc., etc.

> A few colleagues borrowed copies, but they soon fell into the habit of first dropping the "in the style of" and finally omitting my own name as well. Thinking that my colleagues rather exaggerated my modesty, I recalled the outstanding copies and henceforth used the transcriptions exclusively for myself. But I had reckoned without the Newmans of the day, who clamoured in unison with my colleagues that I had no right to monopolise a valuable literature (so they claimed) for myself, and sternly demanded publication in the name of musical ethics.[22]

Again, two of Kreisler's assertions in the above excerpts smack of exaggeration or common truth-stretching. The first is his claim that "hundreds of musicians throughout the world" were aware of his little subterfuge; in all probability it was only a handful. The second is Kreisler's awkward insistence that his earliest programs indicated the works were his own compositions written "in the style" of classical masters. In later interviews—and, indeed, in his second rejoinder to Newman, penned only three weeks later—Kreisler stated flatly that he had attributed the pieces to other composers specifically to pad recital programs with names other than his own.

Newman's second blow in the exchange was almost as low as his first. Once again he aimed not to criticize Kreisler's hoax with legitimate observations about musical integrity but to disparage the compositions as hardly worthy of his attention. "You at once deceive yourself and flatter yourself," Newman wrote in the following week's *Sunday Times*.

> I know practically nothing of these works of yours; I doubt whether in all my life I have heard more than two or three of them; if I have, I have taken no particular notice of them; and I doubt whether what I have scribbled about them in the course of my concert-going during the last twenty-five years or so would occupy, in all, ten lines of the column.[23]

In fact, Newman claimed, the only reason he bothered with the subject at all is that Kreisler had managed to persuade so many people for so many years that the works were genuine. Once more he took swipes at both the violinist and the composers he imitated: "You have demonstrated convincingly that any ordinarily good musician, no matter how modest his endowment for original composition may be, can turn out with perfect ease a manufactured modern article so like the ancient thing it purports to be that listeners everywhere will unquestioningly accept it as genuine."

He attacked Kreisler for raising doubt about the authenticity of other, long-accepted original manuscripts—a fair criticism—and ridiculed the violinist's contention that the disclaimers on his "arrangements" indicated a heavy hand in their revision. To the contrary, Newman wrote, "*you* gave the public to understand that what you had done was to operate upon an *original manuscript* by some famous composer or other when as a matter of fact *there was no such manuscript*" (italics his).[24]

Finally, the critic lambasted his opponent on a fairly silly point: rather than devise fictitious names of faux composers, he said, Kreisler had the gall to assume the identities of "well-known" figures in musical history. It was a peculiar misrepresentation of the truth.

Kreisler did not let it pass unnoticed. He concluded his great feud with Newman with the following letter, repeated here in full from a carbon of the original missive, written in Stockholm. *The Sunday Times* ran it virtually verbatim on 31 March.

> It is with the utmost reluctance that I take up the pen for the second and positively last time in the distasteful public controversy forced upon me by Mr. Ernest Newman, who visibly is growing less and less fastidious in the choice of polemic methods.
>
> His assertion, that I invite the world to laugh with me at the expense of those detested creatures, the critics, is a plain and bold untruth, designed, of course, to bring me into conflict with his colleagues, who, as a body, have shown admirable judgment, fairmindedness, dignity and good humor.
>
> Very likely most of them had all the while suspected the real authorship of the so-called "Classical Manuscripts," and the revelation of *The New York Times* was no news to them. They had moreover long ago accepted my works at

the face value of their own, respective musical merit, and it mattered not the head of a pin whether the pieces were in the end ninety or hundred percent my original work.

It remained for Mr. Newman to take the disclosure as a blow to his prestige and forthwith he burst into rancid print. In my letter to *The Sunday Times* I dealt therefore exclusively with Mr. Newman (aside from some allusions to a few earlier timid anticipators of his now perfected methods, Newmans, as it were, of bygone days), and drew attention to his preposterous assertion, that the achievements of Bach and Handel, when not at their best, were at the reach of "any ordinary, intelligent, modern musician."

In this respect I suggest that Mr. Newman be taken at his word and compelled to prove his simple-formula theory, by turning out in clausura a specified piece in antique style. (If, as an alleged second-grade product by Bach or Handel, this piece succeeds in getting by the caretaker of Queen's Hall, I am prepared to make humble apologies.) Or are we expected to believe that this grandiloquent censor, who for years has been lecturing eminent composers, instrumentalists and singers on their respective art, may in the end not be able to qualify as an "ordinary intelligent musician," according to the standard set up by himself?

Equally false is Mr. Newman's assertion that I had adopted "well-known" old names for my compositions, the sly contention being obviously that I profited by their renown. Who ever had heard a work by Pugnani, Cartier, Francoeur, Porpora, Louis Couperin, Padre Martini or Stamitz before I began to compose in their names? They lived exclusively as paragraphs in musical reference books, and their work, when existing and authenticated, lay mouldering in monasteries and old libraries. Their names were no more than empty shells, dusty old, forgotten cloaks, which I borrowed to hide my identity, when at the outset of my career I saw the necessity of enlarging the snug repertoire of violinists (as far as smaller pieces were concerned) and yet realised the impossibility for a beginner to gain recognition simultaneously as a violinist and as a composer.

It is naive to accuse me of having troubled the calm waters of Musical History and confused its students.

Only the pure, authenticated product of a bygone period can be the subject of scientific research and form the basis for the valuation of its achievements. But who ever dreamed of passing off my compositions as the works of old masters?

Mr. Newman has degraded Bach and Handel in vain. His implication was, that since the second-grade product by Bach or Handel and the first-rate one by other masters of the seventeenth and eighteenth century were à la portée of any ordinary, intelligent musician, my work, which purposed to imitate theirs, was, of course, equally worthless. But he must have been confused by his anger, or else have an unflattering conception of the intelligence of his readers, if he believes that his verbose attempts to befog the issue can detract from the naivety of his argumentation.

How on earth can my compositions fall under the category of eighteenth-century products (be they first-rate or third-rate), when they never purposed to be anything else but modern transcriptions and now are averred to be in each detail the pure expression of my own, specific, however modest talent?

Let me make myself perfectly clear. I am in no way concerned with Mr. Newman's critical opinions. His right to emit them is incontestably vouchsafed by the confidence of his editor. He is at liberty to visualize constructive criticism as a dispenser of dry erudition in the shelter of a well-stocked reference library, rather than as the ally of the artists in their struggle against the growing inertia of concertgoers. We have no voice, when he conceives his right to censure as a license for the expression of facile witticism at the expense of trembling debutants. His utterances, however, are not regarded as the emanation of sober and impartial judgment, and constitute in the main a source of enjoyment to former victims of his rancor who derive some satisfaction from the fact that some other fellow is getting it also.

It is a matter of overwhelmingly small import to me whether this musician by the grace of Grove's Dictionary likes my compositions or not. I am unmoved when he

> chooses to make himself ridiculous by pretending that in twenty-five years he heard no more than two or three of my pieces, whereas there were few violin recitals given during this period that did not include at least one of them in their programs. Had he kept his attack within the decent bounds of his prerogative as a critic, he would never have drawn a word of reply from me.
>
> Mr. Newman is a scholar, a musical writer of great experience, a meritorious compiler of data from musical reference books. Beyond that he may be conceded to be a healthy antidote against the growth of artistic incompetence and as a beneficial irritant, a sort of gadfly that stings artists into better and higher things.
>
> But when he arrogates to himself the office of a musical Cato in England, interrogates these artists in public, impugns their motives and questions their musical ethics, then it is time to call a halt.
>
> For then he is not only ludicrous, but becomes actually irksome and a public nuisance.[25]

Kreisler's debate with Newman, considered more than sixty years after the two men sparred on the pages of *The Sunday Times*, is fascinating for a variety of reasons, none so fascinating as the extent and fervor of Kreisler's anger. This was a side that he rarely if ever showed to the world at large: not in his onstage demeanor, not in his tangles with Harriet, not in his normally gracious relations with music journalists. A listening public accustomed to his gentle and gentlemanly poise must have been shocked to learn that somewhere beneath that tightly buttoned waistcoat beat the raging heart of a pugilist—a pugilist of the pen, perhaps, but a pugilist nonetheless. Indeed, his final attack is composed in that breathless, slightly unbalanced style of a first draft revised barely or not at all before being dropped into the mailbox. He did not "sleep" on this letter; had he, he might have reconsidered his stunningly arrogant reference to the borrowed names of old masters as "empty shells, dusty old, forgotten cloaks." Dusty old cloaks!

The entire letter rings with similar overstatements, motivated by the obvious (and understandable) desire to hit Newman at least as hard as Newman had hit him. In this respect it is surprisingly visceral. But the document rings as well with intellectual pique born of hurt pride and an awareness of extreme professional discourtesy: when Newman impugned not only Kreisler's ethics but his abilities as a composer, he had crossed a line of unforgivable trespass. Fair criticism was acceptable; sweeping dismissals of a good portion of his life's work was not.

Fortunately, Kreisler had few other occasions in which he needed to defend himself in print; criticism of his actions did appear elsewhere, but none was nearly as vituperative as Newman's. The editors of the periodical *The Musician* cast their own vote on the matter in February of 1935, when they published a measured, straightforward, ultimately generous editorial.

> In current musical history no event has commanded wider public attention than Fritz Kreisler's confession that he is the sole author of a large group of popular compositions for the violin which for thirty years had been published and performed the world over as "arrangements" from such classic masters as Vivaldi, Pugnani, Martini, Porpora, Couperin and others. The effect of this startling disclosure among musicians generally, and among violinists particularly has been a composite of amusement, perplexity, resentment and applause. Idol worshippers of the distinguished violinist accept the news as added evidence of the surpassing genius of a great artist who aside from his musical importance long since has earned his right to a place among the world's intellectuals. . . .
>
> In the sister arts—painting, sculpture, drama and literature—there are ugly appellations for those who profess classic authorship for their own brain children. Indeed, the animated comment aroused by the Kreisler "hoax" has not been entirely free from the implication that the distinguished violinist had violated a sacred artistic tradition. The case of the painter who steeps himself in the spirit and technical methods of Corot and then offers his own products as those of the French master is not unlike that of the musician who composes a concerto in C major and causes it to be published as a work of Vivaldi. . . .

> Wholly aside from ethical considerations one cannot escape the conclusion that the violin literature has been precisely richened by this music which has brought unmeasured happiness to thousands of listeners. To return to the parallel of the painter, may it not be said in this case, that Mr. Kreisler is an artist with the genius of a Corot who has preferred to work in anonymity that the glory of Corot might reach greater heights by his subterfuge.[26]

To appreciate the impact of Kreisler's hoax on the music-listening public, imagine a scandal of similar proportions being revealed today: picture, for example, the reaction from the press and the populace if a prominent soprano were accused of lip-synching her arias, or if a world-class cellist confessed authorship for a dozen or so short pieces that he had previously attributed to C. P. E. Bach or Antonio Salieri. The uproar would deafen all concerned and possibly ruin the careers of some fine performers. But such an analogy is ultimately unsatisfactory, and in some sense fallacious, simply because no one performing today is as active and talented a composer—and as prolific a contributor to his instrument's repertoire—as Kreisler was at the time that his "hoax" became public. He was the last (and, not coincidentally, the most enduring) of the nineteenth century's great composer-soloists, and the only such figure to have recorded the bulk of his own work on 78s. Even those who had never heard Kreisler perform in a music hall were familiar with his short works—*Caprice Viennois* was probably one of the most recognized melodies anywhere—and knew him as a composer of established reputation and disarming gifts.

As *The New York Times* observed:

> It was the easier for Mr. Kreisler to adopt these names of old composers and pass off his own music as theirs for several reasons. The first is Kreisler's consummate musicianship, knowledge and taste, which enabled him to write, and write beautifully, in widely varied styles. The second is that he has in many cases written transcriptions of songs and of instrumental pieces, very adroitly and effectively arranged for string instruments. To slip by a number of works as those

of men long since dead was a simple thing and was received without suspicion by the public.[27]

Eventually, all the furious discussion began to fade, and Kreisler plugged ahead with his career—to great success and, in certain parts of the world, great publicity. In May of 1935 the violinist set off sans wife for a month-long tour of South America (a sojourn mentioned briefly in an earlier chapter as an example of Harriet's far-reaching control over her husband's behavior). Accompanied by Franz Rupp, he departed on the *Graf Zeppelin* from Friedrichshafen on 5 May and arrived the following evening in Pernambuco, Brazil, where he gave his first concert before traveling on to Rio de Janeiro.[28] In Rio, Kreisler and Rupp met up with Charles Foley and gave two concerts; from there they went by rail to São Paulo, then back to Rio, then by airplane to Buenos Aires, Argentina. In the days that followed they performed in Montevideo, Uruguay, at the invitation of the president and returned, again, to Rio for a final concert. The pair arrived in Rio following a fifteen-hour flight only one hour before curtain time; Rupp later told Lochner that he and Kreisler performed the concert "virtually deaf" from the noise of the plane. The artists, accompanied by Charles Foley, boarded the *Graf Zeppelin* in Pernambuco and departed for Friedrichshafen in the early hours of 7 June. At no point during Kreisler's voyage did anyone pummel him with questions about his "fakes"; the only journalist who came close to raising the subject was a critic from Rio de Janeiro who tried to take credit for discovering the hoax. Beyond that, his relationship with the South American press was nothing short of a love-fest.[29]

No one doubted, in 1935, that Kreisler had written seventeen pieces beyond the dozens already known to be in the violinist's body of work. No one questioned whether he was capable of writing them. Any protestations of surprise, when voiced, expressed mainly the disbelief that he was capable of deception; this was the beloved Kreisler, after all, a man so universally adored that even the most obvious flaws in his playing and character were either glossed over or ignored by those who admired him. That Kreisler's hand produced the *Praeludium and Allegro* and other such works surprised no one. That he was capable of lying about it so thoroughly and for so long caused tectonic shocks.

In fact, the biggest surprise of all is how few people suspected the truth behind Kreisler's "arrangements." A glaring hint had been dropped roughly a quarter-century earlier, when he confessed to the authorship of two works, *Liebesleid* and *Liebesfreud*, that previously had been presented as transcriptions of works by Joseph Lanner. The decision to reveal himself stemmed not from some spasm of candor but from remarks made by a snide Berlin critic who had taken him to task for presuming to play his own *Caprice Viennois* in the same recital as those much-superior "Lanner" works. This Kreisler could not tolerate, and he promptly informed the critic, and all else who cared, of the works' actual composer.[30] No scandal resulted, no huge flap over the ethics of counterfeit manuscripts, no lingering doubts about the violinist's integrity—and, much to his surprise, no attempt on anyone's part to double-check the authorship of the remaining Kreisler "arrangements." Not a single scholar thought to ask.

In part, the blindness (or, more to the point, deafness) of observers to the true authorship of these fakes makes sense in light of Kreisler's arrangements of well-known, or at least previously existing, works. Those true arrangements display the same flourishes, the same harmonic sensibility and fondness for modulation, that are evidence of Kreisler's style; his handiwork is clearly revealed in his work-overs of Tchaikovsky, Rimsky-Korsakov, Schubert, Paganini, Dvořák, even his version of a traditional tune as simple as the *Londonderry Air*. They are unmistakably altered, sometimes dramatically, by the arranger's hand. "He really absorbed all these musical languages so beautifully," said Eric Wen. "He modulated them and put them in all sorts of different keys. I think it's breathtaking, his arrangements."

Many of these arrangements, Wen continued, "are completely out of character, inauthentic, but just wonderful. . . . I think as an arranger of original violin pieces, he added so much of himself in there—and you can learn so much about his playing by just looking at his arrangements."[31]

Kreisler's "arrangements" of the supposed eighteenth- and nineteenth-century originals by Pugnani and others contain the same flagrant and unmistakable marks of Kreisler's highly idiosyncratic style: his endearing melodies, his frequent use of extended double stops, his intricate, insistent rhythms, his harmonies, even his fondness for fingering on the D-string. All were plain indicators that someone other than the alleged original composers—maybe even the someone who performed these works—had a major role in their creation. Even the magnificent *Praeludium*, ostensibly written by Pugnani and boasting the soaring interior architecture and lambent melodicism characteristic of the period, is distinctly Kreisler's in its employment of multiple stops, its heavy reliance on modulation, and its evident Viennese lyricism. They are, said Eric Wen, "unmistakably Kreisler."[32]

Thus, in a sense—and with a nifty irony—Kreisler's heavy-handed way with arrangements provided a certain cover, or camouflage, for the seventeen hoaxes. As the violinist pointed out to Ernest Newman, only the least observant student of music could have missed the printed disclaimers that declared every such composition to be so thoroughly revised that it was, for practical purposes, a Kreisler original. This deftly worded fib served not only as legal protection but as a reminder to followers of Kreisler's music that the alterations he had made to Pugnani, Martini, Vivaldi, et al., were actually no different from his heavily Kreislerized paraphrases of Glazunov, or Weber, or Falla. He was nearly as well-known for his arrangements as he was for his original works. As a result, anyone who heard in *Chanson Louis XIII and Pavane* an influence distinctly more romantic, and definitely more Viennese, than Couperin's could and would have attributed it to Kreisler's well-known tampering. "There are those who object to Mr. Kreisler's transcriptions of old music. They find them honeyed versions of little pieces from long ago," noted Downes in 1925, finding not fault but cause for magisterial even-handedness in Kreisler's famous arrangements. "But those transcriptions need not be taken too captiously."[33] Because listeners were accustomed to hearing Kreisler's imprint on everything he arranged, there was little cause to suspect that a handful of such "revisions" had no source material beyond Kreisler's own pen. To have such suspicions would have required an intuitive leap, a highly schooled familiarity with compositional styles, and at least minimal awareness of Kreisler's penchant for hyperbolizing.

It must also be remembered, more than sixty years after the scandal broke and nearly a full century after Kreisler wrote the pieces, that the listening public is vastly better educated today than ever before in the styles and structures of baroque and classical music. In part a byproduct of the early-music movement, which has used historically *echt* performances and recordings to publicize and indeed popularize a lode of previously overlooked (and underplayed) music, stylistically savvy audiences are today able to distinguish between compositions of the seventeenth, eighteenth, and nineteenth centuries. Much of baroque music is simply more popular than it was seventy-five years ago.

Yet, the skeptics who questioned the origins of Kreisler's "discoveries"—even those who probably knew the difference between early-eighteenth- and late-nineteenth-century music—rarely claimed the works were stylistically suspect. Years before the hoax was revealed, Carl Flesch examined not the authenticity but the aesthetics of the transcriptions, concluding that their actual authorship mattered little in gauging their worth. "No matter what one's position may be with regard to the transcription question, one thing cannot be denied: Kreisler's transcriptions, within their own consciously contracted frame-work, possess an out-spoken musical value," he wrote. "Whether the composition entitled *Praeludium and Allegro* be by Pugnani or by Kreisler (as many maintain) it is, in its present form, unquestionably the best composition now sailing under Pugnani's flag."[34]

Evidently, if not explicitly, Flesch counted himself among those "many" who believed the arrangements to be Kreisler's handiwork alone. He did not identify others in the same camp, but whoever they were, they were either uninterested in making public accusations or were extremely soft-spoken—and certainly not a member of the Fourth Estate.

Another who spotted the fakes as Kreisler originals was violinist Nathan Milstein. An ardent admirer of the elder man, Milstein had a keen understanding of Kreisler's habits as a composer and a thorough knowledge of the violin repertoire—so thorough a knowledge that he was able to recognize passages that had been lifted from other works. As he remarked in his memoirs:

> I think that such works of Kreisler's in the old style are more pastiche than imitation. Take, for instance, his famous *Praeludium and Allegro* in the style of Pugnani. I know six études for the violin written by Gaetano Pugnani himself—an eighteenth-century Italian composer—and without a doubt Kreisler borrowed from them. But clearly, he changed the rhythm. All these pastiches are smart work, but I think that sometimes Kreisler went overboard on modulations, not knowing when to stop. That's particularly evident in his arrangements of Baroque music.[35]

Milstein's observations also inadvertently point to a contradiction in Kreisler's "confession" to Olin Downes. Kreisler had claimed in revealing the hoax that all of the works, barring the first eight measures of *Chanson Louis XIII*, were wholly original creations; they were not. Accepting Milstein's assertion about the six violin études, either Kreisler lifted from those Pugnani études subconsciously (and guilelessly) or he did so fully aware of their source, adding a further fiction to the heaps already amassed on the subject. Only a composer of such irresistible gifts could have blurred the definitions of plagiarism and counterfeiting and escaped, following heated but ultimately pointless debate, with his reputation intact.

Which leads us back to the implicit but alluring contradiction at the base of Kreisler's deception: that he was able to carry out an elaborate ruse, and then admit that he had carried it out, without ever actually acknowledging it *as* a ruse. He was an innocent deceiver.

Further proof of this contradiction is the fact that Kreisler did so very little to perpetuate the hoax beyond getting it started. He lit the fire and then walked away, clearly expecting someone to discover the flames and douse them before they turned into a genuine blaze. At first they were contained by the violinist's slow rise to prominence, which confined the spurious pieces to Kreisler's own recitals and guaranteed them some measure of obscurity. As Kreisler's reputation grew, however, the "lost masterpieces" took on a life of their own and spread onto the programs of other violinists, becoming recognized works within the instrument's repertoire and showing up as widely accepted fact in books, magazine articles, and newspaper reviews. In this manner the hoax flourished beyond its creator's expectations. It was an organic creature.

Beyond the obvious exception of his "Lanner" dances, Kreisler rarely went out of his way to discourage misconceptions of any sort; it was his habit to let sitting lies lie, choosing to watch quietly as the world swallowed and then disseminated one bald-faced falsehood after another. He was in all likelihood amused by the whole affair. That Kreisler ultimately "confessed" to the hoax neither demonstrated contrition nor in any way implied that he regretted having misled generations of musicians and concertgoers; he was merely answering a direct question that had never before been asked. Had Downes asked him earlier, or had another journalist, decades before, approached the violinist with the same question, he would have responded the same way. He probably wondered why it took so long for the truth to come to light.

Even if Olin Downes had not cabled Kreisler with a question about the *Praeludium and Allegro*, the public would have learned soon enough of the ruse. By 1935 Kreisler had grown tired of his decades-old deception and had apparently lost faith that anyone, any scholar or journalist, might call him on it. In an unusual step toward candor, at the end of 1934 the violinist instructed his American publisher, Carl Fischer, to list the works in question as Kreisler originals in the following year's catalog. The front-page bombshell in *The New York Times* was thus published only months before the news would have been revealed in an official, and considerably more subdued, announcement.[36] The fugitive was at last discovered, on the brink of turning himself in.

It was a poetically just comeuppance. Kreisler had always been a deft manipulator of the press, if only because he seemed so completely ingenuous; few other public figures have so mastered the craft of appearing at once worldly and childlike, sophisticated and driven by the purest motives. His recovery from the hoax of 1935 was a public-relations exercise of magnificent agility, for it demonstrated beyond doubt both Kreisler's spectacularly elastic treatment of hard facts and his bewitching naiveté.

As David Ewen stated in an article for *Esquire* magazine in August 1935, "L'Amico Fritz":

> Fate being what it is, it is not beyond the realm of possibility that the name of Fritz Kreisler will be descended to posterity for a reason other than he is the greatest violinist of our age. One can almost see a musical dictionary of the twenty-first century referring to Kreisler in this fashion:
>
> ". . . He is remembered today only because of a hoax which he perpetrated upon the entire world of music in his time."

History has been lenient on Fritz Kreisler—lenient, and forgetful. The revelation that caused such a stir six decades ago has been reduced to a paragraph or two in the liner notes of historic reissues, and anyone who is familiar with the seventeen fakes knows them not as counterfeit classical works but as Kreisler originals composed "in the style of" Pugnani, or Couperin, or Padre Martini. Despite the enduring pertinence of the debate itself, the scandal that erupted around the pieces dissipated long before Kreisler's death. Ernest Newman's irate accusations of violated ethics are recalled, if at all, only as the windy irrelevancies of an angry journalist. Kreisler was lucky. Had he been less charming, had his noisiest critic made less foolish arguments, and had the public at large been less infatuated with his playing, he might have emerged from the commotion with a permanently sullied reputation. Another artist might have been deemed guilty of counterfeiting ancient masterworks and suffered no small damage to his career. Kreisler, it turned out, was guilty of a few white lies.

Eight

Kreisler the Catholic, Kreisler the Jew

Fritz Kreisler was at least partly Jewish. Of that there is little doubt; the fact was accepted if not mentioned by many who knew him, in musical circles and elsewhere, and accounts of Jewish musicians in the American diaspora invariably include him in the ranks. Although there is some indication that Kreisler's mother was Catholic—which, if true, would have meant that her children were gentiles, according to Jewish tradition—other evidence indicates not only his father's Jewish heritage but also the Jewish identity that seems to have been held by other members of his family. Franz Rupp was convinced of Kreisler's Jewish background despite his mother's "Aryan" ethnicity. Rupp once asked Kreisler's brother Hugo whether the violinist was Jewish. "I'm a Jew," Hugo replied, "but my brother, I don't know."[1] Kreisler's father was Jewish. His brother was Jewish. To a certain extent—by certain definitions—so was he.

This in and of itself would not be revelatory, or even particularly noteworthy, were it not for Kreisler's adamant and lifelong denial of his ethnic and religious heritage. Judging from most printed accounts of his life—including newspaper interviews and Louis Lochner's exhaustive 1950 biography—Kreisler and his wife were both reared as Roman Catholics but fell away from the faith after they married outside the Church and were, according to Church teaching, "living in sin."[2] Such assertions were never doubted by interviewers, most of whom must have questioned some of what they heard but were bound by the conservative rules of decorum exercised by early twentieth-century journalists. If Kreisler said he was not Jewish, if Kreisler said he was born and bred Catholic and had no Jewish family anywhere, fine. That was the story that appeared in print.

On this subject Kreisler never wavered. Throughout the many decades of his highly public life, he recalled often and affectionately his childhood and family in Vienna. He spoke with eloquence of the brotherhood of man. He contributed mightily to a variety of charitable causes, overlooking national boundaries during the nastiest of wars, and he never displayed any racial or religious prejudice of any sort. He was, too, disarmingly candid about his wife, his weaknesses, and other aspects of his personal life, responding easily (albeit not always accurately) whenever confronted with a question. Yet on the subject of his Jewish background, he was quiet. He simply had nothing to say.

Why? Why did Kreisler duck his heritage? Out of shame? Out of self-preservation during the 1930s? Or was he, as a child of Austria, merely a product of his own profoundly antisemitic homeland?

The answers to such questions are not simple, but like many conundrums they are best approached from an oblique angle—in this case, Harriet. Harriet controlled virtually every other aspect of Fritz's life, so it is easy, and easily justifiable, to assume that she also controlled, or at least affected, his attitude toward his own ethnicity. A famous and possibly apocryphal story that circulated for years throughout the musical community told of the great wit and pianist Leopold Godowsky, seated near Kreisler at a social gathering of some significance, leaning across a table and wryly goading him to confess his Jewish roots. When Kreisler's wife snapped, "Fritz hasn't a drop of Jewish blood in his veins!" Godowsky retorted: "He must be very anemic." (In Franz Rupp's version of the tale, recounted in Dennis Rooney's interview with him in *The Strad* in 1987, the conversation took place during the 1930s, at the Kreislers' home outside Berlin.)

Unless Harriet was genuinely ignorant of her husband's background—a far-fetched notion, given her intelligence, her highly suspicious nature, and her ferocious spousal devotion—the only logical conclusion is that Mrs. Kreisler did not want to be married to a Jew. Furthermore, despite the couple's lifelong philanthropy and decency toward the less fortunate, it is doubtful that Harriet championed a liberal attitude toward mixed unions. Harriet championed Fritz—and if championing Fritz meant denying his Jewish heritage, so be it.

What drove her beyond that is open to debate, but according to Franz Rupp and others, it was plain-faced antisemitism. Rupp recalled a visit to the Kreislers' manse in Germany in the decade before World War II, after Hitler had come to power but before German international aggression had begun in full force. There he saw, prominently displayed, a Nazi flag.[3] Rupp attributed its presence in the Kreisler home to Harriet's political inclinations rather than to Fritz's, and he had reason to; Rupp himself had married a Jew, a fact that did not escape Mrs. Kreisler and did not put him in her best graces. "Harriet once said to me, 'I can't understand how you could marry a Jew,'" he recalled to Dennis Rooney. Rupp's rejoinder to Harriet was, simply, "What did you marry?"[4]

That Kreisler tolerated Harriet in this regard is disappointing but not surprising. As we have seen, he spent most of his life and career following Harriet, obeying her rules and putting up with her temper, and throughout their many years together he distinguished himself by his embarrassing and sometimes tragic willingness to submit to her wishes. He did not like conflict, and as a result he submitted even to many of her most outrageous demands. When the two were together, and particularly when they were in public, Harriet was in control; such was the nature of their marriage that, no matter how objectionable her actions or remarks, Fritz rarely openly challenged her. As a result, Kreisler chose to deny his own heritage—indeed, his own family—rather than contradict his wife when she told the world at large that she had married a man with no Jewish blood.

Harriet's power over her husband was undeniably great, yet her influence in no way lessens Kreisler's responsibility in the matter, nor does it fully explain his lifelong submission to such an apparently self-hating lie. For a more illuminating explanation one must return, once again, to Kreisler's origins, the graceful aesthetics and decadent social forces that marked *fin-de-siècle* Vienna.

In the time of Kreisler's birth and childhood, Vienna boasted a large and quite prosperous Jewish population, a highly educated bourgeois presence that benefited from and contributed to the city's rich cultural life. It also had a deeply ingrained fear of its own Jews. As George E. Berkeley describes in his fascinating and disturbing book, *Vienna and Its Jews: The Tragedy of Success*, antisemitism in the city was complex, pervasive, and at odds with its paradoxical admiration for Jewish artists and musicians. Since 1421, when Vienna sanctioned a city-wide extermination campaign that required Jews to convert to Christianity under threat of death or expulsion, Vienna has simultaneously welcomed and reviled the Jewish people. Over the centuries there developed between Jews and the gentiles who controlled the city a fidgety compromise, an understanding that Jewish people who remained in Vienna (and aspired to succeed there) would do so as unobtrusively as possible. In 1670 the Jews were again expelled. Only decades later, more than two hundred years before the rise of Nazism, Vienna forced its Jewish citizens to wear a Star of David.[5]

In the late eighteenth century, Emperor Joseph II ascended to the throne, and in 1781 he issued a Tolerance Ordinance that permitted Jews to work in a variety of trades, venture into public before noon on Sunday, send their children to Christian schools, and, generally, contribute to the working and cultural life of the city. In other words, he encouraged them to assimilate. This they did, and they flourished—causing yet another influx of Jewish immigrants that spurred yet another wave of antisemitic sentiment. So turned the wheel that is the history of Jews in Vienna, a brutally deliberate cycle of acceptance and scorn: hatred led to tolerance, tolerance led to success, and success led, tragically and inevitably, back to hatred.

By the last decades of the nineteenth century the cycle was once again turned against the Jews. For years Jews had been associated with the Liberal movement, itself associated with the cultural and intellectual elite of Vienna's middle class. Liberals promoted economic equity and several significant social and educational reforms, including efforts to wrest education from the control of the Catholic Church. The movement had prospered for so long, and so optimistic were Jewish supporters about its ability to provide them with social and economic equality, that when it finally failed—ousted from government by the anti-Jewish Christian Socials—the city's Jews found themselves without a life-raft in a sea of antisemitism. Many who had been able to prosper for years in business and the arts, frequently overcoming legal and social restrictions designed to hold them back, discovered in the waning years of the century that being Jewish had become an insurmountable hurdle between them and success. Even conversion to Catholicism, long a popular method of assimilation, was no longer a clear path toward acceptance. "By the early 1880s," Steven Beller wrote in his work, *Vienna and the Jews, 1867–1938: A Cultural History*, "Jew-hatred had resurfaced in the modern form of antisemitism; it was no longer a petty bureaucratic annoyance or an endemic but harmless instinct, but something which was to destroy the whole fabric of assimilation."

Intensifying animosity against Jews at the time was their booming numbers. Helped by comparatively low infant-mortality rates and a seemingly unending influx of immigrants from Hungary, Bohemia, Moravia, and Galicia, Vienna's Jewish population grew from roughly 6,000 in 1860 to 147,000 forty years later—making it the largest Jewish community in any Western European city.

So virulent was antisemitism in turn-of-the-century Vienna that it inspired the formation of the Pan-German Party, a political movement led by racial purist and German nationalist Georg von Schönerer, which influenced more moderate politicians for years to come and, just as significantly, drew praise from Adolf Hitler in the pages of *Mein Kampf*. (Hitler used the same work to criticize Vienna's Christian Social mayor, Karl Lueger, as being falsely antisemitic. Lueger himself once sidestepped the issue by declaring, "Who is a Jew is something I determine.")[6] Schönerer himself was not successful politically, but his anti-Jewish activism drew a great deal of public attention (he was once arrested after storming the offices of the *Neues Wiener Tageblatt*, destroying equipment and railing madly against the "Jewish pig scribblers"),[7] lending credence and indeed respectability to sentiments held but not always articulated by many Viennese. As a result, Jews were met with increasing opposition, finding themselves blackballed, mocked, beaten, and harassed in every facet of their daily lives. Freud coped with antisemitic critics. Mahler converted to Catholicism in 1895, smoothing the path to his appointment to the Vienna Court Opera in 1897. As a young man, Arthur Schnitzler was once asked to drop to his knees for asking an orchestra leader at the Polyclinic Ball to postpone playing a quadrille and instead repeat a waltz—the music most closely identified with the bourgeoisie and, by extension, the Jews. (Schnitzler refused to obey.) Further, pan-Germans in parliament tried to pass a bill that would have made it difficult for Jewish people to change their names, making survival in the city considerably more difficult. Whereas once they were allowed to succeed as long as all essential Jewishness had been concealed under several layers of pretense, Jews before the turn of the century were no longer permitted even to assimilate. They were simply not welcome. No matter that Vienna was their home, that they had helped build it into the musical and intellectual hub of Europe, that without them the city would lack much of its cultural vigor. From the antisemitic point of view—from the Viennese point of view—the Jews would always be interlopers.

How did they survive? Long before Kreisler, Austrian Jews had mastered the simplest and most reliable strategy against endemic antisemitism: to prosper in spite of it. But to prosper in spite of it they had to ignore it—and to ignore antisemitism in Austrian society, they were forced to deny their own Jewishness. For some this meant changing their names and ridding their lives of everything remotely Jewish. For many it meant conversion. For others still it meant discreet duplicity, a dual existence that allowed Jewish observances and other traditions only within a close—and closed—community of family and friends.

For all, however, their bond to Vienna had always been a love-hate relationship: they loved the city, and the city hated them. The tension in this relationship and the self-abnegation it implied may baffle outsiders, separated by time as well as culture, who ask why so many Jewish people lived so willingly in a municipality that so clearly despised them. The answer is neither easy nor obvious, and it cannot be fully addressed here. But clearly, Jews remained in Vienna because Jews lived and succeeded there: Johann Strauss was a Jew, Schnitzler was a Jew, Freud was a Jew. The Jewish population was educated, relatively well-off, and, to a limited extent, held positions of power and influence. They were an undeniably productive presence in music, journalism, sports, and academia, contributing hugely to the city's international cultural profile. "Rampant Jew-baiting," George Berkeley wrote, "erected no unbreachable barriers to Jewish achievement."

The Jewish people felt at home in Vienna—that is why they succeeded, and that is why they stayed. Vienna and its Jewish residents shared the same priorities, the same gifts, the same passions for art and erudition; had Vienna been a mansion, old and grand and filled with crystal, the Jews who lived there were its most admiring and liveliest residents. The rest of the household enjoyed their contributions, but wished fervently, loudly, to themselves, to each other, often to the Jews, that the whole accomplished lot of them would leave.

They did not. They liked that fine old house and they stayed there, making music, making news, making lives for themselves, until the specter of Nazism threatened to drive them out forever.

Into this city of beauty and hate was born Fritz Kreisler, the perfect symbol of Viennese grace and the perfect example of the drive to assimilate. Like so many Viennese with Jewish heritage, he was in love with the city, even when it failed to love him back. This unrequited passion informed his playing and dictated many of his decisions, driving him to fight—and potentially die—for an emperor whose mild attitude toward the Jews made him a popular figure among the Viennese Jewish population and inspired many to remain faithful to a country that was in other ways unwelcoming. In none of Kreisler's remarks about Vienna, or indeed about anything associated with his homeland, is there any whispered indication of bitterness or ethnic tension; at no time did he express resentment over his childhood or his family's status; never, in fact, did he speak with anything but the wistfulness of a young man looking back on his first, lost sweetheart. Where Vienna was concerned, Kreisler was a blindly attentive swain.

Perhaps Kreisler's denial—of the antisemitism in Vienna, of the fact of his own (at least partial) Jewishness—was an understandable, maybe even inevitable, reaction to the circumstances of his childhood and youth. There is no evidence that Kreisler's parents schooled their son in Jewish history and practices; to the contrary, there is evidence that the Kreislers made some effort to appear Catholic. It may even be that they were among the nine thousand who actually converted between 1863 and 1903. According to unpublished portions of Louis Lochner's manuscript and notes for *Fritz Kreisler* (held in the Fritz Kreisler Collection of the Library of Congress), Fritz was baptized into the Catholic Church at the age of twelve. To what other lengths the Kreislers went is not known, but, according to Joseph Fuchs, Massart once referred in conversation to "that young man—what is his name?—It was a Jewish name, but he changed it to Kreisler."[8] Kreisler himself recalled attending a Jesuit school in Paris as a teenager, shortly after returning from his first American tour. (In William Stidger's *The Human Side of Greatness*, Kreisler spoke fondly of his experiences at the Jesuit school. He credited the priests there with instilling in him his love of books and of the old masters in art and for "giving me a wider scope of life than music had given me up to that time.")[9]

Fritz Kreisler was reared in a city where Jews were scorned and where discreet assimilation was in some cases the only practical alternative. Many Jewish residents fled or died rather than deny their heritage; many others converted or pretended to be Catholic. Like many who are born under a cloud of prejudice but in otherwise privileged circumstances, Kreisler chose neither to see the prejudice around him nor to see himself as one who was oppressed. Instead, he maintained a carefully constructed portrait of his own background, a portrait as reliant on artifice as the most elaborately staged operetta.

Nothing shook Kreisler's peace of mind and sense of identity so profoundly as the years leading up to World War II—a period when the violinist was living in Germany.

From 1924 to 1939, Fritz and Harriet maintained a home in Grunewald, a wooded residential section of Berlin. Their home, which they had built on property that covered several lush acres, was a considerable luxury for a couple whose tastes had always been avowedly simple: besides their mansion, the estate included a hothouse, an Italian rose garden, a caretaker's house, a graceful lawn, and a grotto complete with white marble seats and bench. Idyllic and secluded, it gave the Kreislers their first truly permanent home base, a place to entertain guests, to relax after concert tours, and to store and admire Kreisler's collection of antique books and objets d'art. The books were Kreisler's pride, gathered over the years (and often against Harriet's wishes) from book and antique shops around the world. At Grunewald they were kept partly in the mansion's parlor-cum-music room—which Lochner, a frequent visitor, called a "veritable museum" of Kreisler paraphernalia—and partly on the floor above. The estate was a space where Kreisler allowed himself, finally, to feel rooted—with his wife, his servants, his two dogs, and whatever occasional guests were invited to lunch. By all appearances, it was a haven of peace amid the tumult of his professional life.[10]

Kreisler's career was not the only source of anxiety. Roughly a year before the Kreislers settled in at Grunewald, Adolf Hitler attempted his first putsch against the Weimar government, preaching racial intolerance. Over the next several years—while Fritz and Harriet were happily ensconced in their mansion home—Hitler focused his hatred on Jews and Communists and mounted a sweeping seize of power and public acceptance that led to his appointment as chancellor in January of 1933. From there he began the steady crescendo that would lead to World War II and the Holocaust: the prohibition of all political parties, other than the Nazi party; the persecution of dissidents and the establishment of concentration camps to that end; the rearmament of Germany in 1935, defying the Treaty of Versailles that ended World War I; the horrors of Kristallnacht; and the annexation of Austria and Sudetenland in 1938. The reach for world domination that ensued was the realization of a decade-long campaign for national glory, a campaign that would have been difficult for anyone living in Germany at the time to misconstrue.

One must assume that Fritz and Harriet Kreisler, well-connected and cosmopolitan, were aware of Hitler's rise to power and the doom it portended for personal and artistic freedom. They were also well aware of the Third Reich's gospel of racial purity and the consequences it implied for Germany's substantial Jewish population. For Fritz especially the 1930s must have been a difficult period, emphasizing ethnicity in a manner that could easily have aroused suspicion in his own background, and requiring him to confront his Jewish heritage as he never had before. He could reveal it and flee or bury it and stay—but no matter how deep he buried his identity, in the end the only option was to abandon Germany in the face of the rising atmosphere of hatred and violence. The events of the late 1930s, and the emotional conflict that resulted, precipitated one of the most anguished states of mind that Kreisler ever experienced, before or after.

In the long months preceding the decision to leave Germany, Fritz's mood had been growing steadily darker; according to Rupp, by as early as 1936 Kreisler had become extremely depressed about the conditions in Germany, so depressed that he was unable to complete his recordings of the Brahms sonatas. Nothing he recorded pleased him.[11] For a devout believer in the human spirit and in the power of art to heal political rifts, the late 1930s must have been a deeply unsettling time. That Kreisler was partly Jewish and was apparently under pressure from his own wife to assimilate could only have worsened his melancholy.

In deference to Harriet Kreisler's demands, Louis Lochner's examination of Kreisler's life in Germany in the 1930s avoided any mention of the violinist's personal travails during this turbulent period. In a letter dated 2 November 1949, Louis Lochner complained to Harold Holt, Kreisler's London manager, that "the unpredictable Harriet today tried to say that I must simply treat as non-existent the period of Hitler's accession to power and the consequences thereof for Fritz."[12] The published manuscript instead focused on Kreisler's public disagreements with the Nazi government's ban on Jewish composers and musicians.

These public disagreements were, at times, surprisingly impassioned. By 1933 Kreisler had become ever more vocal on the subject, objecting to the Reich's racial prohibitions and boycotting performances there in sympathetic protest. In such printed accounts of his protests, there were no explicit or implicit references to what now seems an obvious irony—that of Kreisler, his own semitic roots neatly disguised, voluntarily removing himself from venues closed to Jewish musicians—but his complaints were notwithstanding impressive for their fearlessness and economy of expression. Even when, in late July 1933, the Prussian commissioner for culture lifted the ban against "non-Aryans," Kreisler still refused to perform in Germany, explaining that he "must see it established beyond peradventure of doubt that all of my colleagues in the musical world, irrespective of nationality, race or creed, are not only tolerated but actually welcomed." He would not perform, even at the invitation of Wilhelm Furtwängler, until deed followed declaration and Jewish performers had indeed appeared on German stages. "Art is international," he said in response to the commissioner's move, "and I oppose chauvinism in art wherever I encounter it."[13]

Although Kreisler's belief in the universal and supra-political nature of art was most clearly expressed during the two World Wars, it emerged as a consistent theme throughout the violinist's life. In the period between the wars, as Kreisler was attempting to reestablish his career after the turmoil of World War I but before the rise of fascism, he wrote a treatise for the journal *The Mentor* that examined the role of music in the human experience. The piece, titled "Music and Life" and published in December 1921, is a fascinating and in some ways prescient exploration of the innate and culturally imposed meanings of musical forms. Particularly prophetic are passages in the article that celebrate the diversity and commonality of alien musical forms and predict, decades before the popular acceptance of "world music," the field of ethnomusicology. Kreisler believed fervidly in the global nature of art. "It is passing strange that some would like to nationalize music," he wrote. "Music belongs to no nation. . . . Music, like art and literature, is universal; it transcends all national boundaries."

Kreisler assigns to music both an absolute value and a relative, or contextual, value. Aided by the appropriate music, a person in love feels more romantic; a person "suffering from melancholia" feels more depressed. Amazingly, Kreisler compares music to "hasheesh," seeing parallels between music's mood-enhancing properties and "that powerful drug [which] produces good or bad dreams in keeping with the mental condition and environment of the drug taker." He dismisses the notion of "absolute religious or sacred music" and foretells, with remarkable insight, the development of music therapy.

> A beneficial act, like healing, is quite often accomplished by the art of music. The world is destined to hear more and more of this practical side of music. I shall not be surprised if a book on musical therapeutics, written by a scientist, shall have, before long, a place on the shelves of medical libraries of the world.[14]

His prediction is based on his belief that music, unlike poetry and the fine arts, has no tangible form and is, as a result, "all feeling. For that reason it is the more dynamic, and produces a deeper emotional effect."

"There is only one kind of music, and that is *good* music," he claimed. "When music can be called bad, it ceases to be music. It simply becomes rhythmic noise." Expanding on the relationship between "true" music and one's ability to fully appreciate it, he wrote:

> It is cultural background, intellectual training, specialization, and execution that make the difference in the appreciation of music. If badly played, even Beethoven's symphonies would be a deadly drag. From my earliest days I have been interested in music, and music is my life; and yet, if I do not like the music of a negro in Darkest Africa, that does not make that music less vital, less real to the African. It is my own fault that I do not appreciate such music. The first time I heard Chinese music I did not like it at all. But later on, when I heard a Chinese scholar sing, the deeper and inner message of Chinese music was revealed to me. To understand music of this sort we must study national background and tradition.[15]

Notwithstanding the dated (and offensive) reference to "Darkest Africa," Kreisler's comments were, and are, remarkably universal for an artist schooled in the rigid Western tradition. They also prefigure his 1923 tour of Asia, a trip that more thoroughly familiarized him with the art of the East.

Kreisler wrote of his Asian travels for the *Berliner Tageblatt*, an account that was later reprinted in the 1 March 1924 issue of the journal *The Living Age*. The piece emphasized his admiration for traditions of the Far East, where "art, the artist, and above all the intellectual life are valued far more highly than in Europe." Kreisler was stunned by his reception in Kyoto, where the dignitary Count Otani presented Kreisler with vases containing Otani's own poems (a great honor) and escorted him through a temple arch that had previously been used for the visit of the Prince of Wales. As Otani said goodbye to Kreisler, he murmured: "We wished to do honor to an artist." The violinist was also impressed with the success of German music in China and Japan, and observed:

> For several years both nations have been devoting themselves with especial enthusiasm to the comprehension of German music, and I may add that a field of action lies open to German art and German artists in the Far East which will in the future bear rich fruit. . . . The Japanese people seek to make Western music their own and have sought to emulate its achievements at a distance.[16]

So, to this man—to this musician who held such strong beliefs about the common experience of music, its intrinsically universal quality and its ability to transcend national boundaries—the notion that music should be banned by virtue of the citizenship, race, or creed of its creator was utterly unthinkable. Be it the music of an Austrian in America or of a Jew in Germany, Kreisler believed devoutly in the apolitical pluralism of art.

From such comments made throughout his life, and especially the strong remarks in July 1933 during the early period of Nazi ascendancy in Germany, one might assume that Kreisler was a consistently outspoken opponent of the regime, that his residency in Nazi Germany continued despite frequent and forthright opposition to abuses. In fact, his relationship with the Nazi government throughout his residency in Grunewald was complex and not always combative. Because Kreisler opposed no ideology per se but opposed instead the interference of ideology, or ideological governments, in the business of art and life, his public statements concerning the Reich confounded some observers for their apparent inconsistency. In one remark he excoriated the regime; in another, promoting the notion of art and artists as beyond the political, he seemed to brush aside the extent of Nazi power and the enormity of its deeds.

Consider, for instance, Kreisler's eloquent defense of Arturo Toscanini. In early 1933, the maestro, then based in New York, was invited to conduct at the Bayreuth Festival—the annual celebration of Richard Wagner's music—later that year. He at first agreed to conduct and was assured by Winifred Wagner, the composer's daughter-in-law, that there would be no interference from the Nazi regime. He was nevertheless under extreme pressure from friends and colleagues not to comply. One of the few who supported Toscanini in his desire to conduct at Bayreuth was Fritz Kreisler.

Responding to Toscanini's dilemma, Kreisler released a signed statement to the press. It read:

> I believe that the artists who are responsible for the moral pressure put on Maestro Toscanini are acting in defiance of the very principle which they purpose to defend. Namely: inviolability of artistic utterance under all circumstances and its removal above the sphere of political and racial strife. Moreover, they are performing a poor service to their colleagues.
>
> Bayreuth is an institution cherished in Germany and admired all over the world. Maestro Toscanini's coming there is eagerly anticipated and his gratitude of the many who will be privileged to hear Maestro Toscanini's recreation of the German master's works will constitute a more favorable atmosphere for intercession on behalf of his colleagues than a formal protest or a willful absentation.
>
> I believe that no other interpretation would be put on the maestro's decision to go to Bayreuth than that of his manly and courageous determination to carry out his artistic

> obligation under all circumstances and his desire to uphold the artist's most glorious prerogative of being a herald of love and a messenger of good will from men to men and nation to nation. I solemnly urge Maestro Toscanini to go to Bayreuth. We cannot dispense with such a powerful ambassador of peace and harbinger of good will when the nerves of all nations are on edge and sinister grumblings of war are heard again. Let these harbingers of good will increase and there may be less need for protests.[17]

Kreisler's statement was meant to be published simultaneously with one from Toscanini announcing his decision to honor his Bayreuth contract. Toscanini instead announced that he had decided to decline. The Kreisler statement was released before the violinist was told of Toscanini's decision.[18]

Kreisler was personally and keenly repelled by the events leading to Hitler's takeover and by the subsequent suppression of personal and artistic autonomy. Nevertheless, the combined forces of the "unpredictable" Harriet and the day-to-day reality of living under fascist rule—and Kreisler's own Pollyanna impulse to see in others only the best and noblest motives—meant that he was not always as outspoken and unambiguous in his opposition to the Third Reich as those in the United States might have liked. Occasionally, remarks he uttered against Nazism were parried by startling apologias.

It must be stressed, at this point, that Kreisler rarely voiced his political beliefs. Many decades after this period in the violinist's life, Frederic Kreisler remembered his great-uncle's steadfastly apolitical nature, which he maintained despite—or perhaps because of—Harriet's fiercely articulated opinions. As Frederic described in a letter recalling Fritz and Harriet's relationship in the early 1950s:

> Harriet was a "superpatriot" and a loud supporter of right-wing causes (e.g. Senator Joseph McCarthy). She detested F.D.R. and despised President Eisenhower. She was intolerant and her choice of words reflected that intolerance. My father disagreed with her views and sometimes, unable to contain his anger, challenged her. The result, all too often, was a heated screaming match at the dinner table. Throughout,

> Uncle Fritz never uttered a syllable. My father, who made it his business to find opportunities to talk to Uncle Fritz privately and knew better than anybody what he thought, explained to me after one of these painful scenes that Fritz's silence was his way of avoiding a disagreement that might prompt retribution in the form of a Harriet temper tantrum, or worse.[19]

If the Kreislers' relationship later in life was any indication, Fritz's apparent silence at the dawn of Nazi rule may have been due to Harriet's steamrollering influence. She may simply have overwhelmed and out-muscled his will to argue.

Also significant in this regard is Kreisler's inbred guilelessness: he seemed to regard much of politics and many politicians with bewildering naiveté. For Kreisler, the Emperor Franz Josef was a kind and avuncular presence; the evils of Nazism could be ignored or even nullified through the ideals of art and music; and, equally telling, a leader as openly fascist as Benito Mussolini could be admired and indeed befriended as a charming amateur fiddler with hickeys on his neck from long hours of playing. Kreisler's relationship with Mussolini is illustrated in a February 1930 interview with *America Magazine*, in which he describes evenings spent in Mussolini's villa—and Il Duce's disarming protestations when forced to confess his dalliances with the violin. The telltale marks on his neck, he told the Kreislers, were "from my playing with, not as an artist upon, the violin." As Kreisler remarked to Beverly Smith, his interviewer from *America Magazine*:

> In this Il Duce showed himself, contrary to public opinion of the man, too modest. He plays the violin competently and well. Mussolini, in truth, when you see him at home, with the mask of authority removed from his face, seems a different man. His smile is one of the gentlest I have ever seen.[20]

So apolitical was Kreisler in his devotion to music, and so sure was he in his belief that politics need not enter the realm of art, that he sometimes appeared either unprincipled or aggravatingly unaware in his personal associations and remarks. His deep faith in humanity and deeper faith in the power of music made him, on a few remarkable occasions, look less like a realist than a gull.

In at least one circumstance Kreisler's willingness to equivocate was downright appalling. Franz Rupp once told of a February 1935 visit to Amsterdam, when Kreisler, at Harriet's prompting, firmly established his credentials with the Nazi government. The incident stemmed from an act of real courage: it was during his Amsterdam trip that Kreisler spoke out strongly, publicly, and apparently for the first time against Adolf Hitler. His comments appeared in the Dutch press. The following day, however, Harriet insisted that Fritz make a public statement praising conditions in Germany—which he did, immediately. Upon returning to Berlin, Kreisler learned the effect of his amended public remarks: the Nazis were fully satisfied with his declaration.[21]

So was Harriet. As Rupp told Dennis Rooney, Mrs. Kreisler "kept hoping that the Nazis, whom she supported enthusiastically at first, would agree to make her husband an 'honorary Aryan.' "[22]

They did not. As the years progressed, Kreisler's position in Nazi Germany became more and more tenuous.

Franz Rupp's recollection of the Nazi flag hanging in the Kreislers' home has already been mentioned. What has not yet been addressed—what has never, in fact, been addressed in print, thanks in no small part to Harriet's determination that the real motives never come to light—is the reason behind the Kreislers' eventual flight from Germany. Common sense attributes their exodus to the rise of Nazism, but speculation might lay the blame on almost any aspect of the regime or its ramifications for artists: Kreisler's desire to maintain a global career, fear that the German government might discover his Jewish roots, philosophical and moral differences (on Fritz's part, if not Harriet's) with the Reich. In all likelihood the Kreislers' flight was driven by not one but several impulses.

A letter from Fritz Kreisler to Charles Foley points to one highly compelling reason: he had been drafted by the German army—probably as a result of the Anschluss, which turned all Austrians into German subjects. Dated 28 September 1938 and mailed from London, the letter describes Kreisler's ultimately successful efforts to secure for his nephew Kurt and Kurt's family passage to the United

States aboard the *Empress of Britain*. It was no simple task: his relatives' permit to enter the country ended 14 October, and all ships had been sold out for weeks ahead. Finally, with the help of Harold Holt, Kreisler succeeded in securing passage "through bribe and frantic labour."

The letter continues:

> Altogether the last few days were a nightmare. Aside from the political chaos there were disastrous developments for me here, which are not hard to guess. Raymond exhausted me with conferences, which lead nowhere, and [financial liaison Laurence] Mackie began to get tired of it all. You must realize, that the greatest crisis in the memory of mankind was on hand. The banks feared that the fantastic withdrawals of funds and the transfers to New York could not be endured much longer. Yesterday, when it seemed that war was unavoidable I actually welcomed the solution.
>
> At least one's fate was decided and with the loss of every vestige of hope there ceased the necessity to plan and to struggle. In the coming catastrophe for mankind one's own personal torment seemed puny and ridiculous. Today peace seems almost assured and the personal agony gets the upper hand again. . . .
>
> We both can take counsel after my arrival. I am getting so tired of it all!
>
> I have been drafted as an officer into the German army and in case of war must return immediately. Today that contingency, which yesterday seemed a certainty, is rather remote. There is every hope that I will sail as arranged on the *Queen Mary* Oct. 13.[23]

This horrific turn of events can be viewed through two possible lenses. Through the first, Kreisler appears as a long-time German resident who, prodded by a sympathetic Aryan wife, made occasional positive remarks about the regime despite his own abhorrence. In other words, the Nazis drafted Kreisler because they regarded him as an ally. Through the other lens, a different perspective comes into view, that of a fervid but frustrated dissident whose criticism was tempered by the harsh reality of living under a fascist regime. In that view, the Nazis drafted Kreisler because they wanted to control him. It was a way to force his allegiance.

How the Third Reich actually regarded Kreisler is not known. It may be that the Nazis knew of Kreisler's Jewish background and chose to overlook it for their own purposes; it may also be that they knew nothing, that his lifelong efforts at concealment had, in fact, survived oppression's most vigorous test. If so, his escape from the grip of Hitler's rule was grim cause for celebration.

As it turned out, the circumstances that caused Kreisler's family to flee to the United States in October of 1938 drove the violinist to renounce his own Austrian citizenship only months later. Not long after learning that he had been drafted, Kreisler accepted a long-standing offer from the government of France to become a French citizen. It was not easy for him; he had always been fiercely proud of his Austrian citizenship and did not blithely renounce it. But faced with an unthinkable alternative, Kreisler agreed to the change and, on 13 May 1939, participated in a small but sober ceremony attended by the French minister of fine arts and several members of parliament.[24] (Some confusion surrounds the actual date of his naturalization; *The New York Times* quoted "word from Paris" in reporting his new nationality on 2 May 1939.)

Nine days later Kreisler received his first French passport, which listed his profession as "Professeur de Musique, Violoniste" and his residence as "8, rue de Montpensier, Paris." Stamps on the inside pages indicate that no sooner was Kreisler naturalized in France than he embarked on two trips to Germany—on 27 May and 31 July[25]—for no immediately discernible reason, although it is possible that he made the trips to confirm his French citizenship with German authorities. According to Lochner, the Nazi government at first refused to recognize Kreisler's naturalization, relenting only upon discovery of an obscure law (dating from Napoleon) that allowed Viennese residents to become French citizens.[26] (Lochner's preliminary notes for his book indicate that Harriet had also considered becoming a French citizen, but she abandoned the idea, opting to remain an American.)

The New York Times praised Kreisler's decision to become a French citizen in an editorial that recalled the violinist's ostracism from the American stage following his World War I service in the Austrian army.

> It was hard for any one to think of being at war with Fritz Kreisler, but for a time he played for us no more.
>
> It would have been pleasant if our "war" with Mr. Kreisler could have been ended by his becoming an American citizen. He has done the next best thing by taking out naturalization papers in another country which he happily praises as "a stronghold in which are intact all ideas which make up human dignity: honor, liberty and love of art." His American public will want him to know that such ideas will never be alien here, either, and that we shall not entirely surrender him to France. In a sense his homeland is what it always was, for, whenever and wherever he plays, there is the Vienna of his youth, unconquered and immortal.[27]

He would not remain a French citizen for long. In the fall of 1939 Kreisler sailed to the United States, and there he remained until the end of his life. The impetus to switch citizenship came after France fell to Germany in 1940, and Kreisler was pressed to recognize the collaborationist Vichy government.[28] So, on 8 May 1943, he received his final American citizenship papers at the United States District Court Naturalization Division on the corner of Washington and Christopher streets in lower Manhattan.[29] The documentation was the formal confirmation of what had been, for Kreisler, an informal but deeply felt connection with the country's government and people; even during World War I, when Americans banned him from the stage, he neither severed his ties with the United States nor appeared particularly bitter about his dismal treatment. As he later told Beverly Smith: "It is natural. Patriotism is human and goes deep, in every country. . . . I have only gratitude for all that America has done for me."[30]

Once settled in the United States, Fritz and Harriet occupied themselves with a variety of tasks that included attempts to rescue their two dogs, Airedale Jerry and fox terrier Rexie, who had been left behind in Berlin.

The dogs survived, thanks to efforts made by Louis Lochner to ship the pair of them to Amsterdam and on to America.[31] "Poor Fritz was in great anxiety about them. We had visions of their being ultimately sausage meat," wrote Harriet in a note dated 5 November 1939. "As in England the dogs for various reasons have had to be disposed of by the thousands. They arrived on the *Statendam* early in the morning, but Fritz was there to meet them." She added: "There is little else I can say, except Fritz is playing marvelously and that keeps him happy."[32]

The house in Grunewald did not fare as well. On 7 July 1945, during one of the Kreislers' periodic visits to Saratoga Springs, New York, they picked up a copy of the Albany *Times Union* to discover the following front-page article:

> KREISLER'S BERLIN HOME DESTROYED
>
> Berlin, July 6 (AP)–Violinist Fritz Kreisler's Berlin residence, one of the city's finest, was destroyed December 16, 1942, by five incendiary bombs during an Allied raid, the caretaker disclosed today.

That concise little article was the first the couple had heard of the bombing, the first indication that their grand and gracious home had been reduced to so much debris. Concerned for the well-being of their servants, they sent an immediate and anxious letter to Lochner and his wife, asking them to secure whatever information they could. The Kreislers were thus relieved to learn that the former employees of Bismarck-Allee 30 (including their maid, Manswell Magadalen Hammer, and their chauffeur, Sonntag) had survived the bombing and were, in fact, "fairly well off."[33]

As for the house, it was rubble. Kreisler's beloved book collection had been shipped to England before the war broke out (its owner would not see the collection again until several years later, when all 174 items were sold in a 1949 auction for charity),[34] but the mansion itself, its art objects, Italian rose garden, and white marble grotto, had been obliterated. It was a heartbreakingly definitive symbol of Kreisler's flight from Germany.

Fittingly, he never returned. Even a conciliatory and impassioned plea from the mayor of greater Berlin, written five years after the end of World War II, was not enough to bring the violinist back to his erstwhile home.

Dated 4 February 1950, written in florid German and signed by Dr. Ferdinand Friedensburg, Der Oberbuergermeister von Gross-Berlin, the letter congratulates Kreisler on his seventy-fifth birthday and conveys the Berliners' continuing regard for "your art and your humanity."

> We know the value of what you brought to Berlin as its citizen. We miss you terribly, and it would be a day of great celebration for us if you would return to visit the place of your dramatic triumphs and quiet, gratifying successes. . . . In spirit, I urgently reach out across the long, bitterly evil and bitterly sad times, and across the great sea, to shake your hand.[35]

There is no record of Kreisler's reply to this letter, so there is no way of knowing whether the rift between him and Germany ever fully healed. Even if it had, even if Kreisler was tempted to return to the country that had caused him such anguish, his weakened condition in the 1950s would have made an extended trip impractical and unwise. Whatever peace he made with the city of Berlin was made in silence and across a yawning gap.

Fritz Kreisler never publicly revealed his Jewishness. Nor did he ever formally renounce it. His denials were passive rather than active, allowing Harriet to take a firm stand on the subject while he stood quiet or uttered noncommittal (and, more to the point, nonsectarian) generalities about God and the nature of humanity. Throughout most of his life and career he was given repeated opportunities to sidestep questions about his heritage and simultaneously establish his reputation as a generically spiritual, peripherally Judeo-Christian do-gooder who appeared to have no clear ties to any religious group other than the one Mrs. Kreisler so vigorously denied. He was secular but saintly, a known philanthropist whose deep but vague monotheism effectively camouflaged the complex religious and ethnic identity at his core. Only during his much-publicized conversion to (or reconciliation with) Catholicism in 1947 did the question of their religious backgrounds come once again to the fore.

The story of the Kreislers' conversion is recounted charmingly, albeit sketchily, in Bishop Fulton J. Sheen's memoirs, *Treasure in Clay*. According to Sheen, he first met the Kreislers after receiving a letter from a stranger asking him to visit an uncle who had lost his wife to suicide. Sheen went to the man's Manhattan apartment building along the East River—the River House—but upon arrival learned that he was not home. As the building had only two apartments per floor, Sheen asked the elevator operator whether he knew who occupied the other apartment; Kreisler, he was told. Not one to leave such an opportunity unexplored, the then-Monsignor Sheen rang the Kreislers' doorbell and, "after a short conversation" (one wonders just how short), asked them whether they would like to take instruction in the Catholic Church. They agreed; so began a friendship that would last until Kreisler's death in 1962. Sheen wrote:

> I visited them every week for some years, until the Lord called them from the Church Militant to the Church Triumphant, where I am sure the music of Fritz Kreisler is in the repertoire of Heaven.
>
> Fritz Kreisler was one of the finest and noblest men I ever met in my life. When I would quote a text from the Old Testament, he would read it in Hebrew; when I would quote a text from the New Testament, Fritz would read it in Greek.[36]

Praise for Kreisler's erudition was the only remark Sheen ever made regarding the violinist's entry into Catholicism; nowhere in his memoirs does he discuss Kreisler's religious upbringing, and his account gives no mention of ethnicity. Substantive discussion of his pupils' conversion was clearly out of bounds.

(During Kreisler's funeral Sheen referred to times that he had recited the Lord's Prayer with Kreisler—in Hebrew. That inspired

Mischa Elman to turn to Benno Rabinof and quip, sotto voce, "See? I told you he was Jewish.")[37]

Sheen began instructing the Kreislers in early 1947. Only two months later, on 30 March, Fritz and Harriet received holy communion in the Blessed Sacrament Church in New Rochelle, New York.

Revealingly, the Blessed Sacrament Church has no record of the Kreislers' conversion. Had Kreisler been a lapsed Catholic when he took instruction from Sheen, he would probably have culminated his studies simply by receiving communion at the Easter Vigil Mass; had he been baptized (as an infant or as an older child) and later confirmed, a reintroduction to the Church in his maturity would have involved no sacraments requiring formal paperwork. If, on the other hand, Kreisler had met with Sheen as a Jew who desired to convert, he would have received baptism (usually some weeks before Easter), followed by First Communion and, possibly, confirmation. Assuming Lochner's original notes regarding Kreisler's baptism at the age of twelve are correct, and assuming that the absence of papers at the Church means that no sacraments requiring official documentation actually occurred, the ritual marking his union with the Church would have been nothing more elaborate than communion.

In a letter to *The New York Herald Tribune* dated 5 March 1959 (a carbon of which is held in the Library of Congress), Louis Lochner took pains to correct an article appearing in that day's edition that had referred to the Kreislers' conversion to Catholicism. "Fritz Kreisler was raised a Catholic by his Viennese mother (his father was of a different persuasion)," he wrote. Noting the oft-repeated reason for the couple's lapse from Catholicism (Harriet was a divorcée, and they married outside the Church), Lochner claimed that the Kreislers were not converted by Sheen but "reconverted" by him—and that shortly after this reconversion, in March 1947, he married them again in the Catholic Church.

When news of their conversion—for lack of a better word—was released, *The New York Times* reported dutifully that Harriet's marriage with Fritz was her second, that her first husband was a Protestant, that neither she nor Fritz had attended church for many years. But, Harriet insisted (and the *Times* recounted), "both she and her husband had been born of Catholic parents."[38] (Was she?

Harriet made many public references to a Catholic upbringing, and Lochner believed that she was baptized in infancy.[39] Regardless of which church she was reared in, Frederic Kreisler recalls a woman whose faith, however schooled, seemed superficial.)

What led the Kreislers toward Catholicism? The mystery and grace that define every religious awakening mean that none can ever be understood—not fully—by an outsider. Surely, some moral direction can be discerned from the couple's lifelong philanthropy and commitment to the poor; there is a religious element, too, in many of Kreisler's remarks and writings about music and the role of an artist in society. He was a decent and spiritual man years before he met Fulton J. Sheen and would have remained so had he never formally entered (or re-entered) the Church. Yet Catholicism provided a shape for Kreisler's religious predilections, a framework upon which to hang his deeply held belief in the musical and mystical unseen.

Perhaps, as they had always claimed, the Kreislers were Catholic to begin with. There is every possibility that Fritz Kreisler was indeed born to a Catholic mother—Lochner referred to her as an "Aryan"—and it is indisputable, despite the "different persuasion" of his father, that Fritz had throughout his life never practiced the Jewish faith or appeared to align himself with the Jewish people. Frederic Kreisler, Fritz's great-nephew, has said he was unaware of the Jewish heritage in Kreisler's background or in the family's generally, and that his own family (that is, Kurt's family, Fritz's nephew) was entirely Catholic; he remembers his Uncle Fritz only as a highly devout worshipper who attended Mass faithfully once a week and who regarded his late-life turn toward Catholicism as a re-entry rather than an entry into the Church.[40] Kreisler may have been partly Jewish, but nothing he said, to the press or to his own American relatives, ever acknowledged it.

Why this is so will remain an insoluble puzzle. For all the discussion of Kreisler's upbringing in an antisemitic culture, of his marriage to a woman of dubious or even hostile attitudes toward Jews, and of his own apparent willingness to shirk an ethnic and religious identity acknowledged by his own brother Hugo—for all of that, there is no truer nor more cryptic proof of his denial than the shadow of resignation that darkened his face in the final decades of his life. He had given in: to Harriet, to his own fears, to a story the two had concocted to shield them from potentially dangerous questions. Similarities can be found in the double identities assumed by American communists earlier in this century, or in the so-called "outing" of gays and lesbians who, faced with prejudice in a variety of forms, spend years denying their homosexual identities. In this manner and for even more compelling reasons Kreisler denied his Jewish heritage, choosing to closet himself at a time of murderous racial intolerance. In the end it was his own choice to make, his own selfhood to reveal or disguise.

Ink drawing of young Fritz, around the time he entered the Paris Conservatoire. (Courtesy New York Public Library)

At age 12, having won the Premier Premier Prix at the Paris Conservatoire, with other winners.

The prodigy at age 10, after winning the top award from the Vienna Conservatory.

The beefy young fiddler (second from left) hams it up with friends and fellow members of Vienna's cafe society; the cellist is Arnold Schoenberg.

Kreisler, circa 1910.

Eugène Ysaÿe, the great Belgian violinist whose fame preceded and prefigured Kreisler's.

The seventeen-year-old Jascha Heifetz. (Reprinted from Martens 1919)

Fritz in his army uniform and Harriet in her Red Cross uniform, 1914. (Courtesy New York State Library)

The Kreislers, shortly before Kreisler's arrival at the front during World War I.

Kreisler, gaunt following his service in World War I, making music with Ernest Schelling. (Courtesy New York Philharmonic Archives)

Demonstrating a "walking-stick fiddle," around 1920.
(Courtesy New York Philharmonic Archives)

Photographed at one of his favorite pastimes, reading the newspaper, 1928. (Courtesy New York State Library)

Kreisler at Ernest Schelling's home near Geneva, circa 1920s. Ignacy Jan Paderewski is at the piano; standing behind him is Schelling. The four musicians to the right of Kreisler are the Flonzaley Quartet: Alfred Pochon, Adolfo Betti, Nicolas Moldavan, and Iwan d'Archambeau. (Courtesy David Sackson)

THE MENTOR
SCIENCE
MUSIC
ART
HISTORY
December 1921
Fritz Kreisler and Mrs. Kreisler
MUSIC AND LIFE
By Fritz Kreisler
Dolls of All Nations
Famous Love Letters
The Personality of Kreisler
Mother and Child in Art
A Millionaire Playwright
The Greatest Violin Maker
The Greatest Christian Shrine

Fritz and Harriet Kreisler, gracing a magazine cover at the start of the roaring twenties. (New York State Library)

Fritzi and Harriet, circa 1930. (Courtesy Carnegie Hall Archives)

With Franz Rupp, mid-1930s. (Courtesy Sylvia Rupp)

BELOVED FRITZ KREISLER

. . . Is Badly Hurt in Traffic Accident

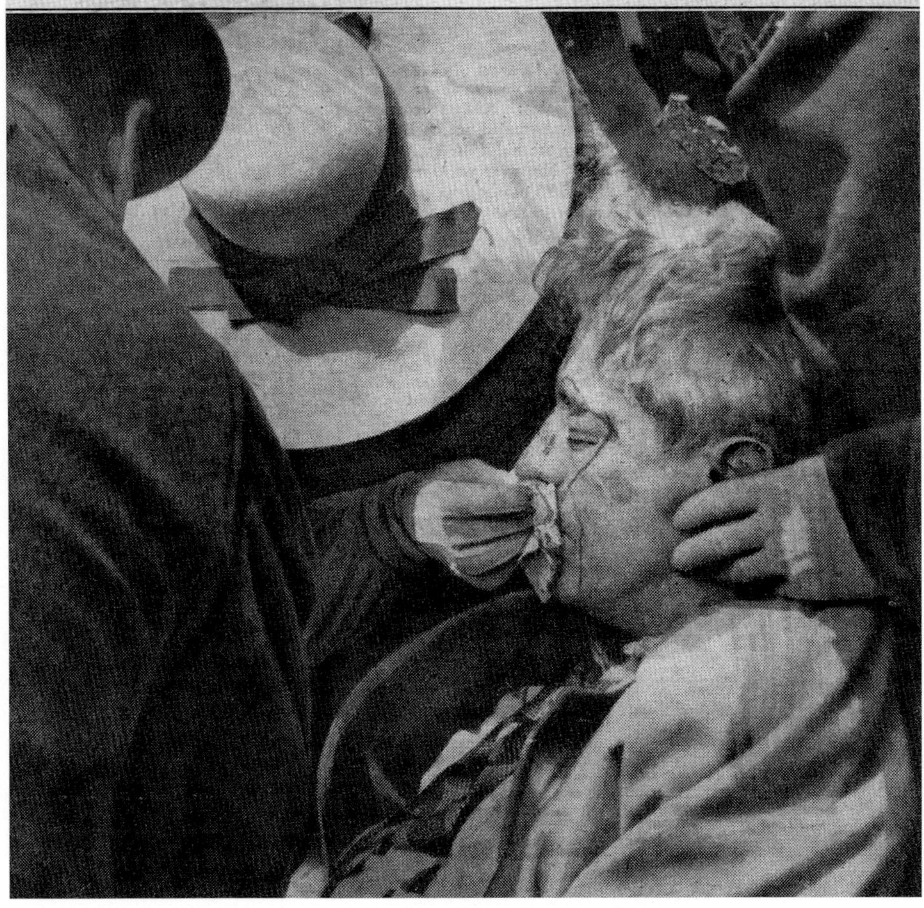

Gory accident-scene photo from the Sunday *Daily News*, 27 April 1941. The caption read: "KINDNESS. A woman spectator wipes face of world-renowned music maker pending arrival of a doctor." (Associated Press/Daily News)

Kreisler performing at Carnegie Hall in the 1940s.
(Courtesy Carnegie Hall Archives)

Kreisler at 85.
(Associated Press)

Nine

The Accident

At fifteen minutes after noon on Saturday, 26 April 1941, Fritz Kreisler was waiting at the intersection of East 57th Street and Madison Avenue in Manhattan, deep in thought. He had just phoned 2 Sutton Place South and left word for Harriet that he would be home for lunch. Then the light changed, and traffic began to move. Kreisler stepped off the curb, onto the street, and into the path of an egg-delivery truck, which slammed into the absent-minded pedestrian and sent him spinning onto the pavement. Bloodied, reeling, and concussed, he was quickly surrounded by passersby who wiped his face and comforted him while waiting for police. They carried him to the lobby of a nearby office building.[1]

At first, no one knew who he was. He was simply a gray-haired man, somewhere in his sixties, distinguished-looking and nattily dressed in a suit and plaid tie. Only when onlookers searched his pockets and discovered letters addressed to him did they realize who had been struck. It was their own beloved Kreisler.

The crowd fell into immediate and genuine mourning. One young man helped prop him against a lamp post; a second soothed him and stroked his neck. A woman gently wiped the blood from his face while another held his head. Even the driver of the truck, a Bronx egg dealer named Patrick Lucadamo, cried when he learned the identity of the victim. "I'll give anything I've got," he said, "to see that this man lives."[2]

So began one of the strangest, and most poignant, periods in Kreisler's life, a time of recuperation and transition that changed him from a performer in his late prime to an adored but aging figure embarked on the last few years of his career. Most, if not all, performers go through such transitions, but few make the change so abruptly. For Kreisler, all it took was a few brief moments in midtown Manhattan.

His injuries were severe. The collision left him unconscious, with internal wounds, a cut on the side of his head, and possible skull fracture—a serious combination of injuries alleviated only by Kreisler's relative good health. After being admitted to Roosevelt Hospital, he was examined by the head surgeon and placed on a seventy-two-hour observation period. What no one realized was just how long the vigil would last.

News of the accident spread quickly, and the city of New York—or much of it, judging from the huge black headlines that dominated the daily newspapers—reacted with anguish and disbelief. "My heart is breaking," moaned Albert Spalding when he tried, unsuccessfully, to visit Kreisler in his room at Roosevelt Hospital. "God forbid that anything should happen. It would be a great loss to the music-loving world."[3] Only hours after the accident, the hospital switchboard was deluged with phone calls inquiring about the violinist's health; the next day, ugly accident-scene photographs of a bleeding, crumpled Kreisler were splashed across the pages of the Sunday *Daily News*, shocking readers with their pathos and gore. More than half a century later, those photos still horrify.

Melvin Spitalnick, at the time an eighteen-year-old messenger boy, spotted the accident scene while riding a Madison Avenue bus. He disembarked to take photos with the Foth-Derby miniature camera that he carried everywhere. When Spitalnick arrived Kreisler was sitting on the sidewalk, surrounded by police, solicitous civilians, and numerous rubbernecking pedestrians. "He was already leaning up against the lamppost when I arrived," Spitalnick said. "It was very distressing. I'd never seen anything like that before. He was coughing up blood."

Unaware, at first, of the victim's identity, Spitalnick snapped a sixteen-photo roll of film in the hopes of selling the images to a wire service. As he worked he heard Kreisler's name bandied about the crowd. After the ambulance arrived and drove the violinist to the hospital, Spitalnick rushed to the Associated Press office at Rockefeller Plaza, where he sold the film. "I've always had mixed emotions about that," he said, "because here was a person I admired, and he was hurt. . . . I had mixed feelings about even getting any publicity for myself."[4]

Anyone in this more cynical age who cannot fathom such public affection for an artist (a violinist, no less) should consider Kreisler's place among performers. Unlike classical musicians today, a soloist of Kreisler's era and stature was as well-known among the working class as he was among the middle and upper classes and literati, and he cut an even more democratic profile among those with access to a Victrola (and, later, a radio). Kreisler was not unique in this regard (witness Enrico Caruso or, among contemporary performers, Luciano Pavarotti), but he was by far the best example, simply because his fame extended beyond mere recognition and became a sort of popular adoration. He was not simply admired; he was cherished. "BELOVED KREISLER," blared the *Daily News* above its spread of gory photographs, and countless others would have chosen that selfsame qualifier.

His friends were on tenterhooks. After the first, most urgent question was answered by physicians—Were his hands injured? (they were not)—music lovers joined Mrs. Kreisler in her watch, combing the newspapers daily for reports of his health.

Harriet took a hospital room next to her husband's and remained at his side constantly. No other visitors were allowed. She tightly controlled all information that was released about the violinist, being careful not to convey in full the seriousness of his injuries.

According to a curious letter, undated but probably written shortly after Kreisler's release from the hospital, the violinist's health was far worse than anyone had realized at the time: his skull had indeed been fractured, and both his hearing and his eyesight were temporarily lost. The letter, addressed to Harold Holt and Laurence

Mackie, is signed in Charles Foley's name, but it was clearly penned by Kreisler himself. It is written in Kreisler's own hand—shaky with infirmity but still identifiable—and with his distinctive use of commas, which are placed unnecessarily after restrictive phrases ("it became known, that . . .") as though he were writing in German rather than English. It is a peculiar letter, a highly detailed summation of his accident and recovery that relates the gravest news with surreal detachment. The tone, style, and word choice are oddly pedestrian—not at all Kreisler's brilliantly purple style—and raise the possibility that he wrote the letter under exact instruction from Harriet.

No matter what its origins, the letter is a remarkable document. In it the author speaks gravely of Kreisler's early chances for survival—more gravely than was ever fully communicated in the newspapers or in later accounts of the accident—and says that no sooner had he been admitted to the hospital than doctors issued a statement "according to which our friend's condition was considered absolutely hopeless and his death believed almost certain within a short time." So severe were Kreisler's injuries that, according to "Foley," church officials "had ordained immediate prayers in all Catholic churches of the United States, begging the Savior to bring about Kreisler's recovery through a miracle." The author of the letter then continues, in a vein that persuades the reader that Harriet must have taken part in composing it:

> The entire Catholic public took care of these prayers. One prayer actually took place through priests and nuns in the hospital where our friend was, and his wife, our friend Harriet, immediately expressed openly her absolute faith in the deliverance of her husband through an immense Catholic miracle. . . . [Her] wonderful behavior has become the topic everywhere here.[5]

(This "miracle" raises yet another question concerning the Kreislers'—at least Harriet's—religious persuasion. Assuming the undated letter was penned in 1941, Harriet's dramatic pronouncement of faith was delivered six years before she and Fritz were "reconverted" by Fulton Sheen. If this is the case, there must have remained within Harriet some vestigial Catholic identity despite having always described herself as a long-lapsed member of the Church. It also indicates that perhaps, despite Frederic Kreisler's recollection to the contrary and in support of Lochner's belief, Harriet was indeed reared as a Roman Catholic.)

Roosevelt Hospital's Chief Surgeon, Dr. James I. Russell, gave periodic bulletins to the press and the public at large, stressing both the seriousness of Kreisler's condition and every incremental change in his health. *The New York Herald Tribune* provided daily reports of his progress: at ten-thirty on the Sunday morning after the accident, it was announced, the violinist had improved but his condition "still remain[ed] serious"; at four in the afternoon he was still improving, but was "not really conscious yet"; by one o'clock in the morning he had improved even further; on Monday night he was still unconscious; on Tuesday night he was still unconscious; on Thursday night, the hospital announced, he had not only failed to regain consciousness but his condition had actually worsened.[6]

This alarming state of affairs dragged on day after day, week after week, as his doctors continued to announce that Kreisler remained in a coma. Finally, on 23 May—almost one month after the accident—the hospital declared him out of danger.[7] When he at last regained consciousness, he did so in a manner strangely well suited for a man of Kreisler's broad erudition: he addressed his listeners not in English, not in French, not even in his native German, but in Latin and ancient Greek. He spoke and understood no other language for several days after he emerged from his coma. (As is the case with such stories, this one might be apocryphal.)

Franz Rupp recalled visiting the hospital some time after Kreisler had awakened—and after his command of modern languages had returned. Rupp later described the scene.

> I went to the hospital, and they announced that Franz Rupp was there. Kreisler said, "I don't know him. I don't know him." So I said to him, "Of course you know me. . . . Do you remember the Copa Cabana? You won a thousand dollars." And he said, "Ahh, Herr Rupp!"—because he won! "Ahh, Herr Rupp"—loud! That brought it back.
>
> Fortunately his wife wasn't there.[8]

Even if Harriet had been there, it is doubtful she would have excoriated her husband with quite the same vigor to which both of them were accustomed. On Harriet's mind throughout this period was not his propensity for gambling or other sundry misdeeds but his health. She also worried about his artistic genius, the likelihood of at least some permanent memory loss and the terrifying possibility that his injuries had severely affected his musical ability. Would he ever again be able to play the violin? And if he could, would he be able to play with the same grace and skill? Driven to find out, Harriet brought Kreisler's Guarnerius into the hospital room one day, kvetching about a concerto passage that, try as she might, she simply could not recall. "It's been bothering me all morning," she complained. "Do you suppose you could play it for me? I mean the motif of the beautiful second movement." Not suspecting her true motives, Fritz lifted the violin to his chin and played the passage perfectly.[9]

"It was a test, but I didn't know it," Kreisler recalled almost three years after the incident.

> I was not aware at that time of the possibility that the part of the brain which controls music—whatever part it is—might be injured. My hands were all right. I could not understand why my wife wanted to hear Mendelssohn, but I wanted to be obliging. I didn't ask myself whether I could play; I took it for granted. After all, I have lived with music all my life. Since I was getting better, music would naturally follow in due course.[10]

So relieved were the press and public when news of this little triumph leaked out that *The New York Times* felt compelled to write an editorial on the subject:

> It must be welcome news to many thousands, even millions, of [Kreisler's] known and unknown friends that the magic which resides in his mind, his fingers and his heart has not been silenced.
>
> A musician who throws a spell over those unlearned in his art, Fritz Kreisler long ago won the critics and the pundits too. The older member of his great audience may

> recall with regret that his Austrian birth shut him out for a time from public performances in this country twenty-four years ago. The younger should know that he refused to serve Nazi Germany, that he gave up his Austrian citizenship after Hitler occupied his beloved Vienna, that he turned over his British royalties to the Red Cross, and that he has consistently stood for the freedom of art, of artists and of human beings.
>
> Yet his playing and his compositions would speak for him if nothing else were known. . . . May his bow and strings soon speak again for more than a hospital audience.[11]

The following day, 30 May 1941, Harriet addressed the masses by way of the *Times*, expressing gratitude for the "many thousands" of well-wishers who had flooded the hospital with letters, flowers, telegrams, and other missives of hope throughout the violinist's ordeal. Roughly one hundred people had offered to donate blood (none was needed); so bountiful were the bouquets crowding the hospital room that Harriet was moved to exclaim, "It's a sin! It's a positive sin!" "I shall never be able to thank the country for its love of him," she said. "It was really this love that pulled him through."

Kreisler was, it seemed, finally out of danger—still on "the slow road" to recovery (and, Harriet added, "going through the headache period"), but clear and free of any threat to his life. Every day he rose from his bed and sat for five minutes in a chair; and, as often as he could, he flicked on the radio and listened to symphonies. "The great thing in his mind, the one thing he keeps harping on, is his love of music," Harriet remarked. "It is the mistress of his entire life. It is the only thing that means anything to him. All else at present has faded out."[12]

According to the letter signed "Charles Foley," by mid-June Harriet had persuaded the doctors that her husband was well enough to be released and cared for by her alone. Slowly, tentatively, Kreisler walked on his own to a waiting car and headed for a friend's home on Long Island, where he continued to convalesce.

Kreisler's condition was "very good," according to George Engles, director of the NBC Concert Service, which managed the violinist. So good was his client's health, Engles said, that he would go ahead as planned with his thirty-four-concert, two-month tour scheduled to begin 14 October and run through the end of the year.[13] By all official reports he was fit and almost ready to return to a demanding work schedule.

In reality, Kreisler was nowhere near well enough to last through a two-month tour. His sight and hearing, although improved, were not fully restored (and indeed never would be), and, according to "Foley," although "both his immense mentality and the strength of his willpower astonished the doctors," he nevertheless faced a long convalescence.

> His recovery goes ahead. Of course he is still partly an invalid and naturally unable to completely lead a normal life. But mentally and musically his advance is amazing.
>
> He has practically gained complete mastery over his violin; he plays often the piano and works over musical arrangements and compositions.
>
> Of course a great number of months will pass, before he will be willing to resume to a certain extent his playing in public, but his hope that this will finally happen makes us all very happy.[14]

So Kreisler remained in seclusion, Harriet overseeing his every hesitant step toward health. Little information is available from this period, as the couple gave no interviews to the newspapers or radio—and Harriet made sure that his exposure even to friends was extremely limited. It was during this time that Kreisler began to loosen his ties with those around him, retreating into the comfort and confines of Harriet's domain and giving in to her insistence that he not overexert himself. Thus he appears to have written very few letters, and correspondence now available for review is minimal.

Nathan Milstein was among the few friends who met with Kreisler shortly after the accident. From Milstein's description it is clear that Kreisler's ability to play, while not destroyed by his injuries, was nevertheless affected by the memory loss and the loss of confidence that accompanied it.

> Soon after the accident, Kreisler was at our house for lunch. I wanted to distract him, so I asked, "Meister, back in Russia

> I owned your recording of Cottenet's 'Meditation.' Who is that composer? I've never heard of him." Kreisler grew animated. "Oh, that's my old friend, an Englishman who lives in America. I haven't performed that piece in a long time." He asked for a violin. I gave him one, and I could see that it was hard for him to handle. He didn't know how to put his finger on F. "Is this F?" he asked me. But then he played a bit from the half-forgotten piece. Even in that condition he was the unique Kreisler, his musicianship full of charm and grace.[15]

Under Harriet's hawkeye supervision, Kreisler's convalescence proceeded, gradually but notably, over the next four months. Finally, on 9 October 1941, Fritz Kreisler put on a black tie and dinner jacket and stepped out for his first public appearance in half a year. The destination was Carnegie Hall; the occasion was the opening concert in the New York Philharmonic's one-hundredth season, led by guest conductor Leopold Stokowski. The program that night was filled with sweep and grandeur: it spanned Beethoven's Fifth Symphony, Stokowski's transcription of the Bach Toccata and Fugue in D Minor, Henry Cowell's *Tales of Our Countryside*, and "Liebestod" from Wagner's *Tristan and Isolde*.[16]

Kreisler's presence at the concert was greeted with a combination of amazement and relief—heads turned at the dapper man—and sparked speculation that he might indeed be able to perform soon. Perhaps he would honor his concert commitments after all.

Unfortunately, this was not the case. Only one month after Kreisler's first public appearance, Marks Levine, the managing director of the NBC Concert Service, announced the cancellation or deferment of virtually all of Kreisler's twenty-six engagements for the 1941–1942 concert season. There would be no tour. At most, it seemed, Kreisler hoped to give one or two recitals in the New York City area; anything more was simply too strenuous.

Yet Levine was insistent that Kreisler had returned to health. He had recovered completely, he told the concert hall managers who had booked him months before. He was well and strong. He was practicing the fiddle and spending a great deal of time on composing. He was fine.[17]

Why, then, the cancellation?

In all likelihood, it was driven by prudence. Despite a remarkable recovery, Kreisler had nevertheless been affected by his accident, and no one could predict the nature and extent of his limits. Certainly, he was able to play the violin with the same warmth and vocal intimacy; just as certainly, he was willing and motivated to attempt a comeback. But twenty-six concert dates meant a big comeback, too big to gamble against the unknown quantity of his abilities and endurance.

The decision to put Kreisler's 1941–1942 tour on hold, therefore, was due not to unstable health but a less-than-granitic faith in the violinist's ability to perform. One assumes that Kreisler himself had few such qualms; he was never one to second-guess his own abilities. But it is easy to picture those who surrounded him—Harriet, of course, flanked by Levine and Foley—wringing their hands over this great but inevitably aging musician, wondering how his sixty-six years would hold up under the pressures of a renewed career and fearing that an unsuccessful, premature return would tarnish both his reputation and his ability to sell tickets. It is easy to picture Kreisler giving in to their concerns, if only because quiescence was his natural state. He always took the path of least resistance, particularly with Harriet. Much as he wanted to tour, he would not fight for it.

So he waited.

Fritz Kreisler's return to performing, when it occurred, was carefully choreographed and extremely gradual; he would not be allowed to make a fool of himself. There was no splashy comeback, no sudden emergence from the shadows, no dramatic announcement of his re-entry into the world of music. His return would proceed one step at a time—small, hesitant, conservative. So long as he shuffled, he would not trip.

He took his first step in mid-January 1942, on the stage of the Academy of Music in Philadelphia.[18] It was not a concert. There were no critics and no audience. Indeed, the only listeners were orchestral players, sound engineers, and assorted techies. Kreisler's first professional outing in ten months was a recording session for

RCA Victor, an artistically unambitious project that returned the violinist to over-familiar musical ground: he recorded nothing but his own works spiffed up with new, full orchestral accompaniments. It was a predictable undertaking in a tightly controlled arena where Kreisler could test his abilities and succeed or fail without public notice. He told reporters at the time that he was ready to play again and would soon start on a national tour, but what he did not add was that any such tour was probably contingent upon the weeks that followed. Clearly, if he played with the same old ease and assurance, he would return to the New York stage sometime the following spring. If not, his comeback would be further postponed.

Everything went well. "I feel like my old self," he was quoted as saying in the 26 January *Newsweek*, and to be sure, it looked like the old Kreisler, striking and poised. The writer Samuel Applebaum later described the scene at the recording session, vividly portraying what must have been an emotionally charged occasion:

> The musicians were tuning up when he walked out to take up his position. As if by signal, they all ceased tuning and as one body, rose. Kreisler stopped, hesitated, seemed to want to speak. Then he did. With tears in his eyes, and a look of tenderness, he gently asked, "Gentlemen, may I have an A, please?"[19]

Step One of Kreisler's return to concertizing had been successfully accomplished. Step Two occurred on 28 January 1942, when the violinist performed his first post-accident recital, at the Palace Theatre in Albany, New York. Like the earlier recording session, the Albany concert was an exercise in caution: it was close enough to New York City for an easy trip but far enough removed that it attracted relatively little attention in the metropolitan press. It was safe.

And it was, by nearly any reckoning, successful. Three thousand concertgoers packed the Palace to capacity—it was a grand old theater with a magnificent interior but spotty acoustics—and welcomed the violinist with a thunderous ovation that subsided only when Kreisler snapped the violin under his chin and played. At the close of the evening the crowd burst into similarly noisy applause, forcing management to darken the stage after the second encore.[20]

Critically, too, Kreisler's Albany recital earned glowing responses. "Throughout the evening," wrote one reviewer, "Mr. Kreisler's tones were whole and beautiful, each passage firm and flowing."[21] Edgar S. Van Olinda, the critic for the Albany *Times Union*, was even more florid in his praise, gushing unabashedly about the "tall man of regal bearing, his patrician countenance crowned by a shock of white hair."

> The man was Fritz Kreisler, beloved artist of three generations. This was not an audience of critics per se, but a vast army of devoted worshippers at the shrine of Apollo whose violinistic apostle Kreisler has been since he first came to America at the age of 13 in joint recital with Moriz Rosenthal. That was half a century ago. He was a great artist then. He is infinitely greater today.
>
> Here was a man of indomitable spirit, whose determination to return to the field he always has dominated reached its zenith last night. Showing no apparent physical evidence of his accident on the streets of New York City last April, his entry on the first concert stage since his convalescence was an experience which might have tried the courage of a less vigorous man.
>
> His program was all too short from the standpoint of pure enjoyment. True, the first half was not on the coddling side of his art. It contained the difficult Grieg Sonata in C Minor and the Bruch Concerto in G Minor, and these were both accomplished with beautiful tone quality and the Kreisler maturity of interpretation. Kreisler does not dazzle the listener with the cold brilliance of technical pyrotechnics—although he has an abundance of this byproduct of the musician's art—but charms with the almost earthy and human quality of his playing.
>
> It is this ability to reach the musical consciousness of the humblest and least tutored member of his audience that has been his great appeal to the laity. . . . We sincerely hope that the concert last night will be the beginning of another distinguished contribution to still another generation.[22]

The second half of the concert was devoted, not surprisingly, to Kreisler's original works and transcriptions—again, unthreatening territory for a man unsure of his abilities and fearful of any lingering deficits. The material he chose for his program was straightforward and familiar: even the Grieg, the most demanding piece of the evening, was a work he had played for years before the accident and knew as well as any in the violin repertoire. The Bruch was a similarly conservative choice, popular with audiences and demanding considerable technical skills from the player, but otherwise a fairly orthodox item on any program. That Kreisler followed it with half a recital's worth of his own short works confirmed better than any public statement the aching hesitancy with which he approached his return to the stage. No contemporary works, no risky premieres, no daring or repertoire-expanding compositions were heard in the Palace Theatre that evening; it was neither the time nor the place for adventurous programming. Kreisler would not tread ground that had not been crossed many times before.

Three months after the Albany concert, Kreisler signed a contract to appear with the Philadelphia Orchestra during the 1942–1943 season, opening up the possibility of a full or at least scaled-back tour. With the Philadelphia he would perform the Mendelssohn concerto; for an appearance with the Chicago Symphony, also scheduled, his share of the program would be the Mendelssohn, and, again, the Bruch.[23] Neither would tax him mightily in the months leading up to the new classical season; equipped with those and equally unthreatening works, Kreisler could look ahead with modest confidence and make himself available for further concert dates.

For music lovers and others who had followed Kreisler's career, however, the greatest test of his post-convalescent ability—and a truer herald of his return—was his Halloween night appearance on the stage of Carnegie Hall. It was his first recital there in twenty-two months, and New Yorkers packed the space to capacity. The ovation they gave him simply for stepping on stage was one of the most thunderous he ever received, a tribute, in Noel Straus's words, "of affection and esteem so whole-hearted and overwhelming that [Kreisler] was visibly touched to the core."[24]

Among those in the crowd was Jeanne Mitchell, a rising young violinist (and the author's mother) and a fervid admirer of Kreisler. She recalled:

> When he came out everyone was standing. No one planned to do it, but everyone leaped to their feet, screaming and clapping. It was a din. He gave little obeisances—sort of military bows and little nods—until he got good and sick of it. Then he put his violin up to his chin and everyone had to shut up—and they were still standing! The accompanist started with the piece, and [Kreisler] started so strong. . . . It was an announcement, you know: "I'm alive." We were speechless. . . . Oh, we were crying—men and women both.
>
> It's so Kreisler, too, to politely acknowledge the greeting and then to say, "Enough." Because, you know, if he hadn't done that, I think it would have gone on for fifteen minutes.[25]

From Mitchell's vantage point in a box seat she could see Jacques Thibaud, Kreisler's great friend and fellow violinist, crouched nervously in an orchestra seat below her. He had come to watch his colleague make a comeback. "I remember that Jacques Thibaud's fingers were unconsciously fingering everything against his cheek, against his left cheek. He was so involved. People loved [Kreisler]—and his colleagues did, too."[26]

Physically, Kreisler appeared to have changed very little: white haired and aristocratic, with a mournful face and the carriage of a soldier, he had at the time of the accident already acquired the look and mien of nobility. Now, onstage in New York City for the first time in almost two years, neither his appearance nor his performance in any way suggested fragility. The accident "had in no wise affected his playing," so claimed a review in the 1 November *New York Herald Tribune*. "His interpretations exhibited the familiar characteristics which have long won him the affection, as well as the admiration, of the musical public at large." Moreover:

> It was gratifying to be able to listen to him again, and to realize that, judging by this performance, there should be further opportunities to do so for many years to come. His

> art now, as before, depends not so much on any single characteristic as an integrated combination of qualities; technical mastery, ingratiating tone, essential musicality, thorough understanding and sympathy for the music which he plays and an ingratiating personality. His interpretations yesterday, as of yore, were personal in the best sense; that of the presentation of the essence of the music by a great artist, as contrasted with a conscious attempt to give an impression of personality in the performance.[27]

The program that afternoon was typical Kreisler, comprising a few core pieces from the violin repertoire, a few original works and transcriptions, and a handful of musical bon-bons. He began the recital with the heavier works: the Bach Concerto No. 1 in A Minor, the Partita No. 3 in E Major, and Mozart's Concerto in E-flat Major. After that, he dipped liberally into the lollipops (including Ravel-Kreisler's *Habanera*, Debussy-Hartmann's *La Fille aux cheveux de lin*, and Rachmaninoff-Kreisler's *Marguerite*). Kreisler closed the recital with his own *Viennese Rhapsodic Fantasietta*, his latest work and, barring the string quartet and the operettas, his largest. It is an odd and affecting piece: melodic, grandly sentimental, and, to skeptical contemporary ears, dated.

Kreisler began writing the *Fantasietta* before the accident and completed it in the long months of convalescence that followed; the work fairly sings with its composer's love of Vienna, a fondness made all the more bittersweet by his exile from it. Even during the Nazi occupation, Kreisler's memories of the city were fixed in the Habsburg era, a time when the waltz ruled and political decay could be facilely ignored; it is a period vividly evoked in the *Fantasietta*, in which up-swept melodic lines that echo his shorter works bounce cheerily over three-four time. In today's concert halls the piece is rarely if ever played. But at the time it was greeted and admired for what it was: a perfectly conceived characterization of Kreisler's musical persona. As such it was ideal for inclusion in his New York comeback recital, which was more than anything else a celebration of the violinist's charms.

(Eric Wen calls the *Fantasietta* "over-the-top," a gorgeous work whose exaggerated Viennese gestures tend to alienate modern violinists. "I think it is a fantastic piece, but it doesn't go down well today. . . . Unless you really get the whole ethos, it seems dated," he said. "That last section—there is so much Richard Strauss—the modulations are all out of *Rosenkavalier*. Like Schubert or Dvořák, I think Kreisler has that natural ease of modulating, and that piece is sort of his virtuoso display of his modulating skill. It reminds me of the *Caprice Viennois*, but darker, with double stops. . . . That piece is quintessential Kreisler. It's the last hurrah of that kind of personality, that kind of musician, writing in that time. Today it doesn't work, sadly.")[28]

The *Rhapsodic Fantasietta* was greeted positively, if not rapturously, by the New York press. The review printed in the 1 November *New York Herald Tribune* remarked:

> [The *Fantasietta*], opening with an extensive introduction and presenting an engaging array of appealing Viennese tunes, is violinistically effective as well as melodically pleasing in its leisurely course. There was mellow warmth and rich color in his playing of these measures, the subtle rhythmic nuances which revealed Mr. Kreisler's Viennese origin and his ability, rivaled by few, to make his hearers conscious of a Viennese atmosphere.[29]

Noel Straus, writing for *The New York Times*, gave the entire recital an unqualified rave.

> It was a foregone conclusion that Mr. Kreisler would not have ventured to give the recital unless he was positive that he could carry it through on a plane consistent with his high ideals and deep integrity as a performer. And this proved definitely true. If there were any who suspected that the artist's violinistic powers would be lessened as a result of his accident, their fears were dispelled as soon as they heard his fiery and vital performance of the Concerto No. 1 in A Minor of Bach, which opened the program. Even in the prefatory playing of the National Anthem it became obvious from the energetic sweep of the bow and the firm grip of the fingers on the strings that his enforced rest brought him back to his public with a new strength noticeable even in his physical appearance.

> There was all of the old brilliance and élan in the corner movements of the Bach concerto, the same supreme authority as interpreter that always has marked his work. The tone, moreover, here as in the other selections that followed, was under absolute control as usual and notable for purity and silkiness, despite the fact that the damp, hot weather was unfavorable for strings and would have severely handicapped a less skilled player.[30]

Thus Kreisler's return to the stage was received with glowing notices from nearly all critical corners. Certainly in retrospect it is difficult to tell whether Kreisler's comeback was as artistically successful as his admirers claimed; certainly, in retrospect, one is tempted to ascribe some of the more effusive praise to sheer relief. A year and a half had passed since the accident, and despite fears that Kreisler would never play again, he had returned to the New York stage with all of his accustomed grace. He had made some errors, yes, but his performances had never been flawless, and any technical glitches in his Carnegie Hall comeback could be waved away as artistically irrelevant. So, too, could any suspicion that the violinist had chosen for his return a program plump with pieces with which he had long been familiar; everything was either penned by his own hand (in whole or in part) or, like the works by Bach and Mozart, was a well-worn member of the violin repertoire. The only new work in the concert was the *Rhapsodic Fantasietta*, and one must assume that the composer was entirely and comfortably aware of its mechanical difficulties. Kreisler did not take chances with his new debut in New York City. Once again, he played it safe.

In the period following the Carnegie recital, the Kreislers returned to some semblance of their lives before the accident—they began to venture out with friends and colleagues, making occasional appearances in and around Manhattan and at social gatherings. A little more than a month after his return to the New York stage, Kreisler was the guest of honor at a dinner given by Elsa Maxwell in the Jansen Suite of the Waldorf-Astoria. Attending was a long list of luminaries, from Deems Taylor and William L. Shirer to William S. Paley and Mrs. William Randolph Hearst.[31]

His friends tried to draw Kreisler out at smaller occasions. Some time during this period violinist Paul Kochansky threw a cocktail party and invited Fritz and Harriet. Jascha Heifetz recalled the uncomfortable atmosphere as partygoers awkwardly tried to avoid all mention of the accident. Finally, someone asked Kreisler about his memory for numbers. He quipped: "I have never been good at numbers. On the other hand, I now remember all sorts of notes which I used to forget."[32]

Kreisler's self-deprecating charm had survived. His humor had survived. His understanding of music, his keen ability to communicate with the violin, his personal and artistic nobility had all survived. He had been hit by a truck at full speed and had lived to joke about it at cocktail parties. He had suffered internal injuries, skull fracture, amnesia, partial permanent memory loss, and a deficit of sight and hearing, and he had recovered to perform again in Carnegie Hall. The audiences that greeted him confirmed that he was still, in musical circles and in the public at large, a beloved figure; the press heralded his comeback with relieved reports of a style and warmth unaffected by his long absence from the stage and the trauma that had precipitated it. By all measures, Kreisler's carefully planned return was a resounding success: he played well, the crowds loved it, critics liked it. The world's most beguiling violinist was back on stage, seemingly little changed.

In truth, much had changed. Over the next few years, as Kreisler resumed some semblance of his former professional life, a few uncomfortable truths emerged. One was the fact that he was, after a prime that had lasted for decades, in the twilight of his career. He performed less frequently, the music he chose for his programs was slightly less demanding, and the crowds that turned out to hear him, while always considerable, had started to advance in age and shrink in size (but not devotion). This is not to imply that Kreisler had alienated any of his former audience, or that his professional efforts during the early to mid-forties were no longer critically lauded; no one questioned the appropriateness of his late career, the depth of artistry with which he played, or the welcome he continued to earn around the country. He had every right to be onstage—but he stood there as a member of the old guard, a reminder of glories past rather than a promise for the future. He had become an elder statesman.

It was a role that suited him well. Gingold described the violinist during that period as "very tall, very stately—he looked like a general."[33] George Neikrug added: "He looked something like Einstein, very kindly. And I remember him sitting up there, with his old-fashioned suits, going to play. He took a great big watch out of his vest."[34] Carrying on the man-of-war image, Sylvia Rabinof Rothenberg said that Kreisler's friends and admirers always referred to him as "the Viking."

> That's the nickname people gave him, because of the way he looked onstage. He was beautiful onstage. He had this wonderful bearing and this noble profile. He wasn't stagey—don't get me wrong; it wasn't conscious on his part—but he looked the role. The way he opened his collar and put his fiddle on his left chin—his whole bearing.[35]

Noble or not, Kreisler had not lost the impish quality that had so long endeared him to his friends and colleagues. Joseph Lippman, husband of press agent Alix Williamson, once toured with Kreisler in the 1940s and used to tell of the violinist's antics before walking out to perform. Just before going onstage, he would check his zipper and say, "It's the last glissando!"[36]

An endearing portrait of Kreisler at this stage of his career has been drawn by Josef Gingold, who was an ardent, lifelong, and outspoken votary of the performer. Gingold was in his first year as concertmaster of the Detroit Symphony when Fritz Kreisler arrived to perform the Beethoven concerto. It was the 1944–1945 season, and although it was then a few years since the accident, "still everybody worried about him, whether he would play," Gingold recalled. "Well, he played the Beethoven concerto at the rehearsal and the concert. It was God's given gift. During the G-minor episode in the first movement, I had to stop playing because I was so choked up. Oh, it was something out of this world."[37]

After the concert Gingold went backstage to congratulate the soloist. "I said, 'Mr. Kreisler, I want to thank you for this evening and for twenty years of listening to you. I never missed a Kreisler concert.' And he looked so pleased." Much to Gingold's delight, Kreisler then invited the younger man to accompany him the following day to his concert in Ann Arbor, Michigan. Not surprisingly, Gingold accepted, and at six o'clock the next evening he met Kreisler, Kreisler's accompanist, Carl Lamson, and his road manager, Paul Stoes, in a limousine outside the Statler Hotel. Gingold climbed in with the limousine driver, not wanting to disturb his idol, but was immediately instructed by Stoes to "'go and sit next to the old man. He loves colleagues. He loves to talk shop.' And so I did, and we started the conversation, and he was utterly charming."[38]

The six hours that followed provided an encounter that Gingold never forgot. Even forty-eight years later he was able to recall his night with Kreisler in great detail, recounting images and conversations with vim and vivid color. So engaging is his description that it deserves direct quotation and is conveyed here in near-entirety. It begins with the limo ride to Ann Arbor.

> I felt myself so small sitting next to him, thinking, "Who am I that Kreisler should even invite me to a concert of his?" It is not false modesty; I speak to you from my heart. And then we came to the hall, it was called the Hill Auditorium in Ann Arbor, and he asked me to come up and join him in the artists' room. He said, "Why don't you hang up your hat and coat here?" Again, I felt very humble, but I hung up my hat and coat and I hung around, hoping to see or hear how Kreisler warms up. What does he do? I was just interested.
>
> So he kept on talking, telling stories about the violin and the piano, and he didn't open it [his violin case]. And I was getting a little sad, thinking, "He's hiding something from me." He wasn't hiding anything. Finally [the hall manager] said, "We'll begin in ten minutes." So he opened his violin case and his bow was still very tight. We always loosened our bows after using them, but he didn't. It was still in there from the night before—it was still very taut, very tight. He hadn't even brushed off the resin, and it was apparent to me that he didn't touch his violin between concerts. [The hall manager] said, "Mr. Kreisler, we are going to start in just about a minute," so he took his violin and stood like an officer in the Austrian army, erect, ready to go out on the stage.

He turned to his pianist, Carl Lamson. He had a terrible lisp, and he said, "Carl, pleath don't hurry me in my variationth, becauth if you hurry me, I am *thunk*." It was so cute. . . .

Just as he was about to step out on stage he said, "Mr. Gingold . . . after the concert we have to go to Detroit. I'm hungry, because I haven't had anything to eat since breakfast." He was on a diet—or it was Harriet's way of punishing him for something.

So he came out on the stage. . . . In this hall, when latecomers arrived, they simply opened the doors and there was the most unbearable draft. Kreisler didn't budge. The whole audience was complaining. Men started putting on their scarves again. So he stood there. All the concerts in those days started with *The Star-Spangled Banner*, every one. Kreisler probably wasn't warmed up, so he did his warm-up in *The Star-Spangled Banner*, playing passages in perfect harmonization to the chords. He was trying to warm up his fingers! But nobody recognized *The Star-Spangled Banner*, and people remained seated. Finally, in the second refrain, he played it with the most heavenly double stops, and people started to rise, very slowly, see, because they weren't sure what was happening.

Then he said, "Everybody sit down," and he was smiling. He had a little bit of a tick in his face. Then he played [Beethoven's] Kreutzer Sonata. In the first movement his fingers were still cold and he had a memory lapse, but he began to improvise with the proper harmonization. Whatever he did, if he didn't know the sonata he would keep playing, improvising, and I'd think, "I wonder what edition he's playing." . . .

[After the concert] I went backstage, and Kreisler was all dressed and ready to go. It was a bitter cold night, and he was wearing a spring coat, no hat, no scarf, and I took my scarf off and said, "Please, put it around your neck." He says, "What for?" I said, "You played a big program tonight, you must be perspired." He said, "You know, with the situ-

> ation that is going on now during the war, I cannot afford to perspire—because I need this shirt for five more concerts."
>
> So we got to Detroit . . . and Mr. Stoes had five martinis. He passed out, and I thought the man died. I wasn't used to people passing out. And Kreisler said, "Leave him alone. It'll be all right. He's not dead. He'll sleep it off," which he did. But he left me in the most enviable position, because Mr. Stoes fell asleep, and Mr. Lamson never opened his mouth, never said "Boo"—he just shook his head, nodded his head when he agreed with something. And then I spoke with Kreisler.[39]

At this point Kreisler regaled Gingold with the famous chest-of-gold Sultan story, described at length in Chapter 6. As the night wore on he spoke of his contemporaries—"He adored Eugène Ysaÿe"—as well as the younger generation, speaking with great admiration for Jascha Heifetz but voicing less complimentary opinions of several others. He asked Gingold to never repeat what he had said on the subject; Gingold kept his word, declining even in 1992 to name the violinists that Kreisler had criticized.

Another encounter with Kreisler—a briefer one—was recalled by Michael Tree, who was a boy of twelve when he won a Young Artist Award in 1946 from the New Jersey Griffith Music Foundation. Kreisler presented Tree with the award and was on hand afterward to chat with him, an occasion that Tree recalled fondly half a century later. "I remember very vividly the impression he made," Tree said. "He was a great personage—tall and erect, almost regal, but in a very friendly way. Of course I was awed."[40]

Tree's parents, Samuel and Sada Applebaum, were also present, and their recollection of Kreisler's remarks are recounted in the book *The Way They Play*. In the conversation that day, Kreisler stressed his long-held belief that "technical proficiency is not the object" and that "speed can never long remain a goal. Though it is attractive, people will get away from it again."[41]

Kreisler's comments to the Applebaums, like his late-night remarks to Josef Gingold, point to another uncomfortable truth revealed in the years following the accident: the concert circuit was packed with speedy young soloists who were poised to seize the audience's attention away from older fiddlers. Kreisler was a great figure—Kreisler was revered—Kreisler was a fine cause for nostalgia. But Kreisler was not Heifetz and his followers, or any of the younger generation whose technique and rapidity of playing set them apart from their romantic forebears; he was, instead, an example so poignant of eras past that even he was aware of his own isolation in the field of players. The old man played at slower tempos, had matured at a slower pace, was born into a slower world—a world fueled by coal and steam and horses, and marked by a pulse no harsher than the waltz. What became apparent in the years that followed Kreisler's accident and preceded his retirement was the acute disjunction between himself and the throng of young musicians who sprang up around him. He was, in many ways, an anachronism.

He was also in decline—in health as well as technical ability. Burdened with heart trouble (according to Frederic Kreisler, in a 1995 interview), Kreisler struggled in his post-accident years with a variety of ailments, some age-related, some related to his head injuries. His hearing and eyesight were never the same. His memory had lost some acuity, and forever after the accident he was unable to recall most details of the years 1928 through 1930 and 1933 through 1936.[42] By June of 1946, when the seventy-one-year-old violinist was rushed to the LeRoy Sanitarium for an emergency appendectomy (reported in *The New York Times* on 9 June 1946), it had already been obvious for some time that he was headed for retirement.

That he probably *ought* to have been headed for retirement was equally apparent. In the period following the accident, Kreisler's intonation had started to miss the mark a little more regularly, and although the intimacy and the charisma in his playing remained, some of the energy did not. Had Kreisler not been hit full-force by a delivery truck at the age of sixty-six—plunging him into a coma, permanently affecting his hearing, and pulling him prematurely from the forefront of violin performance—his career might well have flourished into the mid-1950s. He might have turned out more recordings in slightly better fidelity; he might have retained greater and more permanent influence over the younger generation of violinists; he might even have appeared on television or agreed to be filmed in some other capacity, committing his artistry to a visual (and reproducible) medium available for future study. As it stands, there exists no known film of Kreisler playing, other than a silent, fifteen-second, black-and-white home movie.[43]

Seen in this light, the accident of 1941 was more than a turning point in his career—it was the single, consequential event that forever fixed Kreisler as a pre-World War II artist. The egg truck that hit him at East 57th and Madison did more than crack his skull; it booted him from the upper echelons of violinists and guaranteed that the work he produced after the crash could not ultimately measure up to the work he produced before it. Kreisler was thus frozen in time, planted firmly in the early forties despite a career that pressed ahead haltingly for the remainder of the decade. By the time he died in 1962, Fritz Kreisler had not played professionally for twelve years. He had not been influential for more than twenty.

Ten

Kreisler, Heifetz, and the Cult of Technique

> Everyone thinks, when you read a score, you have a canonical way of playing it. It is not so. Crescendo, accelerando, diminuendo, allegretto, presto, these are merely suggestions, and indicate different things to different composers. It is left to you to play it according to your own subjective character. Each great violinist—if he is really great—must put his personality into the interpretation of a work. Thus, if I hear a record, I know immediately who played it, by his special way of doing it. If a group of violinists stood behind a screen, each playing the same work one after another, I could tell you immediately which one was doing it.[1]

The words are Fritz Kreisler's, but the image they evoke—of shadows behind a screen, each performing the same familiar work—begs us to ask which shadows. Who were these distinctive colleagues of Kreisler's who would by their very playing identify themselves? Mischa Elman, surely; his tone would give him away. Joseph

Szigeti's muscularity and razor edge would announce him, loud and clear. Zino Francescatti, Efrem Zimbalist, Nathan Milstein. And Jascha Heifetz.

When Jascha Heifetz died in 1987, he was eulogized, by nearly all who marked his passing, as the greatest violinist of the century, perhaps of all time. In a sense he was. Unlike Kreisler, who made his name with the emotional and musical wisdom that underpinned his interpretations, Heifetz earned popular fame and professional admiration with the most jaw-droppingly perfect technique ever heard. His intonation was perfect. His tone was perfect. His memory, dynamics, reading—all were perfect. In fact, so perfect was Heifetz's playing, so fast and clean and unmarred by anything resembling human error, that it changed forever the world's perception of how a violinist should sound. Technique was required to be flawless. Tempos were required to be fast. Errant music-making—missed notes, wrong interpretations, or stray "kitchen noise" produced in the heat of performance—was the mark of a performer who was not up to the task of global concertizing.

As Richard Dyer wrote in *The Boston Globe* on 12 December 1987, just two days after the violinist's death:

> He may have lacked the intellectual penetration and zest of Szigeti, the smile that shines through all of Kreisler's playing, the abandon one cherishes in Huberman. But Heifetz is the one who discovered all the resources, all the secrets, the very soul, of his instrument, and no subsequent violinist, or player of any stringed instrument, has escaped his influence or his inspiration.

From Heifetz onward, every student of the violin who aspired to prominence faced a model whose faultlessness might dissuade all but the lionhearted from even trying. Fellow musicians and music critics alike stood in awe, and all recognized Heifetz's dramatic and long-lasting influence: he changed the way violinists make music, and he changed what we hear when they play. He was the single most influential violinist of his and successive generations.

Heifetz earned this position not by sheer force of personality, as Paganini had, or by dramatically reapproaching violin technique, as

Ysaÿe or Kreisler had, but by reshaping the performer's expectations of himself and the listener's expectations of the performer. He revolutionized violin artistry by perfecting the mechanics of it: in so doing, all who came before him were made to seem quaint, or irrelevant, or hopelessly burdened by quirks of style and personality. Kreisler, the greatest and arguably the quirkiest of these predecessors, stood to lose the most from Heifetz's ascension—not as a performer, in which capacity he continued to succeed for many years past the younger man's entry into concert halls, but as a model for future generations of string players. Until Heifetz appeared, Kreisler was the violinist that younger musicians admired and studied and imitated; and although Kreisler remained a significant figure throughout the first half of the twentieth century, Heifetz influenced and indeed seduced a whole wave of student instrumentalists who regarded him as the paragon of violin technique.

Despite overlapping in their lives and careers (Heifetz was younger by twenty-six years), the two represented vastly different styles, eras, even philosophies of artistry. The two men represented approaches to the violin so antipodal that the impact of one cannot be fully grasped without also understanding the impact of the other. Light means nothing without dark, nor dark without light; Kreisler's contributions to violin playing, great or small, enduring or ephemeral, appear in stark relief against Heifetz's. They are the yin and yang of twentieth-century instrumentalism.

As such they rather cleanly divided the ranks of violinists who admired them, separating out those who emulated Kreisler from those who emulated Heifetz. Perhaps "venerated" might be a better word, a more exact and evocative one, since the admiration inspired by both men was peculiarly devotional in character. More than examples, they were idols. Yet even in this regard, they proved different: where Heifetz's genius provoked allegiance to a strict, regimented, and precisely articulated credo of playing, Kreisler's provoked reflection. Heifetz was the god of discipline; Kreisler, the god of song.

Jascha Heifetz was born in Vilnius, Russia (now Lithuania), in 1901, and he started lessons with his father, a violinist, at the age of three. Four years later he was playing in public; two years after that he began studying with Leopold Auer at the St. Petersburg Conservatory. Once there, his rise to the top of the music world proceeded apace; by the age of eleven he had toured all over Russia and Europe, by twelve he had been compared to an "elderly gentleman" in demeanor, by sixteen he had made his Carnegie Hall debut.[2] From then on, the fame of Heifetz was worldwide, his name synonymous with violinistic perfection. He would for the rest of his life be ranked as equal or superior to all other violinists.

Heifetz was a romantic in style and school, but his nature was coolly classical. He was not effusive. He shunned the broad gesture, onstage and off. Possessed of few close friends, he seemed to distance himself even from his family; he married and divorced twice, and relationships with his three children were cordial but never close.[3] While performing, too, he was an icy figure who hardly moved, producing interpretations of such focus and precision that the human element seemed to disappear. Despite the unmistakable imprint of Heifetz's touch on anything he played, he did not trade in sentiment; his readings were as remarkable for their subtlety of emotion as they were for the historical and musicological correctness of every note, every swell, every slight ritard. Some complained he was dull. Others, less comfortable with the unabashed feeling given rein by earlier violinists (including Kreisler), welcomed the Heifetz austerity and heard in it genuine if understated passion. Heifetz was a devout believer in the music he played and a careful student of its art who brought to the instrument a crystalline tone, a fluid bow arm, a flawless left hand, and a meticulous approach to preparation that tolerated no human error. In other words, he was a perfectionist.

Curiously, Heifetz was compared most often to Paganini, who was as shameless a showman and as hungry for publicity as Heifetz was reserved and aloof. "Not since Nicolò Paganini," remarked Zubin Mehta, "has an artist evolved as completely as Heifetz."[4] Paganini altered violin playing as no one had before him and, possibly, no one has since; among his technical innovations were ricochet bowings, multiple stops, heroic use of harmonics, and right- and left-hand pizzicatos.[5] Heifetz made no such innovations, but he represented a culmination—a summation—of violin technique in a manner that galvanized and sometimes terrified those who heard him. Heifetz's prowess was superhuman; Paganini's, demonic. Neither man was merely mortal.

Kreisler, by contrast, was the Everyman of modern violinists, the gifted musician who was either oblivious to his massive popularity or was seemingly unpersuaded by it. Despite being reared in an age and a culture of considerable artifice—and disregarding his numerous acquaintances with kings, sultans, and other assorted despots—he did not appear affected in any way and in fact seemed to regard his own stature and social connections with a wonderment that came close to naiveté. In some ways, his wife would have complained, he was aggravatingly plebeian; he was at heart a man in search of a decent beer. Those who met him found a gracious and approachable man who drew no artificial boundaries between himself and others; one of his most endearing qualities was the fraternal bonhomie with which he greeted workaday musicians and the respect with which he regarded them. He was one of them.

Not surprisingly, that Everyman quality came across in his playing—authoritative but achievable, sublime but somehow grounded in mundane and recognizable truths. There was nothing superhuman about it; it was too organic, too open to interpretation, and even, at times, too flawed.

Unlike Heifetz, whose intensity demanded not merely attention but *belief*—his performances convinced the listener that no other interpretations were advisable or even possible—Kreisler's playing was at once more personal and less final. Heifetz aimed for the definitive; Kreisler did not. While Heifetz's interpretations of the violin repertoire were stunning in their exactness of detail—from performance to performance, his phrasing and fingerings barely wavered—Kreisler's were more fluid, likely to change over time in tempo or bowing. His reading of his own *Liebesleid*, for example, slowed over the years, becoming softer and more sorrowful as the violinist himself aged. Whereas Heifetz strove for one musical idea that he achieved and chiseled to perfection, Kreisler's interpretations changed.

The profoundest differences in philosophy as well as technique are examined in Samuel and Sada Applebaum's *The Way They Play*, which discusses the artistry of twenty-nine prominent string players. Kreisler's chapter is the least specific (and least practical) of the lot, avoiding, as it does, any "how-to" discussion of practicing and performance. Kreisler had little to say on the subject, to the Applebaums or anyone else. The science of violin technique held no interest for him:

> I would rather not talk technically. There is so much that I feel, so much I should like to say, that I welcome this opportunity to express it. There are so many wonderful violinists who will discuss the art from a scientific standpoint, that I should like to talk about violin playing from the human standpoint.[6]

Although he expressed his pleasure in seeing so many youngsters studying music, Kreisler lamented the fact that "too much emphasis is being placed on physical repetition in practice, and not enough on mental control. Muscular technic is not a matter of muscular development alone, but of mental application." He continued:

> Some time ago, I went to the New York Philharmonic concert. Heifetz was playing the Mendelssohn concerto. His tone was beautiful. In every way it was a matured performance. My wife was at my side. We both were delighted with it. Behind us sat a woman with a boy and from their excited bits of conversation I could see the boy was a violinist. When the performance was over, the woman exclaimed, "Wasn't that wonderful!" But the boy replied, "Oh, I can play it faster!" From this episode what can we learn? We learn that there certainly is something drastically wrong with the attitude of the aspiring artist. That boy's senseless attitude makes maturity almost impossible. This experience made much of an impression on me, and I kept thinking about it for days—does technical speed mean so much? . . .
>
> Technical proficiency is not the object in the development of the great art of music. Speed can never remain a goal

> of music. Though it is very attractive, people will get away from it again. And let [the violinist] know Nature, let him go to Nature, to learn that the most wonderful song in the world is the song of the forest![7]

Kreisler's philosophy of the art of music led to what was inevitably the greatest *procedural* difference between these two musical icons, Kreisler and Heifetz: their utterly opposite views on practice. That Kreisler resisted it is well-known, has already been mentioned, and is not likely to shock anyone who is at all familiar with his modus operandi. What does surprise is his passionate belief in extended non-rehearsal and the ornate dialectic he designed to support it. Those who needed to rehearse several hours a day, he theorized in 1909, did so only because they had created that need through self-hypnosis; they had convinced themselves of the necessity of practice, and therefore required it. Kreisler, needless to say, held no such convictions, having mesmerized himself to believe the opposite. "I have hypnotized myself into the belief that I do not need [practice]," he said, tongue only partly in cheek, "and therefore I do not."[8]

Such an approach may seem (and in fact may be) little more than an exercise in wild rationalization, but rationalized or not, he followed it religiously. Explaining that he had not taken his violin out of its case once during an eight-week period "except to clean it," Kreisler told Richard Matthews Hallet in late 1940, "If I played too frequently, I should rub the bloom off the musical imagination. I should drag my melodies like shackles. I prefer to be always thrilled by my interpretations of great music, and so it is well for me to not be always fiddling."[9]

He had a deep and abiding faith in his own fingers and their ability to "remember" passages that the central nervous system may have forgotten. In the same interview with Hallet, Kreisler expounded on this subject at considerable length, returning, as usual, to the artistic benefits of keeping the violin in its case for months at a stretch.

> My craftsmanship loses nothing if I stop playing for a summer. It has been too long building. The intricate human

> machinery of playing is governed by a kind of directing ecstasy that takes its rise in the intellect and flies to the fingers. The fingers in time come to have little intellects in their tips perhaps. Certainly, up to a point they can produce their effects of and by themselves. I have known my fingers to run on by themselves for ten or twenty seconds quite correctly while my mind wandered, just as when exhausted by duty as an officer in the Austrian cavalry, I used to fall asleep for seconds at a time and yet keep erect in the saddle and guide my horse.
>
> My fingers are good honest serving-men, but their physical fitness is all I need think of now. As for technique, if I think in a correct way about music, I arrive at technique without moving my fingers. Let them have their vacation. In the fall, they will perhaps feel the impact of the strings a little more harshly, but then every melody will be new again, and the creative impulses will have more bloom.[10]

Furthering this notion of technique as "truly a matter of the brain," Kreisler proffered in *The Way They Play:* "You think of a passage and you know exactly how you want it. It is like the soldier—he doesn't practice before a battle." As ever fascinated by his own little "serving-men," he remarked,

> These are fingers. Nothing. All you have to do is put them in hot water and they are pliable and warm. The great men I knew practiced very little. They thought and thought. Ysaÿe played more beautifully than anyone and yet he let many notes fall on the floor. He thought only of the greatness. How sad it is that in these days the emphasis is on how many hours one practices. When the Elgar concerto was dedicated to me, I never put a finger on the fingerboard. Then, I saw a passage I thought I could improve, and spent six hours on it.[11]

Despite such waxy protestations, Kreisler did not avoid practice simply because he believed it to be unnecessary and detrimental to his art; he avoided it because he was, to put it mildly, lax. His spontaneous genius—and his extraordinary memory—gave him flexibility while performing and allowed him to appear publicly with little or no preparation beyond the previous night's concert, but it did not make for stainless performances. This is, after all, a man whose idea of warming up before a recital was putting his hands in water. If Monday's concert was a rehearsal for Tuesday's concert was a rehearsal for Friday's, there was no guarantee that Friday's and Monday's appearances would be equally brilliant or, in fact, anywhere near the same concert. Kreisler may have believed that freshness was all, that his goal was to surprise himself as well as the audience, and he may indeed have succeeded; but belief and psychology, while related, are not the same thing, and in this case the credo justified the habit. He did not practice because he did not want to practice. It was more than just a philosophy. It was an excuse.

Consider, once again, those "little intellects" hiding out in Kreisler's fingertips. His faith in them was not always justified; sometimes when his mind wandered, his fingers did, too, taking him on frequent and much-celebrated extemporaneous musical rambles. Kreisler lost his place, with regularity, with élan, with the confidence of one who knew that no matter how far afield he wandered he would always, somehow, find his way back. Such were his gifts that once he strayed from the printed page, he used the occasion as an opportunity to improvise in whatever historical and stylistic idioms were demanded by the piece at hand; when performing Mozart, he spun music in the classical style; if the piece was Bach, he imitated baroque. So good, in fact, were these little improvisations that either audience members did not recognize them as such or, if they did (as his colleagues usually were able), they enjoyed and appreciated them as pointed examples of Kreisler's gifts for ad-libbed music-making.

"At a Kreisler concert, three things would happen," violinist David Sackson said. "He would play out of tune, he'd have a memory lapse—and he'd play so gorgeously that you'd forget about everything."[12]

Kreisler "was anything but a perfectionist," said George Neikrug. "The thing is, when he missed something, nobody cared because the whole audience loved him, and they came to get musical thrills from him."[13]

In his book of memoirs titled *Cellist*, Gregor Piatigorsky recalled a "grand musicale" in London during which Piatigorsky was to share the program with Kreisler and singer Grace Moore. "It was good to see Kreisler again," he wrote, "whose inimitable artistry I loved. Even his slight facial tic had a special charm for me." Kreisler "was in bad humor that night," perhaps due to the fact that Harriet was waiting for him back at the hotel. The violinist asked if he could perform first, and the other artists agreed; as a result, Kreisler was the first to step out onto the specially built stage in a large London drawing room.

> There was no printed program. The familiar Kreisler sound caressed my ears until suddenly he had a memory lapse. I was sure that, if the pianist stopped insisting on playing the music in front of him, Kreisler's improvisations would make it into a better piece, but as it is they were muddling along in search of one another. I did not see the audience, but, judging from the applause following the piece, it was an extremely small one. The second piece he played incredibly beautifully, and there was no third. "Harriet is waiting," he murmured, packing his violin.[14]

Piatigorsky did not say who was serving that evening as Kreisler's accompanist, but it probably was not Carl Lamson. Lamson was the most intuitive and longest-tenured of all Kreisler's accompanists, and he had an inborn talent for sticking with Kreisler even when the violinist took the most unexpected turns. "He looked like an undertaker, you know," Oscar Shumsky said of Lamson. "He was one of the best and coolest accompanists that I can remember. He followed Kreisler like a glove."[15] Most likely the pianist that London evening was another of the skilled musicians who accompanied Kreisler in Britain and Europe.

Another anecdote—this one from roughly the same period and conveyed to the author by Creech Reynolds of Bozeman, Montana—shows just how gifted an improvisational team were Lamson and Kreisler together. This time, the two were appearing at a recital in Rochester, New York, with a program that featured a Mozart sonata. At the beginning of the first movement, Kreisler had a memory lapse; without a break and in no apparent panic, he and Lamson proceeded to improvise the entire development section, seamlessly and in perfect classical style. The two finally returned to the original work at the recapitulation, and none but the most astute of listeners was ever aware of a problem.

(Some observers, Harriet Kreisler included, believed that Lamson had by the end of his association with Kreisler severely overstayed his welcome. Milstein referred to Lamson in his memoirs as an "imperturbable old man" and said Harriet regarded the pianist as phlegmatic, bemoaning the fact that he never seemed to get sick. According to Milstein, Kreisler kept Lamson as his accompanist merely because he did not want to hurt his old friend's feelings. In later years Kreisler apparently became dismissive of Lamson's skills to the point of being rude, even tuning up his fiddle in the middle of the pianist's tuttis. He explained, "Lamson can't hear it anyway!")[16]

So legendary were Kreisler's improvisational skills, and so numerous were the stories that circulated on the subject, that some of the tales were, inevitably, pure inventions. Harold Schonberg, the former critic for *The New York Times*, never personally witnessed one of Kreisler's memory lapses but recalled the following tale:

> One of the famous musical stories said that he [Kreisler] and Rachmaninoff were giving one of their charity concerts in Carnegie Hall, and Kreisler got lost—this was the first movement of the Kreutzer Sonata. And he started to noodle. In the meantime, Rachmaninoff is so amused that his best friend Fritz has lost his place in this piece, that he decides to noodle with him—and of course Rachmaninoff can do anything at the piano. After two minutes of desperate noodling, Kreisler sidles over and says, "Sergei, for God's sake, where am I?" And Rachmaninoff says, "in Carnegie Hall."[17]

Schonberg interviewed Kreisler on the violinist's eighty-fifth birthday, and the resultant article (published in *The New York Times* on 31 January 1960) offered a warm and charming portrait of the great man in his last years. "We got along so well," Schonberg recalled in an interview thirty-five years later, "and he was such a doll, that I asked him, 'What about this story of you and Rachmaninoff?'"

> "What story?" [Kreisler] asked. So I told it to him. And he laughed. He thought it was the funniest thing he'd ever heard. Of course it never happened. Oh, another great story gone to hell!
>
> He said, "First of all, we never played in Carnegie Hall for charity concerts—we played at the Metropolitan Opera. Second of all, I never lost my place in the Kreutzer Sonata!"[18]

Kreisler's ability to mimic the styles of masters past, which allowed him to work such seamless improvisation, is not surprising—how else could he have composed the fakes that so scandalized the music world in 1935? Nor was Kreisler's calm in the face of such memory lapses at all unusual for a man known for his complete lack of performance anxiety. No one was more at ease on stage; Pablo Casals, who suffered terribly and throughout his life from pre-concert nerves, recalled with some wistfulness that Kreisler often spoke of how "at home" he felt on the platform.[19] As one who made his debut in short pants, he could hardly have felt otherwise.

Kreisler's approach to practice, his fluid musical interpretations, and his knack for getting lost meant that his live concerts were mutable phenomena, performances crafted for the audience and himself rather than for the ages. Kreisler recitals were unforgettable but organic, susceptible to the artist's mood and muse and likely to change based on how much he drank with dinner, how inspired he felt by the music at hand, or how recently and under what circumstances he had last spoken with Harriet. "We are subjected, in every performance, to our momentary well-being or disposition," he once told Hope Stoddard.

> We play differently in different halls. Many little things can annoy us. If a lady with a fan fans down in the front seat in another rhythm from my music, it disturbs me. If I hear the echoes of my own playing, it is annoying. There are certain

> halls which affect me adversely and other ones which seem attuned to me. That is why at first I had an aversion to the phonograph. It distorted sound. I could hear the fingernails falling on the strings.[20]

On all occasions Kreisler peppered his concerts with old favorites (his own *Caprice Viennois* or *Liebesfreud*, or a traditional tune like *Londonderry Air*), in later years presenting them not just as encores but fairly stuffing them into the latter half of his programs. He liked to play them, the audience liked to hear them, and he was able to turn them out with little preparation but great panache. This is in strong contrast to Jascha Heifetz, who was loath to perform anything overfamiliar. "Don't you feel that people have heard these enough?" he once snapped at a man who requested Schubert's *Ave Maria* for an encore. "As much as I regret denying your request, it will be a long time before I perform these pieces again."[21] Heifetz's recitals were spectacular and granitic: nothing he produced was ephemeral. Where Kreisler's performances shimmered in the present and then vanished into the past, Heifetz's tilted toward perpetuity.

Kreisler the Mystic told the Applebaums that young violinists should quit fretting over fast tempos and head for the wilderness, "know Nature." Compare those yogi-like utterances with Jascha Heifetz's brass-tack lessons in how to practice, quoted here from the chapter on Heifetz in *The Way They Play:*

> The foundation is the scale. It includes the soundness of each position, and the coordination between the two hands. The scales should be practiced in three- and four- octaves—minor, melodic, harmonic and arpeggios. Of course, I should also like to stress the chromatic scales. Then, also, there are the scales in all types of double stops, in thirds, sixths, octaves, tenths and fingered octaves, in major and the two minors. . . .
>
> If I had a half-hour's time to practice, I would work for twenty minutes on scales in various forms, and on trills. The next ten minutes I would work on pieces, but then I would

> choose the difficult passages only. Once your fingers are in shape, and your right hand is in good form, you can do the pieces as well as your technic and temperament will allow.[22]

Very early on in his career, when the rising young soloist was still a teenager, Heifetz told Frederick H. Martens that he had never been one to over-rehearse. Martens asked Heifetz whether he practiced "six or eight" hours a day, and the violinist replied with a laugh. "No," he said. "I do not think I could ever have made any progress if I had practiced six hours a day. In the first place I have never believed in practicing too much—it is just as bad as practicing too little!" He had never, he said, "believed in grinding"; excessive preparation would show in the execution. Nevertheless, the young Heifetz believed that "to interpret music properly, it is necessary to eliminate mechanical difficulty; the audience should not feel the struggle of the artist with what are considered hard passages."[23]

The advice Heifetz gave in his later years, through example and pedagogy, implied an extremely grueling routine. Even in his youthful interview with Martens, he mused:

> Of course, you must not take me too literally. Please do not think because I do not favor overdoing practicing that one can do without it. I'm quite frank to say I could not myself. But there is a happy medium. I suppose that when I play in public it looks easy, but before I ever came on the concert stage I worked very hard. . . . Have I what is called a "natural" technic? It is hard for me to say, perhaps so. But if such is the case I had to develop it, to assure it, to perfect it. If you start playing at three, as I did, with a little violin one-quarter of the regular size, I suppose violin playing becomes second nature in the course of time.[24]

Heifetz's conversations with Samuel and Sada Applebaum decades later reinforced his view of the primacy of technique. Much as Kreisler bemoaned the new generation's preoccupation with technique and speed, Heifetz worried that students were too "concerto-conscious," trying "to reach artistic status before one is ready, and without the proper background." With this "absolutely incorrect attitude," he admonished, "the technical structure will eventually crumble."[25] Heifetz felt pupils would be well-advised to focus their energies on the trill, practicing this technical building-block with different fingers, positions, and intervals. It was on such exercises that his own extraordinary technique was based. All violinists, he believed, should work in a similar manner. All should work that hard.

Many did—and do. The imitability of Heifetz's playing, the extent to which it could be reduced to its mechanical parts and reproduced, meant that Heifetz influenced and indirectly continues to influence more young musicians than any other performer of this century. Heifetz presented a blueprint for playing that was exhaustive and nearly impossible to realize, but that blueprint promised faultless artistry of a certain type to the student who followed it faithfully to completion. Just as early twentieth-century violinists tried to imitate Kreisler's vibrato, middle- and late-twentieth century aspirants to solo careers used and still use Heifetz as the technical standard *ne plus ultra*. His perfection was seductive, for it was fathomable, concrete, and tantalizingly within reach—like the sculpted physique of a body builder. Follow this regimen, it seemed to say, and you, too, can play like a winner.

The irony in this implication and indeed in Heifetz's legacy is that the essence of his true musical gift—a light-footed phrasing, reserved but always lyrical—was in fact impossible to duplicate. There is cause to be skeptical of any technical innovation inspired by a single virtuoso, simply because exclusivity resists cloning: one or two aspects of a player's technique cannot be reproduced a thousand-fold and stay rooted in the complex musicianship that bore it. Readers will recall Hans Keller's extremely critical assessment of Kreisler's vibrato and its faddish duplication among less talented violinists (presented in Chapter 3 of this book); Flesch's criticism of Heifetz, and of the quest for digital perfection in general, is similar in nature. As he wrote in *The Art of Violin Playing:*

> The false pride of immaculate perfection . . . leads to exaggeratedly meticulous technical studies, which it would be possible to conquer only in practice hours *extended to an exaggerated degree*—while neglecting the spiritual values of the whole. In such cases, absolute mechanization in the shape of gymnastic activity with musical accompaniment

> soon results; while at the same time the final goal can never be reached, because actual infallibility is impossible. In addition, experience has taught us that the highest degree of precision, such as possessed by a Heifetz, is far more due to extraordinary talent than to conscientious toil.[26] [Italics are his.]

Flesch carries this notion further in his memoirs, in which he characterizes Heifetz's superlative technique as "a gift from heaven" bestowed upon him in childhood rather than as the fruit of intensive labor. More specifically:

> The absolute infallibility of his technical apparatus is his worst enemy, because it promotes a certain emotional inertia. As a violinist he invariably is ready for everything, inwardly he isn't. . . . People would forgive Heifetz his technical infallibility only if he made them forget it by putting his personality behind it. He is a living example of the relativity of a virtue which, when it overshadows something more essential, may come to be felt as a defect.[27]

(Flesch also criticizes Heifetz for the accelerating tempos noted earlier by Kreisler. "Since Heifetz's appearance," he wrote, "young fiddlers are possessed by the devil of speed and are trying to establish records.")

Heifetz may indeed have practiced only three hours a day, but mere mortals who aspired to the same technical impeccability were compelled to work considerably harder. He raised the bar; to reach it required, for most violinists, just the sort of over-practice against which Heifetz himself had admonished. Six to eight hours of practice per day may have seemed excessive in 1919, but among today's performers it is the norm. Zeal continues to push most young violinists toward an ever-more stringent work ethic. All but forgotten are Fritz Kreisler's dusty old warnings against the evils of over-rehearsal and the perils of overemphasizing technical skills.

In retrospect, neither Kreisler nor Heifetz had any business telling other violinists—particularly the young and the earnest—how to play their instrument. Each was a musician of such unusual, unique, and inherent gifts that no method of preparation or style of playing could be fully or fairly translated into a comprehensible grammar, and crucial elements of their artistry were invariably left out. It was unfair of Kreisler to advocate limited practice and extended "vacations" from the violin. Kreisler, a veritable guru of sloth, lectured windily on the horrors of over-rehearsing to colleagues, journalists, and anyone else in need of persuasion, yet few if any other performers possess the gifts of spontaneity and mnemonic brawn that allowed Kreisler to stroll unrehearsed onto the concert stage. Those who do (Kreisler included) generally benefit from the work they did as youths. It was likewise unfair of Heifetz to stress the acquisition of technique first, artistic ambition second, for few boasted either Heifetz's innate technical gift or his cool-headed but graceful musicality. The path each man took to pre-eminence could have led to a dead-end or a disaster for a musician of lesser talents.

Wrote Flesch:

> This blind admiration of an alien personality, on the aspirant's part, in many cases has resulted in a loss of his own. To remain true to one's self, to recognize the limitations of one's own nature set up by creation itself, is the secret of a healthy and continuous artistic development. . . . This hopeless chase of a chimaera leads them away from the attainable, and hence forms a danger for artistic development not to be underestimated. The gradual realization that a goal which might have been reached has been sacrificed for a deceitful illusion, is calculated permanently to embitter the spirit, and to rob life and art of all their joy.[28]

Kreisler himself alluded to the inadvisability of using one artist as a model for many others:

> Nobody can write a book for anybody else. We are all mentally subjective. We can't fit other cases. Joachim—I knew him, you know—was looked on as a high priest. He had very long hands. He even had to adjust the fingerboard —so long were his hands. He was an exception, but he

> taught every one of his pupils as though their problems were the same. Me—I have short hands. My problem was entirely different.[29]

How revealing, then, to consider one of the most concrete differences between the two violinists and their disparate legacies: Heifetz had regular pupils, and Kreisler had none. One-on-one and in celebrated master classes, Heifetz instructed many students in the art of the violin, giving them the sort of practical advice that he described in *The Way They Play*. Those in his tutelage sometimes spent months perfecting scales and other purely technical exercises; they were barred from graduating to major works until they had thoroughly mastered the basics. Once they had, Heifetz honed them as he honed himself—demanding the same musical conservatism, the same attention to detail, that he demanded of his own performances. In this manner his coaching produced numerous accomplished professionals—Eugene Fodor and Erick Friedman, among others—but, curiously for the world's greatest violinist, no genuine and enduring superstars. Though many succeeded, none shone as brightly or as long as their teacher.

Why not? Heifetz's pedagogical approach may have been one reason; conceivably, his heavy emphasis on the mechanics of playing may have quashed more daring musical impulses. Perhaps his influence was too strong, his profile too looming. As Richard Dyer wrote, Heifetz "was probably too intimidating a figure, and overpowering an example, to be a successful teacher."[30] For whatever reason, the end result of Heifetz's instruction was a corps of violinists groomed to play as their maestro taught, not as dictated by their own strengths, weaknesses, and interests.

Yet Heifetz was arguably the century's most influential pedagogue. Besides his many private students and his now-legendary master classes at the University of Southern California, he heard many other young musicians who, through their own wit or with help from a friend with pull, played for him in search of encouragement, advice, or both. He was not talkative during such sessions. He was polite but impassive, contributing a comment here, a comment there, and, if he was suitably impressed, offering to take on the violinist as a regular student.

One such violinist was Jeanne Mitchell, a young performer who played for Heifetz in the mid-forties, some time after she had given her New York City debut. The meeting was arranged by a business friend of Heifetz's who had been alerted to Mitchell's talent by an acquaintance at Carnegie Hall. "I went to the Hotel Pierre, and Heifetz was very, very gentlemanly—he was really generous, as a matter of fact. He gave me a lot of time." She played a Schubert sonata and—as a gesture to Heifetz's justly famous recording—the Prokofiev Concerto in G Minor. She hoped he would contribute a few useful insights.

"I thought I could learn something," said Mitchell, who admired and emulated Kreisler. "But all he did was point to one place [in the Prokofiev] and say, 'Why do you use that fingering?' I said, 'Well, I thought it sounded good, but shouldn't I?' Heifetz shrugged. He said nothing else about the Prokofiev, and nothing at all about the Schubert."

> In the middle of this his new wife came in, and she put a damp cloth against my head. . . . I thought, what is this jane doing here?—and thanked her, and he introduced her, and everybody was very nice. But I got the realization that she fully expected me to be fainting dead away.

Mitchell did not faint, however. "I wasn't even scared," she recalled, "because he wasn't the be all and end all for me." When the session was over, Heifetz asked her whether she planned to attend his concert that evening, and urged her to practice ("You must practice a lot to get ahead"). Then he invited her to be his pupil.[31]

Much to Heifetz's surprise, she turned him down. She was not tempted, she said, "out of the opinion I had of what he had to offer, of what I heard when he played. There was nothing in our meeting that suggested that he would be any influence for the good in my playing. . . . If he had had something to say, I think I would have been tempted." As it turned out, however, "If he had put me through that nonmusical regime, I think he would have killed me."

> [Heifetz] didn't have a clue about the other side of music. He had an angelic sound when he did things like, especially, Mozart. He had an angelic sound because he did it correctly

> and he didn't infuse it with any nonsense. But I believe it was his early training that gave him that technique and put him in a bind. . . . He wasn't made of glass, [but] he played like it.[32]

Another aspect of Heifetz's enduring legacy has been the increasing emphasis on competitions as a route to success—and it provides yet another revealing difference in outlook between the two violinists. Kreisler had no success in competitions and (perhaps because of this) was adamantly, philosophically opposed to them. The more sensitive the talent, he believed, the likelier it will fail in competition. Clearly regarding himself as one such artist repelled by the harshness and homogeneity of competitions, he told Joseph Fuchs that he gave them up as a youth because he found it impossible to play well under such artificial conditions. Fuchs recalled Kreisler's words:

> How can you play in a dark hall, with seven people sitting there with yellow pads? You don't play something quite the way you should play it, and somebody puts a mark down. And these marks go down, and you get worried that somebody standing in the wings is waiting to cut your throat.[33]

However disparate their philosophies, Heifetz and Kreisler were not adversaries. The two were cordial and mutually admiring colleagues (at least in print and in public), and Heifetz once confessed that in his youth he did his best to imitate the older man. "Heifetz once said nobody can play like Kreisler, and Kreisler said nobody can play like Heifetz," said Fuchs, who knew both Heifetz and Kreisler. When Fuchs asked Heifetz why he never played Kreisler's *Caprice Viennois*, Heifetz's reply, according to Fuchs, was that "nobody could play it the way the composer plays it. He said, 'I won't touch it.' He had great respect for Kreisler."[34]

If Kreisler had any complaints about his colleague's playing, he did not voice them. The closest he came to criticizing Heifetz was during a 1955 interview for *International Musician*, when he remarked:

> Heifetz brought the most perfect violin technique to his early violin playing. But clinically perfect technique and musicality

> of the inner thing are different. Now Heifetz has gone tremendously ahead. He is not only the head of the technical department, but he is also among those at the top in musicality.[35]

Clearly, Kreisler recognized the differences between himself and Heifetz, sensing in the younger man a technical proficiency that none could match. "Well, gentlemen," he addressed a group of violinists who had just heard the *Wunderkind* play in Berlin, "shall we all now break our violins across our knees?"[36] Franz Rupp recalled a 1935 recording session in London, when Kreisler kept muffing one particularly difficult passage in a Beethoven sonata. He barked, "Get Jascha Heifetz." When Rupp pointed out that Mischa Elman was performing across the English Channel in France and might be more readily available, Kreisler responded, "Franz, we need technique, not tone."[37]

Kreisler knew as well as anyone the flaws in his own performing; he knew, but he did not dwell on them or attempt to remedy them with hours upon hours of practice. Instead he danced around them, retooling pieces to favor his strongest fingers, reworking a bowing to find an easier or more mellifluous approach to a tough passage. He knew that others had greater technique. He knew, as everyone knew, that none was greater than Heifetz's.

The accolades from fellow violinists and musicians flowed freely in eulogies commemorating Heifetz after his death. "Jascha Heifetz was and will remain Number One of violin players," commented Erich Leinsdorf in *The New York Times*. "There is no other branch of music in which one person is as clearly recognized as being nonpareil." Itzhak Perlman added: "Nobody played like him—the strength and the force. His playing had the quality that sizzled and he had such color. He revolutionized violin playing to where it wishes to go today. None of us mortals are going to be able to reach his standard." "We're all children compared to him," Glenn Dicterow, concertmaster of the New York Philharmonic, said. "He never had any competition but himself."[38] In 1987 *The Strad* devoted an issue to Heifetz (much as it had to Kreisler that same year), calling him "the most important violinistic influence of this century." Its pages were filled with laudatory comments from all manner of violinists—including Perlman, who named Heifetz "the king of violinists," and

Isaac Stern, who said, "There has been no player of the violin or any stringed instrument in the last fifty or sixty years who hasn't in some way been affected by the way he played."[39]

Stern was right, of course; for violinists and other string players in this century, Heifetz's influence has been impossible to escape. It was simply too powerful to ignore. Yet many instrumentalists have acknowledged Heifetz's impact while simultaneously recognizing its complex implications for musicianship and the striking contrast it represents with the century's other enormous influence, Kreisler.

Sir Yehudi Menuhin recalled his own boyhood reactions to hearing Heifetz and Kreisler perform. When he heard Heifetz perform, "I was amazed and impressed . . . but I felt all that was within my reach." With Kreisler, "I heard something which was beyond my reach."

> It's like a simple peasant boy, perhaps a provincial boy, who [meets] a person of extreme culture and sophistication who knows society, different kinds of people—who knows the incredible elegance of a distant world. . . . [The boy is] wide-eyed because he doesn't know the first thing about women, doesn't know the first thing about elegance, has never seen the refinement of a society in which the feminine is brought to its peak of entrancing artificiality—is brought to its highest level of artificial refinements. . . .
>
> This was a picture of Vienna, of a distant world, that I knew nothing about at the time.[40]

As a child, Menuhin was able to perform the most virtuosic showpieces in the repertoire. Yet Kreisler's works eluded him.

> To shape *Schön Rosmarin*, to shape those pieces took me—I was twenty before I could do that. And even before I recorded it, I listened and listened and listened to try to catch that combination of twisted rhythm, of elegance, of teasing, of wistfulness, of nostalgia, of carefree. It's a kind of abandonment of the spirit.

When he first heard the piece in his youth, "You can imagine how it struck me. It was something I knew I would never get."[41]

Even more robust in his opinion was Oscar Shumsky, among the last of contemporary violinists whose obvious influences include Fritz Kreisler. Kreisler is evident in Shumsky's tone, his vibrato, his phrasing, and in the emotional intensity of his performances, which balance technical proficiency with a musical gutsiness that can make other performers seem spiritless by comparison. He has been a public and passionately articulate opponent of the tendency among contemporary musicians to sacrifice music-making for the sake and the safety of technique. Those who live and play in fear of errors will make few mistakes but little art. And those who make technical mastery paramount can damage the listener's ability—even desire—to look through a performance to the music at its core.

Heifetz, said Shumsky, had a "chromium plating of sheer ability to get around the instrument."

> You went to hear him in the same sense that you went to hear Houdini, because he'd be pulling rabbits out of the fiddle, doing extraordinary things. You had to admire him for that, and you had to also respect [him as a] very sincere musician and a very caring musician. . . . But he was Heifetz.[42]

As such, Heifetz made it difficult for other violinists to pursue their craft. In contrast to Kreisler's "invitation" to participate in his playing, "Heifetz was discouraging because he made the other violinists despair at what can be accomplished on the instrument," Shumsky said. "Kreisler made you think, 'What a wonderful instrument this is, and what a joy it is to play it.' . . . It wasn't, 'Here I am, look at what I can do.'"[43] (Or, in the words of Josef Gingold: "When you came away from a Heifetz concert, your hair stood on end. When you heard Kreisler, he made you want to dance.")[44]

Shumsky continued:

> With Kreisler, the memory of the way he would play a Franck sonata or a Brahms sonata, the way he would play that would remain with me—and, in fact, has remained with me over the years. I still recall it. I recall the way he played the *Praeludium and Allegro*. I remember the slides that he

> used, the sounds that he produced when he played it. It remains with me.
>
> With Heifetz, somehow, even when I think back to it, I think how amazingly that man played the violin, and I still hear that steely sound, the unwavering onslaught. Heifetz was thrilling, it was exciting, but I don't want to remember it so much.[45]

Was Heifetz the century's greatest violinist? "Well, why not?" said Shumsky. "That title still fits him." Kreisler, on the other hand, "was one of the greatest musicians."

"I think Heifetz," Shumsky continued, "was a destructive influence in a very great sense."

Destructive? Perhaps—if, as Shumsky and others believe, violin artistry has focused more on the "chromium plating" of technique and less on the core metals of musical expression. Heifetz's influence in this regard is undeniable.

When George Bernard Shaw first heard Jascha Heifetz play, he was so struck by his ability that he sent the young man a letter. "If you provoke a jealous God by playing with such superhuman perfection, you will die young," he admonished. "I earnestly advise you to play something badly every night before going to bed, instead of saying your prayers. No mortal should presume to play so faultlessly."[46]

Presumptuous or not, Jascha Heifetz played without error. Countless violinists since have attempted the same feat, with varying but always limited success. Perhaps that is why Heifetz remains a figure of such enduring prominence—he reached a summit that has proved stubbornly out of reach for everyone else—and perhaps, too, that is why Kreisler's profile has faded from modern memory. Kreisler never aimed for perfection; that was never one of his goals. He aimed for a different ideal, a less definable ideal, which he could not articulate in words and could only barely articulate in music. As he stated in the 1955 WQXR radio interview:

> As a composer, my position is a very humble one. As a performer, it may be better, but even there I am in great trouble. When I am judging other artists, it's easy for me, because I

> judge them by the standards, the present standards—by the beauty of their tone, by their musicality and their technical achievements. With me it's different. When I play, I always try to achieve a certain ideal—and I have never been able to achieve it. When I came near it, and when I had advanced in age—well, the ideal had progressed too, so that I came never near it.[47]

Where, in that ideal, is Kreisler's legacy? Where is Heifetz's? Heifetz and Kreisler were different performers, and as such they left remarkably different legacies. For the most part, Heifetz's is easier to track; the lessons he taught were obvious, the effects they had enduring. Every musician who spends the first two hours of a six-hour practice on nothing but scales is a tribute to Heifetz and evidence of the effect he has had on modern performing. Kreisler's influence, while equally significant, was by its very nature intangible, as mutable and mysterious as a line of verse.

The gulf between the two violinists, wide when they were alive and performing, has only widened further over the decades. Kreisler's style of playing—his technique, his philosophy, his execution, and his approach to the violin—seems ever more removed from the contemporary ethos, while Heifetz's seems ever more timely. To many, Heifetz remains the apogee of violin artistry, raising everyone's expectations of what can and should be done with the instrument; no longer excusable are errors in intonation, tone, memory, phrasing. Professional violinists are more proficient now than at any other time in history. What Heifetz accomplished on the violin no one has accomplished since.

As Shumsky, Flesch, and others have already articulated, there may be a downside to this legacy. Heifetz's perfection and mastery of technique (combined with advances in digital recording technology, as will be examined in Chapter 12) have resulted in a certain reluctance among many contemporary performers to take stylistic and emotional risks in their playing, to sweeten a phrase or add a slide or put a little more verve in the bow arm, for fear of making some unforgivable error. Despite the success of a handful of young instrumentalists who, while maintaining a high level of technical proficiency, are carefully inserting unexpected or unorthodox elements into their own playing (Joshua Bell and Nigel Kennedy spring to mind, as does the fiddle virtuoso Mark O'Connor), most contemporary violinists are unwilling or unable to throw every last nickel into the pot. Nor do modern standards require them to. For today, after decades of undeniable progress made in the technical aspects of performance and reproduction, the standard for violin artistry is a stainless technique informed and enlivened by carefully studied, exquisitely judicious musical ideas. In this regard, Jascha Heifetz remains the paragon against which all other violinists are measured.

What of Kreisler? Is he completely irrelevant? To some he is. To others, including many among the ranks of older-generation violinists, Fritz Kreisler was and is the most relevant of all string players, a stirring musical voice who was able to communicate with his listeners as no one else could. For such players, certain Kreislerian touches, be they oversweet glissandos or exaggerated holdbacks or an elastic but disciplined rubato, have less to do with "schmaltz" than with the frank emotionalism of a long-gone era, a time when high emotion was not regarded as low-brow. It is an emotionalism that is heard rarely in the contemporary concert circuit, having disappeared into the musical netherworld along with gramophones and improvised cadenzas. Sentiment is out of style.

Kreisler was a sentimental violinist. As such he was—despite Flesch's belief that he was the first who captured the era's zeitgeist, and despite the fact that he was demonstrably ahead of his time—the least modern of twentieth-century musicians. His interpretations of Bach, Beethoven, and other baroque and classical masters were relatively conservative, free from most romantic flourishes or any other ornamentation that might strike the modern ear as overdone. In that regard they "travel" better than some of his Viennese pieces, whose shifts and swells can sound dated when incorrectly or exaggeratedly played. No contemporary violinist can render *Caprice Viennois* with Kreisler's spark, no one can perform the *Londonderry Air* or *Old Folks at Home* with his charged musical conviction, no one can treat his graceful little melodies with such earnest and learned persuasion. No one, in other words, is as unafraid of affect.

To modern audiences reared on the stern musicianship of Jascha Heifetz and his disciples, the individual voice of Fritz Kreisler might seem brazen, imprudent, even embarrassing in its candor. There are those, Eric Wen among them, who believe that the violinist's artistry (rather than his musicianship) may one day overcome its perceived obsolescence to become, once again, a model for aspiring musicians; it is possible, considering the cyclical nature of musical tastes and the mounting interest in historical recordings, that audiences may someday clamor for vintage romanticism much as they sparked the explosion in baroque and classical performance, which has only lately begun to subside. "If you believe that there's good music and bad music, if you believe in the absolute standards of art—which I do—Kreisler is absolutely good and honest," said Wen. "At some point—this is more of a plea than anything concrete—I think we may come back to that."[48]

If so, the return may be a long way off. Undeniably, unsurprisingly, Heifetz still reigns among the current generation of violinists, influencing them directly via his own recordings and indirectly via the many older performers and pedagogues who matured artistically when Heifetz was at his peak. Thanks to his seductive technique, his fast tempos, and a performing career that lasted well into the latter half of this century, he remains a figure of enduring and daunting sway.

Whether Kreisler has anything similar to offer youthful instrumentalists is open to debate. Were violinists willing to learn, his sixty-, seventy-, and eighty-year-old recordings might have something to teach—about the subtleties of violin artistry, the mysticism and main force of a performer's connection with his audience. Such lessons are there to be learned, said David Sackson, "if [violinists] had the sense to know what to listen for. Heifetz was dazzling, but Kreisler was fascinating. He produced a sound that no one could quite match. . . . No one touched the soul as he did."[49]

Perhaps Oscar Shumsky was correct—perhaps Heifetz was the century's greatest *violinist*, and perhaps Kreisler was its greatest *musician*. Kreisler knew that Heifetz had the better technique. Heifetz admired Kreisler's intimate, intuitive artistry. Yet Kreisler's technique throughout his first fifty years of performing was reliable, and Heifetz was capable of deep, if relatively taciturn, musical interpretation. They were different men, with different priorities.

Although any attempt to contrast Kreisler and Heifetz might seem misguided, mistaken, even wrong (as Fuchs complained, "I think comparisons are odious with great artists. . . . How can you compare Picasso with Matisse? You don't compare. They both had their own way"[50]), comparisons are relevant simply because the two represented such stunningly opposite approaches to violin playing, yielding similarly opposite effects on performance practices. It is worth asking, eleven years after Heifetz's death and thirty-six after Kreisler's, whether classical performance has benefited from its obsession with technique, whether Jascha Heifetz remains a realistic and desirable role model, whether Fritz Kreisler's romantic mysticism has anything to offer the cold, clean world of late-twentieth-century performance practice. As the twenty-first century approaches, it is hard to fathom what will come next—even more dazzling performers? Younger ones? Faster ones? Everyone knows what perfection sounds like; it sounds like Heifetz. The next great soloist will move beyond perfection to visit its far-flung neighbor, an alluring but elusive destination called beauty.

Eleven

"He Was Our God"

Stunned by the brilliance of Heifetz's technique, many young musicians of the late twentieth century are oblivious to the significance and subtleties of Kreisler's genius. Yet few performers before or since were able to evoke the kind of devotion that Kreisler did from audiences, critics, and, perhaps most notably, from colleagues. String players revered Fritz Kreisler. Even many whose style of playing was opposite his regarded Kreisler as the century's greatest instrumentalist, the rare performer whose popular and critical acclaim was matched unequivocally by his colleagues' professional regard; as Harold Schonberg observed in 1985, "the man had no enemies."[1] Everyone acknowledged his shortcomings, but they were accepted as quirks rather than scorned as flaws, much as a loved one's eccentricity is tolerated, forgiven, and to a certain degree cherished. Such was the depth of Kreisler's musicianship and the long reach of his appeal that even technical errors could not mar the nobility of his intent or the humanity in his execution. Whatever he played was musical and unassailably sincere.

None knew this better than his fellow violinists. The violin is an unforgiving instrument, difficult to master and grating, even ugly, if not handled with the proper combination of delicacy and strength. A tense neck, an awkward left hand, too much or too little pressure on the bow, and the most glistening of instruments can sound as mellifluous as a buzz saw. In Kreisler's hands the fiddle sang. No matter what imperfections the demanding listener could discern in a Kreisler recital, everything on the program—even if it did not always follow the score—was performed with unerring grace. Few played the violin with such understanding of its poetry. For that and further reasons, some easier to articulate than others, Kreisler was probably the most beloved soloist *among* soloists of his generation and one or two beyond. In the words of violist Harold Coletta, "He captivated everyone."[2] Or, as David Sackson said, "He was our God."[3]

On one level, this makes perfect sense: Kreisler was a charming man who played the fiddle charmingly and thus charmed entire populations of listeners, colleagues included. But the affection heaped upon him went beyond simple infatuation and points to more deeply rooted causes, a few of which might fall under the general category of blind idolatry. At the very least, such Kreisler adulation belied the younger violinists whose technical equipment was greater than the older man's and who seemed, particularly during the forties, in a position to wipe him off the stage. They could and they did—eventually. But even after Kreisler retired, he was still held in awe by his colleagues and regarded by many as the pinnacle of string artistry.

Why Kreisler was so highly esteemed for so long by so many of his colleagues can be attributed to a number of factors, some of them musical, others psychological. As a complex cultural phenomenon, Kreisler's iconic allure cannot be dissected completely. At the risk of attempting to explicate the inexplicable, his appeal might be broken down into several main considerations.

He represented quiet but groundbreaking changes in violin artistry

The first to play with a full, quick, continuous vibrato, the first to emphasize intimate emotion over ballistic virtuosity, the first to draw from the instrument an eerily human voice, Kreisler made advances in violin musicianship that remain unmatched by any violinist since, even Jascha Heifetz. That Kreisler's role in such advances has been more or less forgotten among the listening public does not lessen its significance, nor does it preclude the possibility of future recognition. It simply means that Kreisler furthered the art of the violin in subtle but significant ways that do not scream for attention but were then, and to a lesser extent are still, valued by those who make their living and their lives from the instrument. The foundation of modern string playing rests on ground that was broken by Kreisler. Those who knew what they were standing on admired and indeed cherished him.

As was discussed in Chapter 3, Carl Flesch believed that Kreisler's style of playing prefigured and ultimately reflected the twentieth-century psyche. Certainly he was the first, and arguably the only, nineteenth-century violinist to greet the new era on its own terms; even Eugène Ysaÿe, who made undeniable advances toward modern playing and continued his career into the 1920s, seemed always the last of the old guard rather than the first of the new. Ysaÿe's name fell naturally with those of Sarasate, Joachim, Wilhelmj. Kreisler retained his rootedness in the nineteenth century but he was not permanently fixed there—perhaps because of his early failures and the fact that he did not succeed in any quantifiable measure until long past the turn of the century. He found success in the modern world; he was the first wholly modern violinist.

Kreisler was thus revered by those who followed him, particularly the two or three generations of young soloists who heard in his manifest but oddly ambiguous charms a perfect exemplar. Despite his Old World grace and carriage, he was not—not for this first wave of followers—an anachronism or nostalgia act. He was instead the first and clearest harbinger of change.

He never publicly criticized another violinist

Despite his (often public) misgivings about contemporary performance in general, Kreisler had only admiring words for the instrumentalists he mentioned by name. If, in private conversation, he expressed reservations about one or another violinist's abilities, he did so in confidence and swore his listener to secrecy. Specific criticisms have, as a result, never made it to print.

Josef Gingold declined to name the violinists that Kreisler admitted to finding distasteful; so did Sam Kissel. Kissel recalled a revealing lunchtime chat (circa 1951) at Del Pezzo's in Manhattan.

> We spoke about current artists. The ones that he liked were Francescatti and Milstein. They both adored Kreisler; he liked them. Then he spoke about the newer ones, and he said he was disappointed. He said, "I don't know what's happened. Sonority is not very rich on the violin any more. I don't know what's happened. The sound isn't right."[4]

Whatever Kreisler's misgivings about other soloists, he kept them to himself.

He was flawed

Fritz Kreisler was nearly as well-known for his fallibility as he was for his genius. Less perfect and hence less daunting than other violinists, he conveyed to musicians and to the world at large the idea that even the greatest artistry could be reassuringly, undeniably human—that no matter how beautiful the sounds he made, they were produced by an imperfect being. He could drop a few notes, slip in intonation, fumble for the first half hour, or suffer a huge memory lapse; none of that detracted from his appeal, for all of it indicated a rather comforting capacity for failure. If Kreisler was admired by fellow violinists, it was in part because he seemed so unfailingly mortal. If I can do it, his music seemed to promise, so can you.

As a result, Kreisler's gifts rarely aroused ungenerous or jealous feelings. Unlike Heifetz, who gave other violinists cause for considerable angst, Kreisler was able to achieve widespread popularity and critical acclaim without terrifying—hence alienating—his colleagues. He was as unthreatening as he was important, a man whose greatest gifts were small in scale: an intimate tone, a lively personality, an even vibrato, a keen sense of rhythm and rubato. Onstage as well as off, Kreisler was approachable. His avuncular geniality blunted any edge he might have had, any threat he might have posed, any challenge he might have presented to the ranks of other violinists awaiting their chance in the spotlight.

That Kreisler liked to eat and gamble and talk and drink, and often did so while his wife was looking the other way, gave his colleagues (particularly the male variety) further reason to regard him as an accessible, "regular guy." He had vices, he made mistakes, and he looked like an absent-minded professor from the old country: he could not have seemed more human.

He bucked conventions

In addition to being old-fashioned, well-mannered, and flawed, Fritz Kreisler was also extremely unorthodox. His playing and his behavior suggested a man unfettered by expectations; he did not practice, did not warm up before playing, did not loosen his bow afterward, did not suffer from stage fright, did not care about money (beyond gambling and book-purchasing), did not belong to any specific school of playing (despite frequent attempts by others to link him with the French school), did not fret over missed notes or historical inaccuracies, did not have regular students, and did not seem to care all that much about his career in general. He simply felt no compulsion to follow the crowd, allowing himself a laxness in preparation and nonconformity in expression that intrigued and bewildered his colleagues.

He performed his own music, emphasizing his own strengths and de-emphasizing his weaknesses

From the very beginning, Kreisler's career (and, later, his celebrity) relied heavily on his own compositions. Notwithstanding his professed motives for writing the faux classical manuscripts, Kreisler ensured, in composing much of the works on his early programs, that listeners would hear exactly the type of music that he performed best. He wrote pieces that fell naturally in his hands, de-emphasizing persistent physical deficiencies (his weak fourth finger, for instance, or his short bow arm) and emphasizing instead the double stops, robust bowings, and first- and second-finger shifts that became such manifestly identifiable aspects of his playing. Whatever flaws he or anyone else perceived were not obvious when he played his own short works, for the works were designed (consciously or unconsciously) to show off his strengths: tone, articulation, rhythm, vibrato.

And melody. Kreisler's fondness for the simple but eloquent melody never left him and served him well throughout his professional life, appealing to audiences on the most elemental levels. His gift in this regard was at once creative and communicative—he could write glorious melodies, and he could realize them *in performance* with such simple persuasion that even the most cynical observers were inevitably won over. Kreisler's melodies charmed, cajoled, seduced. They made his popular image and, in so doing, made his career.

Similarly, Kreisler's great rhythmic ability was never more apparent, or more peerless, than it was in performances of his own music. Other musicians knew this about Kreisler, and they admired him for it. Said Oscar Shumsky:

> No one had a more perfect sense of rhythm. He was just so magnificently attuned to the basic rhythms, to the basic pulse. You just couldn't lose him. . . . I know that Stokowski, for one, found Kreisler very easy to follow. He felt the music in such a way that you knew the music was coming around the corner.[5]

When Kreisler played his own works, his musicianship was unreachable—no one could play the same music and attain the same heights. None realized this better than his colleagues, who performed his celebrated miniatures with humility and respect for the composer.

He played without narcissism

Many who were familiar with Kreisler's playing have said he treated the violin as though it were an extension of himself. More correctly, he treated the instrument as though he and it were equals, partners in the effort to make music devoid of pretension. By no means an absence of personality or ego—Kreisler's playing was marked by a powerful individualism (discussed below)—this lack of bombast implied a purity of intent that is sought and deeply valued by performers of every instrument, and it accounts in large measure for his popularity among colleagues. Surprisingly for a man who made his life appearing in public, he performed without vanity; he somehow managed to render interpretations of great beauty and originality without ever fully taking credit for them. The man was subordinate to the music, the player to the played, as though the concerts Kreisler presented were exercises in discovery rather than creation.

From this sprang the spontaneity that characterized his live performances and many of his recordings, as well as his reluctant attitude toward preparation. If the music is beyond a musician's control—if the musician is merely a conduit, a means of conveyance and communication—then why be a slave to rehearsal? Why, if rehearsing emphasizes the mechanical, the tangible, the technical aspects of performance? Does that serve or subordinate the music? Perhaps the musician who chooses spontaneity over practice is making the music paramount, emphasizing it over his own vainglory. (On the other hand, perhaps the musician is being lazy.)

Whatever the reasons or ramifications, the fact remains that Kreisler's playing always retained an innocent quality, a sense that the music delighted and surprised him even as he played it. He was the holy fool of violinists.

His style of playing was unique

No other violinist played like Kreisler. Many emulated, even imitated him, some with limited success, but none could match the combination of Viennese worldliness and naiveté that characterized his playing and his mien. Nor could anyone else in an era skeptical of overt emotionalism perform the exaggerated shifts, muscular attacks, and other unabashedly romantic flourishes that Kreisler used so often and to such great effect throughout his career. When he moved from a D down to an E on the D-string in *Liebesleid*, the resulting shift was clear, rhythmically focused, and settled with a decisive *snap* on the lower note; similar shifts helped shape renditions of his own works and the works of others, adding further relief to an already hilly musical landscape. Kreisler piled on the gestures and earned praise for it. Anyone who tried the same risked sounding false, self-centered, anachronistic, or all three.

"A great many people attempted to imitate that style of playing in Kreisler's own works—but it could never work," said Michael Tree, the longstanding violist with the Guarneri Quartet. "No one could ever approach it."[6]

Naturally, a lot of people tried. Certain aspects and ornaments of Kreisler's playing could indeed be copied, inspiring large- and small-scale mimicry among performers of varying competency. But because the essence of Kreisler's playing was so dependent upon *non*-musical factors—his Viennese upbringing, his rootedness in the rhythms of Austrian dance, his cosmopolitanism, his warmth of personality, his otherworldly idealism, even his emphatic disinterest in the practical aspect of his own career—those attempts to duplicate the musical tools of his style invariably fell short. Kreisler's playing was an extension and expression of his own distinct personality. For that alone, he was inimitable.

Oscar Shumsky, one in the wave of prodigies who swept the United States in the 1920s, recalled playing for Kreisler at the Park Avenue home of Ernest Schelling circa 1925. Shumsky was eight years old, and (like Yehudi Menuhin) he idolized the Austrian violinist. As Shumsky stated in a 1992 interview:

> It happened at that time that I had heard Kreisler play in Philadelphia with the [Philadelphia] Orchestra. He did the Beethoven concerto and he played his own cadenza—which at that time was new; it had not been published. I heard him in three concerts. He was just a passion of mine. So during that time I actually memorized the cadenza, and I told Schelling that I knew it. Schelling said, "Don't say anything about it."

He didn't. Instead, when Kreisler arrived at Schelling's home, Shumsky simply played the full cadenza, note for note, start to finish. "I asked him if I had any wrong notes in there. He said, 'No, you had wrong harmonies in some places, but the [melody lines] were correct.'"

That was their first meeting. After that, Shumsky would see Kreisler whenever the elder musician came to Philadelphia. "I would go backstage and greet him," Shumsky recalled, "and he had some advice to give where my career was concerned. . . . I can tell you, he was the most gentle person that I'd ever met. He was very kind, very considerate, a very sweet person." Kreisler was "a tremendous personality, and a personality not just in his physical [presence] but a personality in his phrasing. He was very much the musical picture of what he was as a man. . . . The two were inseparable." Shumsky continued:

> He was the personification of what he did [and] the way he did it. He was a very noble, very elegant man, very kind and very sweet individual, and modest. . . . He was certainly the most lovable person, and the most approachable. For that same reason, the way he played . . . was approachable. It invited you to come and listen. It invited you to come and participate in what he was doing.[7]

"Among all the violinists," Shumsky said, "Kreisler was the figure that I most idolized."

Shumsky was among many who venerated Kreisler, including those who knew him personally as well as colleagues who admired him from afar—that is, from the seats of Carnegie Hall. Just how keenly Kreisler affected his fellow musicians is evident from their own testimonies on the subject, which describe better than any paraphrase the intense emotions he aroused. Especially among performers of a certain generation—Shumsky's and Menuhin's, which matured musically when Kreisler was at the height of his powers and his fame—there was no other violinist who so dominated the concert circuit or so influenced their musical upbringing. Later generations turned to later violinists, but Kreisler represented always an ideal of style and romance.

As Paul Hume wrote in the *Saturday Review* in December 1962, eleven months after Kreisler's death: "Kreisler operated on a plane few musicians attain. His colleagues, who were inevitably his rivals, felt for him and spoke of him with a regard, in unreserved praise, a kind of affection rarely encountered in the world of musicians."[8] With this in mind, what follows is a sampling of remarks made by Kreisler's colleagues, culled from articles, printed recollections, and interviews.

Isaac Stern

From an article Stern wrote for the *Saturday Review*, dated 24 February 1962:

> I did not meet Fritz Kreisler more than a half dozen times, and could not say that I knew him well, and yet I, like most string players of our time, must confess that in some subtle way, he influenced us all. Perhaps it was his evident love of every phrase he played, his unashamed enjoyment of being moved by the music, and in turn being able to move his listeners. For in every Kreisler performance that I heard, it was inevitable that in its course there came moments of pure magic, moments where one could forget one was sitting in a concert hall listening to a man performing on an instrument; where only that golden thread of sound entered one's ear and mind, to remain always as a cherished memory. To be taken out of time and place is rare enough as an experience to be cherished, and to do it as consistently as Fritz Kreisler could do it is even rarer.[9]

Josef Gingold

From an interview with Gingold in 1992:

> I never missed a Kreisler concert when I lived in New York. During the Depression I played in a musical show on Broadway, and I was lucky to have a job; bank presidents were throwing themselves out of the window. But every time

> Kreisler played I would ask the contractor if I could send a substitute. He'd say to me, "Joe, what's the matter? The concert pays twelve dollars and the tickets cost five." And I said, "I need it with my soul."
>
> I don't think he understood, because it meant a night's poker game to him. And it meant my soul.[10]

In May 1962 Josef Gingold wrote a brief essay that extolled Kreisler as "a phenomenal, naturally gifted violinist" whose "great talent continued to develop until it reached such artistic heights that Fritz Kreisler became an inimitable interpreter of any composition he chose to play." Gingold then analyzed Kreisler's abilities in one of the pithiest, most lucid breakdowns of the violinist's appeal ever published.

> Kreisler's playing was always vibrant and alive and his sense of rhythm was outstanding. I particularly recall a performance of the Chaconne by Bach which was played with such an impeccable rhythmic sense that, for once, this masterwork came to life as a great unit. Kreisler's way of interpreting his own charming pieces is unforgettable—he combined a tone of ravishing beauty with a highly individualistic artistic sense and fantasy plus a dazzling technical finish. The listener was enchanted by the memory of these performances many years after hearing them. The experience was truly unique. What we consider modern today might be old fashioned in the future. Genius, however, is never old fashioned, and Fritz Kreisler will remain the modern violinist and one who can never be replaced.[11]

Gingold included a copy of the article with a letter he sent to Charles Foley that fairly bursts with affection for the violinist. Mere words did not suffice: so enormous was Gingold's admiration for Kreisler that he felt compelled in the letter to twice underline a reference to him as "this GIANT," a technique also used in the letter's concluding sentence: "He was, for me, the greatest of them all!"[12] Apparently, even a definite article could not define Kreisler's greatness.

Joseph Szigeti

From an article for the May 1962 issue of *High Fidelity Magazine:*

> It so happens that the first work I heard Fritz Kreisler play—at a Nikisch concert in Berlin in 1905—was Viotti's A Minor Concerto, a work seldom heard nowadays, even on records. The fact that I had made my "coming-out" debut at one of the concerts of the Budapest Academy of Music with this same work a few months before the Kreisler "revelation" made this occasion a still more revealing one for the thirteen-year-old that I was. It showed me the magic that the unanalyzable Kreisler alchemy could work on what was (and, alas, still is!) regarded as "student material." It gave me right at the beginning a working model of how Kreisler could transmute baser materials into gold. . . .
>
> His playing of the Viotti gave me an almost palpable demonstration of the essentially Kreislerian attributes of elegance, rhythmic thrust, lyric and parlando sweetness on material that had become "classroom-worn" for me. . . .
>
> It was perhaps Kreisler's capacity to transmute baser materials into gold that was responsible for a certain distortion in the public mind as to what he really stood for. *Londonderry Air*, *Hymn to the Sun*, *Humoresque*, not to speak of his own inimitable compositions, prevented the ordinary listener (in America, particularly) from realizing on what a broad base of musicianship—or better *Musikantentum* (in the sense that the Bach's were *Musikanten*)—all this alchemy rested.[13]

In Szigeti's view, further presented in his contribution to the *Saturday Review*, Kreisler differed from other great violinists in that he always, no matter how venerable and venerated he became, remained a peer:

> What makes Fritz Kreisler's impact on his time so unique is that, while fundamentally changing stylistic concepts of our art, he never became (at least in my opinion) an inhibiting "father image" as, for example, Joachim.

Those who were as much as twenty years his junior could rather call him a "brother image," if such an expression were permissible.

There was that life-affirming, invigorating, youthful essence in his playing that left its mark both on those who (at the turn of the century) were older and those who were younger than he was.

This perhaps not only explains his inescapable imprint on the last sixty years of violin playing, but also insures his continuing influence on coming generations as well.[14]

Louis Kaufman

On hearing the first phrases of a Kreisler program . . . my analytical faculties would melt away under the spell of his Orpheus. His magnetic charm, the incredible beauty of sound that was a direct translation of human sentiment bewitched me and I was in a sort of mystic Nirvana. I was especially entranced by his compelling rhythmic vitality and the radiance of sound produced by his double-stops.[15]

Charles Libove

Though I had heard Fritz Kreisler recordings from my earliest years, I had the privilege and pleasure of hearing and seeing him personally while still a young child. I still remember the phenomenon of his pianissimi that could be heard in the farthest reaches of a large concert hall because of the incredible focus and substance of his beautiful violin sound. His was a beauty of utterance in sound that has not been repeated. It mattered not whether he played his Vuillaume or Guarneri, whether he used gut or steel strings, or whether he played into a primitive recording horn or far more modern recording equipment—that unmistakably gorgeous sound was always there, with its inner light, centered and sonorous. . . .

Fritz Kreisler was truly the complete musician. His playing seemed to reflect goodness of nature, geniality and generosity of spirit and always radiated warmth. It was play-

> ing of uncanny musical honesty and intuition, alive, vibrant, direct and true in his interpretations.[16]

Zino Francescatti

> Kreisler struck me like a thunderbolt the first time I heard him. It was 1913. I had already been playing the violin for many years, though I was only eight. He came on the stage, and already the man was different from the great artists we were accustomed to hear—Ysaÿe, Thibaud, Paderewski, etc. They were personages with very long hair, dressed with a flavor of nineteenth-century romanticism, tremendous redingotes, jabots of lace, elaborate ties.
>
> Kreisler, with his crew-cut hair, sober jacquette, and calm and formidable strength, made me gaze with awe. What came out from his violin was the thing I was waiting for: the revelation, the ideal of my dream not yet revealed to me, the beautiful tone, the clarity and simplicity of the phrases (in the Beethoven concerto), and particularly the rebound inside your chest of the rhythm of his bow. I felt Kreisler pointed to the future for me. He was the artist who speaks to you not only of the wonders of the past, but also of the great things to accomplish your destiny. That night I decided to give all my life to the violin.[17]

Sir Yehudi Menuhin

"As a boy, when I first heard Fritz Kreisler in San Francisco, I was absolutely carried away by that grace and sophistication—the quality of human speech and contact," Yehudi Menuhin recounted in a 1993 interview.

Menuhin was seven or eight years old when he first heard Kreisler, and the experience had a profound affect on the boy. From the beginning, Kreisler impressed him as a violinist and a human being, becoming, in Menuhin's eyes, something close to a fairy godmother.

> He impressed me as a man of such generosity, of such gentleness, of such sweetness, that I used to dream he would

walk out on his stage and give me his Guarnerius. It was a very childish idea, but that's the image I had of the man, and that image never changed—even when I knew him extremely well.

I was enchanted by his playing. It was so human, so human.[18]

Berl Senofsky

From Senofsky's article for *The Strad* of 1 January 1987:

> Fritz Kreisler, apart from being the paramount violinist and artistic standard of his age, was the epitome of a true humanitarian. I was fortunate enough to have spent some time with him, mostly walking in the Berkshires [in Massachusetts] where he vacationed during the summer. We would walk down to Stockbridge and indulge in one of his favourite pastimes: chocolate sodas at the sweet shop. He never failed to elicit from me the feeling that he was my grandfather and should be bouncing me on his knee.[19]

Carl Flesch

> Kreisler has been the most important figure for us violinists since Ysaÿe's decline; he has fundamentally influenced the development of our art as no other violinist of his time has done. In the history of violin playing he will live not only as an artist whose genius stimulated and expanded the art, but as a most valuable symbol of a whole epoch.[20]

Joseph Fuchs

"For me he was a god," said Fuchs. "He was one of the most original violinists that ever lived. He played like no other violinist. They stood in awe of him. . . . His playing was absolutely original. It was not Viennese; it was Kreisleresque." At the same time, Kreisler "was as simple as simple can be. He was a simple person, in that he would address a janitor as well as he would address any great person."[21]

Nathan Milstein

> As a boy in Russia there were two musical names which meant more to me than any others—Chaliapin and Kreisler. From records, of course, for while we had a fine opera in Odessa where I lived, I did not hear Chaliapin until I was taken to St. Petersburg to study with Auer. I did not hear Kreisler until much later in Paris, but always his was the name of a violinist who was above and beyond all others, as the Pope in the Catholic world.
>
> More than anything else I would describe his art as hypnotic. To see him stand there quietly and bring sounds from the instrument unlike anything anybody else produced was to feel what is to me the unique power of the interpreter—to appeal directly, as an individual, to the individual listener. I heard him first in Paris in 1926, but I did not meet him until 1931. I was invited to visit him during the interval. He had just played Bruch, with piano—hypnotically. When I left the room, someone said to me, "You kissed his hand." "No," I said. "That is impossible. I wouldn't do such a thing." But when I thought back—yes, I had, without even realizing it.
>
> Such gifts as Kreisler's come, to a single human being, once in two or three generations—to play as he played, to know what he knew, to create the beautiful expressions of his own personality which we all love and enjoy. For me, in the history of the violin, there is Bach, there is Viotti, there is Paganini—and Kreisler.[22]

The importance of Kreisler to Milstein is revealed in a slight but touching story related by Eric Wen. Wen, who came to know Milstein fairly well in the last years of the violinist's life, said that Milstein deeply admired both Fritz Kreisler and Jascha Heifetz, a violinist of an entirely different species. The closer Milstein drew to the end of his life, however, the more he found himself thinking and even dreaming about Kreisler. "It was very touching," recalled Wen. "He would say, 'Oh, I dreamt about Kreisler again.' The older he got, the more he dreamt about Kreisler. This man who was about to be joined with these immortals—Kreisler meant so much to him, especially at the end. That was his true inspiration."[23]

Sam Kissel

In an interview in 1992, Sam Kissel described Kreisler's imposing—yet familiar—appearance.

> He was such a handsome man. He was about six feet tall, broad-shouldered—there was no fat on him, you know, he was all muscle. He had a wonderful physique. When he came out to play he would hold his violin down from the scroll, and he had a tick on the left side of his face. . . . He looked like the papa of us all.[24]

Philip Dreifus

"He was such an understanding and wonderful performer," said Dreifus, who played for Kreisler shortly before Kreisler went off to fight in World War I.

> He was the most lovable man—that's probably a terrible word to use, but I can't help it—that I have ever known in my life. I really had the greatest respect and love for him. He had the most wonderful smile—he had a smile that would wrap you up. . . . He was kind and probably one of the most gifted men I have ever known in my lifetime, and I have known a great deal.[25]

George Neikrug

Neikrug, the Boston-based cellist and string teacher of considerable renown, recalled hearing Kreisler for the first time at a recital in New York City.

> He always played Saturday at two-thirty, but I thought it was three o'clock. The ticket was for the last row in the balcony. He had already started to play the Franck sonata. Immediately, I was transfixed. He had a pianist [Carl Lamson], an old guy that used to play with him. The second movement of the Franck sonata is very difficult, and he [Lamson] made a total mess of it. But Kreisler looked

and beamed at him as if it was the greatest thing anybody ever heard.[26]

David Oistrakh

In a reverent and respectful letter dated 6 December 1959, David Oistrakh, the Soviet violinist, wrote to Kreisler.

> Dear Maestro,
>
> Throughout my life I have been a deep admirer of your artistic genius. The style which you have created and immortalized in your many compositions and transcriptions has had a tremendous influence on all the violinists of our time without exception and has given joy to countless music-lovers all over the world. From earliest youth I took delight in your recordings and studied them thoroughly. You made an unforgettable impression on me when I finally heard you in person in 1937 in Brussels and London. Many times I have given concerts devoted entirely to your works and transcriptions. In my own work as a teacher I aspire to have my students capture, within the limits of their powers, these qualities of interpretation which you have so generously given to the musical world.[27]

Byron Williams

> I was all ears and eyes in studying the way Kreisler played. At every concert I observed the many unique things he did and listened intently to every sound. Then, inspired anew, I went home to practise what I had seen and heard.
>
> At one of these concerts, my teacher, Roderick White, who knew Kreisler, took me backstage to meet him. I was thrilled to be in his presence and to shake the same hand that could pull those ravishing, glorious tones. . . .
>
> From all the many concerts I heard Kreisler give, his performance of Viotti's Concerto No. 22 in A Minor (with piano) stands out in my memory. It was an unforgettable revelation. In his magical hands, it became a great master-

> piece. Who else could have played those trills with such clarity and brilliant accents, the thirds with such vibrancy, and phrased in such noble style? . . .
>
> In 1961 I had the opportunity to meet Kreisler at the office of Charles Foley in New York. What impressed me most about him was his youthful spirit and insatiable curiosity. I showed him my Storioni, a favorite violin of August Wilhelmj, and, obliging his request to hear it, played two of my own compositions—*Teasing Ballerina*, a capricious virtuoso piece, and *Serenata Veneziana*, perhaps more Viennese than Italian. The latter must have reminded him of Vienna, for his face lit up and he said, "You should always feature this nostalgic, melodic music. People enjoy it. It is not *what* you play, but *how* you play that counts." . . .
>
> I have always cherished the memory of this meeting and, though I never studied with him personally, I consider Kreisler to be my most important teacher.[28]

Williams, it must be added, is the subject of an amusing story (of questionable authenticity) that concerns his admiration for and emulation of Kreisler. Williams apparently looked somewhat like Kreisler and played the Austrian's pieces in a fair imitation of his style. At some point—presumably the meeting described above—Williams told Kreisler of his efforts to duplicate his sound. "My friends say I play just like you," Williams is said to have remarked. "I'd like to play for you." To which Kreisler supposedly responded, "Mr. Williams, that is not necessary. I believe your friends."[29]

Among the briefest but most eloquent illustrations of Kreisler's impact on fellow musicians was a series of greetings recorded by ten colleagues for broadcast on WQXR radio in New York on the evening of Kreisler's eightieth birthday, 2 February 1955. The greetings, most of them addressed to Kreisler directly, are an evocative reminder of the esteem with which the violinist was still regarded five years after his retirement and fifteen years after his prime. They are short, plainspoken, and openly affectionate, clear indications that Kreisler remained a professional model, in spirit if not in practice, for violinists old enough to recall his abiding influence and warmth.

Mischa Elman spoke of Kreisler's "epoch-making influence" and "his inimitable style and great artistry, which will long linger in the memory of those who were fortunate enough to hear him." Yehudi Menuhin, addressing "Fritz, the most beloved of colleagues," conveyed "yet another heart full of reverence and affection. May your benign presence among your younger colleagues long bring us the inspiration we cherish." Nathan Milstein praised Kreisler's artistry and personality. Erica Morini, calling herself one of Kreisler's "most devoted admirers," said that while playing a Kreisler composition "I am thoroughly inspired by the poetic beauty of your spirit and your art. . . . [Y]ou make this world a much more worthwhile one in which to live."

Joseph Szigeti sent "all the affection and admiration and gratitude that I have always felt for our great Fritz Kreisler." Ruggiero Ricci conveyed greetings and admiration. Zino Francescatti declared, in endearingly awkward English: "You always have been my inspiration and model in our difficult career. Let me tell you on this anniversary my everlasting affection, love and respect." Joseph Fuchs spoke of Kreisler's "guiding spirit" and remarked: "Your superb art will long linger in our hearts."

Carl Lamson, Kreisler's accompanist for many years, paid tribute to the violinist "not only as a musician and man, but as a good friend always, in all circumstances." And Isaac Stern, then a young man with a long career ahead of him, delivered the following greeting:

> It is a great privilege to join with my friends and colleagues in this tribute to you—a tribute not only to a great figure in the history of music, but a great man whose warmth and sincerity and nobility of purpose has meant a great deal and will always mean a great deal to all of us. God bless you and many thanks for all that you have done.[30]

Such accolades point to a persistent twist in Kreisler's career: that this least orthodox of soloists should have gained widespread acceptance and even adulation from a musical community that normally, in this century, rewards orthodoxy. All other classical instrumentalists were and are required to follow certain rules—to play a piece as it appears on the page, to hit all the notes properly, to present each recital as an authoritative interpretation of musical manuscripts—but Kreisler was not. Violinists and other soloists admired him despite his eccentricities and even, at times, because of them; his very separateness from other violinists was ultimately what endeared him to them. Without his earnest and sometimes errant philosophizing, without his willingness (some might have said desire) to make mistakes, without his simple faith in the power of art, the arcane world of the violin might have seemed mechanistic and thoroughly, unbearably dry.

At the start of his career, Kreisler was admired for his tangible qualities: the ringing tone, the unyielding vibrato. At its finish, he was admired for the *in*tangibles, the qualities that everyone admired but few could articulate and only the rash tried to imitate. His was an unreachable standard if only because it was, by then, unquantifiable; the apotheosis that promoted him from king of the violin to undisputed "god" simultaneously removed him from the company of relevant string players and reduced his standing as a practical (as opposed to spiritual) model for other musicians. Aspirants looking for step-by-step guidance and high-level instruction in violin technique and string playing looked elsewhere. Those looking for inspiration looked to Kreisler—for Kreisler, the undisputed doyen of violinists, had become a figurehead.

Twelve

Covering Kreisler: The Critics' Dilemma

> What artist is sure when he has played his best? I am perpetually astonished by praise given performances of mine which I am certain were poor, and what seems to me a heart-breaking indifference, or reservation, on the part of the press or public, in instances when I have finished and said to myself, "Old fellow, you came somewhere near it today." Of course, one only comes near it and then one is lucky. For we are the apes of our ideals. We work and we seek. It never comes just right, and we can never completely trust our conclusions. Today we think we have found something of the truth. Tomorrow we feel sadly disillusioned. But the search is the thing which leads and sustains and vitalizes us.[1]

In music as in life, "the truth" is an elusive creature, as inscrutable as a poem and often as difficult to define. Is it the perfect literal translation of printed notes and rests? Is it the authentic realization of historical performance practices? Is it faultless intonation, faultless execution, faultless technique? Or is it something else—something less exact, more metaphorical, more mystical?

Fritz Kreisler's understanding of truth in art was different from that of many modern musicians, but not different from his audience's. In Kreisler's view—in Kreisler's performance—the truth was not something rigidly cerebral but an ideal of beauty that could only be discerned by intuitive means. His belief in the veracity of emotion (and the ability, indeed, the necessity of the individual to express it) was common enough among romantics of his age and schooling and is not by itself remarkable. Where he departed from many of his peers (particularly those younger than he) was in perspective: he viewed the truth from afar, with an eye toward its broadest characteristics rather than its details. In this sense Kreisler was an impressionist at a time when representational art—at least among instrumentalists—was holding sway. His strokes were wider, his interpretations bolder, than the minutely exact paint dabs applied by colleagues whose understanding of the whole (that is, a piece of music) was fixedly reliant on their mastery of its parts (that is, the notes). This is not to say that Kreisler played fast and loose with details, any more than Monet was sloppy with his painting. But Kreisler's eye was simply not focused on minutiae alone. He took the long view.

He expressed this view in several ways: in his reluctance to practice; in his admonitions to younger musicians not to overwork their technique and, in so doing, overwhelm their artistry; and in his admiration for the virtuosos of yore, who scattered many notes in their grand interpretations of the masters. ("More than smoothness is demanded of the artist," he once said. "It wasn't the crack technical performance that the great ones sought. It was quite something else. Why, we have violinists with far more technique than Paganini, and, for all I know, a hundred pianists who could out-play Liszt. What bushels of notes were dropped by Rubinstein! And by Ysaÿe, the incomparable Ysaÿe! One great sweep of the bow, and what vision unfolded.")[2] Most obviously, however, Kreisler's perception of truth in music could, and thanks to recordings still can, be found in his playing. In his earlier career, long before the truck accident and the waning years that followed, Kreisler's performances were perfectly balanced mixes of physical ability and interpretive charm: his intonation was keen, his vibrato was alluring, his style was irresistible. His technique, at least until Jascha Heifetz entered the scene, was regarded as first-rate, and he used it to great effect—not to overwhelm his listeners and not as an end in itself, but as a means to communicate his most fundamental musical ideas. He used it to find and convey his understanding of the truth.

As the years progressed, more and more notes fell away. His memory lapses in the middle of pieces, a likely occurrence even when he was a young man, became more frequent. His intonation began to lose its edge (though some dispute this). His colleagues were younger and sharper and more likely to spend many more hours each day perfecting their skills. The world around him was more cynical, more demanding of its artists, and less likely to forgive the slips of an aging icon.

"I think after the accident he couldn't hear. His sense of pitch was gone," said Oscar Shumsky. "But then, it was gone in many artists who didn't suffer any physical injuries. . . . [With Kreisler] it just deteriorated. The thing that did remain was the bow arm—it seemed to be the last to disappear."[3]

How did the world respond to Kreisler's lapses? Those who heard him and followed him for decades, the core of his admiring public, did not seem to care—not until shortly before his retirement. They attended his recitals as they always had; they patted back tears when he played *Liebesleid* and basked as ever in the warmth of his tone. The mistakes that he made were no more significant than the graying of his hair; he was theirs, as he had always been, and the messages he conveyed were as personal and as revelatory as a bedside diary's. That was all that mattered.

Music critics, on the other hand, were faced with a prickly dilemma: just how honest should they be? Because Kreisler's performances were often technically flawed but always musically seductive, the reviewer usually chose to write not about mechanical or mnemonic errors but the violinist's "inimitable style."

Indeed, critics who were assigned to cover Kreisler's appearances were stymied by the same obstacles that confined anyone who attempted to listen critically. Fritz Kreisler was an attractive musical personality; he was charismatic, cozy, endearingly old-fashioned, and sincerely devoted to the conveyance of beauty. No one listening to his interpretations was immune to his charms; no one wanted to be immune, critics included. It is difficult nowadays to fathom such allegiance, particularly on the part of the press, to an individual performer, but the critics' affection for Kreisler was undeniable and deep. He embodied something that no longer existed, a school of thought steeped in nineteenth-century sensibilities and driven by the eerie theosophy of musical performance, and he embodied it with grace. None but Kreisler carried the Old World so enchantingly as he strode across the stage. None so musically—and none with such alluring ease.

The result was that Kreisler rarely got a bad review, even when he might have deserved one. Take, for instance, a typical review from 1946, five years after Kreisler's accident and four years before his retirement. Written by *The New York Times* critic Noel Straus, the article covered Kreisler's 2 November appearance at Carnegie Hall, a recital that included Saint-Saëns's Concerto No. 3 in B Minor, Kreisler's transcription of Bach's Concerto in D Minor for Piano, and the violinist's own *Viennese Rhapsodic Fantasietta*.

Straus could barely find the words to convey his pleasure with Kreisler's artistry. Kreisler "remains the master musician among the violinists of the day," and his recital "was a triumphant exhibition of interpretive skill. . . . One can but be humble and grateful for superlative music-making on so lofty a plane." Of the Bach, he wrote: "With the magic of his bowing, and the clarity and dispatch of every phrase, combined with the beauty of tone always at his disposal, the corner movements of the concerto came to full life and meaning, while the Adagio . . . was most eloquently and soulfully projected." Kreisler performed the Saint-Saëns, meanwhile, "with true Gallic elegance and refinement," while the *Fantasietta* was performed "with most authentic Viennese nuances in a fascinating and nostalgic unfoldment."

Then, near the bottom of the review, came the following qualification: "If, as in the Bach, there was an occasional lapse from pitch, or other slight imperfection, these mattered not at all in performances so wizard-like in their technical fluency and so unmatchable in their depth of insight."[4]

Straus did not specify which "slight imperfection" marred the recital, but we can take a fair guess: Kreisler got lost. As has already been described, Kreisler often lost his place while performing, not from any grave defect in memory but from sheer lack of practicing. He simply did not practice enough to commit pieces perfectly to memory. To do so would have meant spending far too many hours on the rote rehearsal of notes, something he opposed mightily and which, as a result, he always avoided. Better to give a fresh interpretation with a few slight flaws than a flawless one dulled by practice. Or so he believed.

And, seemingly, so did the critics. As Noel Straus offered in another 1946 review, this one critiquing a Kreisler performance of the Mendelssohn concerto:

> What if a slip in pitch occurred now and then, if rhythms were sometimes rather free, or the tone proved less light in the finale than was awaited. Such details might carry weight in a performance of lesser magnitude, but could not rob so imposing an interpretation of its magnitude and impressiveness. And, by and large, what other violinist of the present day could come near matching this reading in grandeur, dignity, or impact?[5]

Obviously, Straus's definitions of "magnitude" and "grandeur," like those of others who followed Kreisler's career, went beyond the performance and perception of technical accuracy. In a sense it even went beyond the music, if music itself is considered to be the realization of sounds as they appear on a printed or manuscript page. Audiences persuaded by Kreisler's art "filed out into the night, marveling not so much at the music as at the spell Kreisler's warm and generous personality casts over his crowded houses," a writer for *Newsweek* commented in 1940.[6]

As a result, what is most striking in stories that recount Kreisler's performance errors and his relaxed attitude toward them is that no one in the music world ever seemed to care. "Mr. Kreisler has always had his peculiarities of technic and style, and even, as a general rule, certain slight flaws which lesser musicians have not in performance," reads a 1928 review by Olin Downes, one of Kreisler's great apologists. "Yet he remains one of the greatest artists before the public, and it is seldom that he fails to turn what he touches into gold."[7] Musicians regarded his improvisational skills as just another indication of his genius; his core audience (when it noticed at all) did not punish him with diminished ticket sales; and critics throughout Kreisler's career either failed to mention the inevitable mistakes or soft-pedaled them as artistic irrelevancies. Kreisler could do no wrong, even when he did.

Such leniency is unthinkable today, in an era when the most prominent critics are notoriously unforgiving and even the least-schooled of listeners have come to expect flawless performances. This may be attributed to two significant twentieth-century musical developments: the wide availability of recorded music and the perfection of Heifetz's playing, which led to an emphasis on what can best be described as a "digital technique." Pristine in sound and mathematical in precision, this digital technique was part of Heifetz's legacy—a legacy that raised technical expectations, among players, critics, and audiences, forever after. That his recording career flourished well into the latter half of the century, amassing stacks of LPs for later generations to study, only solidifies his reputation as the most modern of modern musicians.

Heifetz in many ways prefigured the culture's current, and apparently enduring, obsession with computers and compact-disc technology. The pandemic cultural change in how people listen to music—at home, ensconced in their arm chairs, or chopping vegetables in the kitchen—and the vast democratization of recording have created an enormous repertoire of works that are available to people who rarely, perhaps never, hear them performed in a live hall. Hence the creation in the minds of many listeners of absolute or definitive renditions against which differently interpreted or somehow flawed performances can barely or rarely compete—and hence the development of an extremely savvy, and extremely critical, musical audience.

The irony here is that this digital technique was best expressed by Heifetz decades before the development and mass availability of digital recording. He was able to achieve on vinyl what performers since then have been able to achieve on disc: flawless renditions of the repertoire. Today the effect is achieved with electronic editing devices, which allow a recording's producer to correct mistakes much as a photographer can airbrush the blemishes off of a movie star's portrait. There is a bit of musical subterfuge involved, as though the recording industry were conspiring to persuade the public that classical performance is more uniform, and thus more predictable, than it actually is. In reality—and at its best—it is the least predictable of art forms, an incalculable sum of tradition, scholarship, divine inspiration, human error, and indulged whim. It is a fascinating mess. Why else would anyone bother to give live performances? Why else would anyone pay to hear them?

Nevertheless, listeners have come to expect perfection. Nowhere is this more apparent than on the concert circuit, where audiences and critics accustomed to the prevailing technology are likely to wince in surprise or disgust when a soloist missteps in recital. Intonation that can be corrected easily and endlessly in the recording booth is on its own onstage, where every missed note or smudged tone stands naked before the judgment of skeptics. What is it we now desire, as a listening public? To be moved? To be impressed? Or to feel assured in the knowledge that we have witnessed perfection?

This purity of sound and technical precision were made possible, Heifetz notwithstanding, by modern technology. Kreisler's early audiences lacked such equipment and thus did not train their ears toward perfection; his listeners were more forgiving because, quite literally, they did not know any better. Neither were they equipped to resist Kreisler's persuasive musical personality, the vast charm of which was enough to overcome any flaws he displayed in performance. How that personality would be received in today's harsh world is an unanswered and unanswerable question, but it is tempting to ask—and to answer. In an era characterized by skepticism, perfectionism, and uniform performance practices, by digital recording and editing so exact that no one with a compact-disc player need ever hear an out-of-tune note, how would Kreisler be judged? With what derision would his muffs and memory lapses be greeted? Perhaps they, and he, would be dismissed as amateurish or tolerated with the patronizing restlessness of a child who endures an old man's nonsensical ramblings. He might fail to grab any critical or popular attention whatsoever. Or he might be hugely successful, creating a career out of CD sales, stadium performances, television specials, best-selling videotapes, and a glitzy "Three Violinists" extravaganza with Pinchas Zukerman and Itzhak Perlman.

In all probability, a Kreisler born to the late twentieth century would be a late-twentieth-century violinist: fast, accurate, his fingers a blur and his carriage cool and detached. He would not, in other words, be Fritz Kreisler. So different is the musical ethos today from what it was seventy or eighty years ago that an artistic personality as pronounced as Kreisler's would either be quashed by the reigning musical conventions or utterly ignored. He would sound like everyone else, or he would have no career at all. So much of what made Kreisler unique, his flaws as well as his virtues, belong to a previous era. Even in the violinist's later career, long after the long-playing record had been introduced and years since Jascha Heifetz had stunned the world with his refitted string technique, Kreisler's most ardent followers remained faithful to the old fiddler and were, as ever, persuaded by his gifts. For most of his career his intonation was superb, his manual dexterity impressive. His flaws, as they became more prominent, did not lessen his standing, for his standing had never depended on flawlessness. In a way it was part of his charm—and a testament to the power of his individuality, which informed everything he played and became a clear if inimitable feature of his interpretations. Kreisler's artistry, the personality and presentation of his music, does not fit comfortably with the age of computers. His playing is a cause for reflection, even nostalgia. His stylistic freedoms, his Viennese buoyancy, his willingness to swap literal precision for interpretive freshness all hail from a time and place far removed from the contemporary American concert hall. Kreisler was a child of conservatories, but he was not a child of international competitions and the sameness of playing that they have inevitably encouraged. He was different. If one of his differences was an occasionally elastic reading of a printed work, well, audiences accepted that. For the most part, so did critics.

Nathan Milstein recalled one such experience, a Kreisler concert he and Vladimir Horowitz attended in Paris. So overwhelmed were the two young men by the violinist's recital—which included Viotti's Concerto No. 22 in A Minor and Bach's Concerto in E Major—that they remained in their seats long after the rest of the audience had departed. "We were destroyed!" he later wrote.

> We had heard exceptional musicians before that, but Kreisler's performance that night was a gift from God. Later I heard Kreisler play not so brilliantly, especially when he hadn't been practicing. But even then, what would have been a catastrophe for others sounded charming from him.[8]

And that is just the point: Kreisler's gifts with the instrument, and the corresponding appeal that spread over a huge cross-section of society, had little to do with technique. People listened to him not for the control in his bowing or the evenness in his vibrato, but the emotion, the elegance, the *voice* behind it. In this regard he was a far more popular and popul*ist* performer than most of his classical colleagues, simply because he was far more sympathetic with (and fond of) less serious types of music. He enjoyed popular music—could *Caprice Viennois* prove otherwise?—and displayed in his own compositions the same emphasis on accessible melodies and dance-inspired rhythms. Vienna of the late nineteenth century was as much a capital of popular culture as New York City or Los Angeles is today, and Kreisler was very much a product of that culture. Just as many young American composers (Todd Levin or Kamran Ince, for example) reveal in their works an innate understanding of and sympathy for rock forms, so did Kreisler inform his own pieces with the infectious lilt of the waltz and the ländler. His understanding of popular music, his relationship to it, was as pure and unshakable as his Austrian accent. He was reared in it.

Onstage, that background translated into a style of playing that spoke directly to audiences of diverse backgrounds and social strata. Despite Kreisler's erudition and the firm classical traditions in which he was trained, there was never a gap between himself and his listeners; the most rarefied music sounded democratic in his hands, the most arcane was approachable. The result was a depth of communication—a relationship with his audience—rarely attained by other classical instrumentalists. He was, as we have seen, one of the century's first great pop stars and a clear forerunner to later popular performers whose appeal has relied almost exclusively on their ability to "connect" with their listeners. It is an apt analogy and a revealing one, for pop musicians are given considerable leeway by concertgoers and critics alike in the technical execution of their music: does it matter, for instance, that Bob Dylan has a nasal voice, that Frank Sinatra's lung capacity diminished over the years, that the Sex Pistols could barely play at all? Hardly. What matters instead is the unquantifiable gold standard of popular performance, the mystical bond that forms—or fails to form—between player and crowd.

In this sense Kreisler's ability was without peer and, unlike other qualities of his playing, tangible—consider the vehemence (and decibel level) of his audience response. Even in the spring of 1921, when the Austrian's career had only begun to recover from the driest years of his wartime ostracism, his popularity was so great that (according to the 27 March *New York Times*) a capacity crowd in Carnegie Hall "hung to every available perch but the chandeliers" and periodically interrupted the concert with noisy bursts of applause. In London over a month later, the scene was similar: "Men and women waved hats and handkerchiefs. Some became hysterical. Others with difficulty controlled their emotion."[9]

The Beatles at Carnegie? No, Fritz Kreisler in Queen's Hall.

Which brings us, once again, to Kreisler's performances, their frequent flaws, and the critics charged with reviewing them. Doing so objectively—hence honestly—was close to impossible, simply because the reviewer was usually bewitched by the same spell that hexed everyone else. The unwritten presumption behind all such reactions to Kreisler's music was the belief that his artistry placed him somehow above the piddling rules followed by more mortal fiddlers. When he missed an entrance and meandered around in his own extemporaneous composition, the lapse itself hardly mattered; more important was the music-making that resulted, which indicated abilities far beyond those of the average performer. To a certain extent his little detours were greeted with the same delight that greeted musical improvisation in the classical era, a mostly lost art that peaked in the lifetime (and at the keyboard) of Mozart. Mozart was a genius as a composer, and prodigious as a performer, but as an improviser he was positively revered. As much if not more than any other quality, it was proof of his distinctive genius. So it was with Kreisler.

Yet Kreisler's errors, and the manner in which they were received, says much about the nature of criticism and the role of the reviewer in shaping public expectations. Like the work of any writer, the critic's job is communication—in this case, communication of a specific musical event to a diverse but somewhat specialized audience. A musician gives a concert, a reviewer tells about it. This is of course self-explanatory. But the assumptions underpinning that communication are so varied, so subtextual, and so utterly subjective that any single critic's review of a given event is likely to vary considerably, often shockingly, from another's. What is significant to one reviewer may be irrelevant to another.

In his brilliant, apoplectic *War on Critics*, Theodore L. Shaw addressed the drawbacks inherent to criticism.

> To put it bluntly, the main function of the critic, *from the angle of scholarship*, is not to render dogmatic and eternally correct verdicts of an art work's so-called "art," but to narrate his adventures in exploring and ascending its cycle, to recount his failures and successes—his final discovery, perhaps, of a clue here and a clue there that might help him respond complexly to the art work's emanations. [Italics are his.]

Moreover:

> To expect a critic, after one attendance at a concert, after one visit to an exhibition of paintings, after one reading of a book, to reach a decision as to the complexity of the art works he has experienced—assuming that they are the products of men of talent—is as ridiculous as to expect him to learn Sanskrit over night, regardless of how great his linguistic aptitudes may be.[10]

Granted, Shaw had quite a low opinion of critics in general.

> Ideologically they are bankrupt, rationally they haven't a leg to stand on, as they themselves well know; and yet they continue their slippery existences and befuddle and frustrate us with their megalomaniac pronouncements, their Tartuffian sanctimonies, their Cheshire grins and cackles. . . . [They are] outright aesthetic criminals, quite aware of the complete fraudulence of their mode of life, deliberately bamboozling us for the benefit of their own pocket-books and to the injury of our health and well-being and laughing up their sleeves at us while doing so.[11]

Criticism has always had its critics; since the field's earliest practitioners, the professional Momus has always had scolds of his own committed to censuring his most acrid observations. Finding fault with the faultfinder is a sport of long and proud history. But Momus himself has changed over the years, becoming at once more exacting—more methodical, more scientific in approach and expectation—and less prone to sweeping hyperbole either positive or negative. "Eviscerated" may seem too strong a word to characterize this transformation, yet there is nevertheless a creeping gutlessness overtaking much of contemporary criticism, as though reviewers were so afraid of affect, so terrified that an opinion might sound intuited instead of informed, that their handiwork reads as though it were drained of emotion much as a skillet is drained of fat. One result of this process—a reduction of criticism to its barest nutrients—is an unwillingness among critics to personalize art, to respond to it not merely as an expert but as an opinionated and independent observer: schooled or unschooled, bilious or forgiving. "Criticism written without personal feeling is not worth reading," wrote another Shaw, George Bernard, who did some criticizing of his own. "It is the capacity for making good or bad art a personal matter that makes a man a critic."[12]

Kreisler's music in particular inspired criticism filled with such "personal feeling." Witness this excerpt from a review describing a 1912 Kreisler appearance with the Boston Symphony Orchestra:

> Mr. Kreisler's playing of Brahms's concerto was the achievement of a great artist, broadly eloquent, exquisitely poetical, free, sometimes, as an improvisation, yet with all its impulse of energy, perfectly symmetrical and perfectly poised. . . . Mr. Kreisler was time and again recalled, and his triumph was pre-eminently deserved.[13]

How extravagant this review seems to a modern reader; how emotional, how overstated, how unapologetic. The critic spent his energy and his column inches not on missed notes or flubbed intonation but on what he perceived as Kreisler's sweeping poeticism—a poeticism answered, and augmented, by the critic's gushing superlatives. Obviously, his role as a reviewer—his duties, defined and executed—was substantially different from that of his modern counterpart, who finds in the riddle of criticism a much more literal answer.

Yet the riddle itself has not changed. Then as now, a critic is faced with several pointed and often unanswerable questions. What, for example, is worth reporting? The audience's reaction to the music? The size of the crowd? The precision of the performer's readings? Or the emotional response evoked in the critic? How should a critic weigh a musician's performance against the parameters laid out on the page? Against the abilities of other performers? Against how the same performer has been reviewed before? One critic may focus on a performer's errors, subtracting points like a red-penned school teacher; another may take the long view, granting clemency for missed marks if the overall interpretation rings with artistic insight. One critic may take copious notes and follow the music with a score; another may take none, instead choosing to sink into the seat and listen. One may perceive her role as that of musical arbiter, judiciously selecting which instrumentalists and ensembles deserve ascension to the next level of success; another may see himself mainly as a lover of music, albeit a lover of music who is knowledgeable, discerning, and skilled in conveying in words alone the attributes of a mostly wordless art.

Most contemporary critics see themselves as musical arbiters—and considering how dramatically performance itself has changed, that is only to be expected. In a world where soloists cannot succeed without winning competitions adjudicated by technically demanding pedagogues, musical performance—and the reporting of musical performance—has assumed a distinctly qualitative aspect. This was an inevitable development. If every young pianist participating in the Tchaikovsky International Piano Competition must perform Tchaikovsky's First Piano Concerto in the final round, how must judges choose a winner? By relying on their own subjective responses to style, to phrasing, to artistic surprises (happy and unhappy) that cannot be tabulated? Or by listening carefully for missed notes and skewed dynamics?

In the era that greeted Kreisler's arrival and ascent, idiosyncrasy was accepted, even valued, in concertizing soloists. Virtuosity was a matter not simply of blazing fingers but of blazing imagination as well; the instrumentalist with the biggest following was not the one who interpreted the works most accurately but the one who changed the music as he played it, a terrifying notion in this, the age of historically informed performances. But as the nineteenth century became the twentieth, music was still ephemeral—it had only started to assume the permanence of shellac, later vinyl—and those who heard it did so only in the fleeting intimacy of a parlor, a living room, a concert hall. Performers were people, not names on the spines of record jackets. The music they played was real and familiar only as long as they played it; listeners could not rush home after hearing Beethoven's Ninth Symphony and compare the performance just heard with that of von Karajan on compact disc. Individual interpretation was less fixed and more valid, and errors did not echo into infinity. They occurred, they were noted, they passed into memory.

Consequently, not only the significance of criticism but its very nature has changed in the decades since Kreisler first rose to fame. In the world before recording—before 78s and long-playing albums and cassettes and eight-tracks and, finally, compact discs—the reviewer played a critical role in the enjoyment and understanding of music. He (and it was almost always a he) described, in vivid terms, a great deal of music that many readers simply would not have had the opportunity to hear. Just as a modern political reporter conveys to the masses remarks and occurrences to which the average citizen is not ordinarily privy, the nineteenth-century and early twentieth-century critic told his readers of pieces and performers whose music could only be heard live and in relatively small concert halls. In other words, he reported on it. As a result, thousands who had never heard Franz Liszt perform were familiar with his virtuosity, and readers who never sat through Wagner's *Ring* could converse on the exploits of Wotan. (It should be noted that newspaper criticism was merely one window into live performance; piano transcriptions were another. Piano versions of symphonies, concertos, and other works were popular during the nineteenth century and allowed anyone with access to a piano—and most middle-class homes had one—to hear music that might otherwise have remained in the concert hall before comparatively small audiences.)

Reviewers are no longer needed in this capacity, at least not to the same degree. Average listeners may never hear a live performance of Henryk Górecki's Third Symphony, but they need not rely on critics to understand its strengths and weaknesses; they must only have access to a stereo to perceive its potent minimalism. Assuming they are patient, music lovers can be confident that most significant new works and performers will eventually appear in that largest of all halls, the recording studio; releases are reviewed regularly in magazines, record guides, and, less commonly, newspapers. Concert reviews are written for and read by the small but fervid segment of the listening population that actually attends live performances, and most of that audience owns just as many CDs as those who never, or rarely, venture into a hall. Modern recording technology and its widespread use and acceptance mean that concertgoers are much more sophisticated than they once were.

(As early as 1924, Kreisler himself commented on the caprice of the modern audience member, claiming that as a species, the American listener is a much more vicious animal than the English. "To play for an English audience is like playing before a trusted friend," he remarked. In the United States, meanwhile, "if a man falls from his standard he is immediately and severely arraigned. They forget here all that the artist may have done or yet may be capable of doing.")[14]

Where, then, does that leave the critic? No longer required for his reportorial skills, the modern-day music journalist often falls back on what had previously been a secondary role, that of the highly qualified nitpicker. Rather than introduce the music to readers, the reviewer instead makes criticisms based on a widely recognized ideal, comparing and contrasting the live version of a piece with every other interpretation available, and hence familiar, to any music lover with a little disposable income. When it is finally unnecessary to describe Bach's *Goldberg Variations* for an uninformed readership, it is necessary to compare each new performance with Glenn Gould's landmark recordings. Conscious or subconscious, intentional or inadvertent, positive or negative, such comparisons are unavoidable and ubiquitous. As Eric Wen remarked,

> I think there's a very different ethos. That whole spiritual element to music—how do you codify that? Today we're so absorbed with trying to define it and capsulate it in some objective way. These things are so subjective and so ephemeral. If you do try to talk about these things you stand the risk of being laughed at, you stand the risk of being mocked.[15]

The ramifications for Kreisler are clear. Modern ears cannot hear Kreisler the way he was heard throughout his career—particularly his early career—because we are simply too knowledgeable *not* to compare him with contemporary violinists. We have heard too many recordings of the Paganini concerto; we have seen too many interviews with rising soloists; we know too well the speed at which this piece can be played, the perfection with which that one was recorded. As consumers we understand and appreciate only definitives: we search compact-disc guides for the ultimate *Water Music*, the most authentic Brandenburgs, the superlative "Ode to Joy." When we find it—if we find it—it becomes the model against which all other performances are judged and upon which all of our expectations are finally based. Most of Kreisler's earliest audiences had no such highly detailed knowledge of previous performers' interpretations, and had, as a result, no such craving for the definitive. They desired merely to hear the definitive *Kreisler*—the Kreisler warmth, the Kreisler lilt, the Kreisler presence. The pieces he played were secondary.

So it was for Kreisler's critics. Faced with reviewing a beguiling instrumentalist whose execution was not always note-perfect, they chose to review not the execution but the artist, the man. Missed notes, sudden improvisations, and other errors all fell under the "occasional lapse" clause that appeared periodically at the end of reviews. Featuring that oblique, intentionally vague language similar to the old Surgeon General's cigarette warnings, the requisite sentence or two gave credence to otherwise glowing reviews and reminded the reader that Kreisler was, after all, a human being. "Mind you," cautioned an Albany critic in a review of Kreisler's 1942 comeback recital, "we do not wish to record that the concert was flawless."[16] Mind you, he never identified the flaws. Why bother? These soft-pedaled complaints lent the critic a respectability he might otherwise have forfeited were his review completely infatuated, but they also emphasized the enormous admiration for Kreisler that was regularly expressed in the mainstream press. To use the vernacular, he was a sacred cow.

"He made the most glorious, intimate, warm, rich, sexy kind of sound I ever heard from any violinist," said Harold Schonberg. "How can you give a player like this a bad review?"[17]

Such an approach to criticism is nearly unthinkable now, but under the circumstances it was understandable, even necessary.

There was simply no other way to cover Kreisler. Whether in so doing critics overlooked or downplayed genuine shortcomings is a valid musical point and an intriguing subject for debate, but it is not historically relevant; one might similarly ponder the fidelity problems of the wax cylinder or the minutest flaws in Johann Strauss the Younger's conducting technique. To dwell on such issues is to miss the greater significance. The wax cylinder was ground-breaking technology; Johann Strauss was a globally popular composer, performer, and leader of waltzes; and Fritz Kreisler was revered and beloved by all who heard him. Did he make mistakes? Did he have memory lapses? Did he, near the end of his career, begin to lose his hearing and hence his grasp of intonation?

Yes. And yes, the critics noticed. But clearly, ultimately, unwaveringly, no one cared.

Thirteen

The Last Years: Kreisler's Retirement and the Failing Public Memory

> It is my opinion that science is having an evil influence on art. I think that life is confused by noises, by acceleration of everything. Everything is judged by how fast it can go, not where it is going. Planes, automobiles, men, everything goes too fast.[1]

Endurance, or perhaps blind stubbornness, had always been one of Fritz Kreisler's surest virtues: he did not give up easily on any long and laborious undertaking, be it marriage to a difficult woman or American concertizing in the face of widespread nationalistic protest. The marriage to Harriet ended only in death. The outcry against him during World War I he acknowledged and succumbed to only when concert appearances became logistically impossible. He did not abandon the violin despite failing his audition for the Vienna Hofoper. He did not abandon Germany until the rise of Nazism nearly consumed him whole in 1938. He did not abandon his career after the accident of 1941, choosing instead to endure a slow and certainly frustrating return to the stage despite permanent damage to his senses and memory.

As a result, it is neither surprising nor remotely out of character that Kreisler took so long to retire, even when it became clear that his virtuosic sheen had started to fade. When his decline began is subject to debate—some say he never fully recovered following the accident, others swear that his age and injuries did not catch up with him until much later—but what remains indisputable is the fact that Kreisler could not have pushed his career any further. Perhaps he should have set aside his violin a year earlier than he did, perhaps two, perhaps five; but by the time he retired he was obviously in decline. Less than a month before his final career performance, on NBC's "Bell Telephone Hour" on 6 March 1950 (as part of a series of radio broadcasts he had agreed to after a decades-long resistance to appearing on the air, which, he initially believed, cheapened the appreciation of music), Kreisler underwent one of several cataract operations intended to repair, at least partially, his deteriorated eyesight. There were no operations for his hearing, or his memory losses, or his bow arm, or his less-than-sure intonation, nor was there a regimen to restore vitality lost to the passage of time. By the end of his five-decade run as a concertizing soloist, he had nowhere to go but home.

To illustrate Kreisler's decline in the final years of his career, one must consider the wildly different perceptions of his musical skills as demonstrated in live performance. Nothing was more consistent, at this stage in his life, than his erraticism. In one concert he was capable of conveying the same grace and conviction that had marked his life on the stage since his Berlin debut in 1899; in another he seemed a sad and ghostly figure, barely able to carry off the contents of an undemanding program. "Was it that bad?" he asked a colleague following one of his last concerts, sensing an old friend's disappointment. "Yes," came the reply. Kreisler knew he was fading, but still, he persisted.

Sometimes, his persistence yielded happy results. On 1 November 1947 Kreisler performed his final recital in Carnegie Hall—not the final recital of his career (he would continue to perform sporadically over the next two years) nor even his last in

New York (there were "Telephone Hour" appearances still to come), but a significant milestone nonetheless. The annual Carnegie Hall appearance had been a staple of the New York City music scene for decades.

Ross Parmenter, covering the recital for *The New York Times*, heard a still-capable violinist performing for a full house of highly appreciative listeners. Recalling the occasion forty-eight years later, Parmenter said that he covered the event as usual, not realizing that it would be the violinist's last in the venue; Kreisler had not announced it as such, and there were no other indications, barring a reduced concert schedule, that the great man was winding down. The critic recalled: "That audience, as might be expected, was somewhat more elderly than audiences of that time. I remember how warmly they were dressed, with many coats trimmed with fur, and how they moved out into the cold after a heart-warming experience."[2]

As was Parmenter's habit—and to his great relief, when he later realized the significance of the occasion—he included in his article not just a straight review of the concert but a sense of it as an event, commenting on the audience and Kreisler's bearing and providing some historical and social context.

> Fitting it in between an appearance up-state and a tour of the Middle West, the unflagging and much loved Fritz Kreisler gave his annual recital yesterday afternoon at Carnegie Hall. The house was filled to its 2,700 capacity, and the warm and continuing applause of the audience proved that the appeal of the 72-year-old violinist is as hardy and as durable as his constitution.
>
> One of the great secrets of that appeal has always been that, as well as being able to meet the masters on equal terms, Mr. Kreisler, perhaps more than any other famous virtuoso, has always been able to play with unwavering sincerity the sort of pieces that ordinary people love to hear.[3]

Among the works on the program were Bach's Sonata No. 2 in B Minor ("stately, vigorous and expressive"), Schumann's *Fantasie* in C Major, Op. 131, and Chausson's *Poème* ("both works had beautiful moments of ardent, poetic feeling"). After the intermission

Kreisler indulged himself and his audience with six short, popular pieces ("all had the old Kreisler magic") and three encores, including, inevitably, *The Old Refrain* and *Schön Rosmarin.*

> Mr. Kreisler stepped onto the stage alone. As it has done in the past, the audience stood to greet him. He started to play before they had barely time to get seated, but such was his command that within a matter of seconds the perfectly silent listeners were hanging on his notes.

Then, at concert's close: "The audience showed it could have gone on listening for much longer, applauding for three minutes after the house lights had been turned up. 'He's a wonderful old man,' one woman was heard to murmur. Everyone seemed to feel the same way."[4]

A similar picture of Kreisler's prowess and appeal was drawn by *The Atlanta Journal*'s Helen Knox Spain, whose enthusiasm for the violinist could hardly be contained.

> When Mr. Kreisler came upon the stage, the audience rose and stood for several minutes paying tribute with mighty applause. . . . The violinist walked upon the stage in a slow gait, but there was little in his playing to indicate his more than 50 years on the concert stage, or the 75 years come February 2, 1950, of his age.

"Kreisler stands supreme," she continued. "He is the king of all violinists. His tone and interpretations stir the emotions of musician and layman alike. A Kreisler recital is that something different in the surging of wonderful music from the fingers and soul of a great man."[5]

Compare these pictures drawn by Parmenter and Spain with another: Harold Schonberg's recollection of a man too old for the stage, half deaf, half blind, playing with poor intonation in a half-filled hall. One of Schonberg's most vivid memories of Kreisler concerns a late-1940s performance with orchestral accompaniment; his account is agonizingly poignant, for it paints the aging Kreisler as a man who could no longer pretend to be a master performer. Gone was Kreisler's mystical connection with the audience; gone, too, was his command of a violinist's most basic tools. Instead of a vigorous man with an old but adoring audience, Schonberg heard a musician weakly hanging on to the glories—and abilities—of his youth.

Discussing the recital many years later, Schonberg said:

> [Kreisler] was old, and he was having bowing problems, and he was out of tune. It was the only time in my life I heard him struggle with the fiddle. The hall was half-empty. It was sad. He did his own cut version of the Paganini Violin Concerto [No. 1 in D], and solo pieces. . . . This was the only time I ever heard him play that way. He was almost deaf at the time, you know. He shouldn't have done it.[6]

The opinionated Harriet Kreisler felt the same way. In an unpublished interview conducted by Louis Lochner in the late 1940s, she brutally criticized her husband's fading powers and said flat-out that he should stop playing publicly. She used a bizarre anecdote to illustrate what she believed was a diminution of the energy that had informed his performances decade after decade: when Kreisler was younger, Harriet said, he gave himself so completely to his music that he was forced to change his underwear at intermission. The full significance of this little detail is not entirely clear, but Harriet's conclusion—that such freshening up was no longer necessary, that one set of undergarments was enough for an evening—was obvious. "He thinks he's still got to teach the world how to fiddle, but what he now plays is flat," she declared.

> He played the *Londonderry Air* correctly but not with that warmth and soul he used to have. Foley and the rest are up in arms if I suggest he stop. But he should. Nobody should play beyond seventy at the latest. What was it that made Fritz what he was? It was a certain warmth, a certain something. I listened closely. That something is gone.[7]

Harriet, always caustic, often right: Kreisler indeed had no business playing for the public when he was all but blind and hard of hearing. It is easy to say so in retrospect, easy to criticize his desire to keep playing so long past his prime. Listening to his later recordings—particularly the *Viennese Rhapsodic Fantasietta* recorded in 1946[8]—leads one to no concrete conclusions about his ability to perform. He in no way embarrassed himself. His intonation is on target, his tone rich and recognizably Kreisler's, his phrasing lyrical if slightly dated. Yet something is clearly missing, some invisible fuel that had fired his engine for more than half a century and had dribbled slowly away. In the interview with Lochner, Harriet attributed this change to a deficit in affect—he was older, she argued, his emotions had dulled, and he did not feel as deeply as he once did. That may be. It may also be that Harriet herself was partly to blame, having so restricted Kreisler's movements outside their home and so weakened his ties to friends and colleagues that a loss in vitality—expressed in his personality and his playing—was perhaps inevitable.

The motivations that drive any soloist, youthful or aging, are complex and not always easily discerned. It is unclear whether Kreisler himself felt driven to perform at his advanced age, or whether he was pushed into it by handlers eager to exploit his name and legacy. Frederic Kreisler said that his great-uncle was "very unhappy" with the decision to retire, that "he loved the stage, he loved the contact with the audience" and was reluctant to give it up.[9] Performance clearly played a significant role in his life—it had defined his world, his marriage, his perception of himself. It is no wonder he found it difficult to leave. Nor was his reluctance to retire particularly foolhardy, considering the extent of his philanthropic obligations, then as always. History may criticize Kreisler's decision to perform, but it cannot so easily dismiss the generosity that drained his pockets and required him, year after year, to keep bringing in the fees. That he was less and less able to earn those big paychecks is a reality that must be faced by all artists who perform into their later years.

"Kreisler hadn't played very often in the last ten years," Schonberg said. "Word had gotten around that maybe he was over the hill, which he was. At the age of eighty [sic] you're entitled. String players don't last as long [as pianists]—you've got a physical problem with the arm and the bow, which you don't have on the piano, which is pretuned."[10]

In truth, Kreisler's concert schedule had been pared back considerably in the last few years before his retirement. Between 6 October 1949 and 6 March 1950, Kreisler's final tour, the violinist performed thirteen concerts, including two appearances on the "Bell Telephone Hour" in New York City, one recital in Syracuse, New York, six in the South, and a smattering of dates in Connecticut and the Midwest. That is a marked cutback from roughly the same period three years earlier (7 October 1946 through 11 February 1947), when Kreisler gave thirty-seven performances throughout the Midwest, South, and Northeast, and it is a far cry from the fifty-eight performances he gave during an even briefer period (14 January through the end of March) in 1926, at the peak of his career.[11] Clearly, he was winding down.

He was also pulling out; as Kreisler's career came to a close, so did his public life. Despite the easy sociability that had characterized his personality since his days in Vienna, Kreisler in his final years assumed a private existence of walks through the neighborhood, afternoon naps, and quiet gatherings with friends and family. He was not entirely cloistered, but he rarely ventured far from their home at the River House on East 52 Street, attracting no more attention than any other aging man sitting on a bench or out for a brief stroll in Manhattan. Even the walks petered out. During an interview with Lochner, Kreisler said that he felt weak in the feet because Harriet prevented his customary walks; she did not want him to go out alone at all.[12] He listened to the radio as well as his ears could hear, read the newspapers as well as his eyes could see, tied up relief packages as well as his hands could manage. He played no music.

He could not have practiced even if he had wanted to. All told, Kreisler acquired more than a dozen world-class violins throughout his life, owning and performing on instruments of venerated beauty and venerable provenance. By the close of his career he had disposed of them all, including his 1734 "Lord Amherst" Stradivarius, purchased by the Rudolph Wurlitzer Company for $10,000[13] and later sold for an undisclosed amount in 1946 to Jacques Gordon, founder of the Gordon String Quartet;[14] Kreisler's 1711 "Earl of Plymouth" Stradivarius, purchased by the Wurlitzer Company for $40,000[15] and later sold for an undisclosed amount to violinist Dorotha Powers;[16] a 1707 instrument by Pietro Guarneri of Mantua, sold to Wurlitzer for $10,000; and violins by Carlo Bergonzi and Daniel Parkes, also sold to Wurlitzer.[17] Kreisler's most famous instrument, his beloved 1733 Guarnerius del Gesù, he donated to the Library of Congress.

So complete was Kreisler's severance from performing that when the copyright for some of his works came up for renewal—and he needed an instrument with which to update or amend fingerings and other details in his compositions—he was forced to borrow a violin and bow from Rembert Wurlitzer.[18] The greatest violinist of his era owned no instrument of his own. "The only thing he had left, at the end, was something he had in the shape of a violin," said Frederic Kreisler, recalling visits with Uncle Fritz at his family's home in Westchester. "It didn't have a back or a front, and it had a fingerboard, and he held on to it. There was no bow, no sound at all. . . . He would put it under his chin and finger it to music he heard on the radio."[19]

At noon every Sunday Frederic and his parents would pick up Fritz and Harriet at the River House and drive them north to Pelham. The family would eat lunch at half-past one or two o'clock, after which the white-haired Uncle would sleep, or walk, or sit around talking. Frederic recalled those days with great fondness:

> He was a great hero to me. He was just wonderful to be with, to be around. He was a very gentle person. I don't know if he was always that way, but certainly at the age that I knew him he was. . . . He would take me by the hand and we would go for a walk. It was very comfortable to be in his presence. He had a great sense of humor. He loved to tell stories.

Most of the stories Fritz and Harriet told during those long, relaxed afternoons were simply tales of people they had known and places they had gone and things they had done. Absent was the elaborate, fictive web-spinning for which the violinist was well-known; this was a time for casual reminiscences, not creative writing.

> What he liked best to remember were the years of playing chamber music together with I guess it was Cortot and Casals and Jacques Thibaud. He always came back to that, and he would think about it and smile about it and remember how much he loved to do it. And he said, "You know, we did that just for fun. It was a pleasure just to be with each other and play with each other."[20]

At the time, Frederic said, his great-uncle wore a hearing aid and "very, very thick lenses" to aid eyesight that had been impaired by cataracts. Harriet was also ailing—with heart trouble and shingles—and "was taking medications all the time." She made frequent visits to hospitals; unlike her husband, who endured old age and its inevitable advance toward death with grace and equanimity borne of faith or philosophic resignation, Mrs. Kreisler noisily lamented her infirmities and regarded the end of life with horror. Death terrified her, wrote Frederic, "because superstition was her substitute for religion and she may have experienced pangs of conscience that conjured up visions of an excruciating eternity."[21]

In another reminiscence, Frederic Kreisler recalled the couple's general appearance:

> They were both tall, and in younger years they were both extremely good-looking. Physically I think they really complemented one another beautifully. His hair was just pure snow white at the end—beautiful. And he had very soft hands, which I knew because he used to hold me by the hand when we walked. His left thumb was very much deformed from the position of holding the fingerboard. The joint where the fingernail is was bent outward from the pressure of the fiddle. Now, whether that's true—it's what I always believed, but it may be that he broke the finger at one point. . . . But it was bent.[22]

Those Sundays in Westchester were the most regular of Kreisler's outings. Occasionally there were others, including a few rare public appearances, which always caused a stir. David Sackson recalled the American debut of Soviet violinist David Oistrakh, who had arrived in New York amid much fanfare (and considerable red tape, thanks to the Cold War) for a 1955 recital in Carnegie Hall. Oistrakh was a lifelong admirer of Kreisler who had always revered him from afar, never having had the opportunity (again thanks to the Cold War) to meet his idol.

Sackson described the scene at Carnegie Hall, which was so crowded that extra audience seating had been arranged on the stage. From that vantage point Sackson witnessed the scene described below.

> Here's the picture:
>
> Everybody's applauding, Oistrakh has just finished [the concert]. He's in and out for applause. I look out, and in about the sixth or seventh row, to my left as I look down from the stage, which would be stage right, of course, I see a person standing up—"Bravo!"—and applauding.
>
> Suddenly it hit me—it's Fritz Kreisler! A gray-haired gentleman with a hearing aid, held by a male nurse, obviously, standing up. Kreisler gets up, I recognize him, and along with my recognizing Kreisler, others sitting on stage recognize him. Suddenly, "It's Fritz Kreisler!"—you know? Like a fire raging through. "Fritz Kreisler!" And by the time poor Oistrakh made his second appearance for applause, the whole place was in turmoil. They knew that something had happened. "Fritz Kreisler!" By this time Kreisler was passing in front of Oistrakh, Oistrakh is taking bows. He doesn't recognize Fritz Kreisler because he never saw him! I mean, this is one of the most anguished moments in his life. . . .
>
> Oistrakh, seeing and sensing this turmoil in the audience, bent down to [his accompanist] . . . and said, "What's happened?" But [the accompanist is] bewildered himself. He doesn't know. He knows that something is happening, but he doesn't know what.
>
> By this time Fritz Kreisler has passed. People are recognizing him, and he makes his way out slowly. Imagine, [Oistrakh] is on stage. The man is going in and out for applause. Fritz Kreisler makes his way down, about six rows down, in front of the stage on his way out to go out the back entrance, and go home. . . .

> This is a heart-breaking thing. It's like your mother or father passing in front of you, and you don't even know them.[23]

(As it turned out, Oistrakh did meet Kreisler—eventually. Months later, when Oistrakh was on his next tour of the United States, he presented to his idol a scroll inscribed with the signatures of master students who had performed an all-Kreisler program for Oistrakh the previous year.)[24]

Another who knew Kreisler in his later years was Yehudi Menuhin, who visited Kreisler on a few occasions (his recollection of meeting Kreisler at Foley's is recounted in Chapter 4). Despite Harriet's best efforts to keep the aging violinist ensconced at home, Menuhin claimed, Kreisler "wasn't a hermit. He wasn't a kind to be a hermit."[25]

Nevertheless, even before Fritz's actual retirement, Harriet had begun to orchestrate his slow but noticeable exodus from public life. Suffering from ill health herself, she had seen her husband lose his keenness of eye and ear and memory, and she was not about to showcase such deficits to a curious world. She had, of course, lobbied long and hard in favor of his permanent retirement. What she also engineered was his quiet departure from society, his retreat into the familiar confines of his home, and his gradual unraveling of relationships that had taken decades to weave. Friends who had grown accustomed to his affectionate missives were at first hurt, then resigned when Kreisler's correspondence grew ever more infrequent and remote. By 1949 Harold Bauer had concluded that his old friend simply no longer liked him; Kreisler, informed by Louis Lochner of Bauer's belief, replied that Harriet "has been sick so long now that we lead a very secluded life, and so I haven't seen much of my old friends and fellow artists. But Harold shouldn't get the impression that I don't care."[26]

So closely did Harriet guard Fritz's public appearances that when Kreisler's old friend Ernest Schelling died, Harriet would not allow her husband to play at his funeral—despite the fact that the music to be performed was the slow movement of Schelling's 1916 Violin Concerto, which was dedicated to Kreisler, and despite Lucie Schelling's emotional appeal to Harriet. Mrs. Kreisler told Mrs. Schelling that Fritz was too tired to perform. When Lucie

Schelling persisted, Harriet blurted: "Do you want me to shout it from the housetops? I'll do that. But Fritz can't play. Ernest is dead anyway, and won't hear it."[27]

A letter from Lochner to Carl and Helen Lamson, dated 8 December 1950, illustrates the sad but inevitable results of the Kreislers' withdrawal from their closest friends.

> How well I understand your hurt feelings! Last summer I was rather ill again part of the time. Harriet and Fritz up in Stockbridge knew about it. Not a peep! Fritz, of course, is getting to be very forgetful, but one word from Harriet would have made him sit down and write me a few lines. But she deliberately tries to make him gaga. Last Monday I wanted to take him to the Bohemians, where that exceptional wunderkind, Michael Rabin, was to play, inter alia, Fritz's Recitative and Scherzo for unaccompanied violin. No soap. Harriet would not allow him. She also would not let him go to [cellist] Willem Willeke's funeral. Fritz is rapidly becoming a recluse, and there is a very sad look about his face. (All this in greatest confidence, of course, but I could weep to think that even now Harriet won't let Fritz have a little fun.) . . .
>
> I have never doubted that Fritz needed an energetic "manager"—but must this continue even after an artist has retired?[28]

In a postscript, Lochner remarked that a "gentleman, formerly of Berlin" had phoned after hearing Lochner discuss his biography on a radio program. He said he agreed with all Lochner said "except considering that 'bitch.'"

Typical of Harriet's control over her husband at this stage was the uproar that erupted when Lochner, encouraged by friends and acquaintances with Hollywood connections, investigated the possibility of using his Kreisler biography as the basis for a film. It was a natural idea, and Lochner was hardly outrageous for pursuing it: the life he had chronicled was theatrical, globe-hopping, musical, and long, certainly fertile ground for a cinematic narrative. In 1952 he approached Kreisler for his approval, sending him a permission to be signed that would have allowed Lochner to collaborate on a dramatization based on the biography that could be sold as the foundation for a movie. The permission outlined the terms for such an agreement—one-third of all money received from the sale, no less than twenty-five thousand dollars, would go to Kreisler. It also used extremely reassuring language in the matter of characterization: "It is to be definitely understood," it said, "that my life must be portrayed in such a manner as to be in keeping with my dignity and stature in the music world and further, that it must not portray me or any member of my family in an unfavorable light."[29] (Exactly *which* member of Kreisler's family might well be portrayed in an unfavorable light is not hard to guess. It is disappointing that the film was, indeed, never made, since any depiction of Harriet—caustic or charming, truthful or bowdlerized—would have been fascinating to observe.)

As might have been predicted, Kreisler's entourage responded immediately and negatively to Lochner's request. "To our amazement Mrs. Kreisler intervened violently. 'Not over my dead body,' she said," Lochner wrote seven years later in a letter to Mrs. John Toth.

> I explained that the prospective producer would submit the script to the Kreislers for any corrections they might wish to make; that later, when the "shooting" had been completed and the picture was being put together, they would have the right to veto anything that did not please them. In vain: Harriet Kreisler remained adamant.
>
> That was the end of our hopes, for in the case of a living person such a picture can only be done with the permission of the person whose life is being dramatized. As poor Fritz is almost blind and very hard of hearing, he has no say in the matter, although I, knowing how much he liked my biography of him, feel sure he would be equally pleased to see his life filmed.
>
> But there you are! Harriet won't even let him read the fine letters I keep receiving since an edition of my book has appeared in England, another in the German language translation in Vienna and a third, a Japanese version, in preparation. She does not want him to be reminded of the past; claims it upsets him. I know the contrary to be true.[30]

Lochner must have pressed the idea just a little too far, for he received a letter from Charles Foley that burned with ire. "My best advice to you, who should know conditions with regard to the health of the two people involved better than a rank outsider," Foley wrote, "would be to drop all thoughts of this matter completely and never refer to it either orally or in writing again."[31] Presumably, Lochner complied.

There was one type of public exposure that Harriet repeatedly, unfailingly approved for her husband: the black-tie birthday bash. So standard were these in their content and purpose that it is a wonder Harriet agreed to them; each occasion was by definition intended to remind the violinist of his past, in such a manner that anyone who happened to parachute in with no previous knowledge of the man might understandably believe that the person being honored was already dead. If Harriet thought that Fritz would be agitated by seeing a dramatization of his life, how would he react to these windy affairs?

Actually, he seemed to enjoy them—or he put on a good face, if only to act like a gentleman and please his friends. Every five years, the music world's brightest lights gathered to pay homage to the great and aging Kreisler, whose watery brown eyes looked sadder and great white head grew bushier with each updated photograph. On such occasions Kreisler's friends, admirers, and onetime colleagues joined in their praises of a man whose artistry had perhaps begun to seem old-fashioned and whose very relevance had long since started to fade. Kreisler's birthday parties were a chance to return him to the spotlight he once commanded and to remind those who attended and the world at large that here, indeed, was one of music's towering figures. Had Kreisler not retreated from performing, had his powers with the fiddle not started to fade, no such celebrations would have been necessary. Whether motivated by guilt, or love, or fear that each passing birthday might be the man's last, the elaborate fetes of his final twelve years served to underscore just how deeply felt—and just how complete—had been Kreisler's absence from music. Long before he died, he was gone. These were living wakes rather than birthday parties.

Ironically, the first such event took place just a month before Kreisler's final public appearance on the "Bell Telephone Hour." On 2 February 1950, Kreisler turned seventy-five years old. The day before, glitterati from around the country and across the decades gathered at the Ritz-Carlton Hotel to honor the man who was once the undisputed apex of violin artistry.

In addition to a celebration of Kreisler's birthday, the occasion was a benefit for the Musicians Emergency Fund. Kreisler had recently taken over as chairman of the board for the organization and its spinoff, the Hospitalized Veterans Service, which provided musical instruction and diversion for ill veterans. Nathan Milstein later described the audience as "rich ladies who had paid a hundred dollars. . . . [T]here were no gentlemen."[32]

Festivities included a lunch, speeches, and a concert performed by many of the prominent musical personalities of the day. Milstein played the *Praeludium and Allegro*. Jennie Tourel sang *The Old Refrain*, with Dimitri Mitropoulos accompanying on the piano. A string quartet played *Liebesfreud* while Kreisler blew out seventy-five candles on an enormous towered cake, inspiring four hundred guests to stand and applaud.[33] Claudio Arrau also performed. Jacques Thibaud cabled from France, congratulations were sent by Serge Koussevitzky and Lawrence Tibbett, and accolades were duly given by the likes of Georges Enesco and Bruno Walter. The committee that planned the event included Zino Francescatti, Jascha Heifetz, Yehudi Menuhin, Joseph Szigeti, Efrem Zimbalist, Isaac Stern, Albert Spalding, Samuel Dushkin, John Corigliano, and Tossy Spivakovsky. Everyone who was anyone was there, or tried to be, or wanted to be. John McCormack's widow sent greetings. So did Myra Hess. As *Musical America* remarked, the personalities who attended the fete amounted to "a virtual *Who's Who* of the upper echelons of the violin-playing world." It was a star-studded memorial.

If this seems too harsh an assessment, consider the telling comments made by Fulton Sheen during the festivities, recalled years later by Milstein:

> I remember that Sheen said to Kreisler, "When God decides that He wants to see you, you will be met by nine angels

> with violins. And they will say to you, 'Maestro, teach us to play the violin as divinely as you do!'"
>
> In response, [Fund president] Mrs. [Helen] Hull pleaded, "Wait a moment, Monsignor, we're not ready for that, let our Fritz stay with us a bit longer!"[34]

Sheen was not alone in trying to whisk Kreisler off to the afterlife. An elegiac tone haunted many of the greetings—*Time* magazine even called them "eulogies"—that were read aloud at the celebration. Bruno Walter opined, "He did not play the violin, he became the violin." Georges Enesco recalled the "revelation" of hearing Kreisler for the first time in 1910, and compared his playing with the more flawed musicianship of other violinists. "With Fritz," he concluded, "there is no 'but.'" President Harry Truman sent "Hearty birthday greetings to one whom the power of music has given the spirit of eternal youth"; Pope Pius XII sent his apostolic benediction.[35] Even Harriet took her turn at the podium, choosing to paraphrase Mary Martin: "I'm in love with a wonderful guy."[36]

Through each little testimonial Kreisler sat, manners intact, handsome head erect, with more dignity than anyone forced to sit through his own dirge could ever be expected to muster. Flattered as he must have been to hear such praise, he could not mistake the bittersweet farewells wrapped so carefully—yet so clearly—in all the approbation. (Fittingly, the musical offerings that evening included Cuban pianist Jorge Bolet playing Liszt's *Funérailles*.) So threnodic were the proceedings that when all was said and done, Kreisler himself was inspired to add, tongue only partly in cheek: "When I listened to all the speeches, I became overwhelmed by the conviction that I had listened to the obituary of my own artistic life."[37]

The honoree confirmed as much in his own remarks, which focused good-naturedly on the vagaries of aging and set himself discreetly apart from more youthful violinists. Not one to "stand in the way of the younger generation," Kreisler said, he stood before them at seventy-five, an age of "physical debilities and moral responsibilities." Regaling his audience with familiar admonitions—young fiddlers should avoid too much practice, should have no teacher past the age of fourteen, should remember that violin playing begins in the brain—he bemoaned the influence of "crazy mothers who drive their children into careers when they're not fitted for it." And he told the usual stories, repeating well-worn accounts of his World War I wounds (those Cossacks again), his "transcriptions" of works by the old masters (it would have been "tactless" to repeat his own name on early programs), his devotion to charities, his stubborn survival through "wars and depressions and catastrophes." Through it all his comments bore the reflective self-invention of someone who, surrounded by overeager eulogists, is determined to write his own obituary.[38]

At the close of the evening, Kreisler addressed his well-wishers with remarks cut short by the ever-present Harriet, who tugged at the table cloth to keep her husband from blathering on. "Accept the profound gratitude," he told his listeners, "of one who will always remain your humble and faithful friend."[39]

Anyone who attended, or even read about, Kreisler's seventy-fifth birthday party could be forgiven for assuming that he was on his last few breaths. What a surprise it must have been to all involved—particularly those who organized the Ritz-Carlton bash—when the old fiddler's lifespan stretched for five more years, requiring everyone to regroup for another fete. This time, the memorializing took place at the St. Regis Roof, again under the auspices of the Musicians Emergency Fund. The Fund was as much a reason for the fete as Kreisler's eightieth birthday: the celebration was an occasion to announce that the newly established Fritz and Harriet Kreisler Fund (part of Musicians Emergency) had already raised fourteen thousand dollars toward its eventual goal of eighty thousand dollars—or one thousand dollars for each year of Kreisler's life. The money would be used to aid musicians starting out, unemployed older musicians, or hospitalized veterans requiring music therapy.[40]

Fulton J. Sheen was again on hand to deliver a tribute, and greetings were read from New York Governor Harriman, Mayor Wagner, Cardinal Spellman, Sir Winston Churchill, Sir John Barbirolli and the Concertgebouw Orchestra of Amsterdam, and Elizabeth, Queen Mother of Belgium. A quartet of female voices (sopranos Eleanor Steber and Hilde Gueden, mezzo-sopranos Rise Stevens and Gladys Swarthout) sang "Happy Birthday"; Mrs. Frederick T. Steinway presented a scroll inscribed with the names of well-wishers and contributors; and five young men associated with the Hospitalized Veterans Music Service at the U.S. Naval Hospital in St. Albans, Queens, presented the violinist with his birthday cake.[41]

Just as Truman sent his hellos for Kreisler's seventy-fifth, Dwight Eisenhower conveyed Presidential greetings with a message read at his eightieth. It said:

> Your musical artistry has become an unforgettable part of the experience of people the world over. The human warmth which is so integral to it is reflected in such responsibilities as your chairmanship of the Hospitalized Veterans Music Service, an organization which has brightened the lives of patients in Veterans Administrations Hospitals by voluntarily bringing them musical instruction and entertainment.
>
> You have my best wishes for many happy years to come.[42]

Nor was the Wednesday night bash at the Regis Roof the only celebration organized in Kreisler's honor. On Tuesday he was honored with a luncheon at Luchow's restaurant, where RCA Victor presented him with a silver pressing of one of his early disks recorded for the label, Smetana's *Aus der Heimat*, recorded on 11 May 1910. The disk was duly played, prompting Kreisler to remark (somewhat cryptically): "If we did it today, it would be quite different." Radio City Music Hall paid tribute to Kreisler the composer with a birthday performance of an "Overture on Kreisler Themes."[43]

Lastly, on the evening of 2 February 1955, WQXR radio in New York City broadcast an interview with the aging violinist, who in his lisping, high-pitched voice recalled his years at the Vienna Conservatory, his early compositions, and his lifelong quest for an artistic ideal. With puckish charm and unfailing self-possession he rehashed once again his rationalization for duping the world with his seventeen "fakes," concluding at last: "So you see, during my whole artistic life, well, the whole thing was nothing but—you might call it a concoction of lies, of white lies."[44] Even at age eighty—even after decades of living in the United States—his English still carried the inflections, the cadences, and the guttural *r*'s of Austria. He was then as ever a child of Vienna.

The New York Times published a tribute of its own on the editorial pages.

> It has been some years since Fritz Kreisler has lifted his bow in public. But in his time he was a virtuoso of the highest rank and a sovereign artist. As Bruno Walter said of him: his right hand was made for the bow, his left hand for the finger board. To this was added the warmth, humanity and insight into the music that characterized all his performances. Today those performances lie mostly in the minds of those who heard them—a recurring spiritual dividend. . . .
>
> Music for him had never been merely a technique but a way of life. To project the lofty architecture of a Bach partita, to help a musician over a rough spot economically, to see that the healing art of music was brought to ill or convalescent veterans were all part of that life. Long before music was considered a therapy for the ill, Fritz Kreisler knew that music was (as he said) "a healing factor, a powerful stimulus to overcoming national animosities, a harbinger of peace and international brotherhood."[45]

Those who had treated Kreisler's eightieth birthday as a final, fond farewell were caught off guard—again—by his eighty-fifth. The man was still alive; what could be done or said in celebration that had not been done and said already? As though Kreisler had not received enough scrolls in his life, on 2 February 1960 he was presented with another—courtesy of Mayor Wagner and Cardinal Spellman, who also gave him a medal. It was an easy way to commemorate the birth of a man whose death seemed always imminent but never actual. This time, however, there was no big bash, no fete at the Regis Roof, no formal dinner featuring cabled greetings from around the world. Indeed, had a party been organized, the honoree himself might not have been able to attend. As he told Harold Schonberg:

> I have the infirmities of eighty-five. Mostly in the ears and eyes: I can walk miles if necessary, only they won't let me. But there is no sense, my dear, in my picking up a violin any

> more. Mostly I listen to the radio and read whatever I can read. My ears and eyes can still do that much.[46]

Decades later Schonberg recalled his interview with Kreisler, remembering most vividly the ageless poise of the man. "He was a Viennese gentleman, probably the uncrowned grand duke of Austria," he said. "He had impeccable manners, and he was still at this age terribly handsome and aristocratic. His hearing was very bad then, and his eyes—well, he wasn't blind, but he was pretty damn close to it."

> I looked at his hands and I said, "Your hands look so young, there's not a mark on them. They look as though you could come out today and play." He said, "I have a terrible left hand." He took his little finger and pushed it way back. He said, "I'm double jointed." He said, "It's very weak." He said, "I had to refinger everything to avoid using the fourth finger."[47]

(Apparently his first finger was weak as well. In an article published in *The New York Times* on 4 February 1962, just a few days after Kreisler's death, Schonberg told of a conversation he had had with the violinist, who claimed that because of the soft bones of his left index finger he had no strength in that finger and therefore had to "refinger the entire repertory to get the middle finger for all high positions. This gave me very much trouble when I was young." In a conversation with Sam Kissel, Kreisler held up his broad hand against Kissel's and complained of the shortness of his fingers: "He said, 'I always had trouble with my goddam little fingers.' I said, 'Which one?' He said, 'The first finger.' ")[48]

Schonberg's written account of that interview, published two days before Kreisler's eighty-fifth birthday, is an unabashed paean to the violinist and a fair indication of just how revered he still was, particularly within music circles. The scroll Kreisler was to receive from the city was a barely adequate gift, Schonberg wrote. Instead, "If the music world had its way, Mr. Kreisler would be receiving a violin studded with diamonds (for his brilliance), sheathed in velvet (for his tone), mounted next to a Botticelli painting (for his style)." In fact:

> By common consent, Mr. Kreisler, who has not played in public for many years, is the greatest and most beloved violinist this century has produced. Old and young musicians, great and mediocre, all have one thing in common: veneration for Mr. Kreisler, the most elegant of violinists, the one more than anybody who could make the violin "speak."[49]

Kreisler sounded subdued, philosophical, in this and other interviews granted during this last period in his life, as though he had lived for so long and was so far removed from his own accomplishments that they, and he, appeared smaller than they actually were. His was the humility of one who outlives his own influence; like many of the giants who had walked before him, he had watched his own great figure shrink in fame and relevance with each passing year. "I have had many beautiful moments in music," he said.

> Do you know I once played the viola? Sometimes I would sit in with Casals and others, and would play the viola in a string quartet. I did not do it too often. It spread my fingers. Ah, my dear, what a joy it was to play chamber music with Casals, Thibaud, Enesco, with Pugno at the piano![50]

Recollections of his earlier glory were wistful, muted, burdened with the knowledge that a golden era had come and gone and now was all but forgotten.

> When I first came to America in 1888, the agencies asked, "Who plays the best Brahms? The best Beethoven?" Now they ask, "Who draws the most?" Times have changed, my dear friend. There was country above Forty-sixth Street. The hares and goats ran around. Ah, America in those days was a cheap place! For twenty-five cents you could get a beautiful lunch. And you got two drinks with it.

"My dear friend," he sighed, "I do not think we are going ahead. There is no peace in the world. Look at Algeria, at the Near East, not to talk of Mr. Khrushchev. And we have plenty of trouble right here."[51]

Nor was Kreisler all that sanguine about the most recent crop of violinists. He admired Francescatti, he said, and Heifetz and Milstein and Stern. Oistrakh he admired the most. "Oistrakh has deep musicianship and a colossal technique. And he has one quality very few have, my dear friend. He does not play too fast. This is very unusual today. We are living in the time of money, and power, and violence," he said, "and, above all, speed."[52]

In April 1961, Ruggiero Ricci organized a concert with the Symphony of the Air to commemorate Kreisler's eighty-sixth—and last—birthday. Sparsely attended, the concert consisted exclusively of Kreisler's compositions and arrangements and served to remind a musical community smitten with youth that one of its oldest members had left an enduring legacy. His birthday passed with little other public notice; Harriet had once again been hospitalized, and the violinist himself was in no shape for public appearances. He had by this time long since ceased performing, and in the fickle world of performance his Old World elegance was but a faint, quaint memory; as a composer of charming melodies, however, he had left his mark. As Winthrop Sargeant commented in *The New Yorker:*

> Mr. Kreisler, of course, passed his peak nearly a generation ago and subsided into a long retirement, though New Yorkers have frequently noticed his aging and dignified figure strolling about the streets of mid-Manhattan, where he has made his home. In his time, he was one of the most celebrated of performing musicians—never the most brilliant of technicians but a personality of truly engaging charm and a man who could bring rare insight to the interpretation of works that demanded maturity of style.

Sargeant remarked on Kreisler's value as a composer as well:

> He was also a man of considerable intellect, and a composer of modest pieces for his instrument, many of which have remained very popular, and none of which strained after self-conscious originality of any sort. Of the grace and formal perfection of these pieces . . . Mr. Kreisler's aim in composing was simply the nowadays almost forgotten one of providing a few moments of enjoyment for his listeners. In this he succeeded wonderfully, being a gifted, if somewhat nostalgic, melodist and a highly skilled craftsman. Actually, along with the late Sergei Rachmaninoff and the late Ernö Dohnanyi, he stands as one of the last of the great composing virtuosos, a type that is today practically extinct, though during the eighteenth and nineteenth centuries a composer who was not also a master of the performing art was so rare that the exceptions to the rule (Berlioz, among very few others) stood out as eccentrics. It could be that all composing should be done by virtuosos, and that the lack of performing virtuosity among contemporary composers explains a good deal about what is the matter with modern music. . . .
>
> Perhaps it is somewhat pompous on my part to make Mr. Kreisler's innocent and melodious little compositions the subject of a general dissertation on the relation of composing to performing. Still, they do exhibit a fastidiousness and appropriateness found in the music of men who are not strangers to the concert platform. . . . They are all unpretentious, tasteful, engaging, and—I suspect—immortal.[53]

This was a prescient assessment, for Kreisler is indeed better known today as a composer than as an instrumentalist. Remarkably clear reissues of many of the violinist's old recordings have renewed some interest in his performances, as have sporadic broadcasts on classical radio. But by far the greatest single indicator of Kreisler's profile among late-twentieth-century listeners is the enduring popularity of his shorter compositions and arrangements, many of which have been performed as encores and recorded by prominent contemporary violinists. Many such modern recordings lack the intangibles that distinguished Kreisler's playing—the whimsy, the Viennese silkiness, the dancing *joie de vivre*—and a few give the music a rather superficial treatment, as though it were less than worthy of their full musical attention. This is a mistake: Kreisler's compositions suffer when they are pandered to or patronized, requiring a skilled and serious interpreter to realize their inherent musicality. Faced with works that are widely regarded as light fare, many modern players are tempted to overdo it, to lay on the schmaltz, to "ham it up." Such interpretations belie the sincerity in Kreisler's short pieces, their eloquent melodicism and often surprising harmonies. Unfortunately—and with a few notable exceptions, including Itzhak Perlman's and Joshua Bell's recordings of Kreisler works—they are rarely if ever taken seriously.

Nevertheless, the mere presence of Kreisler's "lollipops" on modern concert programs and compact disc recordings bears witness to the works' lasting appeal, their very inventiveness as pleasing to audiences today as they were fifty years ago. They are deceptively seductive little tunes. As Harold Schonberg wrote in a tribute written a few days after Kreisler's death, "As a composer, Kreisler enriched the repertory with a large number of delicious morceaux."[54] (Paul Henry Lang's assessment of Kreisler's gift of composition was slightly less laudatory: "Mr. Kreisler was not a great composer, but he was a very agreeable one.")[55]

Even at the end, his compositions did not fail him. His eyesight may have deteriorated, his hearing may have worsened, his intonation may have wobbled, and his bow arm may have slipped, but those short, sweet pieces in their composer's hands were enough to transport listeners from Kreisler's twilight to the height of his career. He had always been the best interpreter, arguably the only true interpreter, of his own music. Near the close of his professional life, Kreisler performances of Kreisler works were the single most persuasive reason to keep listening. No one spoke that language as fluently as he.

Fourteen

Saying Goodbye to "A Beam of Light"

> Is the thing true of an art in one age true of the same art in the next? I sometimes wonder, and it frightens me.[1]

Fritz Kreisler died on 29 January 1962, four days before his eighty-seventh birthday. He died in the Harkness Pavilion of Columbia Presbyterian Medical Center, where he had been since 13 January. His agent said he died following a heart attack.[2] At the time of his death he was already a spectral figure, a wispy-haired man of great dignity and greater modesty whose visage stares knowingly and mournfully out of occasionally published photographs. He had lived twelve years past his retirement, but he had long outlived the pertinence of his own era; to a public preoccupied with expanding technology, a shrinking globe, and Cold War brinkmanship, Kreisler's Old World posture must have seemed quaintly provincial. At the same time, his command of the violin—once considered without peer, without question—had been overlooked, if not entirely forgotten, by a generation of concertgoers reared on Heifetz and his musical progeny. Audiences have a notoriously short memory, even for their most exalted heroes; once a performer leaves the stage, he relinquishes his spot in the public eye to whomever has the skill and pluck to follow. Whether he earns a more permanent place in history is a matter left to scholarship, the opinion of peers, and time's impartial judge. "To an extent, musical performers die when they lay aside their instruments," stated an editorial eulogizing Kreisler in *The New York Herald Tribune*. "There are young musicians today to whom Fritz Kreisler is already a legend."[3]

Kreisler's death brought with it a frank, at times almost worshipful, reassessment of his career. Critics who had not reviewed (or indeed heard) his playing for more than a decade devoted inches of newsprint to nostalgic reflections on the violinist's unquantifiable allure; fellow instrumentalists, some of whom represented Kreisler's antithesis in musicianship or technique, reflected on his ability and legacy as a role model to generations of violinists. Everyone who had anything to say commented on the personal qualities that made Kreisler one of the most admired and least vilified public figures in the world. His greatness was extolled in tribute after blushing tribute.

The *Herald Tribune*, for one, crowned him the greatest violinist of his time. Such a title "is no mean accolade, and no one would have withheld it from Fritz Kreisler. . . . No one has filled his place on the world's musical scene since he ceased to play twelve years ago, and it is unlikely that anyone ever shall." The editorial continued:

> Kreisler had an inherent, uncanny ability to stir the hearts and the imagination of those to whom music was only a pleasant pastime as well as those to whom it was the center of life itself. . . . [N]ot only his memory but his very existence will surely linger in the music he left—not only in such works as the *Praeludium and Allegro* he attributed to Pugnani, but in the ever enchanting *Caprice Viennois* and *Schön Rosmarin*. We are fortunate, too, that he lived in the age of recording, so that many of his matchless performances may continue to be heard and cherished. And there remain those things which no recording and no photograph could ever capture—

> the warmth, the dignity, the love for his art and his fellow men that went side by side with the genius of Fritz Kreisler. In the minds and hearts of those who knew him and heard him, these too will abide.[4]

In *The New York Times*, Harold Schonberg wrote an analysis of Kreisler's musicianship—discussing the length of his bow strokes (short), his mastery of rubato ("infallible"), the quality of his tone ("of unparalleled sweetness"), and the fact, properly stressed, that as a violinist he belonged to no particular school. Kreisler adhered to neither the Paganini style, "with its emphasis on technique and slam-bang virtuosity," nor the "classical" style founded by Louis Spohr and popularized by Joseph Joachim.[5] It might also be pointed out (although Schonberg did not) that Kreisler stayed similarly removed from any later styles of playing, and that he became, by virtue of his individuality, something of a "school" in and of himself. This occurred not because he intended it to be so—remember, Kreisler had no formal pupils—but because his style of playing wielded an influence all its own. From his beginnings as a prominent soloist, Kreisler was mentor, in spirit if not in fact, to uncounted violinists. "The art of Fritz Kreisler was unique, and among his colleagues he was unanimously considered the greatest violinist of the century," Schonberg wrote. Kreisler differed from other violinists "in his charm, and in the sheer aristocracy of his musical conceptions." This aristocratic quality extended to his presence in performing. "There was something regal about Kreisler on the stage; and yet, without condescension, he could take the audience into his confidence and give each member the idea that he was playing for him and him alone."

Schonberg continued:

> With his innate taste, he never distorted a musical phrase. His interpretations were natural, unforced and glowing. Everything about his playing was natural. . . .
>
> As a musician, Kreisler had more of the imponderable elements that go into great playing than any of his contemporaries. His conceptions reflected the charm and aristocracy

> of his nature—a charm that contained elements of the Vienna of Franz Josef's day, of Paris in the Eighteen Eighties, of a more relaxed century and gracious way of doing things.
>
> And yet there was nothing dated about his playing. To his very last days on the concert stage he never could be called an anachronism, because his conceptions were so utterly musical, so completely lacking in eccentricity, and so convincing on their own terms. There was not a living violinist who did not bow to Kreisler as a master.[6]

Schonberg had more to say on the matter. A few days later the *Times* printed a second analysis, a more complete explication of the Kreisler appeal that reiterated the belief, among violinists, that "Kreisler was the only one."

> They would talk about the splendor and accuracy of the Heifetz technique, about the incredible sonority of the Elman tone, about Szigeti's way with Bach. But the conversation would inevitably turn to Kreisler, the complete violinist. Tone, technique and style were fused in him. In his playing were a warmth and a charm that were at once the despair and the admiration of every twentieth-century violinist.
>
> One was never conscious of him playing an instrument. He was the instrument.[7]

The editorial page of *The New York Times* provided another pithy summation of Kreisler's career on the day after the violinist's death:

> Fritz Kreisler, who died yesterday after an incredible career that extended over sixty years, was a beloved musician. His violin playing was beloved not only by the public but also by his colleagues, a notably critical lot. He was beloved as a man and as a composer.
>
> Kreisler was a rare human being who spread a beam of light wherever he passed. He had but to pick up his violin and there was the inimitable Kreislerian aura. Nobody in our time had such elegance of conception, such courtly manners, such a refined way of approaching music.

> As a violinist, in his great days, his playing was magical. It was a combination of tone, style, musicianship and emotional resource all working at an extraordinary level. Certain violinists may have excelled him in this or that aspect of technique, or on the repertory, but none put so many different elements together at one time.
>
> Perhaps the keynote of his playing was charm. Kreisler never was interested in showing off tone or technique; he was interested in making music with as much beauty as possible. His sweet, unforced manner at the violin brought the audience into a living room rather than a concert hall. Those who remember his playing and his platform presence need not be reminded of his greatness. The younger generation, to whom his magic will necessarily remain but legend, will be the losers. Kreisler's art was as much style and period as anything else, and it was an art that has vanished with him.[8]

Paul Henry Lang was equally effusive in *The New York Herald Tribune*.

> Perhaps here we should speak of the man, for this great artist was a remarkable man, possessed of remarkable intelligence and culture, aside from his attractive qualities of gentleness and humor. . . . Those of us who remember Mr. Kreisler's playing in his prime will recall his bow dancing with unerring nonchalance, his fingers squirming on the strings with accuracy, but above all the infectious communication of his playing.[9]

In a remembrance titled "The Paragon," *Newsweek* recalled a comment Kreisler made more than a decade before his death: "Nobody can be claimed as the first violinist in the world. There isn't any one most beautiful woman in the world either, and there isn't one pair of the most beautiful legs in the world."[10] Aside from the remark's winking naughtiness, it captured something that set Kreisler apart from many of his peers—an inherent, obvious modesty. Perhaps taking a cue from his wife, whose assessment of her husband's musicianship so often sank to frank denigration, he almost always downplayed his own abilities.

Such protestations, when uttered in the company of admirers and colleagues, usually fell on deaf ears. *Newsweek*'s account continued:

> There was a first violinist in the world, and for at least a half a century it had been Fritz Kreisler. On occasion, others might have played with more dizzying dexterity or blinding speed, but no one had a warmer, sweeter tone, a nobler sense of purpose, or a finer feeling for the instrument itself. As his friend Bruno Walter observed: "He did not play the violin, he became the violin."[11]

Newsweek's rival *Time* was more matter-of-fact in its assessment of Kreisler's gifts, acknowledging his "taste for melodious schmalz" (same idea, different spelling: *Newsweek* called it "his unblushing sympathy for schmaltz") and calling attention to his occasional tendency to slip off key. The article nevertheless referred glowingly to Kreisler's tone, rhythmic gift, musical imagination, and modesty; as Kreisler himself once said, "the world is a great child and tires easily. You cannot make friends for long with all the world." It quoted Kreisler's assessment of his own career, given when the violinist was 79: "I have achieved only a medium approach to my ideal in music. I got only fairly near."[12]

Other tributes followed, most of them overlooking even the violinist's most obvious failings—nowhere, for example, did anyone mention his predilection for getting lost in performance—and all of them sounding vaguely guilty in their praise, as though his eulogists felt unfaithful for having turned their attention years before from their first true love to younger and flashier swains. We may have ignored you for more than a decade, these tributes seemed to say, but we did not forget. Obituaries and editorials were thus tossed at Kreisler's memory like bouquets thrown regretfully at his grave. Not surprisingly, the most eloquent encomiums came from the violinist's colleagues (many additional such tributes have been offered in Chapter 11).

Joseph Szigeti's farewells effectively touched upon the impact that Kreisler had on many of his fellow musicians.

> These random jottings are not my leave-taking of the incomparable Fritz Kreisler. I silently did this when I listened to him for the last time, at a rehearsal with Donald Voorhis for a "Telephone Hour" broadcast in the late 1940s. And I once again said goodbye to him in the mid-1950s when I looked through stacks of old scratched 78s in most unlikely-looking junk shops, always with the thought in the back of my mind of finding some Kreisler treasures. On one particular foray in Boston I carried back to my hotel a whole boxful of ten-inch records. . . . [including] *Old Folks at Home*, No. 64130. True, they were in a pitiful condition, most of them, but the old Kreisler magic shone right through all these maltreated grooves, and they will help me relive moments that only his genius could give.[13]

Zino Francescatti spoke of Kreisler's gentle and unfailingly generous nature. "I never heard Kreisler be unjust, or have pleasure in criticizing someone," he said. "Intellect, love, modesty, tremendous knowledge, and an immense heart—that was Kreisler for me."[14]

Isaac Stern had similar words, reflecting on Kreisler's place in the great era of performers that included such figures as Casals, Ysaÿe, Rachmaninoff, Cortot, and Thibaud, among others—performers whose music and performances are cherished in the memories of millions. Kreisler's death, Stern said, marked the passing of one of the last links with that era.

> When one spoke of him, the gentle, glowing adjectives seemed to come most quickly to the tongue. His appearance on the stage was the epitome of the wise, understanding grandfather (at least to those of us who knew him in his later years), and in our ears we always carried the immediate impression of a golden, uniquely personal sound, instantly recognizable and unmatched by anyone else.[15]

Stern concluded: "His influence was gentle. He was never dramatic, bombastic, or dazzling as a virtuoso. But he loved music, and music truly loved him. No more can be said of any artist."

On 2 February—Kreisler's birthday—Bishop Fulton J. Sheen delivered the eulogy at the violinist's funeral Mass in the Church of St. John the Evangelist in Manhattan. In his remarks Sheen compared Kreisler's soul and body to the violin and bow; the two had been separated, he said, and the melodies made on earth could be heard no longer.

> One wonders if the soul, the violin, is not like what woodsmen say about the trees that are cut down and become logs that are put in a fire. They give forth many colors. Woodsmen say that every color that ever entered a tree is diffused and spread. . . . One wonders if the violin does not retain every melody, every tune, every concert played upon it. Whether this be true of trees or violins, we are certain it is true of the soul.[16]

Kreisler was blessed, Sheen said, with the gift of music and the gift of faith. He recalled one occasion when the violinist was preparing to give one of his numerous radio concerts. He asked Kreisler whether he planned on practicing beforehand. Kreisler said no—but whenever he played, he returned his gift to God. "That is why I cannot practice," he told Sheen. Sheen prayed that Kreisler would be greeted by angels singing Vieuxtemps's *Fantaisie-caprice*, with which Kreisler had made his American debut in 1888.

The pallbearers included Charles Foley, Mischa Elman, and Franz Rupp; by one count, more than fifteen hundred mourners attended. Harriet, seriously ill and confined to their home at East 52nd Street, did not. Among those present were Kreisler's nephew, Kurt, and Kurt's son, Frederic. Frederic flew home from overseas to attend.[17]

Harold Coletta recalled the mood in St. John the Evangelist.

> When Kreisler's coffin was brought in, there was such a shudder among everyone in the church that we all broke out and wept at the same time. . . . [Sheen said], "When Fritz was dying, I went to visit him [to] prepare him for the afterlife. I was to cleanse his mouth, eyes, ears, hands. But when it came to cleansing his hands, I didn't want to erase the magic and the beauty of what those hands had given us."
>
> Again, we all burst into tears.[18]

Six days after Kreisler's funeral, Mischa Elman interrupted his recital at Carnegie Hall in a gesture to the late violinist. Opening the second half of his program, Elman informed the audience that he wished to pay homage to his "great colleague and friend." He then performed Kreisler's *Preghiera* (Prayer), a quietly elegiac work that requires a mute. It was a fitting and tender tribute from one great violinist to another.[19]

In December, four violinists—Nathan Milstein, Isaac Stern, Zino Francescatti, and Erica Morini—gathered in Carnegie Hall for a memorial concert to benefit the Musicians Memorial Fund. Milstein and Stern played the Vivaldi D Minor Concerto; Milstein and Morini played the Bach Double Concerto; Milstein, Morini, Stern, and Francescatti gathered for the Vivaldi Concerto for Four Violins, in B Minor. Schonberg gave each performer an unqualified rave.[20]

Oddly, no one played anything by Fritz Kreisler, not even an encore.

On 29 May 1963, Harriet Lies Kreisler died in her home at East 52nd Street. She was ninety-three years old. She had survived a year and four months past the death of her husband, to whom she had been married for six decades and from whom she had derived satisfaction both professional and personal. Just as Fritz owed his career to Harriet, so did Harriet owe her raison d'être to Fritz: she was his manager as well as his wife, the woman who controlled every aspect of his life and in so doing controlled her own. That she managed to survive, ailing or not, more than a year without him is a testament to her stubborn spirit and a reminder of the strength that fueled them both for more than half a century.

Shortly after Kreisler's death Charles Foley provided the following assessment of the man and the musician:

> When I say that Fritz Kreisler was the greatest violinist of his era, I am only repeating what hundreds of others have also said. To say that I will miss him would be putting it mildly. He was a great man in many fields. He was a kindly man. He

> was truly one of nature's noblemen. I feel honored to have known him and his departure has created a great void in my life and in the lives of all who love music.[21]

Was Kreisler the greatest violinist of his era? Of the twentieth century? Might he even have been the greatest violinist of all time? Or was he simply one in a crowd—one of the most widely popular, deeply admired, candidly expressive musicians in the world? Nearly thirty-four years before Kreisler's death, Olin Downes was already speculating on the violinist's posthumous significance. "There is one Fritz Kreisler," he wrote. "When he is gone—and may we long be spared the event—we shall not see his like again. There are few more striking exemplifications on the platform of the sheer power of a musical personality."[22] At the very least, Kreisler, more than any other violinist, represented a specific place and time. "There is no doubt a constant change, at least on the surface, perhaps, we could say, in the manners of an art," Kreisler told Downes in 1942. "The artist born of one epoch may find it hard or impossible to understand another."[23]

Indeed, Kreisler's approach *is* dated; no one performing today could (or, more to the point, would) insert the shifts, holdbacks, yawning emphases, and other heavily romantic gestures that dotted his playing. Probably no one would have the nerve. At a time when technology can reduce the Franck sonata to a series of ones and zeros, there is little or no room in music for daring and potentially errant emotionalism. Performance is clean, exact, historically correct, and technically ideal. It is also often dull. As Joseph Fuchs remarked, the current generation of violinists emphasize perfection "at the sacrifice of music." "What good is your technique if you can't play a four-bar phrase beautifully?" he asked.[24] In every discipline conservatism is a paradoxically dangerous trend, and in the classical music industry it has led to a startling homogeneity; with few exceptions, violinists sound alike. Kreisler's playing, in the words of Yehudi Menuhin, had an aspect "of throwing away a gesture, of courting, and it had a certain edge to it, which no one gives it today. He was a great, great artist."[25]

Was Kreisler the most revered violinist of his generation? Yes. Of any generation? Possibly. By almost any reckoning, Kreisler's popularity was of a scope and depth that the world had not seen before and possibly will not again. Aided by the advent of recording equipment, Kreisler reached a populace that performers before him had hardly dreamed of reaching. Unlike the more rigid—and rigidly segregated—audiences of today, Kreisler's public did not draw or even perceive a line between "popular" and "serious" music, "popular" and "serious" musicians, or, for that matter, "popular" and "serious" listeners. Demographically his audience cut across economic, educational, and class lines with a completeness that might surprise late-twentieth-century market analysts. Modern performers should envy the extent of Kreisler's appeal. "All he had to do was turn a phrase or open the *Liebesfreud*, and the audience would go crazy," Oscar Shumsky recalled. "He had tremendous charisma."[26]

Perhaps, in the final analysis, it matters little whether Kreisler was the century's greatest violinist or merely its most beloved. Heifetz's technique was unmatched; Elman boasted the world's most glistening tone; still others had more perfect intonation, a more virtuosic style, or a more reliable memory in the heat of performance. What Kreisler had, and what so many violinists lacked before and since, was the ability to communicate directly with anyone who bothered to listen. This ability was most pronounced during recitals, when Kreisler's sheer physicality—his size, dignity, and bearing—added a significant visual aspect to his presence. Many who heard Kreisler in concert recall the intensely personal nature of his performance and the sense of intimacy that surrounded it; to hear him live was to feel, illogically but unmistakably, that he was playing for each listener alone. "Whenever he played, I always felt that he was playing the concert for me," said Josef Gingold. "It was such a personal thing. He communicated himself so gorgeously."[27]

Kreisler's relationship with his contemporaries, those musicians and music lovers who heard him, enjoyed him, and perceived his worth without the skepticism of history to color their view, has been examined throughout this work. But what of those with no memory of his playing? What must future generations make of this husky man of regal bearing, shrewish wife, and notoriously bad work habits? What has his influence been, and what will it be? Will history forget him? Has it already?

Kreisler left three clear legacies: his recordings; his innovative non-stop vibrato, which set still-relevant performance standards; and his body of compositions. Although many of his works are no longer played, the music remains to be discovered and rediscovered by future generations of violinists. So long as Kreisler's name is printed on the title sheet of *Liebesleid*, he will endure as a composer. In that respect, history will regard him in the bluntest light: as a purveyor of fetchingly melodic short works and a handful of longer ones that evoke a time, a place, and a musical sensibility long since past. On paper his legacy will survive. His technical and stylistic legacy is apparent, too, in his recordings and in the warm tonal character of those modern instrumentalists who continue to look to the past for their inspiration.

Fritz Kreisler is not irrelevant; nor are the ripples of his passage through this world utterly faded. He remains nevertheless a shrunken titan, an artist whose massive umbra shaded musical performance for decades before retreating slowly but inevitably toward the horizon. His time is past. "The biggest trouble in this world is that great people, when they die after a great life, the world has a way of forgetting [them]," said Joseph Fuchs. "And Kreisler is one of the greatest men that ever played on the violin."[28]

There will never be another Fritz Kreisler. The culture that bore and nurtured him has disappeared, as has the community of musicians and music lovers who bade him farewell when he died more than three decades ago. There remain a few who knew him and heard him and can recall his gentle grace, on stage and off. Those who cannot—those who can only listen to reissues of his scratchy, low-fidelity, deeply musical recordings—must keep his life in focus and his legacy intact.

> I am what might be called a mystic. I have no superstition in me, but all artists are mystics. How can one be a real musician and not be a mystic? Music will be, forever, a matter of mysticism. Every form of music is linked to some form of thought; the drums of the jungle, savage love songs, Gregorian chants, modern jazz. They are all alike, save for the association of the thoughts that go with them. African

music and music in the United States, the jazz music to which we dance is all the same, except for the thoughts that are linked with it. What becomes jazz in the United States was religious music to the African. Music is indefinable. It becomes something definite when it is associated with some thought. The nearest approach to the Infinite God available to any of us is through some form of music.

Crossing the Atlantic in mid-winter is like my life in a very marked way. I have had my ups and downs. I have had my successes and failures. I have had sore trials and beautiful friendships on both sides of the sea. I have known war and peace. I have known what it meant to be hooted and hissed by American audiences in the war period; but I have also known what it meant to receive the applause and the praise of American audiences since the war. I have learned that success and money do not make for happiness. . . .

I want to share my thoughts of God and truth. I want to share my music. I want to share my worldly goods. I do not care for things. They bother me. I do not believe that there is any great or lasting comfort in the possession of things. They become burdens to us. I want to give of myself, all of my music and of my possessions, to others. That is supreme happiness.[29]

Appendix A

Chronology of Kreisler's Life

1875 2 February	Fritz Kreisler born, Vienna.
1879	Acquires first violin, a toy; begins lessons with his father.
1882	Enrolls in Vienna Conservatory; studies with Bruckner; meets Brahms.
1885	Wins gold medal for violinists at Vienna Conservatory.
	Enrolls at Paris Conservatoire; studies with Delibes and Massart, his last violin instructor.
1887	Baptized in Catholic Church.
	Concludes study at Paris Conservatoire by winning Premier Premier Prix.
1888 9 November	Makes United States debut in Boston, in appearance with pianist Moriz Rosenthal; tours United States with Rosenthal through spring of 1889.
10 November	Makes New York City debut in Steinway Hall.
1889 summer/fall	Returns to Vienna; abandons violin; attends Piaristen Gymnasium for further schooling.

1892 (or early 1893)	Completes Abitur (high school plus two years of college). Begins medical studies.
1894 (or early 1895)	Abandons medical studies; enters Austrian army as soldier in the Kaiserjaeger Regiment.
1896	Completes mandatory army service; returns to violin.
	Fails audition for Vienna Hofoper orchestra.
1896–98 (circa)	Begins composing "fake" 18th-century manuscripts and other works, including cadenzas for the Beethoven violin concerto.
1898 23 January	Debuts in Vienna with the Vienna Philharmonic.
1899 March	Makes Berlin debut in Beethoven Hall, performing Henri Vieuxtemps's Second Violin Concerto in F-sharp Minor and Paganini's *Non Più Mesta*.
December	Solos with Berlin Philharmonic, Nikisch conducting; first of five performances under Nikisch (also in 1901, 1906, 1909, and 1913).
1901	Tours United States with Josef Hofmann and Jean Gérardy.
	Meets Harriet Lies on the *Prince Bismarck* following American tour; engaged almost immediately.
1902	Marries Harriet Lies in New York City; marries her in a second ceremony conducted by Austrian Ambassador in London shortly thereafter.
1905	Marries Harriet Lies in a third ceremony in Hoboken, New Jersey.
January	Dismissed by New York publication *The Independent* as "deficient in well-rounded emotionality."
1907	Tours British provinces; sells out Queen's Hall.
1908	United States tour; interrupted by typhoid.
	B. Schott's Söhne of Mainz starts publishing Kreisler's short pieces and arrangements.
1909	Anna Kreisler (mother) dies.
October	*The Musician* hails Kreisler's artistry as "unassailable" and declares, "Mr. Kreisler has won his place among the few elect"; Kreisler describes his theory of self-hypnosis and the supposed "need" to practice.
1910	Victor Phonograph Company signs Kreisler to exclusive recording contract.

		Confesses to authorship of *Liebesleid* and *Liebesfreud*, previously presented as transcriptions of works by Joseph Lanner.
	11 May	First recording for RCA Victor, *Aus der Heimat*.
1911		B. Schott's Söhne announce 75,000 copies of Kreisler's music have been sold.
1912		Meets Max Bruch in Berlin.
		Tours Germany, performing 32 concerts in 31 days.
1913	November	The *Musical Courier* openly questions authorship of Kreisler's "arrangements" of 17th- and 18th-century works.
1914	1 August	Receives order to report for duty in Third Army Corps.
	10 August	With regiment, arrives at front line to battle Russian troops.
	6 September	Wounded in attack by Cossacks; taken to field hospital and later to Vienna, where he is reunited with Harriet.
	12 December	Performs first post-injury concert, in Carnegie Hall.
1915		Tours United States; met with widespread acclaim for artistry and heroism; popularity soars.
	May	*Four Weeks in the Trenches* is published; excerpted widely.
1916		Begins work on *Apple Blossoms* for theatrical producer Charles B. Dillingham.
	21 November	Emperor Franz Josef of Austria dies.
1917	27 June	First American troops land in France.
	November	Pittsburgh denies Kreisler permission to perform in Carnegie Music Hall on 8 November; appearance at Union Arcade Auditorium, scheduled for 10 November, is also canceled; other bans around the country follow. Kreisler denies accusations that funds from his American concerts go to support the Austrian war effort. On the same day, the Pittsburgh Orchestra Association bans the performance of music by composers of German or German-allied descent.
	25 November	Cancels remainder of American tour, forfeiting contracts worth $85,000; promises to play without pay for charities.

December *The Christian Science Monitor* recommends placing Fritz and Salomon Kreisler in an American internment camp.

1918 March Following protest against recital in Orange, New Jersey, Kreisler cancels all further performances, including for charities, for duration of war.

April Released from contract for operetta *Apple Blossoms.*

11 November Kaiser Wilhelm of Germany surrenders to Allies; World War I fighting ends.

1919 early Composes String Quartet in A Minor.

7 October *Apple Blossoms* debuts in New York, and runs for more than a year.

November Initiates tentative return to concertizing; more outcry, more cancellations.

10 December Plays in total darkness, and through chants of "Hun! Hun!," when angry members of American Legion cut power to hall in Ithaca, New York.

21 December Earns ovation from 4,000 in appearance at Metropolitan Opera House.

1920 summer Sails with wife to Austria to help distribute food and clothing.

1921 Salomon Kreisler dies.

1923 20 April Departs with wife and accompanist for seven-week tour through Japan and China.

1924 Kreislers take up residence in Grunewald, a residential section of Berlin, where they live for 15 years.

December While performing in Vienna, receives anonymous letter threatening to shoot his arm off unless he pays $700.

1926 14 January Begins two-month tour of Europe.

1930 (circa) In first of several visits, Fritz and Harriet Kreisler socialize with Benito Mussolini at Il Duce's villa.

1932 summer Composes *Sissy, the Rose of Bavaria*, which has successful runs in Vienna, Amsterdam, Munich, and elsewhere.

1933 January Adolf Hitler becomes chancellor of Germany.

Kreisler releases statement supporting Arturo Toscanini's commitment to conducting at the Bayreuth Festival, unaware that Toscanini simultaneously announced his decision to cancel.

1934 December	Instructs Carl Fischer to list "classical manuscripts" as Kreisler originals in following year's catalog.
1935	Records Beethoven sonatas in London.
8 February	Olin Downes reveals the great Kreisler "hoax" in *The New York Times*, only months before new Carl Fischer catalog is released.
	During visit to Amsterdam in February, Kreisler excoriates Hitler to Dutch press; later, at Harriet's urging, he retracts criticism and praises conditions in Germany.
24 February	Ernest Newman launches his attack on Kreisler's "hoax" manuscripts in London's *Sunday Times*, dismissing their musical merits and their ethical basis; thus engages Kreisler in a vitriolic debate in print.
5 May	Kreisler and Franz Rupp depart Germany on the *Graf Zeppelin* for five-week tour of South America.
1936 summer	Depressed about conditions in Germany, begins and then abandons recordings of the Brahms sonatas.
1938	Germany annexes Austria in the Anschluss.
28 September	Kreisler, in London, is drafted as an officer in the German army.
October	Having fled Germany, Kreisler's brother and his family leave the United Kingdom for the United States aboard the *Empress of Britain*.
1939 13 May	Kreisler becomes French citizen in small ceremony attended by French minister and several members of parliament.
fall	Fritz and Harriet Kreisler depart to the United States, where they remain for the rest of their lives.
1941 26 April	Hit by egg-delivery truck in accident in midtown Manhattan, sending him into coma and causing multiple head and internal injuries; prognosis grim.
27 April	The Sunday *Daily News* runs grisly accident photos.
23 May	Hospital announces that Kreisler is finally out of danger; regains consciousness speaking only Latin and ancient Greek.
June	Released from hospital to Harriet's care.

	October	1941–1942 concert engagements are canceled or deferred.
1942	15 January	Records own works with orchestral accompaniment for RCA Victor in Philadelphia.
	28 January	In first concert since accident, Kreisler performs Grieg, Bruch, and own works in Albany, New York; positive reviews.
	28 April	Signs contract to appear with Philadelphia Orchestra during 1942–1943 season, signaling the possibility of a tour.
	summer	Completes *Viennese Rhapsodic Fantasietta*.
	31 October	Gives first Carnegie Hall recital since accident, performing Bach, Mozart, and *Viennese Rhapsodic Fantasietta*, among other smaller works.
	16 December	Allied bombs destroy the Kreisler home at Grunewald in Berlin, though Kreislers do not hear of it until 7 July 1944.
1943	8 May	Receives final American citizenship papers.
1944	fall	Tours with Beethoven concerto.
1946	winter/spring	Tours with Mendelssohn concerto; Records *Viennese Rhapsodic Fantasietta*; Sells several violins, including the 1734 "Lord Amherst" and 1711 "Earl of Plymouth" Stradivariuses.
	June	Rushed to hospital for emergency appendectomy.
	7 October	Begins tour throughout Midwest, South, and Northeast, giving 37 performances through 11 February 1947.
1947	winter	Fulton J. Sheen begins instructing the Kreislers in Catholicism.
	30 March	The Kreislers receive communion in Blessed Sacrament Church in New Rochelle, New York; remarried, with Sheen presiding.
	1 November	Kreisler performs final Carnegie Hall recital of his career, playing Bach, Schumann, and his own works before a capacity crowd.
1948	1 July	Harriet Kreisler falls ill; she and Fritz stay at Heaton Hall in Stockbridge, Massachusetts.
1949	27–28 January	174 items in Kreisler's book collection are auctioned for charity.

6 October	Begins final tour of his career, performing 13 concerts in the South, Connecticut, New York, and elsewhere; tour runs through 6 March 1950.
1950 1 February	Day before his 75th birthday, Kreisler is feted at the Ritz-Carlton Hotel.
4 February	Dr. Ferdinand Friedensburg, the *Oberbuergermeister* of greater Berlin, invites Kreisler to "return to visit the place of your dramatic triumphs and quiet, gratifying successes"; Kreisler remains in the United States.
6 March	In final performance of his career, Kreisler appears on NBC's "Bell Telephone Hour" radio show.
April	Undergoes one of several cataract operations.
1955 2 February	Feted on 80th birthday at the St. Regis Roof; WQXR radio in New York broadcasts interview with Kreisler and tributes from friends and colleagues.
1960 31 January	*The New York Times* publishes an interview in which Kreisler wistfully recalls Vienna, his youth, and earlier musical eras.
2 February	In honor of his 85th birthday, Kreisler receives a scroll from New York City Mayor Wagner and Cardinal Spellman.
1961 April	Ruggiero Ricci organizes concert with Symphony of the Air celebrating Kreisler's 86th birthday.
1962 29 January	Fritz Kreisler dies.
2 February	Fulton Sheen delivers Kreisler's eulogy at funeral mass.
1963 29 May	Harriet Kreisler dies.

Appendix B

Fritz Kreisler: List of Works

This list comprises Fritz Kreisler's known original compositions and arrangements, including published works, recorded works, theatrical works, and additional complete or incomplete autographs, manuscripts, and annotated sheet music held in the Library of Congress Fritz Kreisler Collection.

The vast majority of the published works are designated (CF), indicating Carl Fischer/Charles Foley, Kreisler's primary American publishers. These include all pieces, current and out-of-print, ever published by Fischer/Foley, both before and following the merging of the two publishers. Such pieces are or were published in Europe by B. Schott's Söhne (now Schott Musik International); the few works published by B. Schott's Söhne that cannot be located in available Fischer/Foley lists are designated (BSS). Other publishers are noted in full where relevant.

The notation (LC) indicates that the work can be found among the many musical documents in the Library of Congress's Fritz Kreisler Collection. The collection includes both published and unpublished works, although only the unpublished ones are noted here (LC). Also held in the Library are additional unfinished sketches, not detailed here, and many further examples of sheet music of works by other composers that boast annotations or fingerings in Kreisler's hand. Only the most extensively altered examples of these are included below.

Kreisler's many recordings are described in full by Eric Wen in Appendix C, Discography. Among these, however, are a handful of the violinist's arrangements that were neither published nor donated to the Library of Congress, and do not appear in any other extant list of the composer's works. Several such works are included below and are indicated by a parenthetical note identifying the label, or labels, that recorded them. Not indicated below are the recording labels for the dozens of other pieces that have been published or can be found in the Kreisler Collection.

It should be noted (as Louis Lochner did in his biography of Kreisler) that Fritz Kreisler made additional arrangements of his own works, transcribing many of his well-known morceaux for cello, piano, piano trio (violin, cello, and piano), string quartet, and other combinations. Some of these transcriptions were recorded. He also, in January 1942, recorded new arrangements for violin and orchestra of several of his own compositions; these, again, are included in the discography.

The list that follows does not feature music from *Rhapsody* (or *My Rhapsody*), an operetta from the mid-1940s that included arrangements of a few well-known Kreisler airs. Although Fischer/Foley has for years listed the operetta as Kreisler's, the violinist—and indeed, at the time, his publisher—denied participating in the production and regarded it as creatively misguided.[1]

All works described below are arranged for violin and piano, unless otherwise noted. Quoted remarks, where given, refer to comments written on autographs or sheet music in the Library of Congress Fritz Kreisler Collection.

Original Compositions

Alt-Wiener Tanzweisen.
- No. 1, *Liebesfreud.* (CF)
- No. 2, *Liebesleid.* (CF)
- No. 3, *Schön Rosmarin.* (CF)

Apple Blossoms. Operetta. (CF; originally published by Francis Day Hunter, New York / T. B. Harms.) Kreisler wrote nine of the nineteen musical numbers and co-wrote two. Remaining pieces composed by Victor Jacobi. Book and lyrics by William Le Baron. Manuscripts for one song ("Letter Song," Act I) and one excerpt ("Dance," Act II, unused in final version) are held in the Library of Congress. See also *Who Can Tell?*, transcribed.

As I Tread the Road That Winds. Autograph for voice and piano. ("5 December, 1929, C. J. F.") (LC)

Aucassin and Nicolette (Medieval Canzonetta). (CF)

Ballet: *Einlage*. Incomplete autograph full score. (LC)

Berceuse Romantique. (CF)

A Burst of Melody. Manuscript piano-vocal score. Words by Charles A. Wagner. (LC)

Cadenzas (3) for Beethoven Violin Concerto in D Major, Op. 61. Solo violin. (CF)

Cadenza (1) for Brahms Violin Concerto in D Major, Op. 77. Solo violin. (CF)

Cadenzas (3) for Mozart Violin Concerto No. 3, in G Major, K. 216. Solo violin. (CF)

Cadenzas (3) for Mozart Violin Concerto No. 4, in D Major, K. 218. Solo violin. (CF)

Cadenzas (2) for Mozart Violin Concerto No. 5, in A Major, K. 219. Solo violin. (CF)

Cadenza (1) for Mozart Violin Concerto No. 6, in E-flat Major. Solo violin. (Concerto probably not authentic.) (CF)

Cadenzas (2) for Viotti Violin Concerto No. 22, in A Minor. (CF)

Caprice Viennois. (CF)

Cavatina. (CF)

"Classical Manuscripts" and other works revealed as Kreisler's own:

Andantino (in the style of Padre Martini). (CF)

Allegretto (in the style of Luigi Boccherini). (CF)

Allegretto in G Minor (in the style of Nicola Porpora). (CF)

Aubade Provençale (in the style of Louis Couperin). (CF)

Chanson Louis XIII and Pavane (in the style of Louis Couperin). (CF)

Concerto in C Major (in the style of Antonio Vivaldi). (CF)

Grave (in the style of Wilhelm Friedemann Bach). (CF)

La Chasse (caprice) (in the style of Jean-Baptiste Cartier). (CF)

La Précieuse (in the style of Louis Couperin). (CF)

Menuet (in the style of Nicola Porpora). (CF)

Praeludium and Allegro (in the style of Gaetano Pugnani). (CF)

Preghiera (Prayer) (in the style of Padre Martini). (CF)

Scherzo (in the style of K. von Dittersdorf). (CF)

Sicilienne and Rigaudon (in the style of François Francoeur). (CF)

Study on a Choral (in the style of Stamitz). (CF)

Tempo di Minuetto (in the style of Gaetano Pugnani). (CF)

Variations on a Theme by Corelli (in the style of Giuseppe Tartini). (CF)

Cradle Song (*Ein altes Lied*, according to Lochner). Autograph score for voice and orchestra. ("Based on my *Caprice Viennois*," 1915.) (CF)

Dear Homeland. For voice and piano. (CF)

Drei Nachtgesänge (Three Night Songs). Words by Joseph Freiherr von Eichendorff. For voice and piano. Additional autograph (*Vier Nachtgesänge*) includes "Im Abendrot," not part of the final collection. (CF)

Episode. (CF)

Fantasie für Violine mit Klavier. Autograph. ("19. März 1883.") (LC)

Follow Thy Star. Ozalid of autograph. Incomplete. ("I don't remember whose poem this is and why I did not finish it. I believe it must have been 40 years ago that I wrote this / F. K."—10 March 1950.) (LC)

French Song. Autograph. (LC)

Gemächliches Walzer Tempo. Incomplete autograph sketch. (LC)

Ghasel. Words by Gottfried Keller. For voice and piano. (CF)

La Gitana (Arabo-Spanish Gypsy song of the 18th century). (CF)

Gypsy Caprice. (CF)

He-Uch-la, Wolgalied und anderes Volkslied (Paraphrase). (BSS)

Heut vor fünf und zwanzig Jahr. Autograph sketches for voice and piano. (LC)

Invocation. For organ. (CF)

Irish Song. Autograph sketch for voice and piano. ("Originally conceived for John.") (LC)

Learn How to Lose. For voice and piano. (CF)

Leezie Lindsay. For voice and piano. (CF)

Love Comes and Goes. For voice and piano. (CF)

Liebes-Walzer. Autograph. (LC)

Liebesfreud: Coda. Autograph. ("Fritz Kreisler, Oct. 27th, 1960, New York.") (LC)

Malagueña. (CF)

Marche Miniature Viennoise. (CF)

O Salutaris hostia. For voice and piano. (CF)

The Old Refrain. From Brandl. (CF)

Petite valse. After a poem by Edna St. Vincent Millay. (CF)

Polichinelle Serenade. (CF)

Recitativo and Scherzo Caprice. For unaccompanied violin. (CF)

Romance. (CF)

Rondino on a Theme of Beethoven. (CF)

Serenata. Incomplete autograph sketch. (LC)

Shepherd's Madrigal. (CF)

"Simple, Effective Arrangements in the First Position, also provided with fingering in the Third Position." (CF)

Sissy, the Rose of Bavaria. Operetta. (CF; despite listing, publisher has no current material or information. Schott has material for hire.)

Book and lyrics by Ernst and Hubert Marischka, after a comedy by Ernst Decsey and Gustav Holm. Piano-vocal score. (Pub.: Verlag W. Karczag.) Library of Congress collection includes many autographs (full score and piano-vocal). See also *Stars in My Eyes*, transcribed.

Song, Op. 7. Autograph. (LC)

Spanish Valse. Incomplete autograph. (LC)

Stars in My Eyes. Violin-piano transcription. (CF)

String Quartet in A Minor. (CF) publishes parts only; Schott has parts and study score.

Syncopation. (CF)

Tambourin Chinois. (CF)

Toy Soldier's March. (CF)

Valse in C Major. Unfinished autograph. (LC)

Viennese Love Song. Unfinished autograph. (LC)

Viennese Rhapsodic Fantasietta. (CF)

Who Can Tell? Orchestral version. (Victor)

The Whole World Knows. For voice and piano. (CF)

Arrangements

Albéniz, Isaac

Tango. (CF)

Malagueña. (CF)

Bach, Johann Sebastian

Concerto in A Minor. Arr. August Wilhelmj and James Brown (Novello & Co.). Printed score with extensive Kreisler alterations. (LC)

Concerto in D Minor. Autograph. (LC)

Gavotte in E. (CF)

Prelude in E. (CF)

Suite in E Minor and Fugue in G Minor. Originally for violin and contrabass. (C. F. Peters, n.d.). Printed Bach score with Kreisler alter-ations. (LC)

Balogh, Ernö

Caprice antique. (CF)

Dirge of the North. (CF)

Beethoven, Ludwig van

Andante. For violin, cello, and piano. (CF)

Cavatina in E-flat, from String Quartet No. 13, Op. 130, in B-flat Major. Autograph. (LC)

Minuet in G. For violin, cello, and piano. (Gramophone [HMV] / EMI)

Berlin, Irving

Blue Skies. Autograph. (LC)

Bizet, Georges

Intermezzo (Agnus Dei), from 2nd suite from *L'Arlésienne*. For violin, cello, and piano. (CF)

Boccherini, Luigi

Minuet. For string quintet. (Victor)

Brahms, Johannes

Hungarian Dance No. 5. (Victor)

Hungarian Dance No. 17. (CF)

Cadman, Charles Wakefield

From the Land of the Sky-Blue Water. (Victor; Gramophone [HMV] / EMI)

Chaminade, Cécile Louise Stéphanie

Sérénade Espagnole (Spanish Serenade). (CF)

Chopin, Frédéric

Mazurka, Op. 33, No. 2. (CF)

Mazurka, Op. 67, No. 4. (CF)

Corelli, Arcangelo

La Folia. (CF)

O Sanctissima. For violin, cello, and piano. (Gramophone [HMV] / EMI)

Sarabande and allegretto. (CF)

Dawes, Charles G.

Melody. Orch. Adolf G. Hoffmann. (Gamble Hinged Music Co.). Printed score with Kreisler paste-over and annotations. (LC)

Debussy, Claude

La Fille aux cheveux de lin (Extrait des Préludes). From piano preludes. Autograph. (LC)

Dvořák, Antonin

Humoresque. (Victor; Gramophone [HMV] / EMI)

Indianisches Lamento (Indian Lament). (CF)

Negro Spiritual Melody, from the Largo of the New World Symphony. (CF)

Slavonic Dance No. 1 in G Minor. (CF)

Slavonic Dance No. 2 in E Minor. (CF)

Slavonic Dance No. 3 in G Major. (CF)

Slavonic Fantaisie in B Minor. (CF)

Songs My Mother Taught Me. (CF)

Falla, Manuel de

Danse Espagnole (Spanish Dance), from the opera *La vida breve*. (CF)

Fernández-Arbós, Enrique

Trois morceaux de concert, Op. 6, No. 1, Zambra. Autograph. (LC)

Foster, Stephen Collins

Old Folks at Home (*Swanee River*). (CF)

Friml, Rudolf
La Danse des Demoiselles (Dance of the Maidens), Op. 29. (CF)
Gaertner, Eduard
Viennese Melody (Aus Wien). (CF)
Glazunov, Alexander
Sérénade Espagnole. (Victor; Gramophone [HMV] / EMI)
Gluck, Christoph Willibald
Melodie. (CF)
Godowsky, Leopold
Nocturnal Tangier, from *Triakontameron.* (CF)
Orientale. Autograph. ("Avon, May 22nd, 1915.") (LC)
Grainger, Percy
Molly on the Shore (Irish Reel). (CF)
Granados y Campiña, Enrique
Spanischer Tanz (Spanish Dance), from *Danzas españoles.* (CF)
Handel, George Frideric
Largo. (Victor)
Harrison, Annie
In the Gloaming. (Victor)
Haydn, Franz Joseph
God Save the Emperor Franz, Austrian Imperial hymn. (CF)
Rondo all'ungarese (Hungarian rondo). (CF)
Heuberger, Richard
Midnight Bells, from *The Opera Ball.* In Lochner, Kreisler takes credit for the motif. (CF)
Korngold, Erich Wolfgang
Tanzlied des Pierrot, from the opera *Die tote Stadt.* (Victor)
Krakauer, Anton
Im Paradies (In Paradise), Viennese folksong. (CF)
Leclair, Jean-Marie
Tambourin. (CF)
Lehár, Franz
Frasquita, serenade. (CF)
Leoncavallo, Ruggiero
Mattinata. For violin, cello, and piano. (Gramophone [HMV] / EMI)
Logan, Frederick Knight
Pale Moon, Indian love song. (Forster Music Publisher)
Mendelssohn, Felix
Song Without Words, No. 1 (*May Breeze*, Op. 62, No. 1). (CF)
Song Without Words, No. 2. (CF)
[May Song. (CF)]
[Spring Song. (Victor)]

Mozart, Wolfgang Amadeus
  Rondo, from Serenade in D Major. (CF)
  Violin Concerto No. 3, in G Major. Autograph. (LC)
  Violin Concerto No. 6, in E-flat Major. Autograph. (Concerto probably not authentic.) (LC)
Mussorgsky-Rachmaninoff
  Hopak. (Lochner's *Fritz Kreisler* is the only source that mentions this work.)[2]
Nevin, Ethelbert Woodbridge
  Mighty Lak' a Rose. Autograph. ("played with Geraldine Farrar's recording of it"). (LC)
  The Rosary. (Victor)
Owen, Elwyn
  Invocation. (CF)
Paderewski, Ignacy Jan
  Melody, Op. 16, No. 2. (CF)
  Paraphrase on Menuet, Op. 14, No. 1. (CF)
Paganini, Nicolò
  Caprice No. 13. (CF)
  Caprice No. 20. (CF)
  Caprice No. 24. (CF)
  La Clochette (The Bell), from Concerto No. 2 in B Minor, Op. 7. (CF)
  Concerto in One Movement, from Concerto No. 1 in D, Op. 6. (CF)
  Concerto No. 2 in B Minor, Op. 7. Autograph full score. ("1933") (LC)
  Moto perpetuo. (CF)
  Le Streghe (The Witches' Dance). (CF)
  Theme and Variations (*Non Più Mesta*, Op. 12). (CF)
  Theme and Variations (*I Palpiti*, Op. 13). (CF)
Pergolesi, Giovanni Battista
  Nina (*Tre giorni*). For violin, cello, and piano. (CF)
Poldini, Eduard
  En voyage (autour de Vienne). Autograph. (LC)
  Poupée valsante (Dancing Doll). (CF)
Rachmaninoff, Sergei
  Eighteenth Variation, from *Rhapsody on a Theme of Paganini*. (CF)
  Italian Polka. (CF)
  Marguerite (Albumleaf). (CF)
  Preghiera (Prayer), from the second movement of Piano Concerto No. 2 in C Minor. ("Transcribed by F. K. January 9th, 1940.") (CF)
  Prelude in G Minor. (CF)
Rameau, Jean-Philippe
  Tambourin. (CF)

Ravel, Maurice
Habanera (*Rapsodie espagnole* No. 3). (CF)
Rimsky-Korsakov, Nikolai
Fantasia on Two Russian Themes, Op. 33. (CF)
Hindoo Chant (Song of India). (CF)
Hymn to the Sun, from the opera *Le Coq d'or*. (CF)
Two dances from *Scheherazade*, Op. 35:
No. 1: *Dance Orientale*. (CF)
No. 2: *Chanson Arabe*. (CF)
Saint-Saëns, Camille
Violin Concerto No. 3, Op. 61, in B Minor. Autograph violin part. (LC)
Schelling, Ernest
Irlandaise (CF)
Schubert, Franz
Ballet music from *Rosamunde*. (CF)
Impromptu, Op. 90, No. 3. (CF)
Impromptu, Op. 142, No. 2. Autograph. ("Oct. 26th 1933 on board *S. S. Europe*.") (LC)
Moment Musical. (CF)
Schumann, Robert
Fantasie in C Major, Op. 131. (On autograph full score: "Berlin, 9 Juli 1936.") (CF)
Romanze. (CF)
Scott, Cyril
Lotus Land, Op. 47, No. 1. (G. Ricordi & Co.)
Sibelius, Jean
Violin Concerto in D Minor, Op. 47. Autograph. (LC)
Spohr, Louis
Violin Concerto No. 8, Op. 47. Printed score from C. F. Peters, n.d. (In Form einer Gesangscene), with extensive Kreisler alterations. (LC)
Tartini, Giuseppe
The Devil's Trill. Sonata. (On autograph: "Meinem lieben Freunde Dr. B. Pollack herzlichst zugeeignet.") (CF)
Fugue in A. (CF)
Tchaikovsky, Peter Ilyich
Andante cantabile from String Quartet No. 1, Op. 11, in D Major. (CF)
Berceuse (Lullaby). (Victor)
Chanson sans paroles (Song Without Words). (CF)

Concerto for violin and orchestra, in D Major, Op. 35. With original Kreisler cadenza. (CF)

Humoresque. (CF)

Scherzo, Op. 42, No. 2. (CF)

Traditional: Hawaiian (Liliuokalani)

Aloha Oe, Hawaiian melody. Possibly of Austrian origin.[3] (CF)

Traditional: Irish

Farewell to Cucullain (*Londonderry Air*). (CF)

Traditional: Russian

Paraphrase on Two Russian Folk Songs. (CF)

Traditional: Scottish

Ballads from the Scotch Minstrelsy. Arranged in collaboration with Reinhold Warlich. (CF)

(CF) no longer lists the collection as titled but publishes the following works individually:

The Bonnie Earl O' Moray

Loch Lomond

The Piper O' Dundee

The Praise of Islay

Vieuxtemps, Henri

Violin Concerto No. 2, Op. 19, in F-sharp Minor. Autograph. (LC)

Violin Concerto No. 4, Op. 31, in D Minor. Autograph full score. ("Scored by Fritz Kreisler in 1907.") (LC)

Viotti, Giovanni Battista

Violin Concerto No. 22, in A Minor. Autograph full score. (LC)

Weber, Carl Maria von

Larghetto. (CF)

Wieniawski, Henri

Airs Russes (*Souvenir de Moscow*). (CF)

Caprice in A Minor. (CF)

Caprice in E-flat Major (*Alla Saltarella*). (CF)

Winternitz, Felix

Troika (Capriccio). (CF)

Fritz Kreisler Discography

by

Eric Wen

This listing contains all the studio recordings made by Fritz Kreisler. The recordings span a period of more than forty years—the first record of 1904 predates the invention of Henry Ford's Model T automobile, and the last record, made in 1946, follows the Second World War and the beginning of the atomic age.

Kreisler's violin recordings are grouped into seven parts according to recording company; these are followed by a final section listing recordings made by Kreisler as a pianist for Victor and HMV. Each part lists the recording sessions in chronological order, and within each session the recordings are presented in chronological order. Each recorded side is listed by matrix and take numbers. The published takes are set in bold type and underlined and include the original record catalog number. Due to limitations of space, only the 78 rpm record catalog numbers are given. Catalog numbers for LP and CD reissues have not been listed, but all of Kreisler's commercially issued 78 rpm records have been reissued on CD by BMG, EMI, Biddulph, and Pearl. For items that were unpublished on 78 rpm records and only issued later on LP or CD, a footnote reference is given to its current CD reissue.

As revealed in the discography, most of the items Kreisler recorded with piano accompaniment were single discs of either original works or salon pieces by other composers. Within the time limitations of a 78 rpm record, Kreisler chiseled the violin miniature to perfection. The notion that he simply tossed off these little pieces in the studio is grossly mistaken; the number of takes he would make of a three- or four-minute piece attests to the care and attention he lavished upon them (for example, there are no fewer than twelve takes in three days for Mary Earl's *Beautiful Ohio Waltz* recorded for Victor in May 1919).

This discography does not include: (1) broadcast recordings aired on the "Bell Telephone Hour" between 1944 and 1950; (2) Ampico piano rolls; and (3) noncommercial spoken records. In the last category, it is worth noting that RCA Victor issued two records of Kreisler speaking: the violinist's seventy-fifth birthday speech (with an introduction by Bruno Walter) on four 78 rpm sides and an eightieth birthday interview on one LP side. These records had limited pressings and were made for radio stations to broadcast. Two interviews (with Ben Brower and Abraham Chasins) are also known to exist, as well as an acetate (noncommercial) disc of Kreisler speaking in German.

I would like to acknowledge the help of the late John Pfeiffer of BMG Classics for giving me unlimited access to research Kreisler material in the RCA/BMG archives. His love of great historical performers and his commitment to preserve their recorded legacy remains an inspiration. Bernadette Moore and Jon Samuels of BMG guided me through the intricacies of the Victor file cards and original recording ledgers, and were unstinting in their help.

Ruth Edge, the manager of the EMI archives at Hayes, near London, assisted me with all the relevant information concerning Kreisler's European recordings. Not only did she provide me with photocopies of recording sheets, but she patiently checked the chronology of the individual recordings throughout the discography's many stages, and she answered my endless stream of questions regarding the inner workings of the Gramophone Company.

I am also extremely indebted to the following people (listed alphabetically) for sharing their wealth of knowledge about early recording history and Kreisler's records, as well as their encouragement and support throughout my research: Richard Bebb, Gregor Benko, Rob Cowan, Urs Joseph Flury, Julian Futter, Raymond Glaspole, Ward Marston, Peter Munves, Mark Obert-Thorn, Jim Peters, Dennis Rooney, Jonathan Summers, Alan Vicat, and Richard Warren (Yale University).

Fritz Kreisler: The Violin Recordings

Part 1: The Gramophone Company recordings (Berlin, 1904, and London, 1911)

The Gramophone Company was the most prestigious recording company in the first half of the twentieth century. Established in London in 1897, the Gramophone Company began producing office equipment and electric clocks as well as records in 1900 and became the Gramophone and Typewriter Company (hence the designation "G & T"). In 1903, the company recorded Joseph Joachim and Pablo de Sarasate, two of the most prominent exponents of nineteenth-century violin playing. A year after these landmark documents, four discs made in Berlin by a twenty-nine-year-old Viennese violinist named Fritz Kreisler were added to the G & T catalog. Kreisler had made his concerto debut with the Berlin Philharmonic five years earlier, and he was to usher in a new style of playing that, according to Carl Flesch, "divined in advance and satisfied the specific type of emotional expression demanded by our age."

Kreisler's G & T records were single-sided 10-inch (25-cm) discs. Each recording was given a separate matrix number, and no take numbers were used. (In this discography all Gramophone Company recordings are listed as take 1 within parentheses.)

In 1907, the typewriter division of the Gramophone and Typewriter Company was dissolved, and the company reverted back to the Gramophone Company. By 1911 the company became known as HMV due to their adoption of the familiar "dog and trumpet" logo based on the painting entitled *His Master's Voice* by Francis Barraud of his bull terrier, Nipper, in front of a black horn. Twelve of the sixteen works recorded by Kreisler for HMV in 1911 were original compositions by the violinist. Only four of these works were acknowledged as such at the time, however; the other eight were ascribed to Baroque composers. These "Baroque" pieces figured prominently in Kreisler's repertoire as works by their attributed composers until his confession of the hoax in 1935, over a quarter of a century later. Since then these pastiche works have carried the descriptive authorship of "Kreisler, in the style of . . . ."

All of Kreisler's 1911 HMV recordings were made in Hayes, Middlesex. The letter "e" following the matrix number designates a 10-inch (25-cm) record, and an "f" designates a 12-inch (30-cm) record. The letter prefix before the matrix number identifies the recording engineer (e.g., "ac" = Hancox). In the 1911 sessions, when two recordings of the same piece were made, the first was made for the Gramophone Company, the second for Victor, its American affiliate.

session / *matrix*	*date* / *take(s)*	*original issue on 78 rpm records*	*accompanying artist(s)* / *title of work*	*venue (where known)* / *composer*	*arranger*
1	February 1904		unknown (piano)	Berlin	
2084xCO	(1)	G & T 47944	Chanson sans paroles, Op. 2, No. 3	Tchaikovsky	Kreisler
2085xCO	(1)	G & T 47945	Sarabande/L'abeille	Sulzer/François Schubert	
2086xCO	(1)	G & T 47946	Prelude from Partita No. 3 in E	Bach	Kreisler
2087xCO	(1)	G & T 47947	Air from Suite No. 3 in D "Air on the G string"	Bach	Wilhelmj
2	10 October 1911		Haddon Squire (piano)	London	
ac 5558 f	(1)		Minuet "in the style of Pugnani"	Kreisler	
ac 5559 f	(1)		Minuet "in the style of Pugnani"	Kreisler	
ac 5560 f	(1)		La précieuse "in the style of Couperin"	Kreisler	
ac 5561 f	(1)		La précieuse "in the style of Couperin"	Kreisler	
ac 5562 f	(1)		Andantino "in the style of Martini"	Kreisler	
ac 5563 f	(1)		Andantino "in the style of Martini"	Kreisler	
ac 5564 f	(1)		Scherzo "in the style of Dittersdorf"	Kreisler	
ac 5565 f	(1)		Scherzo "in the style of Dittersdorf"	Kreisler	
14248 e	(1)		Aubade provençale "in the style of Couperin"	Kreisler	
14249 e	(1)		Aubade provençale "in the style of Couperin"	Kreisler	
14250 e	(1)		La chasse "in the style of Cartier"	Kreisler	
14251 e	(1)		La chasse "in the style of Cartier"	Kreisler	
3	6 November 1911		Haddon Squire (piano)	London	
ac 5691 f	(1)	HMV 07957	La précieuse "in the style of Couperin"	Kreisler	
ac 5692 f	(1)		La précieuse "in the style of Couperin"	Kreisler	
ac 5693 f	(1)	HMV 07958	Scherzo "in the style of Dittersdorf"	Kreisler	
ac 5694 f	(1)	Victor 64568	Scherzo "in the style of Dittersdorf"	Kreisler	
ac 5695 f	(1)	HMV 07959	Allegretto "in the style of Boccherini"	Kreisler	

<u>session</u> matrix	<u>date</u> take(s)	original issue on 78 rpm records	<u>accompanying artist(s)</u> title of work	<u>venue (where known)</u> composer	arranger
ac 5696 f	(1)		Allegretto "in the style of Boccherini"	Kreisler	
ac 5697 f	(<u>1</u>)	HMV 07960	Caprice Viennois, Op. 2	Kreisler	
ac 5698 f	(<u>1</u>)	HMV 07961	Tambourin Chinois, Op. 3	Kreisler	
ac 5699 f	(<u>1</u>)	HMV 07962	Liebesleid	Kreisler	
ac 5700 f	(<u>1</u>)	HMV 07963	Liebesfreud	Kreisler	
ac 5701 f	(<u>1</u>)	HMV 07964	Chanson méditation	Cottenet	
ac 5702 f	(<u>1</u>)	HMV 07965	Chanson sans paroles, Op. 2, No. 3	Tchaikovsky	Kreisler
ac 5703 f	(<u>1</u>)	HMV 07966	Hungarian Dance No. 1 in G minor	Brahms	Joachim
ac 5704 f	(<u>1</u>)	HMV 07967	Chanson Louis XIII and Pavane "in the style of Couperin"	Kreisler	
ac 5705 f	(<u>1</u>)	HMV 07968	Gavotte from Partita No. 3 in E	Bach	Kreisler
14413 e	(<u>1</u>)	HMV 3-7943	Aubade provençale "in the style of Couperin"	Kreisler	
14414 e	(1)		Aubade provençale "in the style of Couperin"	Kreisler	
14415 e	(<u>1</u>)	HMV 3-7942	La chasse "in the style of Cartier"	Kreisler	
14416 e	(1)		La chasse "in the style of Cartier"	Kreisler	

Part 2: The acoustic Victor recordings (New York and New Jersey, 1910–25)

The Victor Talking Machine Company, founded in 1901, was the first major record company established in the United States. It was the dominant record label in the U.S., as well as the American affiliate of the European Gramophone Company. In order to distinguish its catalog of serious music, Victor created its special Red Seal label in 1904 for the leading stars of the Metropolitan Opera. Although initially reserved for such illustrious singers as Caruso, Melba, and Tetrazzini, this Red Seal designation was eventually extended to include such star violinists as Mischa Elman and Jan Kubelík, and in May 1910 the name of Fritz Kreisler was added to the illustrious Victor Red Seal roster.

Though no Victor recordings were made of the solo concertos, Kreisler's 1915 recording of the Bach Double Violin Concerto with the Russian-born Efrem Zimbalist (who studied at the St. Petersburg Conservatory with Leopold Auer) was a landmark. Although slightly abridged to fit each movement onto a 12-inch disc, the recording represented the first of a major Bach work. It was also the first time two leading solo violinists were brought together in a recorded performance. Apart from the Bach Double Concerto, all the works Kreisler recorded for Victor were single-sided discs of short pieces. The fact that all the recordings from 1916 until 1920 feature an orchestral rather than piano accompaniment was no small accolade—the Victor studio orchestra was usually reserved for recordings of operatic excerpts by the great singers.

Unlike the recordings in the previous section, the Victor recordings had matrix numbers to designate a specific title. The letter "B" preceding the matrix number designates a 10-inch record, and a "C" preceding the matrix number designates a 12-inch record. The 10-inch and 12-inch records were assigned catalog numbers in the 60000 series and 70000 series, respectively.

In the Victor system, a matrix number would remain with the same work for many years. Alternative recordings of the same title were distinguished by different "takes," and often later takes would replace an earlier one without a change of record number. The differences in alternative takes can involve details of performance (compare the articulation of the final three chords in takes 1 and 2 of the Brahms Hungarian Dance No. 5) or changes in the music itself (take 12 of the violinist's *Caprice Viennois* contains a postlude that is missing in take 3). For remakes of recordings originally made in 1910 and 1912, Carl Lamson replaces George Falkenstein as pianist. Two of the records with the same catalog numbers have completely different accompaniments. Dvořák's *Humoresque* on 74180 with matrix C 8941 has piano accompaniment, yet the same record number is used for matrix C 22887, which has an orchestral backup. Similarly, Kreisler's arrangement of Haydn's "Austrian Imperial Hymn" was issued in two versions on 64408: matrix B 14345 is unaccompanied, and matrix B 15736, made the following year, is with piano.

Three unissued items have survived, and considering that Kreisler never recorded any of the solo violin concertos for Victor, the recordings of movements by Tchaikovsky and Lalo (performed with piano and never released in their original 78 rpm disc form) are especially significant. While it is unfortunate that Kreisler's arrangements of Strauss's *Blue Danube Waltz* and Mendelssohn's "Spring Song" no longer exist, the greatest loss among the unissued recordings is Kreisler playing violin obbligato to Enrico Caruso in Gounod's "Ave Maria."

session / *matrix*	*date* / *take(s)*	*original issue on 78 rpm records*	*accompanying artist(s)* / *title of work*	*venue (where known)* / *composer*	*arranger*
1	11 May 1910		George Falkenstein (piano)	New York	
B 8939	1		Old Folks at Home (Swanee River)	Foster	Kreisler
C 8940	1		Caprice Viennois, Op. 2	Kreisler	
C 8941	1		Humoresque, Op. 101, No. 7	Dvořák	Kreisler
C 8942	1	Victor 74172	Andantino (No. 2 from *Aus der Heimat*)	Smetana	
C 8943	1		Moment musical, Op. 94, No. 3/ Tambourin from *Les fêtes d'Hébé*	Schubert/Rameau	Kreisler
C 8944	1		Méditation from *Thaïs*	Massenet	Marsick
2	13 May 1910		George Falkenstein (piano)	New York	
C 8940	2[1]		Caprice Viennois, Op. 2	Kreisler	
C 8949	1	Victor 74203	Tambourin Chinois, Op. 3	Kreisler	
C 8944	2, 3	Victor 74182	Méditation from *Thaïs*	Massenet	Marsick
C 8941	2	Victor 74180	Humoresque, Op. 101, No. 7	Dvořák	Kreisler
C 8943	2		Moment musical, Op. 94, No. 3/ Tambourin from *Les fêtes d'Hébé*	Schubert/Rameau	Kreisler
C 8950	1[1]		Liebesleid	Kreisler	
C 8951	1, 2	Victor 74196	Liebesfreud	Kreisler	
B 8939	2	Victor 64130	Old Folks at Home (Swanee River)	Foster	Kreisler
B 8952	1		Chanson sans paroles, Op. 2, No. 3	Tchaikovsky	Kreisler
C 8942	2[1]		Andantino (No. 2 from *Aus der Heimat*)	Smetana	
3	18 May 1910		George Falkenstein (piano)	New York	
B 8969	1	Victor 64131	Hungarian Dance No. 5	Brahms	Joachim
C 8940	3	Victor 74197	Caprice Viennois, Op. 2	Kreisler	

C 8943	3	Victor 74202	Moment musical, Op. 94, No. 3/ Tambourin from *Les fêtes d'Hébé*	Schubert/Rameau	Kreisler
B 8952	2		Chanson sans paroles, Op. 2, No. 3	Tchaikovsky	Kreisler
B 8977	1, 2	Victor 64156	Variations on a Theme of Corelli "in the style of Tartini"	Kreisler	
4	20 May 1910		George Falkenstein (piano)	New York	
B 8952	3, 4	Victor 64142	Chanson sans paroles, Op. 2, No. 3	Tchaikovsky	Kreisler
B 8980	1		Gavotte from Partita No. 3 in E	Bach	Kreisler
C 8981	1		Chanson Louis XIII and Pavane "in the style of Couperin"	Kreisler	
C 8982	1	Victor 74330	Chanson méditation	Cottenet	
5	20 May 1910		George Falkenstein (piano)	New York	
B 8980	3	Victor 64142	Gavotte from Partita No. 3 in E	Bach	Kreisler
C 8981	2		Chanson Louis XIII and Pavane "in the style of Couperin"	Kreisler	
6	18 December 1912		George Falkenstein (piano)	New York	
B 8981	1, 2	Victor 64292	Chanson Louis XIII and Pavane "in the style of Couperin"	Kreisler	
C 8982	2		Chanson méditation	Cottenet	
C 8950	2, 3	Victor 74333	Liebesleid	Kreisler	
B 12727	1, 2		Berceuse	Townsend	
C 12728	1	Victor 74332	Prelude from Partita No. 3 in E	Bach	Kreisler
B 12729	1	Victor 64313	Lento (Melodie) from *Orphée ed Euridice*	Gluck	Kreisler
B 12730	1	Victor 64314	Schön Rosmarin	Kreisler	
B 12731	1	Victor 64315	Andantino "in the style of Martini"	Kreisler	

session / *matrix*	*date* / *take(s)*	*original issue on 78 rpm records*	*accompanying artist(s)* / *title of work*	*venue (where known)* / *composer*	*arranger*
7	23 December 1912		George Falkenstein (piano)	New York	
C 8982	3, 4	Victor 74330	Chanson méditation	Cottenet	Kreisler
B 12727	3	Victor 64319	Berceuse	Townsend	
B 12730	2		Schön Rosmarin	Kreisler	
8	19 January 1914		Carl Lamson (piano)	New York	
C 14342	1	Victor 74384	"Ombra mai fu" (Largo) from *Serse*	Handel	Kreisler
B 14344	1	Victor 64406	Aus Wien (Viennese Melody)	Gaertner	Kreisler
B 14343	1		"Du alter Stefansturm" from *Der liebe Augustin* "The Old Refrain"	Brandl	Kreisler
B 14354	1	HMV 3-7969	Song Without Words, Op. 62, No. 1 "May Breezes"	Mendelssohn	Kreisler
			unaccompanied		
B 14345	1	Victor 64408	Theme (Poco adagio cantabile) from String Quartet in C, Op. 76, No. 3, "Austrian Imperial Hymn"	Haydn	Kreisler
9	25 March 1914		John McCormack (tenor) and Vincent O'Brien (piano)	New York	
B 14623	1	Victor 88479	Angel's Serenade	Braga	
C 14624	1		Melody adapted from Bach's Prelude in C "Ave Maria"	Gounod	
C 14625	1	Victor 88482	Le Nil	Leroux	
C 14626	1	Victor 88483	Berceuse from *Jocelyn*	Godard	
C 14627	1	Victor 88484	Ave Maria	Schubert	

10	31 March 1914		John McCormack (tenor) and Vincent O'Brien (piano)	New York	
B 14651	1	Victor 87191	Serenade (No. 4 from *Schwanengesang*)	Schubert	
C 14624	2	Victor 88481	Melody adapted from Bach's Prelude in C "Ave Maria"	Gounod	
B 14652	1	Victor 87192	Intermezzo from *Cavalleria rusticana* "Ave Maria"	Mascagni	
			Vincent O'Brien (piano)	New York	
C 14653	1, 2	Victor 74387	Larghetto from Sonatina in G, Op. 100 "Indian Lament"	Dvořák	Kreisler
11	3 April 1914		Enrico Caruso (tenor) and Gaetano Scognamiglio (piano)	New York	
C 14664	1		Melody adapted from Bach's Prelude in C "Ave Maria"	Gounod	
12	4 January 1915		Zimbalist (2d violin); Rattay, Bianculli, Fruncillo, Bourdon (string quartet) and Rogers (conductor)	Camden (Victor Studios)	
C 15560	1, 2, 3, 4	Victor 76028	Concerto in D minor for two violins, BWV 1043: I Vivace	Bach	
C 15561	1, 2, 3	Victor 76029	Concerto in D minor for two violins, BWV 1043: II Largo ma non tanto	Bach	
C 15562	1, 2	Victor 76030	Concerto in D minor for two violins, BWV 1043: III Allegro	Bach	
13	25 February 1915		Carl Lamson (piano)	New York	
B 15736	1	Victor 64408	Theme (Poco adagio cantabile) from String Quartet in C, Op. 76, No. 3, "Austrian Imperial Hymn"	Haydn	Kreisler
C 15735	1		Slavonic Dance No. 3 in G, Op. 72, No. 8	Dvořák	Kreisler

<u>session</u> *matrix*	*<u>date</u>* *take(s)*	*original issue on* *78 rpm records*	*<u>accompanying artist(s)</u>* *title of work*	*<u>venue (where known)</u>* *composer*	*arranger*
B 15738	<u>1</u>	Victor 64488	Slavonic Dance No. 1 in G minor, from Op. 46, No. 2 and Op. 72, No. 1	Dvořák	Kreisler
C 15742	<u>1</u>	Victor 74437	Slavonic Dance No. 2 in E minor, Op. 72, No. 2	Dvořák	Kreisler
B 14343	2		"Du alter Stefansturm" from *Der liebe Augustin* "The Old Refrain"	Brandl	Kreisler
B 14344	<u>2</u>	Victor 64406	Aus Wien (Viennese Melody)	Gaertner	Kreisler
B 14354	<u>2</u>	Victor 64542	Song Without Words, Op. 62, No. 1 "May Breezes"	Mendelssohn	Kreisler
C 15743	1		Tambourin Chinois, Op. 3	Kreisler	
<u>14</u>	<u>22 April 1915</u>		<u>Carl Lamson (piano)</u>	<u>New York</u>	
B 15937	1, <u>2</u>, 3	Victor 64502	The Rosary	Nevin	Kreisler
B 15938	1, 2, <u>3</u>	Victor 64503	Sérénade espagnole	Chaminade	Kreisler
B 15939	1		Song Without Words, Op. 62, No. 6 "Spring Song"	Mendelssohn	Kreisler
C 15743	<u>2</u>	Victor 74203	Tambourin Chinois, Op. 3	Kreisler	
B 14343	3		"Du alter Stefansturm" from *Der liebe Augustin* "The Old Refrain"	Brandl	Kreisler
<u>15</u>	<u>23 April 1915</u>		<u>Carl Lamson (piano)</u>	<u>New York</u>	
B 15940	1, <u>2</u>	Victor 64504	Mazurka in A, Op. 33, No. 2	Chopin	Kreisler
C 15941	1		Andante Religioso	Thomé	
B 15942	1		"Träumerei" from *Kinderszenen*	Schumann	Kreisler
B 15938	4		Sérénade espagnole	Chaminade	Kreisler
B 15939	2		Song Without Words, Op. 62, No. 6 "Spring Song"	Mendelssohn	Kreisler

16	24 May 1915		Geraldine Farrar (soprano) with Victor Orchestra conducted by Rogers		
C 16043	1, 2	Victor 88537	Mighty Lak' a Rose	Nevin	Kreisler
C 16045	1, 2	Victor 88538	"Connais-tu le pays?" from *Mignon*	Thomas	
C 16046	1		Annie Laurie	Scott	Kreisler
			Geraldine Farrar (soprano) with string quartet and harp		
C 16044	1, 2[1]		Serenata	Tosti	Kreisler
17	10 June 1915		John McCormack (tenor) with Victor Orchestra conducted by Rogers	New York	
C 16089	1, 2		Preislied from *Die Meistersinger von Nürnberg*	Wagner	
B 16090	1, 2	Victor 87230	Serenata	Moszkowski	
B 16091	1, 2	Victor 87231	Carmè "Canto sorrentino"	De Curtis	
			John McCormack (tenor) and Ludwig Schwat (piano)		
B 16092	1	Victor 87232	Flirtation	Meyer-Helmund	
B 16093	1, 2	Victor 87233	Calm as the Night	Böhm	
18	8 January 1916		Carl Lamson (piano)	New York	
C 8944	4		Méditation from *Thaïs*	Massenet	Marsick
C 8941	3		Humoresque, Op. 101, No. 7	Dvořák	Kreisler
B 16985	1, 2		Rondino on a Theme of Beethoven	Kreisler	
C 16986	1		Spanish Dance in E minor, Op. 37, No. 5 "Andaluza"	Granados	Kreisler
B 16986[2]	1		Spanish Dance in E minor, Op. 37, No. 5 "Andaluza"	Granados	Kreisler
B 14343	4		"Du alter Stefansturm" from *Der liebe Augustin* "The Old Refrain"	Brandl	Kreisler
B 16987	1		Wienerisch (No. 12 from Impressions)	Godowsky	

session / matrix	date / take(s)	original issue on 78 rpm records	accompanying artist(s) / title of work	venue (where known) / composer	arranger
C 16987[2]	1	Victor 74463	Wienerisch (No. 12 from Impressions)	Godowsky	
C 8951	3		Liebesfreud	Kreisler	
B 16988	1, 2		Moment musical[3]	Schubert	Kreisler
B 16989	1		Berceuse romantique, Op. 9	Kreisler	
B 8952	5	Victor 64142	Chanson sans paroles, Op. 2, No. 3	Tchaikovsky	Kreisler
B 8980	4	Victor 64132	Gavotte from Partita No. 3 in E	Bach	Kreisler
19	14 January 1916		Carl Lamson (piano)	New York	
B 17013	1, 2	Victor 64563	Songs My Mother Taught Me, Op. 55, No. 4	Dvořák	Kreisler
C 8951	4	Victor 74196	Liebesfreud	Kreisler	
B 16989	2, 3	Victor 64565	Berceuse romantique, Op. 9	Kreisler	
B 14343	5	Victor 64529	"Du alter Stefansturm" from *Der liebe Augustin* "The Old Refrain"	Brandl	Kreisler
C 8944	5	Victor 74182	Méditation from *Thaïs*	Massenet	Marsick
B 16986	2	Victor 64556	Spanish Dance in E minor, Op. 37, No. 5 "Andaluza"	Granados	Kreisler
C 16987	2		Wienerisch (No. 12 from Impressions)	Godowsky	
20	7 February 1916		Carl Lamson (piano)	New York	
B 8939	3, 4	Victor 64130	Old Folks at Home (Swanee River)	Foster	Kreisler
C 8942	3, 4	Victor 74172	Andantino (No. 2 from *Aus der Heimat*)	Smetana	
C 8940	5, 6, 7		Caprice Viennois, Op. 2	Kreisler	
B 8977	2		Variations on a Theme of Corelli "in the style of Tartini"	Kreisler	
B 8969	2, 3	Victor 64131	Hungarian Dance No. 5	Brahms	Joachim
B 17119	1	Victor 64202	Aubade provençale "in the style of Couperin"	Kreisler	

C 17120	1		Scherzo "in the style of Dittersdorf"	Kreisler	
B 17120	1		Scherzo "in the style of Dittersdorf"	Kreisler	
21	10 May 1916		John McCormack (tenor) and Edwin Schneider (piano)	Camden	
C 17653	1		For All Eternity	Mascheroni	
B 17654	1, 2	Victor 87258	Serenade, Op. 1	Raff	
B 17655	1	Victor 87245	Barcarolle from *Contes d'Hoffmann*	Offenbach	
22	11 May 1916		Rattay, Levy, Fruncillo, Bourdon (string quartet) and Rogers (conductor)		
C 17671	1, 2	Victor 74487	Andante cantabile from String Quartet No. 1 in D, Op. 11	Tchaikovsky	Kreisler
23	29 May 1916		Rattay, Levy, Fruncillo, Lennartz (string quartet) and Bourdon (conductor)		
B 17753	1, 2	Victor 64614	Minuet from String Quintet in E, Op. 13, No. 5	Boccherini	Kreisler
B 17754	1, 2	Victor 64600	Rondino on a Theme of Beethoven	Kreisler	
			Rattay, Fruncillo, Lennartz (string trio) and Bourdon (conductor)		
B 17755	1, 2	Victor 64601	Adagietto from *L'arlésienne*	Bizet	Gounod
24	1 March 1917		Victor Orchestra with Pasternack		
B 19321	1, 2	Victor 64660	Underneath the Stars	Herbert Spencer	Pasternack
B 19322	1, 2, 3	Victor 64655	"Poor Butterfly" from *The Big Show*	Raymond Hubbell	
B 19323	1	Victor 64670	Ballet Music from *Rosamunde von Cypern*	Schubert	Kreisler
C 19324	1, 2		Dream of Youth	Winternitz	

session	*date*	*original issue on*	*accompanying artist(s)*	*venue (where known)*	
matrix	*take(s)*	*78 rpm records*	*title of work*	*composer*	*arranger*
25	11 July 1917		Victor Orchestra with Pasternack		
B 20333	1, 2		Minuet in G, Op. 14, No. 1	Paderewski	Kreisler
26	16 July 1917		Victor Orchestra with Pasternack		
B 20339	1, 2	Victor 64731	Polichinelle Serenade	Kreisler	Pasternack
B 20333	3, 4	Victor 64709	Minuet in G, Op. 14, No. 1	Paderewski	Kreisler
B 19324	1, 2, 3	Victor 64730	Dream of Youth	Winternitz	Pasternack
27	25 February 1919		Maurice Eisner (piano)	New York	
C 8943	4, 5	Victor 74202	Moment musical, Op. 94, No. 3/ Tambourin from *Les fêtes d'Hébé*	Schubert/Rameau	Kreisler
C 8941	4, 5		Humoresque, Op. 101, No. 7	Dvořák	Kreisler
28	21 May 1919		Victor Orchestra with Pasternack		
B 22863	1, 2, 3		Beautiful Ohio Waltz	Mary Earl	
C 22864	1, 2		Forsaken (Corinthian Melody)	Korchat	Winternitz
B 22865	1, 2		Paradise	Krakauer	Kreisler
B 22866	1, 2		La Gitana	Kreisler	Lapatino
B 22867	1, 2, 3		Chant, Op. 12, No. 1 "Nobody Knows De Trouble I've Seen"	White	
29	22 May 1919		Victor Orchestra with Pasternack		
B 22863	4, 5, 6, 7		Beautiful Ohio Waltz	Earl	
C 22864	3, 4		Forsaken (Corinthian Melody)	Korchat	Winternitz
B 22865	3, 4, 5, 6		Paradise	Krakauer	Kreisler

B 22868	1, 2		Sérénade du Tzigane	Valdez	
B 22869	1, 2		Chanson indoue [Song of India] from *Sadko*	Rimsky-Korsakov	Kreisler
30	23 May 1919		Victor Orchestra with Pasternack		
B 22863	8, 9, 10, 11, 12	Victor 64817	Beautiful Ohio Waltz	Earl	
C 22864	5, 6, 7		Forsaken (Corinthian Melody)	Korchat	Winternitz
B 22867	4, 5, 6		Chant, Op. 12, No. 1 "Nobody Knows De Trouble I've Seen"	White	
B 22869	3, 4	Victor 64890	Chanson indoue [Song of India] from *Sadko*	Rimsky-Korsakov	Kreisler
B 22865	7, 8, 9	Victor 66023	Paradise	Krakauer	Kreisler
B 22866	3, 4	Victor 64842	La Gitana	Kreisler	Lapatino
B 22868	3, 4, 5	Victor 64857	Sérénade du Tzigane	Valdez	
31	4 June 1919		Victor Orchestra with Pasternack		
B 22864[4]	1, 2, 3, 4, 5	Victor 64873	Forsaken (Corinthian Melody)	Korchat	Winternitz
B 22867	7, 8, 9, 10	Victor 64824	Chant, Op. 12, No. 1 "Nobody Knows De Trouble I've Seen"	White	
C 22887	1, 2, 3, 4	Victor 74180	Humoresque, Op. 101, No. 7	Dvořák	Pasternack
32	2 April 1920		John McCormack (tenor) and Edwin Schneider (piano)	Camden	
B 23905	1, 2, 3	Victor 87571	When Night Descends, Op. 4, No. 3	Rachmaninoff	
B 23906	1, 2, 3	Victor 87574	O Cease Thy Singing, Maiden Fair, Op. 4, No. 4	Rachmaninoff	
33	5 May 1920		John McCormack (tenor) and Edwin Schneider (piano)	New York	
B 24034	1, 2		O Dry Those Tears	Del Riego	
B 24035	1, 2		Where Blooms the Rose	Johns	

session	*date*	*original issue on*	*accompanying artist(s)*	*venue (where known)*	
matrix	*take(s)*	*78 rpm records*	*title of work*	*composer*	*arranger*
B 24036	1, 2	Victor 87576	The Last Hour	Kramer	
B 24037	1, 2	Victor 87573	Since You Went Away	Johnson	
34	1 June 1920		Victor Orchestra with Pasternack		
B 24184	1, 2, 3	Victor 64902	"Who can tell?" from *Apple Blossoms*	Kreisler	
B 24185	1, 2, 3, 4, 5		Blue Danube Waltz	Strauss	Kreisler
B 24186	1, 2, 3, 4		On Miami Shore	Jacobi	
B 24187	1, 2, 3		To Spring, Op. 43, No. 6	Grieg	
B 24188	1, 2		Waltz, Op. 39, No. 15	Brahms	Hochstein
35	2 December 1920		Victor Orchestra with Pasternack		
B 24186	5, 6, 7, 8		On Miami Shore	Jacobi	
B 24185	6, 7		Blue Danube Waltz	Strauss	Kreisler
B 24719	1, 2, 3, 4, 5, 6	Victor 64904	Love Nest from *Mary*	Louis A. Hirsch	Kreisler
36	29 December 1920		Victor Orchestra with Pasternack		
B 24186	9, 10, 11, 12, 13	Victor 64947	On Miami Shore	Jacobi	
C 24185[5]	1, 2, 3, 4		Blue Danube Waltz	Strauss	Kreisler
37	31 March 1921		Carl Lamson (piano)		
B 25132	1, 2, 3, 4	Victor 66104	Aucassin and Nicolette "in the style of Couperin"	Kreisler	
C 25133	1		Hymn to the Sun from *Le coq d'or*	Rimsky-Korsakov	Kreisler
B 24187	4, 5, 6, 7	Victor 64993	To Spring, Op. 43, No. 6	Grieg	

B 25134	1, 2, 3	Victor 64974	Souvenir	Drdla	
B 25130	1, 2, 3	Victor 64961	Melody in A	Dawes	
B 24188	3, 4	Victor 66041	Waltz, Op. 39, No. 15	Brahms	Hochstein
B 25131	1, 2, 3, 4, 5, 6	Victor 66137	Toy Soldiers' March	Kreisler	
38	1 April 1921		Carl Lamson (piano)		
C 25133	2, 3	Victor 74720	Hymn to the Sun from *Le coq d'or*	Rimsky-Korsakov	Kreisler
39	24 April 1922		Carl Lamson (piano)		
C 26427	1[1], 2		Lotus Land, Op. 47, No. 1	Scott	Kreisler
B 26428	1, 2, 3	Victor 66127	Pale Moon (Indian Love Song)	Frederick Logan	Kreisler
B 26429	1, 2		Romance from Sonata No. 3 in C minor	Grieg	
B 26425	1, 2, 3, 4, 5	Victor 66079	Chanson arabe from *Scheherazade*	Rimsky-Korsakov	Kreisler
B 26426	1, 2, 3, 4		Dance orientale from *Scheherazade*	Rimsky-Korsakov	Kreisler
40	25 April 1922		Carl Lamson (piano)		
B 26429	3, 4, 5		Romance from Sonata No. 3 in C minor	Grieg	
B 26426	5, 6, 7, 8	Victor 1075	Dance orientale from *Scheherazade*	Rimsky-Korsakov	Kreisler
B 26431	1, 2, 3, 4, 5	Victor 66196	Cherry Ripe	Scott	
41	30 March 1923		Carl Lamson (piano)		
B 27724	1, 2, 3		The Blue Lagoon	Millöcker	Winternitz
B 27725	1, 2, 3, 4, 5	Victor 66197	Entr'acte, Op. 46, No. 2	Kramer	
B 27726	1, 2, 3, 4, 5	Victor 64504	Mazurka in A minor, Op. 67, No. 4	Chopin	Kreisler
B 27727	1, 2, 3	Victor 66176	Melodie, Op. 16, No. 2	Paderewski	Kreisler
B 27728	1, 2, 3	Victor 66149	"Im Chambre séparée" from *Der Opernball* "Midnight Bells"	Heuberger	Kreisler
B 27729	1, 2		Lullaby (Berceuse)	Tchaikovsky	Kreisler

session	*date*	*original issue on*	*accompanying artist(s)*	*venue (where known)*	
matrix	*take(s)*	*78 rpm records*	*title of work*	*composer*	*arranger*
42	18 January 1924		Carl Lamson (piano)		
B 29299	1, 2, 3	Victor 66231	Love Sends a Little Gift of Roses	Openshaw	Kreisler
B 29400	1, 2, 3	Victor 66232	The World is Waiting for the Sunrise	Seitz	Kreisler
C 29401	1		Canzonetta from Violin Concerto in D, Op. 35	Tchaikovsky	
43	24 January 1924		Carl Lamson (piano)		
C 26427	3, 4		Lotus Land, Op. 47, No. 1	Scott	Kreisler
C 29401	2[1], 3		Canzonetta from Violin Concerto in D, Op. 35	Tchaikovsky	
B 29413	1, 2, 3	Victor 1043	Slavonic Lament	Schuett	Friedberg
B 29414	1, 2, 3	Victor 66250	Minuet from Symphony No. 96 “Miracle”	Haydn	Friedberg
B 29415	1, 2, 3	Victor 66251	Old French Gavotte	traditional	Friedberg
44	27 March 1924		Carl Lamson (piano)		
B 29841	1, 2, 3, 4, 5	Victor 1029	Poupée valsante [Dancing Doll] (No. 2 from Marionettes)	Poldini	Kreisler
B 29842	1, 2, 3, 4		From the Land of the Sky-Blue Water (No. 1 from American Indian Songs, Op. 45)	Cadman	Kreisler
B 29843	1, 2, 3		Largo from Symphony No. 9 “Negro Spiritual Melody”	Dvořák	Kreisler
B 29844	1, 2 ,3, 4, 5		Chansonette	Bass	
B 29845	1, 2, 3, 4		“A Kiss in the Dark” from *Orange Blossoms*	Herbert	Kreisler
C 8940	7, 8, 9		Caprice Viennois, Op. 2	Kreisler	
B 29846	1	Victor 1075	Molly on the Shore	Grainger	Kreisler

45	28 March 1924		Carl Lamson (piano)		
B 29845	5, 6, 7		"A Kiss in the Dark" from *Orange Blossoms*	Herbert	Kreisler
B 29850	1, 2, 3		Dirge of the North	Balogh	Kreisler
B 29841	1, 2, 3, 4, 5, 6		Poupée valsante [Dancing Doll] (No. 2 from Marionettes)	Poldini	Kreisler
B 29851	1, 2	Victor 1062	"Mein sehnen, mein Wähnen" (Pierrotlied) from *Die tote Stadt*	Korngold	Kreisler
B 29852	1, 2		Minuet in G, Op. 14, No. 1	Paderewski	Kreisler
C 8944	6, 7	Victor 74182	Méditation from *Thaïs*	Massenet	Marsick
B 14343	6, 7		"Du alter Stefansturm" from *Der liebe Augustin* "The Old Refrain"	Brandl	Kreisler
B 12727	4, 5		Berceuse	Townsend	
C 15742	2, 3	Victor 74437	Slavonic Dance No. 2 in E minor	Dvořák	Kreisler
46	29 March 1924		Carl Lamson (piano)		
C 14342	2, 3, 4		"Ombra mai fu" (Largo) from *Serse*	Handel	
B 29850	4, 5	Victor 1043	Dirge of the North	Balogh	Kreisler
47	9 April 1924		Carl Lamson (piano)		
C 14342	5, 6		"Ombra mai fu" (Largo) from *Serse*	Handel	
B 29843	4, 5, 6		Largo from Symphony No. 9 "Negro Spiritual Melody"	Dvořák	Kreisler
B 25130	4, 5, 6		Melody in A	Dawes	
B 14343	8, 9	Victor 64529	"Du alter Stefansturm" from *Der liebe Augustin* "The Old Refrain"	Brandl	Kreisler
C 8940	10		Caprice Viennois, Op. 2	Kreisler	

session / *matrix*	*date* / *take(s)*	*original issue on 78 rpm records*	*accompanying artist(s)* / *title of work*	*venue (where known)* / *composer*	*arranger*
48	10 April 1924		Schmidt, Pasternack, Lennartz (string trio)		
B 17755	3, 4, 5	Victor 64601[6]	Adagietto from *L'arlésienne*	Bizet	Gounod
B 20333	5, 6, 7, 8	Victor 64709	Minuet in G, Op. 14, No. 1	Paderewski	Kreisler
			Carl Lamson (piano)		
B 29843	7, 8		Largo from Symphony No. 9 "Negro Spiritual Melody"	Dvořák	Kreisler
C 14342	7		"Ombra mai fu" (Largo) from *Serse*	Handel	
B 25130	7, 8, 9	Victor 64961	Melody in A	Dawes	
B 29845	8, 9, 10		"A Kiss in the Dark" from *Orange Blossoms*	Herbert	Kreisler
49	11 April 1924		Carl Lamson (piano)		
C 14342	8	Victor 74384	"Ombra mai fu" (Largo) from *Serse*	Handel	
B 29843	9, 10, 11, 12, 13		Largo from Symphony No. 9 "Negro Spiritual Melody"	Dvořák	Kreisler
B 29845	11, 12	Victor 1029	"A Kiss in the Dark" from *Orange Blossoms*	Herbert	Kreisler
C 26427	5, 6		Lotus Land, Op. 47, No. 1	Scott	Kreisler
C 8940	11, 12	Victor 74197	Caprice Viennois, Op. 2	Kreisler	
50	15 April 1924		Carl Lamson (piano)		
B 8952	6, 7, 8, 9	Victor 64142	Chanson sans paroles, Op. 2, No. 3	Tchaikovsky	Kreisler
B 16989	4, 5	Victor 64565[7]	Berceuse romantique, Op. 9	Kreisler	
B 127287	6, 7, 8	Victor 64319[8]	Berceuse	Townsend	
B 29844	6, 7	Victor 1062	Chansonette	Bass	

51	11 February 1925	Carl Lamson (piano)	New York	
B 31936	1, 2, 3	Tempo di Minuetto "in the style of Pugnani"	Kreisler	
B 17119	2, 3, 4	Aubade provençale "in the style of Couperin"	Kreisler	
B 31938	1, 2, 3	Hungarian Dance No. 17	Brahms	Kreisler
B 31939	1, 2, 3, 4, 5	The Girl with the Flaxen Hair (No. 8 from Préludes – Book I)	Debussy	Hartmann
B 31940	1, 2, 3, 4	Minuet in G from Anna Magdalena Notebook	(attrib. Bach)	Winternitz
52	13 February 1925	Carl Lamson (piano)	New York	
C 31947	1, 2, 3[1]	Scherzando from *Symphonie espagnole*	Lalo	
B 29842	5, 6	From the Land of the Sky-Blue Water (No. 1 from American Indian Songs, Op. 45)	Cadman	Kreisler
B 31940	5, 6	Minuet in G from Anna Magdalena Notebook	(attrib. Bach)	Winternitz
B 31938	4, 5	Hungarian Dance No. 17	Brahms	Kreisler
B 31946	1, 2, 3, 4	Legend of the Canyon	Cadman	Kreisler
53	18 February 1925	Carl Lamson (piano)	New York	
B 39136	4, 5	Tempo di Minuetto "in the style of Pugnani"	Kreisler	
B 39139	6, 7	The Girl with the Flaxen Hair (No. 8 from Préludes – Book I)	Debussy	Hartmann
54	19 February 1925	Carl Lamson (piano)	New York	
B 31940	7, 8, 9	Minuet in G from Anna Magdalena Notebook	(attrib. Bach)	Winternitz
B 31975	1, 2, 3	Gavotte in F from *La ritrovata figlia de Ottone*	Kozeluh (attrib. Beethoven)	Kramer
B 31938	6, 7	Hungarian Dance No. 17	Brahms	Kreisler
B 17119	5, 6	Aubade provençale "in the style of Couperin"	Kreisler	

session / *matrix*	*date* / *take(s)*	*original issue on 78 rpm records*	*accompanying artist(s)* / *title of work*	*venue (where known)* / *composer*	*arranger*
55	25 February 1925		Carl Lamson (piano)		
B 31939	8, 9, 10, 11		The Girl with the Flaxen Hair (No. 8 from Préludes – Book I)	Debussy	Hartmann
B 31946	5, 6, 7, 8	Victor 1093	Legend of the Canyon	Cadman	Kreisler
B 29842	7, 8, 9		From the Land of the Sky-Blue Water (No. 1 from American Indian Songs, Op. 45)	Cadman	Kreisler
B 31938	8, 9		Hungarian Dance No. 17	Brahms	Kreisler
B 31936	6, 7		Tempo di Minuetto "in the style of Pugnani"	Kreisler	
B 31871	1, 2, 3, 4	Victor 1093	Caprice Antique	Balogh	Kreisler
B 31872	1, 2		Humoresque, Op. 10, No. 2	Tchaikovsky	Kreisler

Part 3: The acoustic HMV recordings (Hayes, Middlesex, 1921–25)

The late acoustic HMV recordings feature Kreisler's first concerto recordings with orchestra: Mozart's Concerto No. 4 in D and Bruch's Concerto No. 1 in G minor. These were made with a studio orchestra (not the Royal Albert Hall Orchestra as has sometimes been claimed). The Bruch concerto was not issued on 78 rpm records, but fortunately it survives in test pressings (now in the Yale University Library) given by the violinist to Elgar; it has been issued on CD.

All the trio recordings with Hugo Kreisler, as well as the one solo piece with piano (Cadman's *From the Land of the Sky-Blue Water*), were made specifically for the Victor Company, the Gramophone Company's American affiliate.

The letters "Bb" and "Cc" preceding the matrix number designate 10- and 12-inch records made at Hayes. The catalog number prefixes for these double-letter matrix numbers are DA and DB, respectively.

session / *matrix*	*date* / *take(s)*	*original issue on 78 rpm records*	*accompanying artist(s)* / *title of work*	*venue (where known)* / *composer*	*arranger*
1	16 December 1921		Hugo Kreisler (cello) and Charlton Keith (piano)	Hayes (Room 1)	
Bb 779	1, 2, 3	Victor 87579	Serenade viennoise, Op. 18	Jeral	
Bb 780	1, 2, 3, 4		Londonderry Air	traditional	Kreisler
2	17 December 1921		Hugo Kreisler (cello) and Charlton Keith (piano)	Hayes (Room 1)	
Bb 787	1, 2, 3, 4		Mattinata	Leoncavallo	Kreisler
Bb 779	4, 5		Serenade viennoise, Op. 18	Jeral	
Bb 780	5, 6	Victor 87577	Londonderry Air	traditional	Kreisler
3	1 November 1923		Hugo Kreisler (cello) and Charlton Keith (piano)	Hayes (Room 2)	
Cc 3775	1, 2		Marche militaire No. 1, Op. 51 (D. 733)	Schubert	
Cc 3776	1, 2, 3[9]		"Morgendlich leuchtend" (Prize Song) from *Die Meistersinger*	Wagner	
Bb 3777	1, 2	Victor 3037	Minuet in G	Beethoven	Kreisler
Bb 3778	1, 2		Andante favori in F	Beethoven	Kreisler
4	20 September 1924		Hugo Kreisler (cello) and Charlton Keith (piano)	Hayes (Room 1)	
Bb 3778	3, 4, 5		Andante favori in F	Beethoven	Kreisler
Cc 3775	3, 4, 5		Marche militaire No. 1, Op. 51 (D. 733)	Schubert	
Bb 5102	1, 2, 3		Abendlied	Schumann	Svendsen
5	22 September 1924		Hugo Kreisler (cello) and Charlton Keith (piano)	Hayes (Room 1)	
Bb 5103	1, 2		Gavotte, Op. 23, No. 2	Popper	
Bb 5104	1, 2, 3		Assad's Song from *The Queen of Sheba* "Magic Tones"	Goldmark	
Bb 5105	1, 2, 3, 4		Polichinelle Serenade	Kreisler	

session / matrix	date / take(s)	original issue on 78 rpm records	accompanying artist(s) / title of work	venue (where known) / composer	arranger
Bb 5106	1, 2, 3	Victor 3035	Marche miniature viennoise	Kreisler	
Bb 5107	1, 2, 3, 4	Victor 3035	Syncopation	Kreisler	
Bb 5108	1, 2		Andante	Bach	Kreisler
Bb 5109	1, 2	Victor 3036	Nina (Tre giorni)	Pergolesi	Kreisler
			Charlton Keith (piano)		
Bb 5110	1, 2, 3, 4		From the Land of the Sky-Blue Water (No. 1 from American Indian Songs, Op. 45)	Cadman	Kreisler
6	23 September 1924		Hugo Kreisler (cello) and Charlton Keith (piano)	Hayes (Room 1)	
Bb 5104	4, 5		Assad's Song from *The Queen of Sheba* "Magic Tones"	Goldmark	
Bb 5105	5, 6		Polichinelle Serenade	Kreisler	
Bb 3778	6, 7	Victor 3037	Andante favori in F	Beethoven	Kreisler
Cc 3775	6, 7, 8, 9		Marche militaire No. 1, Op. 51 (D. 733)	Schubert	
Bb 5102	4, 5, 6	Victor 3036	Abendlied	Schumann	Svendsen
7	24 September 1924		Hugo Kreisler (cello) and Charlton Keith (piano)	Hayes (Room 1)	
Bb 5108	3, 4, 5		Andante	Bach	Kreisler
			John McCormack (tenor) and Edwin Schneider (piano)	Hayes (Room 1)	
Bb 5115	1, 2, 3	HMV DA 644	Morgen!	Richard Strauss	
Bb 5116	1, 2, 3	HMV DA 644	Before My Window	Rachmaninoff	
Bb 5117	1, 2	HMV DA 680[10]	To the Children	Rachmaninoff	
Bb 5118	1, 2, 3	HMV DA 636	Padriac, the Fiddler	John F. Larchet	
Bb 5119	1, 2, 3, 4	HMV DA 636	I Saw from the Beach	Irish Air	Hughes

8	1 December 1924		Orchestra and Sir Landon Ronald (conductor)	Hayes (Room 1)
Cc 5396	1, 2	HMV DB 815	Concerto No. 4 in D, K. 218: I Allegro (part 1)	Mozart
Cc 5397	1, 2	HMV DB 815	Concerto No. 4 in D, K. 218: I Allegro (part 2)	Mozart
Cc 5398	1, 2, 3	HMV DB 816	Concerto No. 4 in D, K. 218: I Allegro (part 3)	Mozart
Cc 5399	1, 2	HMV DB 816	Concerto No. 4 in D, K. 218: II Andante cantabile (part 1)	Mozart
9	2 December 1924		Orchestra and Sir Landon Ronald (conductor)	Hayes (Room 1)
Cc 5400	1, 2	HMV DB 817	Concerto No. 4 in D, K. 218: II Andante cantabile (part 1)	Mozart
Cc 5401	1, 2	HMV DB 817	Concerto No. 4 in D, K. 218: III Rondeau (part 1)	Mozart
Cc 5408	1, 2	HMV DB 818	Concerto No. 4 in D, K. 218: III Rondeau (part 2)	Mozart
Cc 5409	1, 2	HMV DB 818	Concerto No. 4 in D, K. 218: III Rondeau (part 3)	Mozart
10	29 December 1924		Orchestra and Eugene Goossens (conductor)	Hayes (Room 1)
Cc 5508	1, 2		Concerto No. 1 in G minor, Op. 26: I Allegro moderato (part 1)	Bruch
Cc 5509	1[9], 2, 3		Concerto No. 1 in G minor, Op. 26: I Allegro moderato (part 2)	Bruch
Cc 5510	1, 2		Concerto No. 1 in G minor, Op. 26: II Adagio (part 1)	Bruch
Cc 5511	1, 2		Concerto No. 1 in G minor, Op. 26: II Adagio (part 2)	Bruch
11	30 December 1924		Orchestra and Eugene Goossens (conductor)	Hayes (Room 1)
Cc 5512	1, 2, 3		Concerto No. 1 in G minor, Op. 26: III Allegro energico (part 1)	Bruch

session / *matrix*	*date* / *take(s)*	*original issue on 78 rpm records*	*accompanying artist(s)* / *title of work*	*venue (where known)* / *composer*	*arranger*
Cc 5513	1, 2, 3		Concerto No. 1 in G minor, Op. 26: III Allegro energico (part 2)	Bruch	
Cc 5508	3[9]		Concerto No. 1 in G minor, Op. 26: I Allegro moderato (part 1)	Bruch	
Cc 5510	3[9]		Concerto No. 1 in G minor, Op. 26: II Adagio (part 1)	Bruch	
Cc 5511	3[9], 4		Concerto No. 1 in G minor, Op. 26: II Adagio (part 2)	Bruch	
12	2 January 1925		Orchestra and Eugene Goossens (conductor)	Hayes (Room 1)	
Cc 5512	4, 5, 6, 7[9], 8		Concerto No. 1 in G minor, Op. 26: III Allegro energico (part 1)	Bruch	
Cc 5513	4[9], 5		Concerto No. 1 in G minor, Op. 26: III Allegro energico (part 2)	Bruch	

Part 4: The electric Victor recordings (New York and New Jersey, 1925–29)

The electric Victor records are considered by many to be Kreisler's finest recordings. Not only did the improved sonic quality of the electrical recording process capture the playing more vividly than ever, but Kreisler was at the height of his interpretive powers. Among the highlights of these electric Victor recordings are the duo sonatas of Beethoven and Schubert with Sergei Rachmaninoff.

This section contains the most frequently recorded piece: Debussy's *The Girl with the Flaxen Hair*. Of the twenty-seven takes, only take 25 (made on 2 February 1928) was issued. Considering that take 1 was made acoustically on 11 February 1925, it took a span of three years to arrive at a satisfactory take! A number of titles previously recorded acoustically were re-recorded during this period of electric recordings for Victor. There are no significant changes between the acoustic and electric recordings, except in the case of Foster's *Old Folks at Home*. Recorded acoustically in the key of A-flat in 1910 and 1916, it was transposed up a semitone to A major (in order to exploit the resonance of the open A-string) in the 1928 recording.

The last records in this section were made in 1929, following the merger earlier that year with RCA. None of the 1929 recordings was issued on 78 rpm format, but these same titles were remade with HMV the following year.

The letters "BVE" and "CVE" preceding the matrix numbers designate 10- and 12-inch discs, respectively.

session / *matrix*	*date* / *take(s)*	*original issue on 78 rpm records*	*accompanying artist(s)* / *title of work*	*venue (where known)* / *composer*	*arranger*
1	27 August 1925		Carl Lamson (piano)	New York	
BVE 29842	10, 11, 12		From the Land of the Sky-Blue Water (No. 1 from American Indian Songs, Op. 45)	Cadman	Kreisler
BVE 33188	1, 2, 3	Victor 1122	Paraphrase on two Russian folk songs	Kreisler	
BVE 33189	1, 2, 3, 4		Aloha Oe	Liliuokalani	Kreisler
2	28 August 1925		Carl Lamson (piano)		
BVE 31939	12, 13, 14, 15, 16		The Girl with the Flaxen Hair (No. 8 from Préludes – Book I)	Debussy	Hartmann
BVE 31940	10, 11		Minuet in G from Anna Magdalena Notebook	(attrib. Bach)	Winternitz
BVE 33189	5, 6, 7	Victor 1115	Aloha Oe	Liliuokalani	Kreisler
BVE 29843	14, 15, 16	Victor 1122	Largo from Symphony No. 9 "Negro Spiritual Melody"	Dvořák	Kreisler
BVE 29842	13, 14, 15	Victor 1115	From the Land of the Sky-Blue Water (No. 1 from American Indian Songs, Op. 45)	Cadman	Kreisler
3	29 August 1925		Carl Lamson (piano)		
BVE 31975	4, 5, 6	Victor 1136	Gavotte in F from *La ritrovata figlia de Ottone*	Kozeluh (attrib. Beethoven)	Kramer

session / *matrix*	*date* / *take(s)*	*original issue on 78 rpm records*	*accompanying artist(s)* / *title of work*	*venue (where known)* / *composer*	*arranger*
BVE 31940	**12**	Victor 1136	Minuet in G from Anna Magdalena Notebook	(attrib. Bach)	Winternitz
BVE 39139	17, 18, 19, 20, 21		The Girl with the Flaxen Hair (No. 8 from Préludes – Book I)	Debussy	Hartmann
4	1 September 1925		Carl Lamson (piano)		
BVE 31940	13, 14		Minuet in G from Anna Magdalena Notebook	(attrib. Bach)	Winternitz
BVE 31975	7, 8		Gavotte in F from *La ritrovata figlia de Ottone*	Kozeluh (attrib. Beethoven)	Kramer
BVE 33188	4, 5, 6, 7		Paraphrase on two Russian folk songs	Kreisler	
5	17 February 1926		Carl Lamson (piano)	New York	
BVE 34703	1, 2, 3, 4, 5		Deep in my Heart, Dear	Romberg	Kreisler
BVE 34704	1, 2, 3, 4, 5		Indian Love Call from *Rose Marie*	Friml	Kreisler
6	22 February 1926		Carl Lamson (piano)	New York	
BVE 34703	**6**, 7, 8, 9	Victor 1151	Deep in my Heart, Dear	Romberg	Kreisler
BVE 34704	6, **7**, 8, 9, 10, 11	Victor 1151	Indian Love Call from *Rose Marie*	Friml	Kreisler
7	7 April 1926		Carl Lamson (piano)	New York	
BVE 35121	1, **2**, 3, 4, 5	Victor 1165	Andantino	Lemare	
BVE 35122	1, 2, **3**, 4, 5, 6	Victor 1165	At Dawning, Op. 29, No. 1	Cadman	Rissland
BVE 35123	1, 2, 3, **4**, 5, 6	Victor 1158	"Kreisler" Serenade	Lehár	
BVE 35124	1, 2, 3, 4, 5		"Hab' ein blaues Himmelbett" (Serenade) from *Frasquita*	Lehár	Kreisler

8	8 April 1926		Carl Lamson (piano)	New York	
BVE 35125	1, 2, 3, 4, 5, 6		In the Gloaming	Annie Harrison	Kreisler
BVE 35126	1, 2, 3, 4, 5, 6		Mighty Lak' a Rose	Nevin	Kreisler
BVE 35127	1, 2, 3	Victor 1209	Invocation	Owen	Kreisler
BVE 35128	1, 2, 3, 4	Victor 1209	The Rose and the Nightingale, Op. 2, No. 2 "Oriental Romance"	Rimsky-Korsakov	Borrisoff
BVE 31872	3, 4, 5, 6	Victor 1170	Humoresque, Op. 10, No. 2	Tchaikovsky	Kreisler
BVE 35129	1, 2, 3, 4	Victor 1170	Albumblatt, Op. 38, No. 3 "Daisies"	Rachmaninoff	Kreisler
9	9 April 1926		Carl Lamson (piano)	New York	
BVE 31872	7, 8, 9, 10		Humoresque, Op. 10, No. 2	Tchaikovsky	Kreisler
CVE 8950	4, 5		Liebesleid	Kreisler	
CVE 8941	6, 7, 8		Humoresque, Op. 101, No. 7	Dvořák	Kreisler
BVE 35124	6, 7, 8, 9, 10, 11, 12	Victor 1158	"Hab' ein blaues Himmelbett" (Serenade) from *Frasquita*	Lehár	Kreisler
BVE 35123	7, 8		"Kreisler" Serenade	Lehár	
BVE 35129	5		Albumblatt, Op. 38, No. 3 "Daisies"	Rachmaninoff	Kreisler
BVE 35122	7, 8		At Dawning, Op. 29, No. 1	Cadman	Rissland
CVE 8940	13, 14		Caprice Viennois, Op. 2	Kreisler	
10	14 April 1926		Carl Lamson (piano)	New York	
BVE 35125	7, 8, 9		In the Gloaming	Harrison	Kreisler
BVE 35126	7, 8, 9		Mighty Lak' a Rose	Nevin	Kreisler
CVE 8941	9, 10		Humoresque, Op. 101, No. 7	Dvořák	Kreisler
CVE 8940	15, 16, 17	Victor 6692	Caprice Viennois, Op. 2	Kreisler	
CVE 8951	8, 9	Victor 6608	Liebesfreud	Kreisler	
CVE 8950	6, 7	Victor 6608	Liebesleid	Kreisler	
BVE 35124	13		"Hab' ein blaues Himmelbett" (Serenade) from *Frasquita*	Lehár	Kreisler

session / *matrix*	*date* / *take(s)*	*original issue on 78 rpm records*	*accompanying artist(s)* / *title of work*	*venue (where known)* / *composer*	*arranger*
11	16 March 1927		Carl Lamson (piano)	Camden	
BVE 38215	1, 2, 3, 4		Blue Skies	Berlin	Kreisler
BVE 38216	1, 2, 3		Dance of the Maidens, Op. 48	Friml	Kreisler
CVE 38219	1, 2		Shepherd's Madrigal	Kreisler	
BVE 38220	1		Malagueña, Op. 165, No. 3	Albéniz	Kreisler
BVE 38221	1, 2		Tango, Op. 165, No. 2	Albéniz	Kreisler
12	17 March 1927		Carl Lamson (piano)	Camden (Victor Studio No. 3)	
BVE 38215	5, 6	Victor 1233	Blue Skies	Berlin	Kreisler
BVE 38219	4, 5, 6	Victor 6712	Shepherd's Madrigal	Kreisler	
BVE 38216	4, 5, 6		Dance of the Maidens, Op. 48	Friml	Kreisler
BVE 38221	3, 4, 5		Tango, Op. 165, No. 2	Albéniz	Kreisler
BVE 38220	2, 3		Malagueña, Op. 165, No. 3	Albéniz	Kreisler
				Camden (Church Building)	
BVE 38215	7, 8		Blue Skies	Berlin	Kreisler
BVE 38219	7, 8		Shepherd's Madrigal	Kreisler	
BVE 38216	7, 8	Victor 1233	Dance of the Maidens, Op. 48	Friml	Kreisler
BVE 38220	4, 5		Malagueña, Op. 165, No. 3	Albéniz	Kreisler
13	25 March 1927		Carl Lamson (piano)	Camden (Victor Studio 3)	
BVE 38221	6, 7, 8		Tango, Op. 165, No. 2	Albéniz	Kreisler
BVE 38220	6, 7, 8	Victor 1244	Malagueña, Op. 165, No. 3	Albéniz	Kreisler
CVE 37461	1, 2, 3, 4, 5, 6	Victor 6712	Gypsy Caprice	Kreisler	
BVE 38216	10, 11		Dance of the Maidens, Op. 48	Friml	Kreisler
BVE 14343	10, 11		"Du alter Stefansturm" from *Der liebe Augustin* "The Old Refrain"	Brandl	Kreisler

BVE 12730	3, 4, 5	Victor 1387	Schön Rosmarin	Kreisler	
CVE 15743	3, 4, 5		Tambourin Chinois, Op. 3	Kreisler	
BVE 37462	1, 2	Victor 1244	Canción (No. 6 from Seven Popular Spanish Songs)	Falla	Kochánski
14	26 March 1927		Carl Lamson (piano)	Camden (Victor Studio 3)	
CVE 8941	11, 12, 13	Victor 6692	Humoresque, Op. 101, No. 7	Dvořák	Kreisler
BVE 38215	9, 10		Blue Skies	Berlin	Kreisler
CVE 37461	7, 8		Gypsy Caprice	Kreisler	
CVE 15743	6, 7		Tambourin Chinois, Op. 3	Kreisler	
BVE 38221	9, 10		Tango, Op. 165, No. 2	Albéniz	Kreisler
BVE 38220	9, 10		Malagueña, Op. 165, No. 3	Albéniz	Kreisler
15	12 January 1928		Carl Lamson (piano)	New York (Victor Studio 1)	
BVE 40358	1, 2, 3, 4, 5	Victor 1358	En bateau (No. 1 from Petite Suite)	Debussy	Choisnel
BVE 31939	22, 23, 24		The Girl with the Flaxen Hair (No. 8 from Préludes – Book I)	Debussy	Hartmann
BVE 38221	11, 12, 13, 14, 15, 16		Tango, Op. 165, No. 2	Albéniz	Kreisler
BVE 40359	1, 2, 3, 4, 5		Danza espagñola from *La vida breve*	Falla	Kreisler
16	1 February 1928		Carl Lamson (piano)	New York (Victor Studios)	
BVE 41598	1, 2, 3, 4	Victor 1428	Presto from *Ruralia hungarica*, Op. 32c	Dohnányi	
BVE 41599	1, 2, 3, 4	Victor 1429	Andante (part 1) from *Ruralia hungarica*, Op. 32c	Dohnányi	
BVE 42400	1, 2, 3, 4, 5	Victor 1429	Andante (part 2) from *Ruralia hungarica*, Op. 32c	Dohnányi	
BVE 42401	1, 2, 3, 4, 5	Victor 1428	Molto vivace from *Ruralia hungarica*, Op. 32c	Dohnányi	

session / *matrix*	*date* / *take(s)*	*original issue on 78 rpm records*	*accompanying artist(s)* / *title of work*	*venue (where known)* / *composer*	*arranger*
17	2 February 1928		Carl Lamson (piano)	New York (Victor Studios)	
CVE 8944	8, 9, 10, 11	Victor 6844	Méditation from *Thaïs*	Massenet	Marsick
BVE 25134	4, 5, 6, 7, 8	Victor 1325	Souvenir	Drdla	
BVE 31939	25, 26, 27	Victor 1358	The Girl with the Flaxen Hair (No. 8 from Préludes – Book I)	Debussy	Hartmann
BVE 8939	5, 6, 7		Old Folks at Home (Swanee River)	Foster	Kreisler
18	7 February 1928		Carl Lamson (piano)	Camden (Victor Studio 1)	
BVE 35126	10, 11, 12	Victor 1320	Mighty Lak' a Rose	Nevin	Kreisler
BVE 15937	4, 5, 6	Victor 1320	The Rosary	Nevin	Kreisler
19	27 February 1928		Carl Lamson (piano)	Camden (Victor Studio 1)	
BVE 8939	8, 9, 10, 11	Victor 1325	Old Folks at Home (Swanee River)	Foster	Kreisler
BVE 40359	6, 7, 8	Victor 1339	Danza espagñola from *La vida breve*	Falla	Kreisler
BVE 38221	17, 18, 19	Victor 1339	Tango, Op. 165, No. 2	Albéniz	Kreisler
CVE 15743	8, 9, 10, 11	Victor 6844	Tambourin Chinois, Op. 3	Kreisler	
20	28 February 1928		Carl Lamson (piano)	Camden (Victor Studio 1)	
BVE 41758	1, 2, 3, 4, 5	Victor 1501[11]	Dance of the Marionettes	Winternitz	
			Sergei Rachmaninoff (piano)		
CVE 41759	1, 2, 3		Sonata No. 8 in G, Op. 30, No. 3: I Allegro assai	Beethoven	
CVE 41760	1, 2, 3		Sonata No. 8 in G, Op. 30, No. 3: II Tempo di Menuetto, ma molto moderato e grazioso (part 1)	Beethoven	

CVE 41761	1, 2		Sonata No. 8 in G, Op. 30, No. 3: II Tempo di Menuetto, ma molto moderato e grazioso (part 2)	Beethoven	
CVE 41762	1, 2, 3		Sonata No. 8 in G, Op. 30, No. 3: III Allegro vivace	Beethoven	
21	29 February 1928		Sergei Rachmaninoff (piano)	Camden (Victor Studio 1)	
CVE 41759	4, 5, 6		Sonata No. 8 in G, Op. 30, No. 3: I Allegro assai	Beethoven	
CVE 41762	4, 5, 6		Sonata No. 8 in G, Op. 30, No. 3: III Allegro vivace	Beethoven	
22	22 March 1928		Carl Lamson (piano)	Camden (Victor Studio 1)	
BVE 41599	5, 6, 7, 8		Andante (part 1) from *Ruralia hungarica*, Op. 32c	Dohnányi	
BVE 42400	6, 7		Andante (part 2) from *Ruralia hungarica*, Op. 32c	Dohnányi	
BVE 40359	9, 10, 11		Danza espagñola from *La vida breve*	Falla	Kreisler
			Sergei Rachmaninoff (piano)		
CVE 41759	6, 7, 8	Victor 8163	Sonata No. 8 in G, Op. 30, No. 3: I Allegro assai	Beethoven	
CVE 41760	4, 5	Victor 8163	Sonata No. 8 in G, Op. 30, No. 3: II Tempo di Menuetto, ma molto moderato e grazioso (part 1)	Beethoven	
CVE 41761	3, 4, 5	Victor 8164	Sonata No. 8 in G, Op. 30, No. 3: II Tempo di Menuetto, ma molto moderato e grazioso (part 2)	Beethoven	
CVE 41762	7, 8	Victor 8164	Sonata No. 8 in G, Op. 30, No. 3: III Allegro vivace	Beethoven	

session / *matrix*	*date* / *take(s)*	*original issue on 78 rpm records*	*accompanying artist(s)* / *title of work*	*venue (where known)* / *composer*	*arranger*
23	30 November 1928		Carl Lamson (piano)	Camden (Victor Studio 1)	
CVE 14653	3, 4, 5, 6		Larghetto from Sonatina in G, Op. 100 "Indian Lament"	Dvořák	Kreisler
BVE 49146	1, 2, 3[1]		Habañera from *Rapsodie espagnole*	Ravel	Kreisler
BVE 49147	1[1], 2, 3, 4		Nocturnal Tangier (from *Triakontameron*)	Godowsky	Kreisler
BVE 49148	1, 2, 3, 4		Songs My Mother Taught Me, Op. 55, No. 4	Dvořák	Kreisler
24	6 December 1928		Carl Lamson (piano)	Camden (Victor Studio 1)	
BVE 15738	2, 3, 4	Victor 1414	Slavonic Dance No. 1 in G minor	Dvořák	Kreisler
CVE 15737	2, 3	Victor 7225	Slavonic Dance No. 3 in G	Dvořák	Kreisler
BVE 16985	3, 4, 5	Victor 1386	Rondino on a Theme of Beethoven	Kreisler	
BVE 14343	12, 13, 14		"Du alter Stefansturm" from *Der liebe Augustin* "The Old Refrain"	Brandl	Kreisler
BVE 27728	4, 5, 6, 7		"Im Chambre séparée" from *Der Opernball* "Midnight Bells"	Heuberger	Kreisler
BVE 22869	5, 6, 7		Chanson indoue [Song of India] from *Sadko*	Rimsky-Korsakov	Kreisler
BVE 49168	1, 2		Pièce en forme d'habanera	Ravel	Catherine
25	20 December 1928		Carl Lamson (piano)	New York (Victor Studios)	
BVE 27728	8, 9		"Im Chambre séparée" from *Der Opernball* "Midnight Bells"	Heuberger	Kreisler
			Sergei Rachmaninoff (piano)		
CVE 49280	1, 2, 3		Sonata in A, Op. 162 "Duo": I Allegro moderato (part 1)	Schubert	
CVE 49281	1, 2, 3		Sonata in A, Op. 162 "Duo": I Allegro moderato (part 2)	Schubert	
CVE 49282	1, 2	Victor 8217	Sonata in A, Op. 162 "Duo": II Scherzo: Presto	Schubert	

CVE 49283	1, 2, 3		Sonata in A, Op. 162 "Duo": III Andantino	Schubert	
CVE 49284	1, 2, 3	Victor 8218	Sonata in A, Op. 162 "Duo": IV Allegro vivace (part 1)	Schubert	
CVE 49285	1, 2, 3		Sonata in A, Op. 162 "Duo": IV Allegro vivace (part 2)	Schubert	
26	21 December 1928		Carl Lamson (piano)	New York (Victor Studios)	
CVE 14653	7, 8, 9	Victor 7225	Larghetto from Sonatina in G, Op. 100 "Indian Lament"	Dvořák	Kreisler
BVE 49148	5, 6, 7	Victor 1414	Songs My Mother Taught Me, Op. 55, No. 4	Dvořák	Kreisler
BVE 27728	10		"Im Chambre séparée" from *Der Opernball* "Midnight Bells"	Heuberger	Kreisler
			Sergei Rachmaninoff (piano)		
CVE 49280	4, 5	Victor 8216	Sonata in A, Op. 162 "Duo": I Allegro moderato (part 1)	Schubert	
CVE 49281	4, 5	Victor 8216	Sonata in A, Op. 162 "Duo": I Allegro moderato (part 2)	Schubert	
CVE 49282	3, 4		Sonata in A, Op. 162 "Duo": II Scherzo: Presto	Schubert	
CVE 49283	4	Victor 8217	Sonata in A, Op. 162 "Duo": III Andantino	Schubert	
CVE 49284	4		Sonata in A, Op. 162 "Duo": IV Allegro vivace (part 1)	Schubert	
CVE 49285	4	Victor 8218	Sonata in A, Op. 162 "Duo": IV Allegro vivace (part 2)	Schubert	
27	16 December 1929		Carl Lamson (piano)	New York (RCA 44th Street Lab)	
BVE 57918	1, 2, 3, 4		Jota (No. 4 from Seven Popular Spanish Songs)	Falla	Kochánski
BVE 49168	3[1], 4, 5		Pièce en forme d'habanera	Ravel	Catherine
BVE 57920	1, 2		Lento (Melodie) from *Orphée ed Euridice*	Gluck	Kreisler
BVE 19323	2		Ballet Music from *Rosamunde von Cypern*	Schubert	Kreisler

session / *matrix*	*date* / *take(s)*	*original issue on 78 rpm records*	*accompanying artist(s)* / *title of work*	*venue (where known)* / *composer*	*arranger*
28	17 December 1929		Carl Lamson (piano)	New York (RCA 44th Street Lab)	
CVE 57924	1[1], 2, 3, 4		Londonderry Air	traditional	Kreisler
BVE 27728	11, 12, 13		"Im Chambre séparée" from *Der Opernball* "Midnight Bells"	Heuberger	Kreisler
BVE 57925	1, 2, 3, 4, 5		Polichinelle Serenade	Kreisler	
29	18 December 1929		Carl Lamson (piano)	New York (RCA 44th Street Lab)	
BVE 57930	1, 2[1], 3		Chanson Louis XIII and Pavane "in the style of Couperin"	Kreisler	
BVE 57931	1[1], 2, 3		Schön Rosmarin	Kreisler	
BVE 57932	1, 2[1]		"Du alter Stefansturm" from *Der liebe Augustin* "The Old Refrain"	Brandl	Kreisler
30	23 December 1929		Carl Lamson (piano)	New York (RCA 44th Street Lab)	
BVE 57947	1, 2, 3, 4		Sérénade espagnole	Glazunov	Kreisler
BVE 57918	5[1], 6		Jota (No. 4 from Seven Popular Spanish Songs)	Falla	Kreisler
BVE 57920	3[1], 4		Lento (Melodie) from *Orphée ed Euridice*	Gluck	Kreisler
BVE 57925	6, 7, 8[1]		Polichinelle Serenade	Kreisler	
BVE 57932	3, 4		"Du alter Stefansturm" from *Der liebe Augustin* "The Old Refrain"	Brandl	Kreisler

31	24 December 1929	Carl Lamson (piano)	New York (RCA 44th Street Lab)	
BVE 57950	1, 2[1], 3	La précieuse "in the style of Couperin"	Kreisler	
BVE 19323	3, 4[1], 5	Ballet Music from *Rosamunde von Cypern*	Schubert	Kreisler
BVE 27728	14, 15	"Im Chambre séparée" from *Der Opernball* "Midnight Bells"	Heuberger	Kreisler
BVE 57951	1	Larghetto from Violin Sonata in F, Op. 10, No. 1	Weber	Kreisler

Part 5: The Electrola recordings (Berlin, 1926–30 and 1935–36)

The recordings made by Kreisler for Electrola, the German branch of the Gramophone Company in Berlin (where the violinist lived at the time), feature the three great concertos by Beethoven, Mendelssohn, and Brahms. All the short pieces with piano as well as the Grieg Sonata No. 3 with Rachmaninoff were designated as "recorded for Victor." However, two of the short pieces—the Adagio movement from Bach's Sonata No. 1 and the Schumann Romance in A—were intended as "filler" sides to the concerto recordings. (The Schumann work, used as the filler side for the Brahms concerto, appears as side 5, following the first movement.)

Although the complete Beethoven sonata cycle was initiated by Electrola, it was aborted due to adverse pressure from the Nazi government. It is interesting to note, however, that Kreisler recorded his two most popular works (*Caprice Viennois* and *Tambourin Chinois*) in Berlin as late as September 1936.

The letters "BW" and "BL" preceding the matrix number designate a 10-inch record, with a DA prefix in the catalog number. "CW" and "CL" preceding the matrix number designate a 12-inch record, with a DB prefix in the catalog number. The letters following the B and C represent the codes for a particular recording engineer (BW and CW = A. D. Lawrence, and BL and CL = D. E. Larter). After 1934, the engineer code was dropped, and the "0RA" and "2RA" prefixes were adopted for HMV recordings made in Germany by Electrola. The 0RA matrix number prefix designates a 10-inch record, with a DA prefix in the catalog number, and 2RA designates a 12-inch record, with a DB prefix in the catalog number.

The letter "R" following the matrix prefix indicates a relay transmission (i.e., location recording). At this time two different cutting machines were often used in recording, and the letter A following a take number represents the second cutting machine.

session / *matrix*	*date* / *take(s)*	*original issue on 78 rpm records*	*accompanying artist(s)* / *title of work*	*venue (where known)* / *composer*	*arranger*
1	8 December 1926		Michael Raucheisen (piano)	Berlin (Studio)	
BW 611	1, 1A, 2, 2A[12], 3		Danza española from *La vida breve*	Falla	Kreisler
CW 612	1, 1A, 2, 2A, 3	Victor 6706	Hungarian Dance No. 17	Brahms	Kreisler
BW 613	1, 1A[12], 2, 3		The Girl with the Flaxen Hair (No. 8 from Préludes – Book I)	Debussy	Hartmann
2	9 December 1926		Berlin Staatskapelle and Leo Blech (conductor)	Berlin (Singakademie)	
CWR 614	1, 1A, 2, **2A**, 3	HMV DB 997	Concerto in E minor, Op. 64: I Allegro molto appassionato (part 1)	Mendelssohn	
CWR 615	1, **1A**, 2, 2A, 3	HMV DB 997	Concerto in E minor, Op. 64: I Allegro molto appassionato (part 2)	Mendelssohn	
CWR 616	1, **1A**, 2, 2A	HMV DB 998	Concerto in E minor, Op. 64: I Allegro molto appassionato (part 3)	Mendelssohn	
CWR 617	1, **1A**	HMV DB 998	Concerto in E minor, Op. 64: II Andante (part 1)	Mendelssohn	
CWR 618	1, 1A, 2, **2A**	HMV DB 999	Concerto in E minor, Op. 64: II Andante (part 2)	Mendelssohn	
3	10 December 1926		Berlin Staatskapelle and Leo Blech (conductor)	Berlin (Singakademie)	
CWR 619	1, 1A, 2, **2A**, 3, 3A	HMV DB 999	Concerto in E minor, Op. 64: III Allegro molto vivace (part 1)	Mendelssohn	
CWR 620	1, 1A, 2, 2A, 3, 3A	HMV DB 1000	Concerto in E minor, Op. 64: III Allegro molto vivace (part 2)	Mendelssohn	
4	11 December 1926		Arpad Sandor (piano)	Berlin (Studio)	
CW 621	1, 1A		Lotus Land, Op. 47, No. 1	Scott	Kreisler

5	14 December 1926		Arpad Sandor (piano)	Berlin (Studio)	
CW 621	2, 2A, 3	Victor 6706	Lotus Land, Op. 47, No. 1	Scott	Kreisler
CW 622	1, 1A, 2, **2A**, 3	HMV DB 1000	Song Without Words, Op. 62, No. 1 "May Breezes"	Mendelssohn	Kreisler
			Berlin Staatskapelle and Leo Blech (conductor)	Berlin (Singakademie)	
CWR 620	4, 4A		Concerto in E minor, Op. 64: III Allegro molto vivace (part 2)	Mendelssohn	
CWR 631	1, **1A**	HMV DB 990	Concerto in D, Op. 61: I Allegro ma non troppo (part 1)	Beethoven	
CWR 632	1, 1A, **2**	HMV DB 990	Concerto in D, Op. 61: I Allegro ma non troppo (part 2)	Beethoven	
CWR 633	1, **1A**, 2	HMV DB 991	Concerto in D, Op. 61: I Allegro ma non troppo (part 3)	Beethoven	
CWR 634	1, 1A, 2, 2A, 3		Concerto in D, Op. 61: I Allegro ma non troppo (part 4)	Beethoven	
CWR 635	1, 1A, **2**	HMV DB 992	Concerto in D, Op. 61: I Allegro ma non troppo (part 5)	Beethoven	
CWR 636	1, 2, 2A		Concerto in D, Op. 61: I Allegro ma non troppo (part 6)	Beethoven	
			Arpad Sandor (piano)	Berlin (Studio)	
BW 643	1[12], 1A, 2		En bateau (No. 1 from Petite Suite)	Debussy	Choisnel
BW 644	1, 1A, 2A, 3		Canción (No. 6 from Seven Popular Spanish Songs)	Falla	Kochánski
6	15 December 1926		Berlin Staatskapelle and Leo Blech (conductor)	Berlin (Singakademie)	
CWR 637	1, 2, **2A**, 3	HMV DB 993	Concerto in D, Op. 61: II Larghetto (part 1)	Beethoven	
CWR 638	1, 1A, **2**	HMV DB 993	Concerto in D, Op. 61: II Larghetto (part 2)	Beethoven	
CWR 639	1, 2, 2A, **3A**, 4	HMV DB 994	Concerto in D, Op. 61: III Rondo (part 1)	Beethoven	
CWR 640	1, 1A, **2**	HMV DB 994	Concerto in D, Op. 61: III Rondo (part 2)	Beethoven	
CWR 641	1, 1A		Concerto in D, Op. 61: III Rondo (part 3)	Beethoven	

session / matrix	date / take(s)	original issue on 78 rpm records	accompanying artist(s) / title of work	venue (where known) / composer	arranger
			Arpad Sandor (piano)		
BWR 645	1, 1A		En bateau (No. 1 from Petite Suite)	Debussy	Choisnel
BWR 646	1, 2, 2A		Canción (No. 6 from Seven Popular Spanish Songs)	Falla	Kochánski
BWR 647	1, 1A, 2, 2A[12]		Danza española from *La vida breve*	Falla	Kreisler
CWR 648	1, 1A, 2		Hungarian Dance No. 17	Brahms	Kreisler
CWR 649	1, 1A		Lotus Land, Op. 47, No. 1	Scott	Kreisler
CWR 650	1		Song Without Words, Op. 62, No. 1 "May Breezes"	Mendelssohn	Kreisler
7	16 December 1926		unaccompanied	Berlin (Singakademie)	
CWR 642	1, **1A**, 2A	HMV DB 995	Adagio from Sonata No. 1 in G minor	Bach	
			Berlin Staatskapelle and Leo Blech (conductor)		
CWR 641	2, **2A**	HMV DB 995	Concerto in D, Op. 61: III Rondo (part 3)	Beethoven	
CWR 631	2, 3		Concerto in D, Op. 61: I Allegro ma non troppo (part 1)	Beethoven	
CWR 632	3, 2A		Concerto in D, Op. 61: I Allegro ma non troppo (part 2)	Beethoven	
CWR 634	**4A**	HMV DB 991	Concerto in D, Op. 61: I Allegro ma non troppo (part 4)	Beethoven	
CWR 635	3, 3A		Concerto in D, Op. 61: I Allegro ma non troppo (part 5)	Beethoven	
CWR 636	3, **3A**	HMV DB 992	Concerto in D, Op. 61: I Allegro ma non troppo (part 6)	Beethoven	
			Arpad Sandor (piano)		
BWR 645	2, 2A		En bateau (No. 1 from Petite Suite)	Debussy	Choisnel

BWR 646	3, 3A		Canción (No. 6 from Seven Popular Spanish Songs)	Falla	Kochánski
BWR 647	3, 4A		Danza espagñola from *La vida breve*	Falla	Kreisler
CWR 649	2A		Lotus Land, Op. 47, No. 1	Scott	Kreisler
CWR 650	2, 2A		Song Without Words, Op. 62, No. 1 "May Breezes"	Mendelssohn	Kreisler
BWR 651	1, 2A		Song Without Words, Op. 62, No. 1 "May Breezes"	Mendelssohn	Kreisler
8	13 October 1927		Hugo Kreisler (cello) and Michael Raucheisen (piano)	Berlin (Studio)	
CW 1237	1, 2, 3, 4	HMV DB 1166	O Sanctissima	Corelli	Kreisler
CW 1238	1, 2, 3	HMV DB 1166	Intermezzo from *L'arlésienne*	Bizet	Kreisler
BW 1239	1, 2, 3, 4	HMV DA 961	Syncopation	Kreisler	
BW 1240	1, 2, 3	HMV DA 961	Marche miniature viennoise	Kreisler	
9	21 November 1927		Berlin Staatskapelle and Leo Blech (conductor)	Berlin (Singakademie)	
CWR 1355	1, 2, 3	HMV DB 1120	Concerto in D, Op. 77: I Allegro non troppo (part 1)	Brahms	
CWR 1356	1, 2, 3	HMV DB 1120	Concerto in D, Op. 77: I Allegro non troppo (part 2)	Brahms	
CWR 1357	1, 2	HMV DB 1121	Concerto in D, Op. 77: I Allegro non troppo (part 3)	Brahms	
CWR 1358	1, 2, 3, 4	HMV DB 1123	Concerto in D, Op. 77: II Adagio (part 1)	Brahms	
10	23 November 1927		Berlin Staatskapelle and Leo Blech (conductor)	Berlin (Singakademie)	
CWR 1366	1, 2	HMV DB 1121	Concerto in D, Op. 77: I Allegro non troppo (part 4)	Brahms	
CWR 1367	1, 2, 3		Concerto in D, Op. 77: I Allegro non troppo (part 5)	Brahms	

session / *matrix*	*date* / *take(s)*	*original issue on 78 rpm records*	*accompanying artist(s)* / *title of work*	*venue (where known)* / *composer*	*arranger*
CWR 1368	1, 2	HMV DB 1123	Concerto in D, Op. 77: II Adagio (part 2)	Brahms	
CWR 1369	1		Concerto in D, Op. 77: III Allegro giocoso (part 1)	Brahms	
11	25 November 1927		Berlin Staatskapelle and Leo Blech (conductor)	Berlin (Singakademie)	
CWR 1369	2, 3, 4	HMV DB 1124	Concerto in D, Op. 77: III Allegro giocoso (part 1)	Brahms	
CWR 1376	1, 2, 3, 4, 5	HMV DB 1124	Concerto in D, Op. 77: III Allegro giocoso (part 2)	Brahms	
CWR 1355	4		Concerto in D, Op. 77: I Allegro non troppo (part 1)	Brahms	
CWR 1356	4		Concerto in D, Op. 77: I Allegro non troppo (part 2)	Brahms	
CWR 1357	3		Concerto in D, Op. 77: I Allegro non troppo (part 3)	Brahms	
CWR 1366	3		Concerto in D, Op. 77: I Allegro non troppo (part 4)	Brahms	
CWR 1367	4	HMV DB 1122	Concerto in D, Op. 77: I Allegro non troppo (part 5)	Brahms	
CWR 1358	5		Concerto in D, Op. 77: II Adagio (part 1)	Brahms	
CWR 1368	3		Concerto in D, Op. 77: II Adagio (part 2)	Brahms	
12	13 December 1927		Arpad Sandor (piano)	Berlin (Studio)	
CW 1434	1, 2, 3, 4	HMV DB 1122	Romance in A, Op. 94, No. 2	Schumann	Kreisler

13	14 September 1928		Sergei Rachmaninoff (piano)	Berlin (Studio)
CL 4511	1, 2, 3		Sonata No. 3 in C minor: I Allegro molto ed appassionato (part 1)	Grieg
CL 4512	1, 2, 3		Sonata No. 3 in C minor: I Allegro molto ed appassionato (part 2)	Grieg
CL 4513	1, 2		Sonata No. 3 in C minor: II Allegretto espressivo alla Romanza (part 1)	Grieg
CL 4514	1, 2, 3		Sonata No. 3 in C minor: II Allegretto espressivo alla Romanza (part 2)	Grieg
CL 4515	1, 2, 3, 4		Sonata No. 3 in C minor: III Allegro animato (part 1)	Grieg
CL 4516	1, 2, 3		Sonata No. 3 in C minor: III Allegro animato (part 2)	Grieg
14	15 September 1928		Sergei Rachmaninoff (piano)	Berlin (Studio)
CL 4511	4, 5	HMV DB 1259	Sonata No. 3 in C minor: I Allegro molto ed appassionato (part 1)	Grieg
CL 4512	4, 5	HMV DB 1259	Sonata No. 3 in C minor: I Allegro molto ed appassionato (part 2)	Grieg
CL 4513	3, 4, 5	HMV DB 1260	Sonata No. 3 in C minor: II Allegretto espressivo alla Romanza (part 1)	Grieg
CL 4514	4, 5	HMV DB 1260	Sonata No. 3 in C minor: II Allegretto espressivo alla Romanza (part 2)	Grieg
CL 4515	5, 6	HMV DB 1261	Sonata No. 3 in C minor: III Allegro animato (part 1)	Grieg
CL 4516	4, 5	HMV DB 1261	Sonata No. 3 in C minor: III Allegro animato (part 2)	Grieg

session matrix	date take(s)	original issue on 78 rpm records	accompanying artist(s) title of work	venue (where known) composer	arranger
15	13 February 1930		Michael Raucheisen (piano)	Berlin (Beethovensaal)	
BLR 6059	1, 2, 3		Lento (Melodie) from *Orphée ed Euridice*	Gluck	Kreisler
BLR 6060	1, 2, 3		Pièce en forme d'habanera	Ravel	Catherine
BLR 6061	1, 2, 3	HMV DA 1138	"Du alter Stefansturm" from *Der liebe Augustin* "The Old Refrain"	Brandl	Kreisler
16	14 February 1930		Michael Raucheisen (piano)	Berlin (Beethovensaal)	
BLR 6062	1, 2, 3	HMV DA 1157	Sérénade espagnole	Glazunov	Kreisler
CLR 6063	1, 2, 3	HMV DB 2117[13]	Londonderry Air	traditional	Kreisler
BLR 6064	1, 2, 3	HMV DA 1215[14]	Polichinelle Serenade	Kreisler	
BLR 6065	1, 2, 3, 4	HMV DA 1157	Jota (No. 4 from Seven Popular Spanish Songs)	Falla	Kochánski
BLR 6066	1, 2, 3	HMV DA 1138	"Im Chambre séparée" from *Der Opernball* "Midnight Bells"	Heuberger	Kreisler
BLR 6067	1, 2, 3	HMV DA 1137	Ballet Music from *Rosamunde von Cypern*	Schubert	Kreisler
17	15 February 1930		Michael Raucheisen (piano)	Berlin (Beethovensaal)	
BLR 6068	1, 2, 3	HMV DA 1139	La précieuse "in the style of Couperin"	Kreisler	
BLR 6069	1, 2, 3	HMV DA 1139	Chanson Louis XIII and Pavane "in the style of Couperin"	Kreisler	
BLR 6070	1, 2, 3	HMV DA 1137	Larghetto from Violin Sonata in F, Op. 10, No. 1	Weber	Kreisler
BLR 6071	1, 2, 3[12]		Schön Rosmarin	Kreisler	
18	22 February 1935		Franz Rupp (piano)	Berlin (Electrola Studio B)	
2RA 404	1		Sonata No. 1 in D, Op. 12, No. 1 (part 1)	Beethoven	
2RA 405	1, 2		Sonata No. 1 in D, Op. 12, No. 1 (part 2)	Beethoven	
2RA 406	1		Sonata No. 1 in D, Op. 12, No. 1 (part 3)	Beethoven	

2RA 407	1, 2	Sonata No. 1 in D, Op. 12, No. 1 (part 4)	Beethoven
2RA 408	1, 2	Sonata No. 1 in D, Op. 12, No. 1 (part 5)	Beethoven
2RA 409	1, 2	Sonata No. 2 in A, Op. 12, No. 2 (part 1)	Beethoven
2RA 410	1	Sonata No. 2 in A, Op. 12, No. 2 (part 2)	Beethoven
2RA 411	1	Sonata No. 2 in A, Op. 12, No. 2 (part 3)	Beethoven
2RA 412	1, 2	Sonata No. 2 in A, Op. 12, No. 2 (part 4)	Beethoven
2RA 413	1, 2	Sonata No. 2 in A, Op. 12, No. 2 (part 5)	Beethoven
19	23 February 1935	Franz Rupp (piano)	Berlin (Electrola Studio B)
2RA 414	1, 2, 3	Sonata No. 5 in F, Op. 24 (part 1)	Beethoven
2RA 415	1, 2	Sonata No. 5 in F, Op. 24 (part 2)	Beethoven
2RA 416	1, 2, 3	Sonata No. 5 in F, Op. 24 (part 3)	Beethoven
2RA 417	1, 2, 3	Sonata No. 5 in F, Op. 24 (part 4)	Beethoven
2RA 418	1, 2, 3	Sonata No. 5 in F, Op. 24 (part 5)	Beethoven
20	25 February 1935	Franz Rupp (piano)	Berlin (Electrola Studio B)
2RA 419	1, 2, 3	Sonata No. 4 in A minor, Op. 23 (part 1)	Beethoven
2RA 420	1, 2	Sonata No. 4 in A minor, Op. 23 (part 2)	Beethoven
2RA 421	1, 2	Sonata No. 4 in A minor, Op. 23 (part 3)	Beethoven
2RA 422	1, 2, 3	Sonata No. 4 in A minor, Op. 23 (part 4)	Beethoven
2RA 423	1, 2	Sonata No. 4 in A minor, Op. 23 (part 5)	Beethoven
21	26 February 1935	Franz Rupp (piano)	Berlin (Electrola Studio B)
2RA 424	1, 2	Sonata No. 3 in E-flat, Op. 12, No. 3 (part 1)	Beethoven
2RA 425	1, 2	Sonata No. 3 in E-flat, Op. 12, No. 3 (part 2)	Beethoven
2RA 426	1, 2	Sonata No. 3 in E-flat, Op. 12, No. 3 (part 3)	Beethoven
2RA 427	1, 2, 3	Sonata No. 3 in E-flat, Op. 12, No. 3 (part 4)	Beethoven

session / *matrix*	*date* / *take(s)*	*original issue on* / *78 rpm records*	*accompanying artist(s)* / *title of work*	*venue (where known)* / *composer*	*arranger*
22	28 September 1936		Franz Rupp (piano)	Berlin (Saal 2)	
2RA 1484	1, 2, 3, 4	HMV DB 3050	Caprice Viennois, Op. 2	Kreisler	
2RA 1485	1, 2, 3	HMV DB 3050	Tambourin Chinois, Op. 3	Kreisler	

Part 6: The electric HMV recordings (London, 1935–39)

In 1931, the Gramophone Company merged with the Columbia Recording Company to become Electrical and Musical Industries (E.M.I.). The individual labels continued to preserve their separate identities, however, and the electrical HMV recordings of Kreisler include remakes of the three major concertos by Beethoven, Brahms, and Mendelssohn, as well as Mozart's Concerto No. 4 in D. (The second recording of Mendelssohn's concerto is distributed onto six, instead of seven, sides.)

Perhaps the most important corpus of works in this section is the ten violin and piano sonatas of Beethoven, recorded with pianist Franz Rupp. This "Beethoven Society" edition of the complete sonatas was offered on subscription. Mozart and Brahms sonatas as well as other Mozart concertos were intended but, sadly, never attempted.

The "0EA" matrix number prefix designates a 10-inch record made in England, with a DA prefix in the catalog number, and "2EA" designates a 12-inch record, with a DB prefix in the catalog number.

The concertos and Beethoven sonatas were brought out in two formats: DB 2000 and 3000 series in manual coupling (i.e., sides 1 and 2 on the same disc), and DB 7000 and 8000 series in automatic coupling (i.e., successive sides on separate records, allowing for stacking of discs for "continuous" playback). This section also contains one spoken record: an advertisement for Marconiphone (which the Gramophone Company bought in 1929).

session / *matrix*	*date* / *take(s)*	*original issue on 78 rpm records*	*accompanying artist(s)* / *title of work*	*venue (where known)* / *composer*	*arranger*
1	1 April 1935		Petrie (2d violin), Primrose (viola) and Kennedy (cello)	London (Abbey Road Studio No. 3)	
2EA 1370	1, 2, 3	HMV DB 2483	String Quartet in A minor: I Fantasia: Moderato (part 1)	Kreisler	
2EA 1371	1, 2, 3	HMV DB 2483	String Quartet in A minor: I Fantasia: Moderato (part 2)	Kreisler	
2EA 1372	1, 2, 3	HMV DB 2484	String Quartet in A minor: II Scherzo: Allegro vivo con spirito (part 1)	Kreisler	
2EA 1373	1, 2, 3	HMV DB 2484	String Quartet in A minor: II Scherzo: Allegro vivo con spirito (part 2)	Kreisler	
2EA 1374	1, 2, 3, 4	HMV DB 2485	String Quartet in A minor: III Einleitung und Romanze: Allegretto – Andante con moto	Kreisler	
2EA 1375	1, 2, 3, 4	HMV DB 2485	String Quartet in A minor: IV Finale: Allegro molto moderato (part 1)	Kreisler	
2EA 1376	1, 2, 3, 4	HMV DB 2486	String Quartet in A minor: IV Finale: Allegro molto moderato (part 2)	Kreisler	
2	2 April 1935		Franz Rupp (piano)	London (Abbey Road Studio No. 3)	
2EA 1377	1, 2, 3		Sonata No. 1 in D, Op. 12, No. 1: I Allegro con brio (part 1)	Beethoven	
2EA 1378	1		Sonata No. 1 in D, Op. 12, No. 1: I Allegro con brio (part 2)	Beethoven	
2EA 1379	1, 2	HMV DB 2555[15]	Sonata No. 1 in D, Op. 12, No. 1: II Terna con variazioni: Andante con moto (part 1)	Beethoven	

session / *matrix*	*date* / *take(s)*	*original issue on 78 rpm records*	*accompanying artist(s)* / *title of work*	*venue (where known)* / *composer*	*arranger*
2EA 1380	1	HMV DB 2555[15]	Sonata No. 1 in D, Op. 12, No. 1: II Terna con variazioni: Andante con moto (part 2)	Beethoven	
2EA 1381	1, 2	HMV DB 2556[15]	Sonata No. 1 in D, Op. 12, No. 1: III Rondo: Allegro	Beethoven	
2EA 1377	4	HMV DB 2554[15]	Sonata No. 1 in D, Op. 12, No. 1: I Allegro con brio (part 1)	Beethoven	
2EA 1378	2	HMV DB 2554[15]	Sonata No. 1 in D, Op. 12, No. 1: I Allegro con brio (part 2)	Beethoven	
3	3 April 1935		Franz Rupp (piano)	London (Abbey Road Studio No. 3)	
2EA 1382	1, 2	HMV DB 2556[16]	Sonata No. 2 in A, Op. 12, No. 2: I Allegro vivace (part 1)	Beethoven	
2EA 1383	1, 2	HMV DB 2557[16]	Sonata No. 2 in A, Op. 12, No. 2: I Allegro vivace (part 2)	Beethoven	
2EA 1384	1, 2, 3	HMV DB 2557[16]	Sonata No. 2 in A, Op. 12, No. 2: II Andante, più tosto Allegretto (part 1)	Beethoven	
2EA 1385	1, 2, 3	HMV DB 2558[16]	Sonata No. 2 in A, Op. 12, No. 2: II Andante, più tosto Allegretto (part 2)	Beethoven	
2EA 1386	1, 2, 3	HMV DB 2558[16]	Sonata No. 2 in A, Op. 12, No. 2: III Allegro piacevole	Beethoven	
2EA 1387	1		Sonata No. 3 in E-flat, Op. 12, No. 3: I Allegro con spirito (part 1)	Beethoven	

2EA 1388	1, 2		Sonata No. 3 in E-flat, Op. 12, No. 3: I Allegro con spirito (part 2)/ II Adagio con molt'espressione (part 1)	Beethoven
2EA 1389	1, 2	HMV DB 2560[17]	Sonata No. 3 in E-flat, Op. 12, No. 3: II Adagio con molt'espressione (part 2)	Beethoven
4	4 April 1935		Franz Rupp (piano)	London (Abbey Road Studio No. 3)
2EA 1387	2, 3	HMV DB 2559[17]	Sonata No. 3 in E-flat, Op. 12, No. 3: I Allegro con spirito (part 1)	Beethoven
2EA 1388	3, 4	HMV DB 2559[17]	Sonata No. 3 in E-flat, Op. 12, No. 3: I Allegro con spirito (part 2)/ II Adagio con molt'espressione (part 1)	Beethoven
2EA 1389	3, 4		Sonata No. 3 in E-flat, Op. 12, No. 3: II Adagio con molt'espressione (part 2)	Beethoven
2EA 1390	1, 2, 3, 4	HMV DB 2560[17]	Sonata No. 3 in E-flat, Op. 12, No. 3: Rondo: Allegro molto	Beethoven
2EA 1391	1, 2		Sonata No. 5 in F, Op. 24: I Allegro (part 1)	Beethoven
2EA 1392	1, 2		Sonata No. 5 in F, Op. 24: I Allegro (part 2)/ II Adagio molto espressivo (part 1)	Beethoven
2EA 1393	1, 2		Sonata No. 5 in F, Op. 24: II Adagio molto espressivo (part 2)	Beethoven
2EA 1394	1, 2, 3		Sonata No. 5 in F, Op. 24: III Scherzo: Allegro molto/ IV Rondo: Allegro ma non troppo (part 1)	Beethoven
5	5 April 1935		Franz Rupp (piano)	London (Abbey Road Studio No. 3)
2EA 1394	4, 5, 6		Sonata No. 5 in F, Op. 24: III Scherzo: Allegro molto/ IV Rondo: Allegro ma non troppo (part 1)	Beethoven

session / *matrix*	*date* / *take(s)*	*original issue on 78 rpm records*	*accompanying artist(s)* / *title of work*	*venue (where known)* / *composer*	*arranger*
2EA 1395	1, 2, 3		Sonata No. 5 in F, Op. 24: IV Rondo: Allegro ma non troppo (part 2)	Beethoven	
2EA 1396	1, 2, 3, 4, 5	HMV DB 2781[18]	Sonata No. 4 in A minor, Op. 23: I Presto	Beethoven	
2EA 1397	1, 2	HMV DB 2781[18]	Sonata No. 4 in A minor, Op. 23: II Andante scherzoso, più Allegretto (part 1)	Beethoven	
2EA 1398	1, 2		Sonata No. 4 in A minor, Op. 23: II Andante scherzoso, più Allegretto (part 2)	Beethoven	
2EA 1399	1, 2		Sonata No. 4 in A minor, Op. 23: III Allegro molto (part 1)	Beethoven	
2EA 1400	1, 2		Sonata No. 4 in A minor, Op. 23: III Allegro molto (part 2)	Beethoven	
6	6 April 1935		Franz Rupp (piano)	London (Abbey Road Studio No. 3)	
2EA 1398	3, 4	HMV DB 2782[18]	Sonata No. 4 in A minor, Op. 23: II Andante scherzoso, più Allegretto (part 2)	Beethoven	
2EA 1399	3, 4, 5	HMV DB 2782[18]	Sonata No. 4 in A minor, Op. 23: III Allegro molto (part 1)	Beethoven	
2EA 1400	3	HMV DB 2783[18]	Sonata No. 4 in A minor, Op. 23: III Allegro molto (part 2)	Beethoven	

7	7 April 1935		Petrie (2d violin), Primrose (viola) and Kennedy (cello)	London (Abbey Road Studio No. 3)
2EA 2001	1, 2, 3, **4**	HMV DB 2486	Scherzo "in the style of Dittersdorf"	Kreisler
8	8 April 1935		LPO and Sir Landon Ronald (conductor)	London (Abbey Road Studio No. 1)
2EA 1465	1, 2A, 3, 3A, 4, **4A**	HMV DB 2460[19]	Concerto in E minor, Op. 64: I Allegro molto appassionato (part 1)	Mendelssohn
2EA 1466	1, 1A, 2, **2A**, 3, 3A	HMV DB 2460[19]	Concerto in E minor, Op. 64: I Allegro molto appassionato (part 2)	Mendelssohn
2EA 1467	**1**, 1A, 2, 2A	HMV DB 2461[19]	Concerto in E minor, Op. 64: I Allegro molto appassionato (part 3)	Mendelssohn
2EA 1468	1, 2, **2A**	HMV DB 2461[19]	Concerto in E minor, Op. 64: II Andante (part 1)	Mendelssohn
2EA 1469	1, **1A**, 2, 2A	HMV DB 2462[19]	Concerto in E minor, Op. 64: II Andante (part 2)/ III Allegro molto vivace (part 1)	Mendelssohn
2EA 1470	1A, 2A, 3, 3A, 4, **4A**	HMV DB 2462[19]	Concerto in E minor, Op. 64: III Allegro molto vivace (part 2)	Mendelssohn
9	4 February 1936		Franz Rupp (piano)	London (Abbey Road Studio No. 3)
2EA 3081	1, 2, **3**	HMV DB 3296[20]	Sonata No. 6 in A, Op. 30, No. 1: I Allegro (part 1)	Beethoven
2EA 3082	1, **2**, 3	HMV DB 3296[20]	Sonata No. 6 in A, Op. 30, No. 1: I Allegro (part 2)	Beethoven
2EA 3083	**1**, 2	HMV DB 3297[20]	Sonata No. 6 in A, Op. 30, No. 1: II Adagio molto espressivo (part 1)	Beethoven
2EA 3084	**1**, 2, 3	HMV DB 3297[20]	Sonata No. 6 in A, Op. 30, No. 1: II Adagio molto espressivo (part 2)	Beethoven

session / matrix	date / take(s)	original issue on 78 rpm records	accompanying artist(s) / title of work	venue (where known) / composer	arranger
2EA 3085	1, 2, 3	HMV DB 3298[20]	Sonata No. 6 in A, Op. 30, No. 1: III Allegretto con variazioni (part 1)	Beethoven	
2EA 3086	1, 2, 3	HMV DB 3298[20]	Sonata No. 6 in A, Op. 30, No. 1: III Allegretto con variazioni (part 2)	Beethoven	
10	5 February 1936		Franz Rupp (piano)	London (Abbey Road Studio No. 3)	
2EA 3087	1, 2, 3	HMV DB 2786[21]	Sonata No. 8 in G, Op. 30, No. 3: I Allegro assai	Beethoven	
2EA 3088	1, 2	HMV DB 2786[21]	Sonata No. 8 in G, Op. 30, No. 3: II Tempo di Minuetto, ma molto moderato e grazioso (part 1)	Beethoven	
2EA 3089	1, 2, 3	HMV DB 2787[21]	Sonata No. 8 in G, Op. 30, No. 3: II Tempo di Minuetto, ma molto moderato e grazioso (part 2)	Beethoven	
2EA 3090	1, 2		Sonata No. 8 in G, Op. 30, No. 3: III Allegro vivace	Beethoven	
11	6 February 1936		Franz Rupp (piano)	London (Abbey Road Studio No. 3)	
2EA 3090	3	HMV DB 2787[21]	Sonata No. 8 in G, Op. 30, No. 3: III Allegro vivace	Beethoven	
2EA 3091	1, 2	HMV DB 3068[22]	Sonata No. 7 in C minor, Op. 30, No. 2: I Allegro con brio (part 1)	Beethoven	
2EA 3092	1, 2	HMV DB 3068[22]	Sonata No. 7 in C minor, Op. 30, No. 2: I Allegro con brio (part 2)	Beethoven	
2EA 3093	1, 2, 3	HMV DB 3069[22]	Sonata No. 7 in C minor, Op. 30, No. 2: II Adagio cantabile (part 1)	Beethoven	

2EA 3094	1, 2, 3	HMV DB 3069[22]	Sonata No. 7 in C minor, Op. 30, No. 2: II Adagio cantabile (part 2)	Beethoven
2EA 3095	1, 2	HMV DB 3070[22]	Sonata No. 7 in C minor, Op. 30, No. 2: III Scherzo: Allegro/ IV Finale: Allegro (part 1)	Beethoven
2EA 3096	1, 2, 3	HMV DB 3070[22]	Sonata No. 7 in C minor, Op. 30, No. 2: IV Finale: Allegro (part 2)	Beethoven
12	7 February 1936		Franz Rupp (piano)	London (Abbey Road Studio No. 3)
2EA 1391	3, 4	HMV DB 2783[23]	Sonata No. 5 in F, Op. 24: I Allegro (part 1)	Beethoven
2EA 1392	3, 4	HMV DB 2784[23]	Sonata No. 5 in F, Op. 24: I Allegro (part 2)/ II Adagio molto espressivo (part 1)	Beethoven
2EA 1393	3, 4	HMV DB 2784[23]	Sonata No. 5 in F, Op. 24: II Adagio molto espressivo (part 2)	Beethoven
2EA 1394	7, 8	HMV DB 2785[23]	Sonata No. 5 in F, Op. 24: III Scherzo: Allegro molto/ IV Rondo: Allegro ma non troppo (part 1)	Beethoven
2EA 1395	4, 5	HMV DB 2785[23]	Sonata No. 5 in F, Op. 24: IV Rondo: Allegro ma non troppo (part 2)	Beethoven
13	16 June 1936		LPO and John Barbirolli (conductor)	London (Abbey Road Studio No. 1)
2EA 2974	1, 1A	HMV DB 2927[24]	Concerto in D, Op. 61: I Allegro ma non troppo (part 1)	Beethoven
2EA 2975	1, 1A	HMV DB 2927[24]	Concerto in D, Op. 61: I Allegro ma non troppo (part 2)	Beethoven
2EA 2976	2, 2A	HMV DB 2928[24]	Concerto in D, Op. 61: I Allegro ma non troppo (part 3)	Beethoven
2EA 2977	1, 2, 2A		Concerto in D, Op. 61: I Allegro ma non troppo (part 4)	Beethoven

session / matrix	date / take(s)	original issue on 78 rpm records	accompanying artist(s) / title of work	venue (where known) / composer	arranger
2EA 2978	1, 1A	HMV DB 2929[24]	Concerto in D, Op. 61: I Allegro ma non troppo (part 5)	Beethoven	
2EA 2979	1, 2, 2A		Concerto in D, Op. 61: I Allegro ma non troppo (part 6)	Beethoven	
14	17 June 1936		LPO and John Barbirolli (conductor)	London (Abbey Road Studio No. 1)	
2EA 2980	1, 2, 2A	HMV DB 2930[24]	Concerto in D, Op. 61: II Larghetto (part 1)	Beethoven	
2EA 2981	1, 2, 2A		Concerto in D, Op. 61: II Larghetto (part 2)	Beethoven	
2EA 2982	1, 2, 2A	HMV DB 2931[24]	Concerto in D, Op. 61: III Rondo (part 1)	Beethoven	
2EA 2983	1, 1A	HMV DB 2931[24]	Concerto in D, Op. 61: III Rondo (part 2)	Beethoven	
2EA 2984	1, 2, 2A		Concerto in D, Op. 61: III Rondo (part 3)	Beethoven	
			Franz Rupp (piano)	London (Abbey Road Studio No. 3)	
2EA 3705	1, 2, 3	HMV DB 3071[25]	Sonata No. 9 in A, Op. 47 "Kreutzer": I Adagio sostenuto – Presto (part 1)	Beethoven	
2EA 3706	1, 2		Sonata No. 9 in A, Op. 47 "Kreutzer": I Adagio sostenuto – Presto (part 2)	Beethoven	
15	18 June 1936		Franz Rupp (piano)	London (Abbey Road Studio No. 3)	
2EA 3706	3, 4	HMV DB 3071[25]	Sonata No. 9 in A, Op. 47 "Kreutzer": I Adagio sostenuto – Presto (part 2)	Beethoven	
2EA 3707	1, 2, 3	HMV DB 3072[25]	Sonata No. 9 in A, Op. 47 "Kreutzer": I Adagio sostenuto – Presto (part 3)	Beethoven	
2EA 3708	1, 2	HMV DB 3072[25]	Sonata No. 9 in A, Op. 47 "Kreutzer": II Andante con variazioni (part 1)	Beethoven	

2EA 3709	1, 2	HMV DB 3073[25]	Sonata No. 9 in A, Op. 47 "Kreutzer": II Andante con variazioni (part 2)	Beethoven
			LPO and John Barbirolli (conductor)	London (Abbey Road Studio No. 1)
2EA 2986	1, 1A, 2A	HMV DB 2915[26]	Concerto in D, Op. 77: I Allegro non troppo (part 1)	Brahms
2EA 2987	2A	HMV DB 2915[26]	Concerto in D, Op. 77: I Allegro non troppo (part 2)	Brahms
2EA 2988	1A, 2A	HMV DB 2916[26]	Concerto in D, Op. 77: I Allegro non troppo (part 3)	Brahms
2EA 2989	1, 1A	HMV DB 2916[26]	Concerto in D, Op. 77: I Allegro non troppo (part 4)	Brahms
2EA 2990	1, 1A	HMV DB 2917[26]	Concerto in D, Op. 77: I Allegro non troppo (part 5)	Brahms
2EA 2991	1, 1A	HMV DB 2917[26]	Concerto in D, Op. 77: II Adagio (part 1)	Brahms
2EA 2992	1, 1A	HMV DB 2918[26]	Concerto in D, Op. 77: II Adagio (part 2)	Brahms
16	19 June 1936		Franz Rupp (piano)	London (Abbey Road Studio No. 3)
2EA 3713	1, 2, 3	HMV DB 3073[25]	Sonata No. 9 in A, Op. 47 "Kreutzer": II Andante con variazioni (part 3)	Beethoven
2EA 3714	1, 2, 3	HMV DB 3074[25]	Sonata No. 9 in A, Op. 47 "Kreutzer": III Finale: Presto (part 1)	Beethoven
2EA 3715	1, 2	HMV DB 3074[25]	Sonata No. 9 in A, Op. 47 "Kreutzer": III Finale: Presto (part 2)	Beethoven
2EA 3716	1, 2	HMV DB 3299[27]	Sonata No. 10 in G, Op. 96: I Allegro moderato (part 1)	Beethoven
2EA 3717	1, 2	HMV DB 3299[27]	Sonata No. 10 in G, Op. 96: I Allegro moderato (part 2)	Beethoven
2EA 3718	1, 2	HMV DB 3300[27]	Sonata No. 10 in G, Op. 96: II Adagio espressivo (part 1)	Beethoven
0EA 3712	1		Speech for Marconiphone machine	

session / *matrix*	*date* / *take(s)*	*original issue on 78 rpm records*	*accompanying artist(s)* / *title of work*	*venue (where known)* / *composer*	*arranger*
17	20 June 1936		Franz Rupp (piano)	London (Abbey Road Studio No. 3)	
2EA 3719	1, 2	HMV DB 3300[27]	Sonata No. 10 in G, Op. 96: II Adagio espressivo (part 2)/ III Scherzo: Allegro	Beethoven	
2EA 3720	1, 2	HMV DB 3301[27]	Sonata No. 10 in G, Op. 96: IV Poco Allegretto (part 1)	Beethoven	
2EA 3721	1, 2	HMV DB 3301[27]	Sonata No. 10 in G, Op. 96: IV Poco Allegretto (part 2)	Beethoven	
18	22 June 1936		LPO and John Barbirolli (conductor)	London (Abbey Road Studio No. 1)	
2EA 2987	3A		Concerto in D, Op. 77: I Allegro non troppo (part 2)	Brahms	
2EA 2997	1, 1A, 2A, 3		Concerto in D, Op. 77: III Allegro giocoso (part 1)	Brahms	
2EA 2998	1, 1A, 2A, 3, 3A		Concerto in D, Op. 77: III Allegro giocoso (part 2)	Brahms	
2EA 2977	3A	HMV DB 2928[24]	Concerto in D, Op. 61: I Allegro ma non troppo (part 4)	Beethoven	
2EA 2979	3A	HMV DB 2929[24]	Concerto in D, Op. 61: I Allegro ma non troppo (part 6)	Beethoven	
2EA 2981	3A	HMV DB 2930[24]	Concerto in D, Op. 61: II Larghetto (part 2)	Beethoven	
2EA 2984	3A	HMV DB 2932[24]	Concerto in D, Op. 61: III Rondo (part 3)	Beethoven	
2EA 2990	2A, 3		Concerto in D, Op. 77: I Allegro non troppo (part 5)	Brahms	

2EA 2997	**4A**	HMV DB 2918[26]	Concerto in D, Op. 77: III Allegro giocoso (part 1)	Brahms	
2EA 2998	**4A**	HMV DB 2919[26]	Concerto in D, Op. 77: III Allegro giocoso (part 2)	Brahms	
19	8 February 1938		LPO and Malcolm Sargent (conductor)	London (Abbey Road Studio No. 1)	
2EA 6212	1, 1A, 2		Concerto No. 4 in D, K. 218: I Allegro (part 1)	Mozart	
2EA 6213	1, 1A, 2, 3		Concerto No. 4 in D, K. 218: I Allegro (part 2)	Mozart	
2EA 6214	1, 1A		Concerto No. 4 in D, K. 218: II Andante cantabile (part 1)	Mozart	
2EA 6215	1, 1A		Concerto No. 4 in D, K. 218: II Andante cantabile (part 2)	Mozart	
2EA 6216	1, 1A, 2, 2A		Concerto No. 4 in D, K. 218: III Rondeau (part 1)	Mozart	
2EA 6217	1, 1A, 2		Concerto No. 4 in D, K. 218: III Rondeau (part 2)	Mozart	
20	14 February 1938		Franz Rupp (piano)	London (Abbey Road Studio No. 3)	
0EA 6094	1, 1A, 2	HMV DA 1627	Chanson indoue [Song of India] from *Sadko*	Rimsky-Korsakov	Kreisler
2EA 6095	1, 1A	HMV DB 3443	Andante cantabile from String Quartet No. 1 in D, Op. 11	Tchaikovsky	Kreisler
0EA 6096	1, 1A, 2	HMV DA 1631	Mazurka in A minor, Op. 67, No. 4	Chopin	Kreisler
0EA 6097	1, 1A	HMV DA 1628	Gavotte from Partita No. 3 in E	Bach	Kreisler
0EA 6098	1, 1A	HMV DA 1628	Rondino on a Theme of Beethoven	Kreisler	
2EA 6099	1A, 2A	HMV DB 3444	Lotus Land, Op. 47, No. 1	Scott	Kreisler
2EA 6100	1, 1A	HMV DB 3443	Humoresque, Op. 101, No. 7	Dvořák	Kreisler
2EA 6101	1, 1A, 2, **2A**	HMV DB 3731	Rondo from "Haffner" Serenade (part 1)	Mozart	Kreisler
2EA 6102	1, 1A	HMV DB 3731	Rondo from "Haffner" Serenade (part 2)	Mozart	Kreisler

session / *matrix*	*date* / *take(s)*	*original issue on 78 rpm records*	*accompanying artist(s)* / *title of work*	*venue (where known)* / *composer*	*arranger*
21	15 February 1938		Franz Rupp (piano)	London (Abbey Road Studio No. 3)	
0EA 6094	3, 3A		Chanson indoue [Song of India] from *Sadko*	Rimsky-Korsakov	Kreisler
0EA 6103	1, 2	HMV DA 1629	La Gitana	Kreisler	
0EA 6104	1, 1A, 2, 2A	HMV DA 1631	Waltz, Op. 39, No. 15	Brahms	Hochstein
0EA 6105	1A, 2, 2A	HMV DA 1622	Poupée valsante [Dancing Doll] (No. 2 from Marionettes)	Poldini	Kreisler
0EA 6106	1, 1A, 2, 2A	HMV DA 1630	Danza espagñola from *La vida breve*	Falla	Kreisler
0EA 6107	1, 1A, 2	HMV DA 1622	Londonderry Air	traditional	Kreisler
2EA 6108	1, 1A, 2, 2A	HMV DB 3444	Hymn to the Sun from *Le coq d'or*	Rimsky-Korsakov	Kreisler
0EA 6109	1, 1A	HMV DA 1627	Schön Rosmarin	Kreisler	
0EA 6110	1, 1A	HMV DA 1629	Liebesleid	Kreisler	
0EA 6111	1A	HMV DA 1630	Liebesfreud	Kreisler	
22	11 February 1939		LPO and Malcolm Sargent (conductor)	London (Kingsway Hall)	
2EA 6212	3	HMV DB 3734[28]	Concerto No. 4 in D, K. 218: I Allegro (part 1)	Mozart	
2EA 6213	4	HMV DB 3734[28]	Concerto No. 4 in D, K. 218: I Allegro (part 2)	Mozart	
2EA 6214	2	HMV DB 3735[28]	Concerto No. 4 in D, K. 218: II Andante cantabile (part 1)	Mozart	
2EA 6215	2, 3	HMV DB 3735[28]	Concerto No. 4 in D, K. 218: II Andante cantabile (part 2)	Mozart	
2EA 6216	3, 4	HMV DB 3736[28]	Concerto No. 4 in D, K. 218: III Rondeau (part 1)	Mozart	
2EA 6217	3, 4	HMV DB 3736[28]	Concerto No. 4 in D, K. 218: III Rondeau (part 2)	Mozart	

Part 7: The RCA Victor recordings (London, 1936–46)

In 1936, Kreisler was re-engaged by RCA Victor (formerly the Victor Company) to record his own arrangement of the first movement of Paganini's Concerto No. 1 in D. In addition to providing an original cadenza, Kreisler composed a new introduction and coda, and he rewrote all the transitional sections. The works recorded at Kreisler's next Victor session in 1942 were issued in an album entitled *My Favorites*. This album of three records (six pieces) marked Kreisler's return to the studio following his emigration to the United States. The violinist composed new orchestral accompaniments for six original works, and the Philadelphia Orchestra (called the "Victor Symphony Orchestra" for contractual reasons) was engaged. This was the first recording Kreisler made after the accident in which he was hit by a truck while crossing a street in New York in April 1941. Following the 1942 Philadelphia session, due to the ban on recordings in 1943–44, Kreisler would not record again until after the Second World War.

The letters "BS" and "CS" preceding the matrix numbers designate 10- and 12-inch records, respectively. For the recordings made after 1945, the matrix number prefixes "RB" and "RC" are substituted for the 10- and 12-inch records. The catalog numbers were also altered: all 10-inch discs had the number 10 preceding a four-digit catalog number, and all 12-inch discs used the number 11 before the four-digit catalog number.

Appropriately enough, Kreisler's final recording was his *Viennese Rhapsodic Fantasietta*, a work he described as a nostalgic portrayal of a bygone Vienna. Although the piece ends in an atmosphere of gaiety, there is more than a hint of melancholy in this loving portrayal of the composer's home city, which he never revisited after the Second World War. Nearly seventy-two years old when he made the recording, Kreisler's remarkable performance confirms Nathan Milstein's observation (made in 1949) that "there is a natural superiority about Fritz Kreisler which age cannot destroy. His technique is still indescribable." This exhilarating performance brings the recorded career of a revered master to a glorious close.

session / *matrix*	*date* / *take(s)*	*original issue on 78 rpm records*	*accompanying artist(s)* / *title of work*	*venue (where known)* / *composer*	*arranger*
1	13 December 1936		Philadelphia Orchestra and Eugene Ormandy (conductor)	Philadelphia (Academy of Music)	
CS 03149	1	RCA Victor 14420[29]	Concerto No. 1 in D, Op. 6: I Allegro (part 1)	Paganini	Kreisler

session / *matrix*	*date* / *take(s)*	*original issue on 78 rpm records*	*accompanying artist(s)* / *title of work*	*venue (where known)* / *composer*	*arranger*
CS 03150	1, 1A	RCA Victor 14420[29]	Concerto No. 1 in D, Op. 6: I Allegro (part 2)	Paganini	Kreisler
CS 03151	1, 1A, 2, 2A	RCA Victor 14421[29]	Concerto No. 1 in D, Op. 6: I Allegro (part 3)	Paganini	Kreisler
CS 03152	1, 1A, 2, 2A	RCA Victor 14421[29]	Concerto No. 1 in D, Op. 6: I Allegro (part 4)	Paganini	Kreisler
2	15 January 1942		Victor Symphony Orchestra and Charles O'Connell (conductor)	Philadelphia (Academy of Music)	
CS 071315	1, 1A, 2, **2A**	RCA Victor 11-8230[30]	Caprice Viennois, Op. 2	Kreisler	
CS 071316	1, 1A, 2, 2A, 3, 3A, **4R**[31]	RCA Victor 11-8230[30]	Tambourin Chinois, Op. 3	Kreisler	
CS 071315	1, 1A	RCA Victor 11-8231[30]	Liebesfreud	Kreisler	
CS 071315	1, 1A	RCA Victor 11-8231[30]	Liebesleid	Kreisler	
CS 071315	1, 1A	RCA Victor 11-8232[30]	La Gitana	Kreisler	
CS 071315	1, 1A	RCA Victor 11-8232[30]	Schön Rosmarin	Kreisler	
3	2 May 1945		Victor String Orchestra and Donald Voorhees (conductor)	New York (Lotos Club)	
D5-RC 0949	1, 1A, 2, **2A**	RCA Victor 11-9264[32]	Concerto in C "in the style of Vivaldi": I Allegro energico ma non troppo	Kreisler	
D5-RC 0950	1, 1A, 2, 2A	RCA Victor 11-9265[32]	Concerto in C "in the style of Vivaldi": II Andante doloroso	Kreisler	
D5-RC 0951	1, 1A, 2, **2A**	RCA Victor 11-9265[32]	Concerto in C "in the style of Vivaldi": III Allegro molto	Kreisler	

4	4 May 1945		Victor Symphony Orchestra and Donald Voorhees (conductor)	New York (Lotos Club)	
D5-RB 0739	1, 1A	RCA Victor 10-1203[33]	Rondino on a Theme of Beethoven	Kreisler	
D5-RB 0740	1, 1A, 2, 2A	RCA Victor 10-1202[33]	"Du alter Stefansturm" from *Der liebe Augustin* "The Old Refrain"	Brandl	Kreisler
D5-RB 0741	1, 1A, 2, 2A	RCA Victor 10-1204[33]	Londonderry Air	traditional	Kreisler
D5-RB 0742	1, 1A, 2, 2A	RCA Victor 10-1203[33]	"Im Chambre séparée" from *Der Opernball* "Midnight Bells"	Heuberger	Kreisler
5	9 May 1945		Victor Symphony Orchestra and Donald Voorhees (conductor)	New York (Lotos Club)	
D5-RB 0750	1, 1A	RCA Victor 10-1202[33]	Marche miniature viennoise	Kreisler	
D5-RB 0751	1, 1A, 2, 2A	RCA Victor 10-1204[33]	"Gypsy Rondo" from Trio No. 25 in G	Haydn	Kreisler
D5-RC 0954	1, 1A, 2, 2A	RCA Victor 11-9264[32]	Chanson Louis XIII and Pavane "in the style of Couperin"	Kreisler	
6	20 December 1946		RCA Victor Orchestra and Donald Voorhees (conductor)	New York (Lotos Club)	
D6-RC 6642	1, 1A, 2, 2A	RCA Victor 11-9952	Viennese Rhapsodic Fantasietta (part 1)	Kreisler	
D6-RC 6642	1, 1A, 2, 2A	RCA Victor 11-9952	Viennese Rhapsodic Fantasietta (part 2)	Kreisler	
D6-RB 3497	1, 1A, 2, 2A, 3, 3A	RCA Victor 10-1395	The Rosary	Nevin	Kreisler
D6-RB 3498	1, 1A, 2, 2A, 3, 3A	RCA Victor 10-1395	"Stars in my Eyes" from *Sissy* (later *The King Steps Out*)	Kreisler	

Fritz Kreisler: The Piano Recordings

Between February and April 1914 Kreisler made a number of test recordings for the Victor Company as pianist. Such perennial favorites as *Caprice Viennois*, *Liebesfreud*, *Liebesleid*, and *Schön Rosmarin* were recorded, as well as Dvořák's *Humoresque*. That the Victor Company seriously considered issuing recordings of Kreisler as pianist was a reflection of his selling power.

Although only *Humoresque* survives, it vividly documents the violinist's marvelous piano playing. Kreisler especially loved to delight guests at parties by performing Viennese waltzes on the piano, and among the fans of his piano playing were Leopold Godowsky (who remarked that Kreisler "has an exquisite touch on the piano and plays simply in a captivating way") and Ignacy Paderewski ("I'd be starving if Fritz had taken up the piano. How beautifully he plays!").

Part 1: The Victor recordings (New York, 1914)

session *matrix*	date *take(s)*	*original issue on 78 rpm records*	accompanying artist(s) *title of work*	venue (where known) *composer*	*arranger*
1	6 February 1914		unaccompanied	New York	
C 14423	1, 2		Liebesfreud	Kreisler	
C 14424	1		Liebesleid	Kreisler	
C 14425	1, 2		Schön Rosmarin	Kreisler	
B 14426	1		Andantino "in the style of Martini"	Kreisler	
C 14427	1, 2		Caprice Viennois, Op. 2	Kreisler	
C 14428	1		Humoresque, Op. 101, No. 7	Dvořák	
2	31 March 1914		unaccompanied	New York	
B 14425	3		Schön Rosmarin	Kreisler	
C 14428	2, 3[1]		Humoresque, Op. 101, No. 7	Dvořák	

B 14650	1		La précieuse "in the style of Couperin"	Kreisler	
C 14423	3, 4		Liebesfreud	Kreisler	
C 14427	3		Caprice Viennois, Op. 2	Kreisler	
C 14424	2		Liebesleid	Kreisler	
3	3 April 1914		unaccompanied	New York	
C 14423	5, 6		Liebesfreud	Kreisler	
C 14424	3		Liebesleid	Kreisler	
B 14425	4		Schön Rosmarin	Kreisler	
C 14427	4		Caprice Viennois, Op. 2	Kreisler	
C 14428	4, 5		Humoresque, Op. 101, No. 7	Dvořák	
B 14650	2		La précieuse "in the style of Couperin"	Kreisler	

Part 2: The HMV recordings (Hayes and Berlin, 1921–27)

session	*date*	*original issue on*	*accompanying artist(s)*	*venue (where known)*	
matrix	*take(s)*	*78 rpm records*	*title of work*	*composer*	*arranger*
4	17 December 1921		accompanying Hugo Kreisler (cello)	Hayes (Room 1)	
Bb 788	1, 2	Victor 66185[9]	"Letter Song" from *Apple Blossoms*	Kreisler	
Bb 789	1, 2	Victor 66116[9]	"I'm in Love" from *Apple Blossoms*	Kreisler	
Bb 790	1, 2, 3, 4	Victor 66219[9]	Serenade	Drigo	Wolf-Israel
Bb 791	1, 2, 3	Victor 66040[9]	Sérénade espagnole	Chaminade	Kreisler
Bb 792	1, 2, 3	Victor 66218[9]	Liebesleid	Kreisler	
Bb 793	1, 2, 3		Songs My Mother Taught Me, Op. 55, No. 4	Dvořák	Kreisler
Bb 794	1, 2, 3	Victor 66082[9]	Viennese Waltz Fantasy	traditional	H. Kreisler

session	*date*	*original issue on*	*accompanying artist(s)*	*venue (where known)*	
matrix	*take(s)*	*78 rpm records*	*title of work*	*composer*	*arranger*
5	1 November 1923		accompanying Hugo Kreisler (cello)	Hayes (Room 2)	
Bb 3779	1, 2	Victor 1039[9]	Melody in F	Rubinstein	
Bb 3780	1, 2		Rondino on a Theme of Beethoven	Kreisler	
Bb 3781	1, 2	Victor 1039[9]	La Cinquantaine	Gabriel-Marie	
6	5 November 1923		accompanying Hugo Kreisler (cello)	Hayes	
Bb 3797	1, 2		Nocturne in D	Chopin	
Bb 3781	3, 4		La Cinquantaine	Gabriel-Marie	
7	20 September 1924		accompanying Hugo Kreisler (cello)	Hayes (Room 1)	
Bb 5103	1, 2		Gavotte No. 2, Op. 23	Popper	
8	22 September 1924		accompanying Hugo Kreisler (cello)	Hayes (Room 1)	
Bb 5104	1, 2, 3		Assad's Song from *The Queen of Sheba* "Magic Tones"	Goldmark	
Bb 5105	1, 2, 3, 4		Polichinelle Serenade	Kreisler	
9	23 September 1924		accompanying Hugo Kreisler (cello)	Hayes (Room 1)	
Bb 5104	4, 5		Assad's Song from *The Queen of Sheba* "Magic Tones"	Goldmark	
Bb 5105	5, 6		Polichinelle Serenade	Kreisler	

10	14 October 1927	accompanying Hugo Kreisler (cello)	Berlin (Studio)	
BW 1245	1, 2, 3	Cantabile	Cui	
BW 1246	1, 2, 3, 4	Märchen (Legend)	Drdla	
BW 1247	1, 2, 3	Assad's Song from *The Queen of Sheba* "Magic Tones"	Goldmark	
BW 1248	1, 2, 3, 4	Adagietto from *L'arlésienne*	Bizet	Weidinger

Notes

1. Issued on CD: BMG 09026 61649 2.
2. In this session two selections were initially recorded on different sized discs. The Granados Spanish Dance in E minor, originally intended to be released as a 12-inch disc (with a C matrix number prefix), was altered to become a 10-inch disc (with a B matrix number prefix). Similarly, the Godowsky *Wienerisch*, originally intended to be released as a 10-inch disc (with a B matrix number prefix), was altered to become a 12-inch disc (with a C matrix number prefix).
3. The exact Schubert *Moment musical* is not designated in ledgers.
4. Change of 12-inch record size to 10-inch; old matrix number reused with a B matrix number prefix instead of a C prefix.
5. Change of 10-inch record size to 12-inch; old matrix number reused with a C matrix number prefix instead of a B prefix.
6. Assigned catalog number Victor 64601, but may not have been issued.
7. Assigned catalog number Victor 64565, but may not have been issued.
8. Assigned catalog number Victor 64319, but may not have been issued.
9. Issued on CD: Biddulph LAB 009/10.
10. Coupled with Rachmaninoff's *How Fair this Spot* featuring McCormack accompanied at the piano by Edwin Schneider.
11. Coupled with Kreisler's *Polichinelle Serenade* recorded by HMV on 14 February 1930.
12. Issued on CD: Biddulph LAB 049/50.
13. Coupled with Mendelssohn's *Song Without Words* recorded by Electrola on 14 December 1926.
14. Coupled with Winternitz's *Dance of the Marionettes* recorded by Victor on 28 February 1928.
15. DB 2554/6 was also issued in an "automatic coupling" set as DB 7892/6.

16. DB 2556/8 was also issued in an "automatic coupling" set as DB 7892/4 and 7897/8.
17. DB 2559/60 was also issued in an "automatic coupling" set as DB 7895/8.
18. DB 2781/3 was also issued in an "automatic coupling" set as DB DB 8054/5 and 8058/60.
19. DB 2460/2 was also issued in an "automatic coupling" set as DB 7889/91.
20. DB 3296/8 was also issued in an "automatic coupling" set as DB 8349/54.
21. DB 2786/7 was also issued in an "automatic coupling" set as DB 8054/7.
22. DB 3068/70 was also issued in an "automatic coupling" set as DB 8235/40.
23. DB 2783/5 was also issued in an "automatic coupling" set as DB 8056/60.
24. DB 2927/32 was also issued in an "automatic coupling" set as DB 8210/5.
25. DB 3071/4 was also issued in an "automatic coupling" set as DB 8235/41.
26. DB 2915/9 was also issued in an "automatic coupling" set as DB 8127/31.
27. DB 3299/301 was also issued in an "automatic coupling" set as DB 8349/54.
28. DB 3734/6 was also issued in an "automatic coupling" set as DB 8637/9.
29. Issued in set M-361.
30. Issued in set M-910.
31. Take 4R is a composite of takes 2 and 3A, reconstructed on 29 May 1942.
32. Issued in set DM-1070.
33. Issued in set M-1044.

Notes

All interviews are by the author unless otherwise noted.

Chapter 1: Vienna

1. Schorske 1981, 4.
2. Schorske 1981, 36.
3. Hofmann 1994, 1.
4. Hofmann 1994, 140.
5. Fritz Kreisler, interview by Louis Lochner, 2 June 1949, Library of Congress Fritz Kreisler Collection. *See also* Lochner 1950, 3–4.
6. Lochner 1950, 8, 13.
7. Lochner 1950, 3–5.
8. Hofmann 1988, 86.
9. Quoted in Roy 1921.
10. Lochner 1950, 6.
11. Antrim 1944.
12. Lochner 1950, 9, 17.
13. Quoted in Lochner 1950, 11.
14. Lochner 1950, 12–13.

15. Quoted in Flesch 1958, 16.
16. Lochner 1950, 17.
17. Quoted in Martens 1919, 102.
    In fact, the young Kreisler probably heard Anton Rubinstein play during the pianist's 1884 visit to Vienna, his first in six years, not his first ever. Kreisler would have just turned nine years old and would have been as agog as everyone else at Rubinstein's densely programmed three-hour recitals. "Rubinstein moves among our swarm of ivory crushers like Gulliver among the Lilliputians," wrote composer and critic Hugo Wolf, "utterly his own man, a fixed star among the miserable shooting stars, a personality through and through" (quoted in Henry Pleasants, ed., trans., and annot., *The Music Criticism of Hugo Wolf*, New York and London: Holmes & Meier Publishers, 1979, 13).
18. Fritz Kreisler, interview by WQXR radio, broadcast tape, 2 February 1955.
19. Bachmann 1966, 365.
20. Fritz Kreisler, interview by WQXR radio, broadcast tape, 2 February 1955.
21. Quoted in Downes 1942.
22. Lochner 1950, 21–22.
23. Lochner 1950, 23–24.
24. Breuer 1948, 8–9.
25. Josef Gingold, interview, 13 July 1992.
26. Flesch 1930, 55.
27. Ross Parmenter, interview, 17 February 1995.

Chapter 2: Prodigy

1. "Ysaÿe, Kreisler, Vecsey."
2. Slenczynska and Biancolli 1958, 163.
3. Quoted in Scheinert 1934.
4. Scheinert 1934.
5. Lochner 1950, 26–27.
6. Lochner 1950, 26–27.
7. Lochner 1950, 28.
8. Quoted in Lochner 1950, 28.
9. "A Wonderful Pianist," *The New York Times*, 10 November 1888, 1.
10. Lochner 1950, 8.
11. "Mr. Seidl's Concert," *The New York Times*, 11 November 1888, 4.
12. "Music," *The Independent*, 15 November 1888, 9.
13. "Mr. Seidl's First Concert," *New-York Daily Tribune*, 12 November 1888, 4.

14. "Moriz Rosenthal's First Concert," *New-York Daily Tribune*, 14 November 1888, 7.
15. "Herr Moriz Rosenthal," *The New York Times*, 14 November 1888, 5.
16. *Chicago Tribune*, quoted in Lochner 1950, 31.
17. Lochner 1950, 31.
18. "Fritz Kreisler, Now 83, Feels All Beauty Is Lost," *Los Angeles Times*, 17 August 1958, 1A, 2.
19. Charles D. Isaacson, "Why Great Artists Succeeded," *Etude* (October 1930): 746.
20. Lochner 1950, 34–35.
21. Lochner 1950, 35.
22. Quoted in Lochner 1950, 35.
23. Lochner 1950, 37–38.
24. Lochner 1950, 40.
25. Lochner 1950, 40–41.
26. Quoted in Lochner 1950, 42.
27. Flesch 1958, 119.
28. Flesch 1958, 118.
29. Flesch 1958, 118–120.
30. Slenczynska and Biancolli 1958, 7.

Chapter 3: From Ysaÿe's Shadow to the Birth of a Pop Star

1. Martens 1919, 1.
2. Quoted in Corredor 1956, 58.
3. G. B. Shaw 1981, 639, 954–955.
4. Philip Dreifus, interview, 26 May 1993.
5. Philip Dreifus, interview, 26 May 1993.
6. Quoted in Richard Aldrich, "Two Great Violinists," *The Outlook* (6 May 1905): 33.
7. Spalding 1943, 58.
8. Quoted in Lochner 1950, 53–54.
9. See Pearl records (Gemm CD 9125), Pavilion Records Lt., England.
10. See Pearl records, *Joachim-Sarasate-Ysaÿe* (OPAL CD 9851), Pavilion Records Lt., England.
11. See *The Kreisler Collection: The Complete Acoustic HMV Recordings*, Biddulph Recordings (LAB 009-10).
12. Lochner 1950, 21.
13. Flesch 1930, 75.
14. Eric Wen, interview, 29 September 1995.
15. Eric Wen, interview, 29 September 1995.
16. Keller 1984, 148–149.

17. Fritz Kreisler, interview by Louis Lochner, 2 June 1949, unpublished portions, Library of Congress Fritz Kreisler Collection.
18. Quoted in "Fritz Kreisler, Now 83, Feels All Beauty Is Lost," *Los Angeles Times*, 17 August 1958, 1A, 2.
19. Quoted in "Fritz Kreisler, Now 83, Feels All Beauty Is Lost," *Los Angeles Times*, 17 August 1958, 1A, 2.
20. Josef Gingold, interview, 13 July 1992.
21. Flesch 1958, 37.
22. Quoted in Arthur Abell birthday letter to Fritz Kreisler, Library of Congress Fritz Kreisler Collection.
23. Arthur Abell birthday letter to Fritz Kreisler, Library of Congress Fritz Kreisler Collection.
24. Arthur Abell birthday letter to Fritz Kreisler, Library of Congress Fritz Kreisler Collection.
25. In his letter, Abell quoted Bruch in the original German. Translated here by Susanne Dopierala Richardson.
26. Quoted in Arthur Abell birthday letter to Fritz Kreisler, Library of Congress Fritz Kreisler Collection.
27. Arthur Abell birthday letter to Fritz Kreisler, Library of Congress Fritz Kreisler Collection.
28. Translated by Susanne Dopierala Richardson.
29. Quoted in Arthur Abell birthday letter to Fritz Kreisler, Library of Congress Fritz Kreisler Collection.
30. Quoted in Arthur Abell birthday letter to Fritz Kreisler, Library of Congress Fritz Kreisler Collection. Translated by Susanne Dopierala Richardson.
31. Louis Lochner unpublished notes, Library of Congress Fritz Kreisler Collection.
32. "W.E.B." 1909.
33. "Ysaÿe, Kreisler, Vecsey."
34. "Ysaÿe, Kreisler, Vecsey."
35. Louis Lochner unpublished notes, Library of Congress Fritz Kreisler Collection.
36. Louis Lochner unpublished notes, Library of Congress Fritz Kreisler Collection. *See also* Lochner 1950, 121.
37. "W.E.B." 1909.
38. Lochner 1950, 131.
39. "Men and Women of Interest," *Harper's Bazar*, January 1910, 38.
40. Louis Lochner unpublished notes, Library of Congress Fritz Kreisler Collection.
41. Louis Lochner unpublished notes, Library of Congress Fritz Kreisler Collection.
42. Casals and Kahn 1970, 143.

43. Casals and Kahn 1970, 143.
44. Flesch 1930, 107.
45. Flesch 1930, 75.

Chapter 4: Fritzi and Harriet

1. Kreisler quoted in Lochner 1950, 82.
2. Quoted in Stidger 1940, 76.
3. Quoted in "How Kreisler Finds Musical Novelties," *The New York Times*, 8 November 1909, 7.
4. Lochner 1950, 76.
5. "Estate to Mrs. Kreisler," *The New York Times*, 25 October 1924, 25.
6. Stidger 1940, 68.
7. "Fritz Kreisler Talks on a Variety of Subjects," *Musical America* (9 November 1907): 15.
8. Franz Rupp quoting Josef Hofmann, in an interview by David Sackson, January 1992.
9. Quoted in Lochner 1950, 77.
10. Franz Rupp, interview by David Sackson, January 1992.
11. Quoted in Stidger 1940, 76.
12. Franz Rupp, interview by David Sackson, January 1992.
13. Franz Rupp, interview by David Sackson, January 1992.
14. Quoted in Rooney 1987.
15. Lucie Schelling quoting Harriet Kreisler, in an interview by Louis Lochner, 24 May 1949, unpublished portions, Library of Congress Fritz Kreisler Collection.
16. Harold Coletta, interview, 12 July 1992.
17. Franz Rupp, interview by Louis Lochner, 12 April 1949, unpublished portions, Library of Congress Fritz Kreisler Collection.
18. George Neikrug, interview, 19 August 1992.
19. Sir Yehudi Menuhin, interview, 27 February 1993.
20. Edward S. Naumburg, interview, 13 February 1995.
21. Alix Williamson, interview, 28 March 1995.
22. Philip Dreifus, interview, 26 May 1993.
23. Frederic Kreisler, interview, 9 August 1995.
24. Sylvia Rabinof Rothenberg, interview, 3 November 1992.
25. Louis Lochner letter to Charles Cunningham, 28 August 1949, Library of Congress Fritz Kreisler Collection.
26. Louis Lochner unpublished notes, Library of Congress Fritz Kreisler Collection.
27. Quoted in Lochner 1950, 81–82.
28. Sylvia Rabinof Rothenberg, interview, 3 November 1992.

29. Sir Yehudi Menuhin, interview, 27 February 1993.
30. Milstein and Volkov 1990, 178.
31. Milstein and Volkov 1990, 170.
32. David Sackson, interview, 16 September 1992.
33. Sam Kissel, interview, 14 September 1992.
34. Milstein and Volkov 1990, 169.
35. Rooney 1987.
36. Quoted in Stidger 1940, 73.
37. Quoted in "Kreisler, Fritz," *Current Biography* (1944): 359.
38. Quoted in "Kreisler, Fritz," *Current Biography* (1944): 359.
39. Quoted in "Kreisler, Fritz," *Current Biography* (1944): 359.
40. Albert Spalding, interview by Louis Lochner, unpublished portions, Library of Congress Fritz Kreisler Collection.
41. Quoted in Rooney 1987.
42. Franz Rupp, interview by David Sackson, January 1992.
43. Frederic Kreisler letter to the author, 17 March 1997.
44. Frederic Kreisler, interview, 9 August 1995.
45. Fritz Kreisler letters to Charles Foley, 11 January and 9 July 1937, Library of Congress Fritz Kreisler Collection.
46. Fritz Kreisler letters to Louis Lochner, 1 July and 15 September 1948, Library of Congress Fritz Kreisler Collection.
47. Harriet Kreisler letter to George F. Denney, Jr., 18 October 1948, Library of Congress Fritz Kreisler Collection.
48. Franz Rupp, interview by David Sackson, January 1992.
49. Sir Yehudi Menuhin, interview, 27 February 1993.
50. "Kreisler Returns With His 'Manager,'" *The New York Times*, 5 October 1934, 25.
51. "Kreisler Returns With His 'Manager,'" *The New York Times*, 5 October 1934, 25.
52. Quoted in "Kreisler Returns With His 'Manager,'" *The New York Times*, 5 October 1934, 25.
53. "Fritz Kreisler, Now 83, Feels All Beauty Is Lost," *Los Angeles Times*, 17 August 1958, 1A, 2.
54. Quoted in "Kreisler Here, Finds He's Lost," *The New York Times*, 6 January 1933, 22.
55. Quoted in Stidger 1940, 75.
56. Quoted in Stidger 1940, 76.
57. Quoted in Stidger 1940, 77.
58. Lochner 1950, 84.
59. Josef Gingold, interview, 13 July 1992.
60. Milstein and Volkov 1990, 177.
61. Quoted in Lochner 1950, 80.

Chapter 5: Shunned: An Enemy in America

1. Kreisler quoted in "Kreisler Here, Wounded," *The New York Times*, 25 November 1914, 5.
2. Kreisler 1915, 3–4.
3. Kreisler 1915, 4–5.
4. Quoted in "Kreisler, Wounded, Tells of War," *The New York Times*, 29 November 1914, V, 4.
5. Quoted in "Kreisler, Wounded, Tells of War," *The New York Times*, 29 November 1914, V, 4.
6. Casals and Kahn 1970, 143.
7. Kreisler 1915, 27–29.
8. Quoted in "Kreisler, Wounded, Tells of War," *The New York Times*, 29 November 1914, V, 4.
9. Kreisler 1915, 85.
10. "Kreisler, Wounded, Tells of War," *The New York Times*, 29 November 1914, V, 4.
11. H. Kreisler 1914.
12. "Mr. Kreisler's Recital," *The New York Times*, 13 December 1914, II, 14.
13. "Dinner to Fritz Kreisler," *The New York Times*, 20 December 1914, II, 13.
14. "Kreisler's Second Recital," *The New York Times*, 31 December 1914, 9.
15. Lochner 1950, 104. A slightly different wording of this exchange is quoted in Lochner's notes of his interview with Kreisler, 6 April 1949, Library of Congress Fritz Kreisler Collection.
16. Henry T. Finck, "Lion of the Musical Season," *The Nation*, 18 March 1915, 313.
17. Konrad Bercovici, "Little Stories of Big Men," *Good Housekeeping*, January 1934, 148.
18. Konrad Bercovici, "Little Stories of Big Men," *Good Housekeeping*, January 1934, 148.
19. Quoted in "Fritz Kreisler's Tribute to His Emperor."
20. "Franz Joseph and Fritz Kreisler," *The Outlook* (27 December 1916): 895.
21. Quoted in "Fritz Kreisler's Tribute to His Emperor."
22. Quoted in "Fritz Kreisler's Tribute to His Emperor."
23. Nathaniel Ferguson, "When Kreisler Played," *The Musician* (May 1917): 223.
24. Quoted in "Fritz Kreisler Denies Anti-American Actions," *Musical Courier* (22 November 1917): 5.

25. "Warlich-Kreisler Recital," *The Pittsburgh Post*, 4 November 1917, II, 8.
26. Quoted in "Hot Protests Made Against Fritz Kreisler," *The Gazette Times*, 4 November 1917, 1.
27. Quoted in "Hot Protests Made Against Fritz Kreisler," *The Gazette Times*, 4 November 1917, 1.
28. "Musical Comments and Current Events," *The Pittsburgh Post*, 11 November 1917, II, 6.
29. "Police Refuse Permit for Kreisler," *The Gazette Times*, 8 November 1917, 7. *See also* "Pittsburgh May Bar Muck," *The New York Times*, 7 November 1917, 11; "Kreisler Concert Permit Is Refused" and "Cancelling of Kreisler Concert," *The Pittsburgh Post*, 8 November 1917, 6.
30. "Karl Muck Refused to Appear in Baltimore," *The Gazette Times*, 6 November 1917, 9.
31. "Police Close Pittsburgh to Fritz Kreisler," *The Pittsburgh Dispatch*, 8 November 1917, 4. *See also* "Police Refuse Permit for Kreisler," *The Gazette Times*, 8 November 1917, 7.
32. "Arts and Patriotism," *The Pittsburgh Sun*, 8 November 1917, 6.
33. "Lieut. Kreisler," *The Washington Post*, 10 March 1918, II, 4.
34. "Old Agonies Revive: Israel Philharmonic to Perform Wagner," *The New York Times*, 16 December 1991, 1.
35. "Statement Issued by Fritz Kreisler."
36. "German Orchestra Music Is Barred," *Pittsburgh Sun*, 8 November 1917, 18.
37. "Hot Protests Made Against Fritz Kreisler," *The Gazette Times*, 4 November 1917, 1.
38. "Bar Kreisler and Hempel," *The New York Times*, 10 November 1917, 8.
39. "Agitation Continues Against Enemy Music," *Musical Courier* (15 November 1917): 5.
40. "Agitation Continues Against Enemy Music," *Musical Courier* (15 November 1917): 5.
41. "German Songs Omitted," *Christian Science Monitor*, 24 November 1917, 1.
42. Philip Dreifus, interview, 26 May 1993.
43. "Kreisler Calls on Hillis to Retract," *The New York Times*, 27 November 1917, 9.
44. "The Enemy Music Peril," *The World*, 9 November 1917, 8. Reprinted in the *Musical Courier*, 15 November 1917.
45. "Kreisler Wildly Cheered," *The New York Times*, 25 November 1917, I, 23.

46. "Kreisler Quits Concert Tour," *The New York Times*, 26 November 1917, 1.
47. Quoted in "Artist, Officer, and Gentleman," *The Touchstone* (November 1917): 143.
48. "Fritz Kreisler in a Statement of Great Frankness Tells of His Conduct in War," *The New York Times*, 25 November 1917, VII, 5.
49. Jonas 1917.
50. Quoted in "Kreisler Quits Concert Tour," *The New York Times*, 26 November 1917, 1.
51. "The Banishment of Kreisler," *The World*, 27 November 1917, 8. Reprinted in "Kreisler Cancels All His Concerts," *Musical Courier*, 29 November 1917, 5.
52. Quoted in "More Patriotic Agitation Against Alien Musicians," *Musical Courier*, 6 December 1917, 5.
53. "Topics of the Times: An Artist Shows His Sense," *The New York Times*, 27 November 1917, 12.
54. Quoted in "Kreisler Quits Concert Tour," *The New York Times*, 26 November 1917, 1.
55. Quoted in "More Patriotic Agitation Against Alien Musicians," *Musical Courier*, 6 December 1917, 5.
56. "Kreisler Fails to Appear," *The New York Times*, 3 December 1917, 13.
57. "Kreisler Plays Quartet," *The New York Times*, 22 December 1917, 9.
58. "Fritz Kreisler Delights," *The New York Times*, 2 February 1918, 9.
59. "Objects to Kreisler Concert," *The New York Times*, 5 March 1918, 4.
60. "Kreisler Quits Concert," *The New York Times*, 9 March 1918, 11.
61. "Kreisler Out as Composer," *The New York Times*, 9 April 1918, 14.
62. Farrar 1938, 142.
63. "Fritz Kreisler's Tribute to His Emperor."
64. Quoted in "Kreisler on His Opera," *The New York Times*, 12 October 1919, IV, 3.
65. Quoted in "Operetta's New Life," *Arts and Decoration* (November 1919): 30.
66. Lochner 1950, 181–182. *See also* "Kreisler on His Opera," *The New York Times*, 12 October 1919, IV, 3.
67. Quoted in "Kreisler on His Opera," *The New York Times*, 12 October 1919, IV, 3.
68. Quoted in Lochner 1950, 181–182.
69. *The New York Times* 22, 24, and 30 November 1919.
70. "The Kreisler Case, *The Boston Herald*, 6 December 1919, 16. Reprinted in "States of Mind Over Kreisler," *Literary Digest*, 27 December 1919, 30.
71. "Legion Invites Kreisler," *The New York Times*, 24 November 1919, 15.

72. "Ask Ruling on Kreisler," *The New York Times*, 27 November 1919, 19.
73. "Crowd Hoots Kreisler and Cuts Off Lights," *The New York Times*, 11 December 1919, 3.
74. Quoted in "States of Mind Over Kreisler," *Literary Digest*, 27 December 1919, 30.
75. "Give Ovation to Kreisler," *The New York Times*, 22 December 1919, 19.
76. "Fritz Kreisler Discusses America's Attitude Toward Him."
77. Quoted in "Kreisler on Vienna's Woe," *The New York Times*, 29 December 1921, 14.
78. "Kreisler Cancels Concert in Paris," *The New York Times*, 12 November 1924, 24.
79. "Fritz Kreisler Discusses America's Attitude Toward Him."

Chapter 6: Tall Tale Teller: The Kreisler Apocrypha

1. George Neikrug, interview, 19 August 1992.
2. Josef Gingold, interview, 13 July 1992.
3. Quoted in Lochner 1950, 34.
4. Kreisler 1915, 86.
5. Milstein and Volkov 1990, 173.
6. "An Unconquered Viennese," *The New York Times*, 2 May 1939, 22.
7. Ernö Balogh, interview by Louis Lochner, 5 August 1949, unpublished portions, Library of Congress Fritz Kreisler Collection.
8. Franz Rupp, interview by David Sackson, January 1992.
9. Joseph Fuchs, interview, 17 February 1994.
10. Frederic Kreisler, interview, 9 August 1995.
11. Lochner 1950, 357–358.
12. George Neikrug, interview, 19 August 1992.
13. Flesch 1930, 84.
14. Lochner 1950, 61.
15. Lochner 1950, 75.
16. Quoted in Lochner 1950, 43–44.
17. Quoted in Lochner 1950, 44.
18. Quoted in Lochner 1950, 45.
19. Josef Gingold quoting Kreisler, in an interview by the author, 13 July 1992.
20. Antrim 1944.
21. Lochner 1950, 379–380.
22. Milstein and Volkov 1990, 175.
23. Library of Congress Fritz Kreisler Collection.

24. Milstein and Volkov 1990, 175.
25. David Sackson, interview, 22 May 1993.
26. Quoted in Stoddard 1955.
27. Josef Gingold, interview, 13 July 1992.
28. Frederic Kreisler, interview, 9 August 1995, and letter to the author, 17 March 1997.

Chapter 7: Hoaxes All: Pugnani, Vivaldi, Martini, and Kreisler

1. Sir Yehudi Menuhin, interview, 27 February 1993.
2. Quoted in "Kreisler Reveals 'Classics' As Own. . . ."
3. "Fritz Kreisler Back for Concert Tour," *The New York Times*, 10 January 1934, 24; "Fritz Kreisler Returns," *The New York Times*, 11 January 1925, 31; "Kreisler on German Intellectuals," *Literary Digest*, 2 February 1924, 29; "Kreisler on Love and Art," *The New York Times*, 15 April 1926, 24.
4. Lochner 1950, 208–222.
5. "Threaten Kreisler at Vienna Concert," *The New York Times*, 17 December 1924, 8.
6. Lochner 1950, 264–266.
7. "Kreisler's Secret Kept by Musicians," *The New York Times*, 9 February 1935, 17, 1.
8. Quoted in "Kreisler's Secret Known by Heifetz," *The New York Times*, 10 February 1935, II, 2.
9. Quoted in Lochner 1950, 296.
10. Quoted in "Kreisler's Secret Known by Heifetz," *The New York Times*, 10 February 1935, II, 2.
11. Sir Yehudi Menuhin, interview, 27 February 1993.
12. Kreisler 1951.
13. Kreisler 1951.
14. Kreisler 1951.
15. "W.E.B." 1909.
16. "How Kreisler Finds Musical Novelties," *The New York Times*, 8 November 1909, 7.
17. "How Kreisler Finds Musical Novelties," *The New York Times*, 8 November 1909, 7.
18. "Kreisler Soloist at Philharmonic," *The New York Times*, 5 January 1905, 11.
19. "Kreisler's Violin Art," *Musical Courier* (26 November 1913): 3.
20. Downes 1942.
21. Newman 24 February 1935.

22. Kreisler 10 March 1935.
23. Newman 17 March 1935.
24. Newman 17 March 1935.
25. Fritz Kreisler letter to the editor of *The Sunday Times*, carbon of original letter, Library of Congress Fritz Kreisler Collection.
26. "The Kreisler Hoax."
27. "Kreisler Reveals 'Classics' As Own. . . ."
28. "Kreisler's Concert Tour To Be Made on Zeppelin," *The New York Times*, 4 May 1935, 16.
29. Lochner 1950, 288–290.
30. Lochner 1950, 295–296.
31. Eric Wen, interview, 29 September 1995.
32. Eric Wen, interview, 29 September 1995.
33. Olin Downes, "Music: Fritz Kreisler Plays," *The New York Times*, 20 January 1925, 19.
34. Flesch 1930, 122.
35. Milstein and Volkov 1990, 174.
36. Lochner 1950, 297.

Chapter 8: Kreisler the Catholic, Kreisler the Jew

1. Franz Rupp quoting Hugo Kreisler, in an interview by David Sackson, January 1992.
2. Lochner 1950, 76.
3. Franz Rupp, interview by David Sackson, January 1992.
4. Quoted in Rooney 1987.
5. The information in this section relating to the history of Jews and anti-semitism in Vienna is taken primarily from the works of Berkeley 1988 and Beller 1989, unless otherwise noted.
6. Sked 1989, 227.
7. Morton 1979, 62.
8. Joseph Fuchs quoting Massart, in an interview by the author, 21 February 1994.
9. Stidger 1940, 71.
10. Lochner 1950, 231–232.
11. Rooney 1987.
12. Louis Lochner letter to Harold Holt, 2 November 1949, Library of Congress Fritz Kreisler Collection.
13. Quoted in "Kreisler Is Firm on Reich Concerts," *The New York Times*, 21 July 1933, 5.

14. Kreisler 1921.
15. Kreisler 1921.
16. Kreisler 1924.
17. Library of Congress Fritz Kreisler Collection.
18. Louis Lochner, early manuscript of *Fritz Kreisler*, Library of Congress Fritz Kreisler Collection.
19. Frederic Kreisler letter to the author, 17 March 1997.
20. Quoted in B. Smith 1931.
21. Franz Rupp, interview by Louis Lochner, 12 April 1949, unpublished portions, Library of Congress Fritz Kreisler Collection.
22. Quoted in Rooney 1987.
23. Fritz Kreisler letter to Harold Holt, 28 September 1938, Library of Congress Fritz Kreisler Collection.
24. Lochner 1950, 283–284.
25. Passport, Library of Congress Fritz Kreisler Collection.
26. Lochner 1950, 285.
27. "An Unconquered Viennese," *The New York Times*, 2 May 1939, 22.
28. Louis Lochner unpublished notes, Library of Congress Fritz Kreisler Collection.
29. Citizenship papers, Library of Congress Fritz Kreisler Collection.
30. Quoted in B. Smith 1931.
31. Lochner 1950, 110.
32. Harriet Kreisler letter to Louis Lochner, 5 November 1939, Library of Congress Fritz Kreisler Collection.
33. Fritz Kreisler letters to Mr. and Mrs. Louis Lochner, 5 July, 8 July, and 20 August 1945, Library of Congress Fritz Kreisler Collection.
34. Lochner 1950, 384–385.
35. Ferdinand Friedensburg letter to Fritz Kreisler, 4 February 1950, Library of Congress Fritz Kreisler Collection. Translated by Susanne Dopierala Richardson.
36. Sheen 1980, 258–259.
37. David Sackson quoting Mischa Elman, in an interview by the author, 22 May 1993.
38. "Sheen Aids Kreislers to Return to Church," *The New York Times*, 1 April 1947, 29.
39. Louis Lochner unpublished notes and early manuscript, Library of Congress Fritz Kreisler Collection.
40. Frederic Kreisler, interview, 9 August 1995.

Chapter 9: The Accident

1. Details of the accident are gathered from accounts published on 27 April 1941 in *The New York Times*, *New York Sunday News*, and *The New York Herald Tribune*.
2. Quoted in David Charnay and Gerald Duncan, "Fritz Kreisler Hit by Truck, Gravely Hurt," *New York Sunday News*, 27 April 1941, 4.
3. Quoted in "Kreisler, Violinist, Suffers Skull Fracture When Knocked Down in Traffic by Truck," *The New York Times*, 27 April 1941, 1.
4. Melvin Spitalnick, interview, 25 October 1994.
5. "Charles Foley" letter to Harold Holt and Laurence Mackie, undated, Library of Congress Fritz Kreisler Collection.
6. *The New York Herald Tribune*, 28 April–3 May 1941.
7. Lochner 1950, 316.
8. Franz Rupp, interview by David Sackson, January 1992.
9. Lochner 1950, 316.
10. Quoted in Taubman 1944.
11. "Kreisler Plays Again," *The New York Times*, 29 May 1941, 18.
12. Quoted in "Kreisler Safely on 'Slow Road' to Recovery, Wife Thanks Thousands of Well-Wishers," *The New York Times*, 30 May 1941, 17.
13. "Kreisler Quits Hospital, Plans Concerts in Fall," *The New York Herald Tribune*, 18 June 1941, 17.
14. "Charles Foley" letter to Harold Holt and Laurence Mackie, undated, Library of Congress Fritz Kreisler Collection.
15. Milstein and Volkov 1990, 174.
16. "Packed House Hears Philharmonic at Concert Opening 100th Season," *The New York Times*, 10 October 1941, 26.
17. "Packed House Hears Philharmonic at Concert Opening 100th Season," *The New York Times*, 10 October 1941, 26.
18. Reports of this recording session in Philadelphia are taken from "Kreisler Plays Again," *The New York Times*, 16 and 29 January 1942, and "Comeback," *Newsweek*, 26 January 1942, 67.
19. Applebaum 1972, 109.
20. "Kreisler Plays Again," *The New York Times*, 29 January 1942, 21.
21. "Kreisler Plays Again," *The New York Times*, 29 January 1942, 21.
22. Edgar S. Van Olinda, "Kreisler's Art Thrills Large Audience Here," Albany *Times Union*, 29 January 1942, 17.
23. Lochner 1950, 318. *See also* "Fritz Kreisler Signs," *The New York Times*, 29 April 1942, 26.
24. "Kreisler Heard in Recital at Carnegie Hall," *The New York Herald Tribune*, 1 November 1942, 47.
25. Jeanne Mitchell Biancolli, interview, 15 February 1994.

26. Jeanne Mitchell Biancolli, interview, 15 February 1994.
27. Francis D. Perkins, "Kreisler Heard in Recital at Carnegie Hall," *The New York Herald Tribune*, 1 November 1942, 47.
28. Eric Wen, interview, 29 September 1995.
29. "Kreisler Heard in Recital at Carnegie Hall," *The New York Herald Tribune*, 1 November 1942, 47.
30. Noel Straus, "Fritz Kreisler Receives Ovation at First Recital Since Accident," *The New York Times*, 1 November 1942, 54.
31. "Kreisler Is Honored by Society and Arts," *The New York Times*, 10 December 1942, 36.
32. Quoted in Lochner 1950, 366
33. Josef Gingold, interview, 13 July 1992.
34. George Neikrug, interview, 19 August 1992.
35. Sylvia Rabinof Rothenberg, interview, 4 November 1992.
36. Alix Williamson quoting Kreisler, in an interview by the author, 28 March 1995. Glissando is the musical term for a rapid slide down or up a scale.
37. Josef Gingold, interview, 13 July 1992.
38. Josef Gingold, interview, 13 July 1992.
39. Josef Gingold, interview, 13 July 1992.
40. Michael Tree, interview, 3 January 1996.
41. Quoted in Applebaum 1972, 99.
42. Lochner 1950, 316.
43. Eric Wen, interview, 29 September 1995.

Chapter 10: Kreisler, Heifetz, and the Cult of Technique

1. Kreisler quoted in Stoddard 1955.
2. Schonberg 1985, 374.
3. Schonberg 1985, 378–381.
4. Quoted in Schonberg 1987.
5. Schonberg 1985, 105.
6. Quoted in Applebaum 1972, 95.
7. Quoted in Applebaum 1972, 98–99.
8. Quoted in "W.E.B." 1909.
9. Quoted in Hallet 1940.
10. Quoted in Hallet 1940.
11. Quoted in Applebaum 1972, 98–99.
12. David Sackson, interview, 16 September 1992.
13. George Neikrug, interview, 19 August 1992.
14. Piatigorsky 1965, 209–210.

15. Oscar Shumsky, interview, 16 September 1992.
16. Milstein and Volkov 1990, 171–172.
17. Harold Schonberg, interview, 18 January 1995.
18. Harold Schonberg, interview, 18 January 1995.
19. Corredor 1956, 200.
20. Quoted in Stoddard 1955.
21. Quoted in Applebaum 1972, 64.
22. Quoted in Applebaum 1972, 74–75.
23. Quoted in Martens 1919, 79–80.
24. Quoted in Martens 1919, 80–81.
25. Quoted in Applebaum 1972, 75.
26. Flesch 1930, 106.
27. Flesch 1958, 337.
28. Flesch 1930, 107.
29. Fritz Kreisler, interview by WQXR radio, broadcast tape, 2 February 1955.
30. Dyer 1987.
31. Jeanne Mitchell Biancolli, interview, 15 February 1994.
32. Jeanne Mitchell Biancolli, interview, 15 February 1994.
33. Joseph Fuchs quoting Kreisler, in an interview by the author, 17 February 1994.
34. Joseph Fuchs, interview, 21 February 1994.
35. Quoted in Stoddard 1955.
36. Quoted in Schonberg 1987.
37. Franz Rupp quoting Kreisler, in an interview by David Sackson, 21 November 1991.
38. Quoted in Schonberg 1987.
39. Quoted in Lois Timnick, "Jascha Heifetz, 86, Hailed as Greatest Violinist, Dies," *Los Angeles Times*, 12 December 1987, 1.
40. Sir Yehudi Menuhin, interview, 27 February 1993.
41. Sir Yehudi Menuhin, interview, 27 February 1993.
42. Oscar Shumsky, interview, 16 September 1992.
43. Oscar Shumsky, interview, 16 September 1992.
44. Josef Gingold, interview, 13 July 1992.
45. Oscar Shumsky, interview, 16 September 1992.
46. Quoted in Joseph McLellan, "The Sound of Perfection," *The Washington Post*, 12 December 1987, IV, 1.
47. Fritz Kreisler, interview by WQXR radio, broadcast tape, 2 February 1955.
48. Eric Wen, interview, 30 September 1995.
49. David Sackson, interview, 29 December 1993.
50. Joseph Fuchs, interview, 17 February 1994.

Chapter 11: "He Was Our God"

1. Schonberg 1985, 240.
2. Harold Coletta, interview, 12 July 1992.
3. David Sackson, interview, 16 September 1992.
4. Sam Kissel, interview, 14 September 1992.
5. Oscar Shumsky, interview, 16 September 1992.
6. Michael Tree, interview, 3 January 1996.
7. Oscar Shumsky, interview, 16 September 1992.
8. Paul Hume, "The Ageless Kreisler," *Saturday Review*, 29 December 1962, 53.
9. Stern 1962.
10. Josef Gingold, interview, 13 July 1992.
11. Gingold 1962. Article included in the Library of Congress Fritz Kreisler Collection.
12. Josef Gingold letter to Charles Foley, 21 May 1962, Library of Congress Fritz Kreisler Collection.
13. Szigeti May 1962.
14. Szigeti February 1962.
15. Kaufman 1987.
16. Libove 1987.
17. Francescatti 1962.
18. Sir Yehudi Menuhin, interview, 6 March 1993.
19. Senofsky 1987.
20. Flesch 1958, 125.
21. Joseph Fuchs, interview, 21 February 1994.
22. Milstein 1962.
23. Eric Wen, interview, 30 September 1995.
24. Sam Kissel, interview, 14 September 1992.
25. Philip Dreifus, interview, 26 May 1993.
26. George Neikrug, interview, 19 August 1992.
27. David Oistrakh letter to Fritz Kreisler, 26 December 1959, Library of Congress Fritz Kreisler Collection.
28. Williams 1987.
29. George Neikrug, interview, 19 August 1992.
30. WQXR broadcast tape, 2 February 1955.

Chapter 12: Covering Kreisler: The Critics' Dilemma

1. Kreisler quoted in Downes 1942.
2. Quoted in Downes 1942.

3. Oscar Shumsky, interview, 16 September 1992.
4. Noel Straus, "Kreisler Scores at Carnegie Hall," *The New York Times*, 3 November 1946, 54.
5. Noel Straus, "Kreisler Cheered in Violin Concerto," *The New York Times*, 11 January 1946, 16.
6. "Music: The Great Kreisler: Now 65 and Tiring, but He Plays On as Legendary Stature Grows," *Newsweek*, 25 March 1940, 39.
7. Olin Downes, "Music: Fritz Kreisler Plays," *The New York Times*, 19 January 1928, 16.
8. Milstein and Volkov 1990, 169.
9. "London Cheers Kreisler," *The New York Times*, 5 May 1921, 3.
10. T. Shaw 1952, 87–88.
11. T. Shaw 1952, 3–4.
12. G. B. Shaw 1955, 34.
13. "Boston Orchestra Again," *The New York Times*, 8 December 1912, 18.
14. Quoted in "Fritz Kreisler Leaves," *The New York Times*, 18 April 1924, 16.
15. Eric Wen, interview, 29 September 1995.
16. Edgar S. Van Olinda, "Kreisler's Art Thrills Large Audience Here," Albany *Times Union*, 29 January 1942, 17.
17. Harold Schonberg, interview, 18 January 1995.

Chapter 13: The Last Years: Kreisler's Retirement and the Failing Public Memory

1. Kreisler quoted in Stoddard 1955.
2. Ross Parmenter letter to the author, 7 January 1995.
3. Ross Parmenter, "Kreisler Cheered at Annual Recital," *The New York Times*, 2 November 1947, 62.
4. Ross Parmenter, "Kreisler Cheered at Annual Recital," *The New York Times*, 2 November 1947, 62.
5. Helen Knox Spain, "Audience Pays Stirring Tribute to Kreisler," *The Atlanta Journal*, 12 November 1949, 3.
6. Harold Schonberg, interview, 18 January 1995.
7. Harriet Kreisler, interview by Louis Lochner, 5 October 1948, unpublished portions, Library of Congress Fritz Kreisler Collection.
8. See *The Immortal Fritz Kreisler—Legendary Performances*, 1987 RCA/Ariola International (5910-2-RC).
9. Frederic Kreisler, interview, 9 August 1995.
10. Harold Schonberg, interview, 18 January 1995.
11. Concert itineraries, Library of Congress Fritz Kreisler Collection.

12. Fritz Kreisler, interview by Louis Lochner, 2 June 1949, unpublished portions, Library of Congress Fritz Kreisler Collection.
13. Library of Congress Fritz Kreisler Collection.
14. "Stradivarius Sold by Fritz Kreisler," *The New York Times*, 26 October 1946, 10.
15. Library of Congress Fritz Kreisler Collection.
16. "Fritz Kreisler Sells His Famed Stradivarius," *The New York Times*, 10 April 1946, 29.
17. Library of Congress Fritz Kreisler Collection.
18. David Sackson, interview, 22 May 1993.
19. Frederic Kreisler, interview, 9 August 1995.
20. Frederic Kreisler, interview, 9 August 1995.
21. Frederic Kreisler letter to the author, 17 March 1997.
22. Frederic Kreisler, interview, 9 August 1995.
23. David Sackson, interview, 22 May 1993.
24. David Sackson, interview, 22 May 1993.
25. Sir Yehudi Menuhin, interview, 6 March 1993.
26. Louis Lochner quoting Kreisler, in letter to Harold Bauer, 1 March 1949, Library of Congress Fritz Kreisler Collection.
27. Lucie Schelling quoting Harriet Kreisler, in an interview by Louis Lochner, 24 May 1949, unpublished portions, Library of Congress Fritz Kreisler Collection.
28. Louis Lochner letter to Carl and Helen Lamson, 8 December 1950, Library of Congress Fritz Kreisler Collection.
29. Library of Congress Fritz Kreisler Collection.
30. Louis Lochner letter to Mrs. John Toth, 19 June 1959, Library of Congress Fritz Kreisler Collection.
31. Charles Foley letter to Louis Lochner, 29 May 1952, Library of Congress Fritz Kreisler Collection.
32. Milstein and Volkov 1990, 172–173.
33. "A Great Human Being," *Time*, 13 February 1950, 41.
34. Milstein and Volkov 1990, 172.
35. "A Great Human Being," *Time*, 13 February 1950, 41.
36. Quoted in "Grand Old Man," *Newsweek*, 13 February 1950, 82.
37. Quoted in "Grand Old Man," *Newsweek*, 13 February 1950, 82.
38. "A Great Human Being," *Time*, 13 February 1950, 41.
39. Quoted in "A Great Human Being," *Time*, 13 February 1950, 41.
40. "Kreisler Is Feted on 80th Birthday," *The New York Times*, 3 February 1955, 18.
41. "Kreisler Is Feted on 80th Birthday," *The New York Times*, 3 February 1955, 18.

42. Quoted in Howard Taubman, "Eisenhower Hails Kreisler, 80 Today," *The New York Times*, 2 February 1955, 29.
43. "Octogenarians," *Musical America* (1 February 1955): 3.
44. Fritz Kreisler, interview by WQXR radio, broadcast tape, 2 February 1955.
45. "Fritz Kreisler at 80," *The New York Times*, 2 February 1955, 26.
46. Quoted in Schonberg 1960.
47. Harold Schonberg, interview, 18 January 1995.
48. Sam Kissel, interview, 14 September 1992.
49. Schonberg 1960.
50. Quoted in Schonberg 1960.
51. Quoted in Schonberg 1960.
52. Quoted in Schonberg 1960.
53. Sargeant 1961.
54. Schonberg February 1962.
55. Lang 1962.

Chapter 14: Saying Goodbye to "A Beam of Light"

1. Kreisler quoted in Downes 1942.
2. "Fritz Kreisler Dies in Hospital at 86," *The New York World-Telegram & The Sun*, 29 January 1962, 1.
3. "Fritz Kreisler, Master Violinist," *The New York Herald Tribune*, 30 January 1962, 22.
4. "Fritz Kreisler, Master Violinist," *The New York Herald Tribune*, 30 January 1962, 22.
5. Schonberg January 1962.
6. Schonberg January 1962.
7. Schonberg February 1962.
8. "Fritz Kreisler," *The New York Times*, 30 January 1962, 28.
9. Lang 1962.
10. Quoted in "The Paragon," *Newsweek*, 12 February 1962, 56.
11. "The Paragon," *Newsweek*, 12 February 1962, 56.
12. Quoted in "Last of a Breed," *Time*, 9 February 1962, 64.
13. Szigeti May 1962.
14. Francescatti 1962.
15. Stern 1962.
16. Quoted in "Kreisler 'Gift of Faith' Stressed in Sheen Eulogy," *The New York Herald Tribune*, 2 February 1962, 4.
17. Frederic Kreisler, interview, 9 August 1995.
18. Harold Coletta, interview, 12 July 1992.

19. "Music: Homage to a Great Colleague," *The New York Times*, 8 February 1962, 24.
20. Harold C. Schonberg, "Music: Four Violins," *The New York Times*, 28 December 1962, West Coast edition, 5. Because of the city-wide newspaper strike, Schonberg's article never ran in New York, but appeared only in the West Coast edition of the *Times*.
21. Quoted in "Fritz Kreisler," *Musical America* (March 1962): 15.
22. Olin Downes, "Music: Fritz Kreisler Plays," *The New York Times*, 19 January 1928, 16.
23. Quoted in Downes 1942.
24. Joseph Fuchs, interview, 21 February 1994.
25. Sir Yehudi Menuhin, interview, 27 February 1993.
26. Oscar Shumsky, interview, 16 September 1992.
27. Josef Gingold, interview, 13 July 1992.
28. Joseph Fuchs, interview, 21 February 1994.
29. Quoted in Stidger 1940, 76–77.

Appendix B

1. Lochner 1950, 423–424.
2. Lochner 1950, 415.
3. Lochner 1950, 241.

Bibliography

Amis, John, and Michael Rose. 1989. *Words About Music*. New York: Marlowe and Company.

Antrim, Doron K. 1944. "The Maestro Plays On." *Readers Digest* (August): 83. Condensed from *The Washington Post* (2 July).

Applebaum, Samuel and Sada. 1955. *With the Artists: World Famed String Players Discuss Their Art*. New York: John Market and Co.

——. 1972. *The Way They Play*. Book I. Neptune City, NJ: Paganiniana Publications.

Auer, Leopold. 1980. *Violin Playing As I Teach It*. New York: Dover Publications. Original edition, New York: Frederick A. Stokes Company, 1921.

"W.E.B." 1909. "Fritz Kreisler." *The Musician* (October): 453.

Bachmann, Alberto. 1966. *An Encyclopedia of the Violin*. Edited by Albert E. Wier. Translated by Frederick H. Martens. New York: Da Capo Press. Original edition, New York and London, 1925.

Beller, Steven. 1989. *Vienna and the Jews, 1867–1938: A Cultural History*. Cambridge, England: Cambridge University Press.

Berkeley, George E. 1988. *Vienna and Its Jews: The Tragedy of Success*. Lanham, MD: Madison Books.

Breuer, Katharina. 1948. *Dances of Austria*. New York: Chanticleer Press, under the auspices of the Royal Academy of Dancing and the Ling Physical Education Association.

Campbell, Margaret. 1981. *The Great Violinists*. Garden City, NY: Doubleday and Co.

Casals, Pablo, and Albert E. Kahn. 1970. *Joys and Sorrows: Reflections by Pablo Casals As Told to Albert E. Kahn*. New York: Simon and Schuster.

Corredor, J. Ma. 1956. *Conversations with Casals*. Translated by Andre Mangeot. New York: E. P. Dutton and Co.

Downes, Olin. 1935. "Kreisler's 'Classics.'" *The New York Times* (3 March): VIII, 5.

——. 1942. "Talk with Kreisler: Violinist Discusses His Early Days and Some Contemporary Problems." *The New York Times* (8 November): VIII, 7.

Dubal, David. 1992. *Conversations with Menuhin*. New York: Harcourt Brace Jovanovich.

Dyer, Richard. 1987. "Heifetz Unrivaled on Violin." *The Boston Globe* (12 December): 1.

Elman, Mischa. 1962. "The Kreisler Career." *Saturday Review* (24 February): 45.

Ewen, David. 1935. "L'Amico Fritz." *Esquire* (August): 12. This article can also be found in the Library of Congress Fritz Kreisler Collection, which holds an unpublished little "chat book" put together by "book designer G. Alan Chidsen" from Great Neck, New York.

Farrar, Geraldine. 1938. *Such Sweet Compulsion*. New York: The Greystone Press.

Flesch, Carl. 1930. *The Art of Violin Playing*. Vol. 2. Translated by Frederick H. Martens. New York: Carl Fischer.

——. 1958. *The Memoirs of Carl Flesch*. Translated and edited by Hans Keller, in collaboration with C. F. Flesch. New York: Macmillan and Co. Original edition, Rockliff Publishing, 1957.

Francescatti, Zino. 1962. "The Kreisler Career." *Saturday Review* (24 February): 46.

"Fritz Kreisler Discusses America's Attitude Toward Him." *Literary Digest*, 3 January 1920, 48.

"Fritz Kreisler's Tribute to His Emperor." *The New York Times Magazine*, 3 December 1916, 2.

Gingold, Josef. 1962. "My Tribute to Fritz Kreisler." *Yes #XI* (May).

Hallet, Richard Matthews. 1940. "Fritz Kreisler, and What's in Him." *The Christian Science Monitor Magazine* (7 December): 5.

Hofmann, Paul. 1988. *The Viennese: Splendor, Twilight and Exile*. New York: Anchor Press, Doubleday.

——. 1994. *The Spell of the Vienna Woods: Inspiration and Influence from Beethoven to Kafka*. New York: Henry Holt and Company.

Johnson, William M. 1980. *Vienna Vienna: The Golden Age, 1815–1914.* New York: Clarkson N. Potter Inc.

Kaufman, Louis. 1987. "L'Amico Fritz." *The Strad* (1 January): 42.

Keller, Hans. 1984. "Violin Technique: Its Modern Development and Musical Decline." In *The Book of the Violin*, edited by Dominic Gill. New York: Phaidon Press Limited.

Kreisler, Fritz. 1915. *Four Weeks in the Trenches: The War Story of a Violinist.* New York: Houghton Mifflin & Co. Reprint, Neptune City, NJ: Paganiniana Publications, 1981.

——. 1921. "Music and Life." *The Mentor* (December): 5.

——. 1924. "A Violinist in the Orient." *The Living Age* (1 March): 412.

——. 1935. "Mr. Kreisler's Defence: He Replies to Mr. Newman." *The Sunday Times* (10 March): 15.

——. 1935. "A Letter from Fritz Kreisler." *The Sunday Times* (31 March): 7.

——. 1951. "The Great Kreisler Hoax." As told to Louis Biancolli. *Etude* (June): 18.

Kreisler, Harriet. 1914. "With Fritz Kreisler at the Front." *Musical Courier* (14 October): 5.

"The Kreisler 'Hoax.'" *The Musician* (February 1935): 3.

"Kreisler Reveals 'Classics' As Own; Fooled Music Critics for 30 Years." *The New York Times*, 8 February 1935, 1.

Lang, Paul Henry. 1962. "The Genius of Kreisler, Dead at 86." *The New York Herald Tribune* (30 January): 1.

Lawrence, Vera Brodsky. 1995. *Strong on Music: The New York Music Scene in the Days of George Templeton Strong.* Chicago: University of Chicago Press.

Ledbetter, Gordon T. 1977. *The Great Irish Tenor.* New York: Charles Scribner's Sons.

Libove, Charles. 1987. "L'Amico Fritz." *The Strad* (1 January): 44.

Lochner, Louis P. 1950. *Fritz Kreisler.* New York: The Macmillan Company. Reprint, St. Claire Shores, MI: Scholarly Press, 1977.

Martens, Frederick H. 1919. *Violin Mastery: Talks with Master Violinists and Teachers.* New York: Frederick A. Stokes Company.

Menuhin, Yehudi. 1962. "The Kreisler Career." *Saturday Review* (24 February): 47.

Milstein, Nathan. 1962. "The Kreisler Career." *Saturday Review* (24 February): 47.

Milstein, Nathan, and Salomon Volkov. 1990. *From Russia to the West: The Musical Memoirs and Reminiscences of Nathan Milstein.* Translated by Antonina W. Bouis. New York: Limelight Editions.

Morton, Frederic. 1979. *A Nervous Splendor: Vienna 1888/1889.* London: Weidenfeld and Nicolson.

Newman, Ernest. 1935. "The Kreisler Revelations: Debit and Credit." *The Sunday Times* (24 February): 5.

——. 1935. "An Open Letter to Fritz Kreisler: The 'Classical Manuscripts.'" *The Sunday Times* (17 March): 7.

Piatigorsky, Gregor. 1965. *Cellist*. Garden City, NY: Doubleday and Co.

Rooney, Dennis. 1987. "Instinctive Partnership: Franz Rupp Reminisces About Playing with Fritz Kreisler." *The Strad* (January): 31.

Roy, Basanta Koomar. 1921. "The Personality of Kreisler." *The Mentor* (December): 31.

Rubinstein, Artur. 1973. *My Young Years*. New York: Alfred A. Knopf.

Sablosky, Irving. 1986. *What They Heard: Music in America, 1852–1881*. Baton Rouge, LA: Louisiana State University Press.

Sadie, Stanley, ed. 1980. *The New Grove Dictionary of Music*. 20 vols. London: Macmillan Publishers Limited.

Sargeant, Winthrop. 1961. "Musical Events: And So to Mr. Kreisler." *The New Yorker* (15 April): 87–88.

Scheinert, Carleton A. 1934. "Kreisler and the Prodigy." *The Etude* (September): 516.

Schonberg, Harold C. 1960. "City Will Honor Kreisler at 85." *The New York Times* (31 January): 60.

——. 1962. "An Individual Musician: Fritz Kreisler Stood Apart from the Two Mainstreams of Violin Playing." *The New York Times* (30 January): 33.

——. 1962. "The Only One: Kreisler Was the Complete Violinist with His Unique Style and Charm." *The New York Times* (4 February): II, 5.

——. 1985. *The Virtuosi: Classical Music's Great Performers, from Paganini to Pavarotti*. New York: Vintage Books.

——. 1987. "Jascha Heifetz is Dead at 86: A Virtuoso Since Childhood." *The New York Times* (12 December): 1.

Schorske, Carl E. 1981. *Fin-de-Siècle Vienna: Politics and Culture*. New York: Vintage Books.

Schwartz, Boris. 1983. *Great Masters of the Violin*. New York: Simon and Schuster.

Senofsky, Berl. 1987. "L'Amico Fritz." *The Strad* (1 January): 48.

Shaw, George Bernard. 1955. *Shaw on Music: A Selection from the Music Criticism of Bernard Shaw*. Edited by Eric Bentley. Garden City, NY: Anchor Books, Doubleday.

——. 1981. *Shaw's Music: The Complete Musical Criticism in Three Volumes*. Edited by Dan H. Laurence. New York: Dodd Mead and Company. Originally published by G. B. Shaw as *London Music in 1888–9 as Heard by Corno di Bassetto*, 1937.

Shaw, Theodore L. 1952. *War on Critics*. Boston: Stuart Art Gallery.

Sheen, Fulton J. 1980. *Treasure in Clay: The Autobiography of Fulton J. Sheen*. Garden City, NY: Doubleday and Co.

Sked, Alan. 1989. *The Decline and Fall of the Habsburg Empire, 1815–1918*. London and New York: Longman.

Slenczynska, Ruth, and Louis Biancolli. 1958. *Forbidden Childhood*. London: Peter Davies.

Slonimsky, Nicolas. 1993. *Baker's Biographical Dictionary of Musicians*. Eighth edition. New York: Schirmer Books.

Smith, Beverly. 1931. "He Plays on the World's Heartstrings." *America Magazine* (February): 66.

Smith, Helena Huntington. 1928. "Profiles: A Gentleman from Vienna." *The New Yorker* (24 November): 29.

Spalding, Albert. 1943. *Rise to Follow: An Autobiography*. New York: Henry Holt and Company.

"Statement Issued by Fritz Kreisler." *The Pittsburgh Sun*, 8 November 1917, 18.

Stern, Isaac. 1962. "The Kreisler Career." *Saturday Review* (24 February): 48.

Stidger, William L. 1940. *The Human Side of Greatness*. New York and London: Harper and Brothers Publishers.

Stoddard, Hope. 1955. "Kreisler on Relativity in Music." *International Musician* (March): 10.

Stowell, Robin. 1992. "Other Solo Repertory." In *The Cambridge Companion to the Violin*. Edited by Robin Stowell. Cambridge, England: Cambridge University Press.

Szigeti, Joseph. 1962. "The Kreisler Career." *Saturday Review* (24 February): 48.

——. 1962. "Memories of Kreisler." *High Fidelity Magazine* (May): 40.

——. 1979. *Szigeti on the Violin*. New York: Dover Publications.

Taubman, Howard. 1944. "Grand Master of the Bow." *The New York Times Magazine* (9 January): 12.

Taylor, Deems. 1937. *Of Men and Music*. New York: Simon and Schuster.

Williams, Byron. 1987. "L'Amico Fritz." *The Strad* (1 January): 50.

"Ysaÿe, Kreisler, Vecsey." *The Independent*, 19 January 1905, 145.

Index